Belonging to the Army
Camp Followers and Community during the American Revolution

BELONGING TO THE ARMY

Camp Followers and Community
during the American Revolution

Holly A. Mayer

UNIVERSITY OF SOUTH CAROLINA PRESS

© 1996 University of South Carolina

Cloth edition published by the University of South Carolina Press, 1996
Paperback edition published in Columbia, South Carolina,
by the University of South Carolina Press, 1999

www.sc.edu/uscpress

Manufactured in the United States of America

19 18 17 16 15 14 13 12 11   13 12 11 10 9 8 7 6 5 4

The Library of Congress has cataloged the cloth edition as follows:
Mayer, Holly A. (Holly Ann), 1956–
  Belonging to the Army : camp followers and community during the American Revolution / Holly A. Mayer.
    p.   cm.
  Includes bibliographical references and index.
  ISBN 1-57003-108-8 (cloth)
  1. United States. Continental Army—Military life. 2. Camp followers—United States—History—18th century. I. Title.
E259.M39   1996
973.3—dc20   96-10074

ISBN 978-1-57003-339-1 (pbk.)

To my parents

Jack Mayer, Colonel, U.S. Army Retired,
and
Ruth Beckstein Mayer, Army Wife, never retired

Contents

Preface	ix
Acknowledgments	xiii
1 Custom, Conflict, and Camp Followers	1
2 The Army: A Continental Community	30
3 The Mercantile Community: Sutlers and Other Suppliers	85
4 Retainers to the Camp: The Conjugal Family	122
5 Retainers to the Camp: The Extended Family	162
6 All Persons Serving with the Army	192
7 Subject to Orders and the Discipline of War	236
8 Contributors to a Glorious Work	270
Bibliography	279
Index	292

Preface

The American Revolution was a fascinating epoch defined by noble ideals and dispiriting contradictions. The War for American Independence, that armed conflict that resulted from and continued this revolution, certainly embodied those ideals and contradictions, as did the Continental Army itself, the very agency that secured independence for the new nation. A number of historians have illuminated this tension between ideology and reality, between policy and practice. They have shown how the revolutionaries came to rely on a regular army as the limits of their vaunted militias, though worthy enough in limited, local engagements, became obvious; and they have provided evidence that citizen-soldiers did not always meet the description of either citizen or soldier. Intrigued—and already interested in how the war affected people's lives and, in turn, how people's actions influenced the outcome of the war—I decided to do more research on the army's role in the American Revolution, and, even more specifically, on those who peopled that army. It was about that time, when I was a graduate student casting about for a dissertation topic, that a piece of mental flotsam bobbed up in my memory: if the United States Army thought it proper to celebrate their importance in "The Year of the Military Family," as it did in 1984, then the Continental Army's civilian adjuncts, its camp followers, certainly merited attention.

When I began my research, I was primarily interested in the attitudes and actions of women with the Continental Army, but I quickly discovered that the other camp followers—men as well as women, black and white—could not be ignored, for they too have been overlooked in most historical literature. While researching the Continental Army, I became more and more disturbed by a lack of published information on camp followers. Except for a few notable exceptions, authors either disregarded these people or only referred to them in passing. I set out to find these forgotten "revolutionaries." In the process, I found a vital, sometimes chaotic, sometimes highly disciplined, and singular community—a Continental Community.

What had begun as a rather narrow study of a particular group of individuals ended as an examination of the legal, labor, and social relationships and interactions between the Continental Army, its uniformed personnel, and its civilian attachments. The study of the army as a community rather than just as a formal military organization not only gave the army more of a personality, but also suggested other possibilities about why and how that army, despite the odds and the naysayers, managed not only to survive but achieve victory in the War for American Independence.

George Washington, as historians, including Robert Middlekauff in *The Glorious Cause* (p. 463), have mentioned, clearly recognized that "the army was the Revolution." If the army did not survive, if it did not succeed, then neither would the Revolution. These historians have then gone on to present a number of reasons as to why and how the Continental Army survived to achieve victory. Some, taking the high road so-to-speak, have focused on the Americans' sense of purpose, their mission, and their virtue in adversity. Others (shall we say taking the low road?) have pointed to such things as luck, leadership, and British unpreparedness or errors—both in policy and strategy. Certainly both avenues of inquiry have resulted in some valid conclusions; nevertheless, they are not complete until notice is taken of the cloud of persons who performed multitudinous tasks to keep the army going.

This study actually began with some very simple questions. Who were the camp followers? What did they do? Why did they do it? And what was the result of their actions? Then, as I came to realize that I was dealing with a community, the questions increased in difficulty: what kind of community did these people form, why and how did it work, and what did it mean for the army and the war effort? These questions helped direct and define the major themes of this book: the relationship between the army and its community, and the contributions of that community and its people to the army and thus the Revolution.

In studying the formation, organization, and administration of this community, I was able to delve into some other issues. These developed into the secondary themes—the subtext, if you will—of this book. There is the issue of the Revolution itself: how far did it go? As this community worked to effect independence—thus guaranteeing a successful political revolution—were there any indications of it engendering a social revolution? What were class, gender, and race relations like in the Continental Community? Thus I include some— though, as I am sure some readers will be quick to point out, by no means exhaustive—analyses of such relationships in my examination of the social organization of the army. But all of these issues always brought me back to the subject of how the community worked—which I approached by way of a focus on how the army controlled the people who contributed to it.

The camp followers could have easily overwhelmed the Continental Army and confounded the war effort, so administration of them was essential. To be of benefit to the cause, they had to be controlled. That control was contingent on the army recognizing their value to its existence. At first, it simply wanted to be rid of most of them and to incorporate most if not all support functions within the organization itself. Then, when it could not do that, the army incorporated them—thus giving an expansive meaning to the term *belonging to the army*. Their presence and production may have meant survival, but control meant success. Furthermore, as it did with its soldiers, the army also tried to make camp followers fit the image of the army (for the army was supposed to reflect the visionary quest of the new nation), but when it could not do that, it tried to make them "invisible." It was not very successful in that endeavor during the war, but afterward it was another story.

The focus of this book is on Washington's main army; thus most of the incidents discussed occurred in the Eastern, Northern, and Middle Departments. There are, of course, some Southern Department references for comparison and contrast, especially from when the main army moved into Virginia for the 1781 campaign. Most of the evidence comes from units attached to the main army, such as the 1st Pennsylvania Regiment and, in particular, the 2nd Continental Artillery. The latter unit was properly titled "continental" in that although it drew most of its soldiers from New York, it also had soldiers from the other middle states of New York, New Jersey, and Pennsylvania, and from New England, specifically Connecticut. As a result it may not have been quite as provincial as some other units. The 2nd Continental Artillery also had quite a few camp followers due to its need of artificers to maintain the equipment, and because many of the areas from which the unit drew its personnel experienced British occupation.

In rendering quotations, I have retained the original spelling and grammar (or lack thereof) whenever possible. Changes and additions appear in brackets. Empty brackets indicate that a word was obscured in the original text. Superscript letters have been brought down to the line, and most dashes have been transcribed into periods. Words repeated at the end of one page and at the beginning of the next appear only once.

Acknowledgments

Although a book ultimately represents the vision and labor of its author, who must accept responsibility for all faults found therein, it can only be completed with the assistance and support of many people. This book began as a dissertation under the supervision of James P. Whittenburg at the College of William and Mary. I thank him for his constant interest in my topic (a challenge for all advisers) and gentle guidance. My thanks also go to Michael McGiffert, Thad Tate, and Cam Walker for their insightful comments on the same; and to Don Higginbotham for the excellent advice that helped set me on course when I began to make the revisions for the book.

The metamorphosis of dissertation into book was aided substantially by the discerning criticisms and suggestions of many other people. I offer my profound appreciation to Fred Anderson, who read two versions of this project and made detailed, helpful comments each time. Harold E. Selesky also offered many excellent suggestions. Among the others who have read or listened to parts of this project and offered much helpful information and advice were Jean B. Lee, the participants at an Institute of Early American History and Culture seminar in 1990, and John Rees and the other many reenacters whose enthusiasm for the topic and willingness to share the results of their own research constantly energized me. Thanks are certainly also due here to Warren Slesinger of the University of South Carolina Press for his support.

During the course of my research, I was assisted by numerous people at various institutions, all of whom I thank profusely. The David Library of the American Revolution in Washington Crossing, Pennsylvania, is a wonderful place in which to work. The library's late president and director, Ezra Stone, offered me warm hospitality at the Feinstone Research Center; David J. Fowler, the research director, answered my numerous queries and suggested additional materials; and Marilynn Huret took care of anything they did not. While in that part of the country, I also worked at the Historical Society of Pennsylvania where I was very grateful for Linda Stanley's, and the rest of the staff's, patient assistance. At Carlisle Barracks, John J. Slonaker and David Keuogh showed me what the United States Army Military History Institute had on the Revolutionary War, as did the helpful souls up the road at the Pennsylvania State Archives in Harrisburg. Various librarians very courteously assisted me in the Manuscript Division of the Library of Congress, as did others at the National Archives. At the latter, William E. Lind of the Military Reference Branch, who

I believe has since retired, proved especially helpful. Robert K. Wright, formerly of the U.S. Army Center of Military History, gave me extensive bibliographic assistance when I was still formulating my topic. In Richmond the staff of the Virginia Historical Society delivered many a manuscript to my table. Conley L. Edwards III and Minor Weisiger helped my investigations at the Virginia State Library, while Sandra Gioia Treadway, of the same institution, proffered much good advice. The staff of The New-York Historical Society made sure my short trip there was pleasant and productive. And in the "backcountry" my efforts were aided by the folks at the Filson Club in Louisville and at the William L. Clements Library of the University of Michigan. I wish especially to thank Rob Cox and John Harriman at the latter institution for their friendly assistance.

I am very grateful to the College of William and Mary in Virginia and its Department of History for the fellowships, assistantships, and research grants that made it possible for me to pursue both the Ph.D. and the research on this topic. I also extend my appreciation to the State Council for Higher Education in Virginia for the Commonwealth Fellowship in 1988, the Board of Trustees of the David Library of the American Revolution for the generous research grant I received in 1989, and the National Society Colonial Dames XVII Century for scholarships in 1985 and 1986. To Duquesne University I give thanks for the Presidential Scholarship Award that helped support my efforts as I finished the manuscript. And I salute my colleagues in the history department at Duquesne who murmured sympathetically and then got out of my way as this novice stalked down the halls muttering about the impossibility of teaching, researching, and writing all at once.

Finally, and with great pleasure, I now turn to thank friends and family who have lived through this lengthy process with me. Gail S. Terry and John M. Hemphill II were most generous in their advice and support. Another pair of both personal and professional friends, Janet L. Coryell and Christine Styrna Devine, gave me much-needed "reality checks." To the 6AITAAS/6RFI "Squints" at Fort Huachuca: Yes, here it is, finally finished! Most of all, I thank my parents, Ruth and Jack Mayer, and my brother, Jon, for all their loving guidance and support. And while this book is dedicated to my parents, I also present it as a memorial to my grandmother, Anna Maria Schrepfer Beckstein, who saw me start this project—and reminded me to take "Alles mit Humor" in this as in life—but did not live long enough to see me finish it.

Belonging to the Army
Camp Followers and Community
during the American Revolution

1

Custom, Conflict, and Camp Followers

> Last Sunday the Rebel army was Mustered at the W[hite] plains, when it was reported amongst them that they have 20000, but the Friends to Government say if they be 14000 that is the outside of them. [T]hat the Women and Waggoners make up near the half of their Army.
>
> *British Intelligence Report*
> *New York, 11 August 1778*[1]

Soldiers alone do not make an army. They are the most fundamental part of that military force, but as hard as they work, and as much as they do, an army seldom marches out on their efforts alone. A great number of other people join the soldiers and their officers to build and maintain these martial organizations. That number rises and falls in response to such actions as recruiting for war and restructuring for peace. At times then, as the above description of the American army in 1778 indicates, "near the half" or more of an army may be people not actually in the army. Such women, wagoners, and others are camp followers: those people who live and work with the military and accept, willingly or not, its governance of their affairs. While their endeavors both complicate and enrich military life and actions, their very existence suggests that an army can be seen as something more than a simple hierarchical organization of brigades, regiments, battalions, companies, officers, and soldiers arranged and coordinated to do combat against an enemy. Such an assembly of both military and civilian persons, as bound together by duty, economics, or affection, and governed by military rule and custom, is a community.

Military communities generally reflect the times and the states that create them. They can serve to illuminate national ideologies, illustrate social stratification and mobility, and delineate a culture's customs. These communities can do this, especially in the modern era, because they encompass people from all walks of life and with all manner of speech and thought. Of course there are also distinctions that differentiate this kind of community from civilian ones. The very heterogeneity that allows it to represent a national community sets it off from most other, more homogeneous, local communities. It is, furthermore, a highly mobile society marked by individuals moving in and out of the association, and by the group moving as a body as well. Finally, and perhaps most importantly, this community as a whole and the individuals within it accept military superintendence and promote the military mission: the defense of a nation's property and policy. As an army serves its nation, it in turn is supported by its followers.

This symbiotic existence was especially marked in the Continental Army during the War for American Independence. Camp followers were necessary to the survival of the military, just as the military, in turn, was necessary to the success and survival of the fledgling nation. People on both sides of, and at various times in, the conflict acknowledged the latter point: a British officer observed in October 1776, "if that Army is destroyed or dispersed, the subjugation of the American Colonies, may be said to be nearly effected: for it is highly improbable they will be able to assemble another army in the field able to face that of Britain"; while an American officer in 1780 remarked that "an army is essential to the American union."[2] Recognition of and concern about these connections resulted in discussions and decisions at various levels in the army and governments on the civilian-military relationship. Most revolutionaries accepted the fact that they needed an army to secure their cause, but they worried about establishing an instrument of state that could become instead a threat to the states and their peoples. At issue were such things as authority and accountability.

The representatives to the Continental Congress in June 1775 recognized the possible threat at the same time they acknowledged the need for a unified force. Their response was to assume control over the armies of Massachusetts, Connecticut, New Hampshire, and Rhode Island, which were assembled at Boston. The congressional delegates then requested that the other colonies also provide troops. Thus the "Army of the United Colonies" was the legislative creation of the Continental Congress in Philadelphia, and by so placing the power of creation within itself, Congress established its authority over the military. That did not mean it had sole authority. As was evident throughout the war, the army was the servant of both this federal assembly and the state governments, and as a result had to endure the corresponding troubles one servant has when forced to please too many masters. Indeed, in trying to ensure that the army did not destroy their revolutionary gains, the state governments sometimes seemed hell-bent on destroying the army. They were "extremely tenacious of their rights of making new appointments and conferring promotions in their lines of Infantry," though they were generally good enough not to interfere with (but correspondingly slow enough to support) the artillery or cavalry, which were "understood to be lines belonging to the Continent at large."[3]

Congress strengthened its authority versus that of the states over the military, and, in turn, strengthened the military's authority, by appointing George

Washington commander in chief. He professed, and throughout the war acted upon, a deeply held belief that the army must remain accountable to the provincial governments, but he felt it must especially answer to Congress and the federal interest.[4] Whereas, however, the issue of dominion and subordination was settled rather quickly and easily at the national level, Washington soon found that he also had to establish the nature of the civilian-military association when symbiosis was desirable at a local level. There were times when military needs had to outweigh civilian desires, though not concerns, so that the army could fulfill its obligations to the state. Thus, at the same time it had to serve all the people, the army had to master some of them. One way of doing that was to show that this was an army created by, for, and of the people in terms of recruitment and, especially, administration.

The task fell upon Washington, and he had to surmount tremendous difficulties not so much to command this army as to create, re-create, and administer it. In contrast to his favorite model—the established, professional, British army—this American force was a new army formed out of citizen volunteers and then filled in with almost everyone else. Furthermore, it was formed to fight a defensive crusade on the home front, not to ship out for a foreign campaign (though for some soldiers, duty in different states appeared equal to duty in foreign parts). He also had to deal with the congressional, state, and military leaders who in creating this instrument of the Revolution looked to the precedents set by both the colonial militias and the provincial armies recruited to fight alongside the British in the colonial wars. While the latter expeditionary forces showed that the colonists had evolved militarily by the French and Indian War, militias still defined the American way of warfare. Revolutionary leaders heralded that heritage and wanted the army to reflect it, and in doing so to be not only an instrument but a model of and for the new American republic. Washington, backed by some other leaders, refuted the army-as-militia idea and over the next eight years trained and promoted his force—his main army becoming the standard-bearer—into a regular, "respectable," army.[5]

Complicating Washington's task, however, and an offshoot of the militia tradition, was that this was to be a unified army of virtuous volunteers, not companies of subjects. But such a policy placed power with those who would volunteer as opposed to within the organization that needed them. One result was that some people volunteered to serve with the military but not in it; and others offered their service in or with the military only so long as their personal and families' needs were met. Thus some of Washington's problems were due to the fact that he could not focus solely on the army alone; he had to deal with an evolving social organism—in effect, a "Continental Community." This was the people's army, and many wanted to belong to the army that belonged to them, but on their terms. The army in its acceptance, use, and maintenance of followers met some of those terms, deflected others, and then made considerable demands of its own. The Continental Community, then, was the result of the people's desires, the army's needs, and the repercussions of the Revolution.

The Continental Community was peopled by both combatants, those who bore arms in the military, and noncombatants, including the civilians with the army. The attitudes and actions of each group can only be fully understood when one is offset by the other, when the community as a whole is presented and when the administration of that community is analyzed. Officers, soldiers, and camp followers need to be examined as separate groups as well as interrelated ones in order to understand the military community and how such an association sustained the army. Each group as a whole, as well as the individuals within them, helped create an environment conducive to perseverance. By their informal interpersonal relations and official personnel actions, these people defined a new community and, to some degree, a new country.

Community may be defined by mental or spiritual as well as physical ties. "It may be found in, or be given symbolic expression by, locality, religion, nation, race, occupation, or crusade.... Fundamental to the strength of the bond of community is the real or imagined antithesis formed in the same social setting by the non-communal relations of competition or conflict, utility or contractual assent." A community can be formed because of individual beliefs and practices or in spite of them. In creating the American military establishment, Washington tried to build what was essentially a community based on a common calling—what the Puritans would have called *mission.* Yet Washington realistically recognized the necessity of establishing a network of legal relationships and contracts to structure the community into an organization able to achieve a specified end by specified means.[6] For although the Continental Community began as essentially a camp full of crusaders, its members, especially those now called camp followers, sometimes forgot the "cause" in their concentration on their occupations, locations, and personal relations. Revolutionary leaders—both civilian and military—had to try to engender in people such internal compulsions as patriotism and a desire for liberty so as to get them to fight in the army for independence, but they often had to rely on such external compulsions as contractual agreements (enlistments, commissions), money, and military discipline to keep them.

The story of this particular community is thus also one of generation, degeneration, and regeneration.[7] The Revolution begat the Continental Army: an army that, in turn, reproduced much of the structure of the British army. Army needs and army life, however, severely challenged revolutionary beliefs, practices, and peoples. The conflict between the ideal and real, theory and application, meant that revolutionaries both in and out of the army saw in the military community the deterioration or degradation of their cause and its institutions. Both its similarities and dissimilarities to the British army were pointed out as proof of this descent from grace. Yet with each reestablishment of the army, with every year survived, every drill learned, and every speech or order heeded, the officers, soldiers, and camp followers of the American army made progress in establishing a "camp upon a hill."[8]

In fostering the image of a successful republican, volunteer army, both contemporaries and later historians tended to overlook or dismiss camp followers. One reason was that many equated "camp follower" with "whore," or even if they were not quite so derogatory, they saw such a being as part of the lower orders that did not quite seem representative of or equal to the ideal of the American citizen. Yet to so define *camp follower* is not only to ignore the legions of civilians, other than prostitutes, who also followed the drum but slander many of them as well. Camp followers of the Continental Army, those "others belonging to the army" referred to by contemporaries, were male and female, young and old, and professed a variety of connections and occupations. They were people who were not officially in the army: they made no commissioning or enlistment vows. What kept them with the army was their desire to be near loved ones, to support themselves, and/or, in some cases, to share in the adventure. This diverse company encompassed both patriots, those who embraced the cause of independence with a fervor equaling or surpassing that of any soldier, and leeches, who were there merely for personal gain. A few prostitutes and scavengers trailed after the army, but family members, servants, and other authorized civilians outnumbered them by far. Article 23 in Section XIII of the 1776 American Articles of War provided a definition of camp followers: "all sutlers and retainers to a camp, and all persons whatsoever serving with the armies of the United States."[9]

Sutlers were merchants or traders permitted to sell provisions to the troops. Business-minded individuals, whether self-employed peddlers or representatives of some of America's bigger mercantile concerns, saw opportunity beckon as early as the spring of 1775 when New England militia units camped around Boston. They carted their goods in and set up shop. Some then attempted to stay with the forces that were united into the Continental Army. Their desire to profit from soldiers' needs and desires, however, could and did cause difficulties. Military commanders tried to prevent problems by permitting only a select few merchants to sell their goods within the army's lines. Furthermore, before they gave a trader a license to sell in camp, they demanded that he abide by army regulations and officers' orders. Although other peddlers were allowed in—or sneaked into—camp from time to time, only those merchants who had a regimental sponsor and who agreed to the terms set before them were allowed to set up booths within the camps and, sometimes, even follow the army on campaign.

Retainers followed the army because of personal inclination, pleasure, or the possibility of provisions and paying positions; they included women, children, servants, and volunteers. By attaching themselves to officers or soldiers, retainers helped form domestic units, families, or circles of intimates within the broader military community. Most could be labeled attendants: persons who accompanied officers or soldiers to attend or serve them. They were family members, servants, friends, and companions. Wives and other family members, friendly partisans though they may have been, acted as attendants when they visited male relatives in garrison or accompanied them on campaigns, for they provided domestic comforts and companionship. Servants and slaves, whether willing or unwilling, were there to relieve their employers of domestic chores: to attend to their gear, meals, and quarters, among other things. A few other retainers, who could be more properly called adherents rather than attendants, were partisans, or friends and companions who acted as aides and allies. Volunteers, the term referring in this case to gentlemen warriors, whether in search of a commission or not, and to men who wished to become officers and thus gentlemen, performed as companions-in-arms. Commanders accepted them within their military families so as to utilize their talents and promote their training. A few volunteers were men who just preferred to fight as independents, but most planned to join the service. After presenting their petitions for officer's appointments at headquarters, they socialized and even fought side-by-side with the officers and units they wished to join as they awaited word on their commissions. They could have returned home to await the answer, but volunteers generally were men who preferred action in the interim.

These camp followers had personal, as opposed to official, ties to the army (if they received and then operated an official suttling concession or if they accepted jobs within the civil or staff departments, they essentially moved out of this category of followers and into one of the others). The retainers, more than any of the other types of camp followers, seemed to fit the later British phrase that described such people as the army's human impedimenta.[10] Their ties to the military may have been somewhat tenuous and ill-defined, but commissioned and noncommissioned officers regulated them as they did everyone else they perceived as "belonging to the army." If a retainer did not obey military orders, he or she could be punished and dismissed from camp. The military community's need for order and security meant that everyone within it, including those not directly employed or contracted to the army, had to accept military discipline.

Finally, civilian employees working in or affiliated with the military's staff departments received the designation "persons serving with the army."[11] They were employed in the public service and often maintained at public expense. Their work was supposed to facilitate army operations and release soldiers from noncombatant duties. These army civilians served in various positions, including those of deputies, clerks, conductors, wagoners, artificers, nurses, and laborers. And they, like their uniformed counterparts, were subject to army regulations.

All of these people helped create the Continental Community: a society made unique by its American social, political, and military origins. The fact, however, that civilians did gather around the army and that a sense of community developed was not unheard of or even unusual. The Continental Army in developing its own military community reflected and followed precedents set by ancient, medieval, and contemporary military forces. As long as there have been armies, there have been camp followers: they are a military tradition.

The ability to endure privation marked the careers and characters of camp followers from the Roman to the early modern eras. The lives of female followers were particularly illustrative of the hardships and hazards of attaching oneself to the military, for their difficulties were compounded by the expectations and prejudices attendant on their gender and the biological consequences of their sex. Carrying babes in their arms and their household goods on their backs, these women trudged after the men and armies that gave them work and bread. The equation was set: the troops provided these women with a livelihood, and the work performed by these women contributed to the operations of the early European armies. Their work proved necessary but not extraordinary, for their tasks tended to be identical to the everyday chores of their sisters at home. They cooked the food, did the wash, mended clothing, took care of the sick and wounded, helped their fellow women, lay with men, and then bore and raised their children.[12]

Some of these women labored outside the purely domestic sphere in order to support themselves and their families. Female sutlers were often soldiers' wives or widows, not outsiders. Like their male counterparts, most women merchants made their living selling liquor and other staple items to the soldiers; some, however, did supplement their incomes by engaging in prostitution. In the seventeenth and eighteenth centuries, army women exercised many options to adjust to circumstance and ensure survival. The fact that the army was a community aided them in their efforts. The army had to serve itself. As armies grew larger, becoming direct instruments of state and king rather than private formations gathered and led by princelings and barons, they took greater control of support services instead of contracting out. Although military transportation was often directed by the civilian government and driven by civilian workers, and military supply continued to remain partly in the hands of noncombatant followers, sutlers and other service support groups came increasingly under direct military control during the eighteenth century. The result was not necessarily bad for the followers: the loss of some of their independence was offset by their achieving a semiofficial status.[13]

In line with other European armies, the British army developed both formal and informal policies to regulate camp followers, but there were differences. Whereas prostitutes were an accepted part of the Italian armies in the Renaissance, and the Spanish armies in the sixteenth and seventeenth centuries acknowledged their value, the English army chased the women of that particular profession out of camp. It banned them again and again over the years, but those indomitable women always came back. Even as the army tried to rid itself of them, policy assured such entrepreneurs an open market by making it difficult for the soldiers to engage in "legal" sex. By the late seventeenth century the army strongly discouraged marriage for soldiers. In 1671 soldiers in the Foot Guards were forbidden to marry without their captain's permission; in 1685 this became the policy for the whole army.[14] Soldiers were to think only of duty, not of family.

A few men did receive permission to marry and maintain their wives "on the strength" of the regiment. The British army generally allocated women "on the strength" a space in the barracks and a portion of the rations. As a number of men married without permission, there were also many "off the strength" wives living around the camps and garrisons. Such women did not receive the housing and ration privileges of the others, nor could they participate in the pool from which was drawn the names of the wives allowed to accompany the regiments on campaign (the British used a quota system to limit the number of wives traveling with the troops). Many women without permission followed the army anyway. Some made their own way out to join the regiment, while others managed to gain a berth by accompanying officers as servants.[15]

As a soldier's pay barely covered his own needs, let alone those of a family, the wives had to work. They formed a readily available and cheap labor force for the army. At the same time, the army in effect legitimized their position within the organization by giving them work. These followers found a niche for themselves as washerwomen, cleaning women, and, most especially, nurses. Almost all of the British army's nurses were female by 1750 (a few came from civilian hospitals, but most were soldiers' wives). Women also filled a number of other positions within the eighteenth-century army hospitals. They were laundresses, cooks, and matrons. The matron was the highest-paid woman in the medical services and had considerable respect and prestige. She supervised the nurses and had the general responsibility of overseeing the patients' comfort. Charlotte Browne was a matron of the British army hospital organized for General Edward Braddock's campaign against the French and Indians in 1755. During her service that season she dealt with recalcitrant servants (dismissing one for theft), absent nurses who preferred to be with their soldier-husbands, miserable roads, desolate camps, her brother's death, and her own illness. She also had to deal with the wounded refugees of Braddock's defeat and follow the remnants of that force to Fredericks Town, Maryland. While there, she was visited, probably to be examined for propriety, by the town's ladies.[16] Nursing and associated caregiver positions, then, assured women places within the military organization and, at least for matrons, gave them some respectability in civilian communities.

Americans became familiar with British camp-follower practice and policy by way of their participation in the colonial wars, especially the French and Indian War. The experience left provincials with mixed feelings about the value of such arrangements. A love-hate relationship existed between colonists and regulars to begin with; camp women only aggravated the situation. Most of these female followers were attached to the British regular forces, for although the Marylanders and Virginians with Braddock's expedition had women with them, the more strongly religious New Englanders did not permit women to accompany their regiments on campaign. The limitation or elimination of American women in and from the camps apparently served only to increase colonial prejudices; the provincials were generally not impressed by the examples of British womanhood accompanying the king's army. Even though the British army regulated women by way of general orders and subjected them to martial law, the provincials tended to regard them all as doxies. It did not seem to matter that most of the British soldiers' wives in America were legally married and often very loyal to their husbands.[17]

A few were not only loyal to their husbands, but were recognized as heroines. During the later war, the one for American independence, when the British and Americans were dealing with the follower question again, a woman's death gave a writer the chance to commend her earlier service. Mrs. Stone died at age forty-three in Ireland in June 1779.

> This woman ... being married when very young to a Mr. Stone, a serjeant in a marching regiment ... accompanied him, though she was rather of a small and handsome make, through most of the hardships our armies underwent in America during the last war; no consideration of fear could make her leave her husband's side, thro' *nine engagements* in which he was concerned; in the course of which she twice helped to carry him off wounded from the field of battle; and it is a fact which can be testified by living witnesses, now in Dublin, that at the siege of Louissburg, at a time when many of our troops were killed, she supplied the living with the powder cartridges of the dead, and animated the men in the ranks next to her by her words and actions. Though a woman of the most surprising intrepidity, she was never known to be guilty of any thing that could impeach her delicacy, or violate the modest demeanour of her sex.[18]

Mrs. Stone, however, was apparently the exception rather than the rule, and thus the British high command had the same reservations as the Americans. Many officers reluctantly accepted the presence of women even though some of them believed they debauched the troops, spread venereal disease, and were prone to stealing. Not only was it costly to maintain wives and children, but they were deemed lazy and recalcitrant as well. Officers tried to cow the women into obedience by threatening them with being drummed out of camp, having their rations revoked, or even confinement, whipping, and death. Yet even as commanders barked out orders and threats, camp women often found ways to circumvent the regulations, or they ignored them altogether.[19]

Not many army wives were allowed to accompany the troops from Britain to America during the period 1755 to 1783. During the French and Indian War approximately six women per company had permission to follow the army. This number actually decreased during the American Revolution. One result was that the British army in America lacked the usual contingent of experienced nurses who commonly followed the army on the European Continent. The army in the colonies had to rely on untrained soldiers' wives who generally disliked the duty, both for the miserable labor and because it separated them from their spouses. The hard, poorly paid work could also prove dangerous to the nurses if an epidemic raged through a hospital.[20]

Americans absorbed the lessons on handling auxiliary personnel at the same time they were learning strategy and tactics. The provincials saw that the British command allowed women to accompany the forces, but limited the number. They observed that the army regarded the women with suspicion, threatened them with harsh discipline, but seldom followed through. They noted that while some women provided essential services, others shirked their duty. Americans absorbed all this contradictory information and came to the conclusion that camp women were more trouble than they were worth.

The colonials more readily accepted the other, preponderantly male, camp followers: sutlers, contractors, and staff or civil department employees. British expeditionary troops and their colonial counterparts often resorted to sutlers to replenish personal supplies and supplement their rations. These retailers were very important to troop morale—that is, when they were not gouging the soldiers' pay with high prices. Contractors were generally less conspicuous, though at times no less cursed, as they moved in and out of encampments delivering equipment or excuses and conferring with officials in the army's military branches and public departments. Civil department personnel were everywhere. By the mid to late eighteenth century the British army had fully operational civil or public divisions; they included the adjutant general, quartermaster general, commissary general of stores and provisions, and deputy paymaster general departments, among others. Although they eventually became militarized in the nineteenth century, all commissaries and paymasters serving during the difficulties in America were civilians. There were also civilian storekeepers, clerks, and artificers.[21] Americans, familiar with these positions from their service with the British, incorporated them into their own military establishment when the time came.

There were a great many similarities in the types and treatment of camp followers with both sides during the War for American Independence. Americans had imbibed deeply of British military traditions, and it showed in their management of camp followers. Yet both forces had to adjust their administration of followers due to the nature of the conflict. Winning was contingent on the support of the civilian populace, including those who flocked to the camps. But winning was also contingent on controlling civilians, especially those in camp. The equation was complicated by the fact that not all were with the armies voluntarily. On the one hand, there were the poor families who were financially attached and the slaves who were legally fettered to soldiers and officers. On the other hand, there were the refugees who had been forced out of neutrality and into one camp or another.

As the armies ranged over the countryside combating the issue of independence, they alienated and displaced thousands from both sides. Many of the displaced then supported or, going one step further, joined one or the other of the armies because they believed in the cause or, especially in the case of the loyalists, had nowhere else to go. Some men enlisted so as to regain what they had lost. They joined those who served in the hopes of preventing enemy occupation or destruction of their property. Families joined their men when they had nowhere else to go.[22]

This movement of peoples was due to both the British-loyalist and American communities trying either to control or drive out all hostile and subversive civilians in their occupied areas. Revolutionaries viewed loyalists as malcontents and possible spies and thus often officially invited them to leave. Governing bodies were most severe with male suspects, but women also suffered persecution. In November 1777 two men, a woman, and two children loaded a small boat with provisions and valuables and crossed over to the British-held island in Rhode Island. They said that they fled "from the persecution of the Rebels who have filled the Jails of the Country with those who have shewn the least attachment to the King's Government."[23] A month later "between 3 and 400 women and children arrived [in New York City] from Fish-Kills, Poughkeepsie and Newburgh, being the wives and children of the friends of government that fled from persecution in different parts of this province; they were sent off by order of committees, councils of safety, &c. with little more than their wearing apparel, being robbed of their furniture, cattle, &c. and their farms given to strangers."[24] Political cleansing moved south when the Pennsylvania Assembly, on 6 June 1780, resolved that the wives and children of men with the enemy had to depart the state within ten days. If they remained after that time they were to be given no protection and considered enemies of the state.[25]

When conditions were reversed and the British controlled an area, families sympathetic to the American cause often tried to flee. Sometimes they made it out of the occupied zone; sometimes they did not. The British under siege in Savannah in the fall of 1779 refused a request by the American generals to release trapped women and children. On the other hand, the British allowed a number of women to ship out of Charleston in August of 1780. Upon their arrival in Philadelphia they said that they had been well treated by the British when they applied for permission to leave. The mitigating factor in that case may have been the onslaught of sickness in the city.[26]

The dispossessed persons who were forced to, or chose to, follow the armies heightened the sense of injustice and gave an added impetus to mission on both sides. In particular, refugee-followers with the Continental Army helped ensure that the contention that Americans had just grievances against Britain remained fresh. Common complaint fed into common cause, which, in turn, fostered a sense of common community.

Not all refugees became camp followers, however, and not all followers were refugees. Refugees huddled close to the armies for succor and safety, but often beyond that there was a relative passivity in the military sense. Camp followers, too, wanted aid and security, but they tended to be more actively involved in their own fate and that of their army. The armies encouraged that identification, for they needed active supporters in order to succeed, not passive parasites. This is not to say that all refugees were parasites—most were simply unfortunate victims of war—but if they would not help the army, then commanders did not want them. Washington preferred that most disperse around the countryside to be charges upon friends, families, and civilian governments, and that did occur. British commanders generally did not have that option due to the revolutionaries' control of most of the country. Thus strongholds such as New York became refugee centers.[27] Both armies as a result became very aware of the significance of such intimate civil-military relations over the course of the war, and their dealings with camp followers were part of that. The British army's acceptance, regulation, and relief of followers and refugees stand as comparison and counterpoint to the American army's acceptance, regulation, and integration of the camp followers who became so significant to its success in war.

The Continental Army collected a contingent of followers shortly after it took to the field in 1775. General Washington and other leaders were dismayed, but not surprised. When they tried to deal with these civilians, officers frequently turned to British precedents for guidance. That did not mean that they copied the model precisely. While their practices reflected the English example, they also often used common sense to adapt to ever-changing situations. Local arrangements were the rule rather than the exception, for although it was discussed, there was no concerted armywide policy, as in the British army, that covered all followers at all times.

As sutlers, women and children, servants and slaves, and other civilians followed the soldiers into the opposing camps, the armies had to decide what to do with them. Generally, commanders either welcomed or repelled the sutlers depending on their services and savoriness, tried (with varying degrees of force and success) to discourage the women and children from staying, put the servants and slaves to work assisting their masters, and—especially in the American army—engaged most other able-bodied civilians in tasks that supported the military mission. To make sure followers at least did not hinder, even if they did not help, the mission, commanders regulated them as they did their soldiers. They kept an eye on everything: from hygiene to housing; from recreation to business.

Soldiers are consumers—out to buy goods that fill their bellies, cover their bodies, make them feel good, or while away time—and there have always been plenty of people eager to sell them everything and anything that met those requirements and more. The American Revolution saw no exception to this maxim. As a result, both the British and American armies paid strict attention to the activities of the sutlers in their camps. Section VIII of the British Articles of War of 1765 (which were in force at the beginning of the Revolution) regulated suttling by limiting hours of operation and allowing the army to determine what goods could be sold and at what quality and price. Sutlers, however, also received a certain amount of protection under the section's Article IV: it forbade commanders to charge exorbitant rents for the buildings let out to the merchants. The American Articles of War of 1775 included almost verbatim most of the British regulations; the articles of 1776 contained them all.[28]

The armies could not control the merchants in city or countryside, but they could control who sold what in camp. If needed, a regiment would advertise for a qualified sutler, as British regiments did in July 1778 and September 1779, but generally—especially for the Americans—the problem was one of limiting the number of sutlers.[29] In either camp an appointment as camp sutler was extremely valuable, especially when the sale of liquor was authorized. No matter how high they raised the prices, sutlers could always find buyers for liquor. Both commanders and other citizens interested in the health and wealth of the soldiers were aware of this and tried to curb profiteers. But sutlers could only be controlled, not disposed of entirely. They were too important for the needs and morale of the troops. Besides these authorized concessionaires, numerous other peddlers hawked their wares in and around camp, including peddlers of the flesh. Armies were good for business.

Armies also offered employment to their followers. The British army saw nursing as one of the most important jobs available to women. Indeed, it was a job that could not be declined, for refusal meant banishment: "The Commander in Chief is Determin'd not to Allow any women to Remain with the Army That Refuses to take a Share of this Necessary Duty."[30] The British army also commonly gave wives "on the strength" (and some of those "off the strength," even though they were not supposed to be encouraged to remain with the troops) laundry detail. In addition to that, wives generally sewed and mended uniforms.

When in garrison, some camp women took on the cooking for a mess (a group of officers or soldiers who dined together) or filled positions as servants to officers and their families. When following the troops on the march, they performed the same tasks, although cooking was often done by the men themselves. The women also accepted any other odd jobs that popped up. At times these dependents herded cattle or sheep, or sold merchandise to the troops.[31]

The American army provided its women with the same sort of work their counterparts performed for the British army. The prevailing sentiment seemed to be that if the army had to accept their presence, they could at least earn their keep, contribute to the cause, and stay out of trouble. Although Washington complained that there were too many women with the army, he knew that if he did not supply them with rations or a way to provide for themselves he would lose their husbands and fathers as soldiers. Thus, even though some officers recommended and implemented a quota system in their units, it was never adopted as an armywide policy during the Revolution. Indeed, whereas some people thought the army was burdened with too many followers, others thought there were too few of these supporters. One man who observed the troops during the war thought that the Americans' ragged and unkempt appearance was due to the lack of enough women to tend to their clothing.[32]

Neither force took much care of its followers during march or battle. The British commonly ordered women to walk (no matter how burdened with packs or children) behind the army's baggage, especially when complaints were made that "the Regiml. Waggons are work'd Upon every Occasion which has Render'd many of their horses unfit for use."[33] When the troops engaged in battle, commanders expected camp followers to remain out of the way. The noncombatants usually clustered around the baggage, where they were safe enough unless the army had to make a quick retreat or the enemy attacked the supply train.[34] American camp followers received the same orders. Washington and other officers repeatedly commanded the women to stay off the wagons and walk alongside them. The women just as repeatedly ignored such commands and climbed aboard.

Even when camp women and other followers did obey orders to accompany the baggage and stay out of the way, they were still exposed to the hazards of war. Armies could not always provide adequate protection for their baggage trains or transports, and enemies took advantage of that, subjecting some camp followers to the terror of ambush and capture and even death. Such was the case in the summer of 1777 in New York, probably following the fall of Ticonderoga, when a British detail on Wood Creek captured boats laden with baggage, women, and invalids making for safety at Fort Anne. Sometimes the enemy was nature: in March 1779 the British ship *Mermaid,* transporting troops of the 82nd Regiment from Halifax to New York, ran aground and broke up. A total of 145 people died, including 13 women and 7 children. Among the 42 saved was not one woman or child.[35]

Although the vast majority of female followers were soldiers' wives, some officers had their consorts with them. Officers rarely, if ever, ordered their visiting wives to the same labor assigned to the other women with the army; they were also more attentive to their desires. Officers' wives were deemed to be ladies, and there was a distinct difference in the courtesies accorded them in garrison and on the march. It was not uncommon in the British army for officers to take their wives along on military expeditions. A number of officers' wives were with General John Burgoyne's troops in 1777; they included Christian Henrietta Acland ("Lady Harriet") and the wives of Major Harnage and Lieutenant Reynel. Lady Harriet became known for her perseverance in overcoming all the difficulties that beset her during that campaign. When her husband, Major John Acland, was wounded and taken prisoner on 7 October (at what has been called the second battle of Freeman's Farm or the battle of Bemis Heights), Lady Harriet requested and received permission to enter the enemy's lines to nurse him. The German contingent also had a resolute distaff side, including Baroness Frederika Riedesel and her three children.[36] But many officers' families, like those of the soldiers, spent a good deal of their days separated from their military men. Captain Frederick Mackenzie's wife and family "were left at Halifax, Nova Scotia in June 1776, when the Army embarked there to go against New York, and wintered there." They rejoined Mackenzie in Rhode Island in August 1777.[37]

American officers' wives, in comparison to their British and German counterparts, were not as likely to follow their husbands on campaign as to join them in camp. Most waited until the marches and battles of the season were over and the army was tucked into winter quarters before entering the military's realm. This tradition began early in the war when Martha Washington (often referred to as Lady Washington), Catharine Greene, and others joined their husbands in the camp outside Boston during the winter of 1775–1776. These women did contribute to the war effort by sewing and knitting and visiting with the troops to offer encouragement, but their exertions were always primarily for their husbands. Camp time, for some of these women, took on the aura of a social season; it was a time for formal calls, dinners, and dances.[38] This pattern of visiting and activities continued throughout the war, from Cambridge to Valley Forge and on to Morristown and the New York Highlands.

A great many of the officers and their wives had servants or waiters to attend to their needs. Some of the servants in the military community were soldiers detailed to the duty; some of the others, those not in uniform, were actually slaves. British officers often selected uniformed personal servants, or batmen, from the ranks, but they could also choose to have civilian servants with them. *The Royal Gazette* in New York ran advertisements for officers seeking servants. Not just anyone would do for these gentlemen; some were especially interested in finding an attendant who could dress hair. Those people in service to military personnel did not have an easy time of it: their work was hard, and as with any other soldier or camp follower, they were subject to the vicissitudes of war, including capture and death. The 20 July 1779 return of the prisoners taken by the Americans at Stony Point included two attendants left at Kakeal and twenty-five officers' servants sent to Easton. American officers also engaged military and civilian personal servants, but the practice was limited by manpower and financial shortages.[39]

Both the American and British armies employed African Americans as soldiers, servants, and laborers. John Murray, earl of Dunmore and royal governor of Virginia, issued a proclamation on 7 November 1775 freeing all indentured servants and slaves belonging to the rebels if they could and would bear arms in His Majesty's army. Lord Dunmore hoped not only to deprive rebel planters of their workers, but also to gain valuable laborers for the royal regiments as well. Many slaves accepted his offer. The governor enlisted many of them as soldiers, but the British army and navy put others to work as sailors, foragers, guides, artificers (the Royal Artillery had great need of them), and manual laborers. Adding insult to the injuries they caused the Americans, when the British raided the countryside, they not only burned down houses and destroyed crops, they also carried away slaves. The British agenda was, of course, to break the rebels; the African-American agenda was liberty. Some slaves simply slid through the British ranks and out to freedom, a move that certainly aggravated their liberators.[40] Most, however, even though British service often proved detrimental to their health (especially for refugees billeted on transport ships teeming with parasites and disease), stayed with that army and provided valuable services to the royal effort. One of the reasons given for the American failure at Savannah in the fall of 1779 was that Colonel Maitland used perhaps "2000 negroes" to strengthen and add to the British earthworks.[41]

African Americans were valuable to the Continental Army as well. The American army had numerous blacks in military service by 1778. Most of them were in the infantry, but many of these soldiers were sidelined into personal service as waiters or supporting roles such as cooks. Other African Americans acted as spies, guides, messengers, and laborers. Public levies procured slaves to clear land, repair roads, and construct redoubts and other fortifications. Black women also aided the army. Usually slaves, they served as nurses and cooks. Their employment released soldiers for other tasks.[42]

Other followers also released soldiers and officers for other duties. While many volunteers lived with and fought alongside the regiments into which they wished to be commissioned, others took positions in the staff (such as quartermaster and commissary) departments. The British army brought along most of its necessary civil department personnel and then hired the rest, as needed, in America. The American army built up its staff departments over the course of the war, but because of staffing difficulties the distinction between military and civil branches was never as great as in the British army. Due to a lack of qualified civilians, especially for the higher positions, many officers accepted additional staff duties, and many soldiers received either temporary or permanent artificer (mechanic) assignments. The militarization of these departments in the American army thus preceded the event in the British army. The Continental Army did, nonetheless, employ a great number of civilians for various jobs. Then as now, war created a demand for skilled artisans and laborers. The army joined battle with civilian manufacturers over these people, and although it generally lost out to the higher pay offered by domestic industries, the army did manage to hire many carpenters, blacksmiths, forge men, nailers, wagoners, and others. Some actually enlisted in the army; others worked for the army in a noncombatant status. In either case, their pay generally exceeded that of the ordinary soldier.[43]

One staff division in the American army, the hospital department, following the precedent set by the British service, hired many female as well as male civilians. In great need of nurses throughout the war, military hospitals recruited among the camp followers and the local populaces. Although army wives often nursed the sick and wounded, the army did not acknowledge them as army nurses unless they were actually hired for that task. The army engaged many dependent wives for nursing duties, but it also employed other women previously unconnected with the military as matrons and nurses for the army hospitals. Legislation passed in 1777 and after did not specify sex, but nurses were usually women because commanders did not want to release precious manpower for that duty.[44] Female nurses and male attendants not drawn from the line were camp followers: they did not enlist in the army, nor were they given the titular designation of officer as the physicians and surgeons-mates were, but they provided a valuable service.

There were some followers who had nothing in goods or skills to offer the army and took from it instead. Thieves recognized neither politics nor noble causes. Vagabonds on the road and inhabitants from nearby communities scurried into the camps and carried away just about everything on which they could get a grip. Some villains even impersonated soldiers in order to draw rations for themselves.[45] This meant that even as the American army battled with Congress for more supplies, it found itself hard-pressed to hang on to the stores it did have. It was besieged on more than one front.

The Continental Army struggled to survive not just physically but in spirit as well—and, as it did in the former, its community contributed to both the problem and solution of the latter. This was an army built upon anger, patriotism, and an incipient nationalism, and one maintained by sheer stubbornness as well as coercion and discipline. It was an army created out of fighting men, not one created to make men fight, though it soon had that duty too. Even after the *rage militaire* vanished, and both army and nation settled down to deal with limited pools of manpower and learned to accept, or at least tolerate, military discipline and training, most revolutionaries still preferred to think of the army as a voluntary association that aided the cause rather than a standing army necessary to its success.[46]

When the War for American Independence began, it pitted a crisis-born (and crisis-prone) citizen army against a long-standing professional one. American volunteers fought against British soldiers, most of whom had enlisted for life.[47] Revolutionaries, in contrast, joined militias and Continental regiments for varying lengths of time, to serve for as little as a matter of weeks or for as long as the war's duration. Over those weeks and years the farmers who had turned in their plowshares for swords, and the tradesmen their tools for guns, did evolve into a rather formidable fighting force. But the miracle was that they had gained the time to develop, for confronting them across the battlefield was a national army whose techniques and tactics had been honed in battle for over a hundred years, and with traditions that extended even further back in time. The British officers, many of whom belonged to Britain's upper classes, commanded soldiers (and soldiers' wives) drawn from the lowest level of the social order whose livelihood was the army and whose sense of community was "regimental esprit."[48] Their raison d'être was the military mission: the implementation of Britain's national policy via warfare whenever and wherever needed.

Some Americans, mirroring their British counterparts, joined the Continental Army in search of a livelihood, but revolutionaries had other reasons for serving in or with their army: they were defending the home front and trying to implement an ideological program. The war was fought on their domain. They looked around and saw "the remains of burnt and destroyed houses, once the fair fruit of hard industry, and now the striking monuments of British brutality," and walked over the dead bodies of people whom they had once loved. They fought the "Sons of Tyranny" for "their own estates and property, their own rights, liberties and government."[49] They joined the army to repel an invading force that threatened everything they had come to hold dear.

This perceived threat—as well as their shared experiences—contributed to a growing sense of unity and community among the people belonging to the army. That development, in turn, tied into a growing identification with the nation. While the newspapers, battling on the ideological front in this war, had promoted the growth of American nationalism, the army nurtured it.[50] The newspapers had presented the recipe for American patriotism, but the army was the cauldron in which the ingredients boiled and simmered and then boiled again. Washington reminded his suffering soldiers at Valley Forge that as citizens engaged in the glorious task of founding an empire they should scorn to cower from the "rigours of war, which Mercinary hirelings fighting in the Cause of lawless ambition, Rapine Devastation, Encounter with Cheerfulness and Elacrity. We should not mearly be equal, we should be superior to them in every qualification that dignifies the man or Soldier in proportion as the motives from which we act and the final hopes of our toils are superior to theirs."[51]

Service with the Continental Army, just as service in it, seems to have expanded many men's allegiances to include nation as well as colony or state. As success appeared to be dependent on a common identity as well as unified action, that was no small matter. Officers and soldiers professed their allegiance via their commissioning and enlistment papers, but volunteers and staff department personnel also identified with the military's expression of the national mission. The volunteers, in their enthusiasm and desire for action and appointments, helped at times, ephemeral as it might have been, to reinvigorate jaded or discouraged officers and confirm the value of both position and cause. Those who joined the staff departments, dedicating their efforts to tasks that turned them into the scapegoats for frustrating failures if ill-performed but into saviors if performed well, released officers and soldiers for duty in the fields of combat. These people were sure—and had it confirmed by others who stated that the army could not do without them—that their work contributed to the achievement of independence, and their sense of importance as well as worthiness of recognition and recompense grew accordingly.[52]

In contrast to some of their male counterparts, many of the women who served the army did so for personal reasons rather than broad political convictions. Their contributions to the war effort were on a secondary level: they supported the men who fought the war. Even those who did harbor strong convictions usually channeled their patriotic efforts through appropriate female work. Their identities remained fixed in the domestic sphere. That identification was promoted by the Continental Army's officers and soldiers who were fighting for the rights and property of men. The hierarchy, regulations, and exigencies of military life generally gave most camp women little opportunity to develop or exercise autonomous political expression.[53]

Women within camp, as those without, did, however, use the intrusion of the public, political world into their domestic one to speak out. They did so through petitions, boycotts, and personal behavior (including cutting ties with friends now deemed enemies, and associating only with men and women of like opinions—the Continental Community certainly being an example of that) and thereby discovered how their actions could affect public acts and opinions. Abigail Adams declared that a woman's patriotism was the most disinterested of all human virtues because such patriotism was without thought of ever attaining public office or honor. She gave proof to her own analysis when she continued to support American independence and her husband John's struggles toward that goal even after he brushed aside her calls for new laws in favor of the female sex.[54] Others believed, as she did, that the women of America wanted to contribute actively to the cause; and the *Pennsylvania Gazette* was pleased to publish such sentiments: "Our ambition is kindled by the fame of those heroines of antiquity, who have rendered their sex illustrious, and proved to the universe, that, if the weakness of our constitution, if opinion and manners did not forbid us to march to glory by the same paths as the men, we should at least equal, and sometimes surpass them in our love for the public good."[55]

American men, in response, both privately and publicly honored women for their patriotic stands even as they continued to accord them no political power. Alexander Hamilton considered women who kept their men in the army to be heroines. He both believed and encouraged his fiancée, Elizabeth Schuyler, to be one when he wrote her, "I know . . . that if you saw me inclined to quit the service of your country, you would dissuade me from it."[56] She not only did what he expected, after they were married she also accompanied him to camp on occasion. On the public stage, when the widow Mary Fishbourne died in October of 1781, the *Pennsylvania Gazette* lauded her not only for her excellent social and maternal character but also for her "steady and zealous regard to the rights of her country."[57] Americans, male and female, began over the course of the war to believe that women had a national, if not political, identity as well as a domestic one.

Of course a few women patriots did march out of their domestic province. Army life gave them a unique, though dangerous, opportunity to do so. Women disguised as men had served in European armies throughout the last half of the seventeenth and into the eighteenth centuries. Their ability to perform as soldiers may have been advanced by changes in military technology that led to a decline in the use of the pike and matchlock musket and the issue of lighter flintlocks and other weapons. Female participation in military actions continued into the American Revolution. Thousands of women were involved in military operations (some only as "baggage," but a few as actual combatants) during the war. Some disguised as men enlisted in the army, others following the army took up arms when the situation seemed to demand it, and even some women at home found it necessary to defend person and property.[58] Assuming such a role could be hazardous, however, not just for the possibility of physical danger but of social censure as well. The latter could be a profoundly humiliating experience, as one young woman found out. Running away from a father who would not permit her to marry the man she desired, she decided to enlist in the American army (thus a patriotic as well as personal gesture) at Elizabethtown in 1778. Suspected of being a she rather than a he, the young enlistee was forced to undergo a physical examination which revealed the truth. The next day Lieutenant William Barton "orderd the Drums to beat her [while still in men's clothing] Threw the Town with the whores march."[59]

An act of heroism or suffering, as in being shot, could mitigate contemporary censure and ensure future renown for women in and with the military. That was the result with Deborah Sampson and Samuel Gay (only her pseudonym is known), both of whom enlisted in the army, were wounded, and upon being treated were discovered and discharged. The camp follower Mary Ludwig Hays, who found a place within American mythology as "Molly Pitcher," supposedly not only carried buckets of water to the soldiers but "manned" an artillery piece at Monmouth during the heat of battle.[60]

Most camp followers, however, both male and female, were not with the army to do battle; they were there to do service. As with numerous soldiers and officers, some failed the test of virtue and patriotism, but many others proved their mettle. Although some camp followers certainly hindered the army's efforts, others helped it become a more effective fighting force. Some provided much-needed supplies and spirits: at a price to be sure, but welcome all the same. Others raised spirits by engendering a sense of domestic comfort and continuity, or by volunteering their admiration and active support. Still others took up pen and hammer, awl and whip, scalpel and shovel, so that soldiers could lay those down and pick up their muskets.

The Continental Army was thus both the reason for and a part of a Continental Community of people both in and with the military. Army and community were continental in that, although neither reflected a United States at war's beginning, both mirrored the process and problems of unification during the war and helped establish the United States by their survival to and success at war's end. In 1775 the army was essentially a militia force composed of men who saw themselves as warriors fighting for their country—and not all saw themselves as belonging to the same country. Over the course of the war the army had to train them to be the nation's soldiers. It also had to convince followers of the importance of the state over the individual. The army did not succeed with every person, but the measure of its success with many, if not most, was seen in the victories of the troops and the eventual cohesion of the community.

The Continental Community reflected eighteenth-century American society and culture. Social stratification was made obvious by the rank and file: who gained rank, who earned it, and who did not. Yet American egalitarianism was made evident by the struggles to maintain deference and order in the face of democracy and individualism. Some members of the community strove to create a conventional army, while others celebrated its unconventional facets; both groups adapted as circumstances and community dictated. Perhaps the one stable element was that gender roles remained essentially the same in principle if not always in practice. Finally, reflecting the development of some other American communities, some people joined the Continental Community for material reasons, whereas others did so for idealistic ones—and staying was the result of an amalgam of the two.

The survival of the Continental Army rested upon this community: on the perseverance of its officers and soldiers, the labors of its camp followers, and the effective regulation of both. In particular, as the army accommodated itself to meet its followers' needs, it in turn insisted that they accommodate themselves to its rules: military orders and law. In its emphasis on legality and accountability, the administration of this community certainly reflected the American heritage and revolution, but it also shows that the army's leaders wanted to make soldiers not only out of warriors but out of women, waiters, and wagoners.

Notes

1. Entry, 11 August, British Intelligence Journal, New York, 1778, Manuscript Division, Library of Congress, Washington, D.C. Henry Knox's estimate of the size of the Continental Army in 1778 was 32,899; the number of troops at White Plains in August had to be considerably less. For Knox's estimates, see Fred Anderson Berg, *Encyclopedia of Continental Army Units: Battalions, Regiments, and Independent Corps* (Harrisburg, Pa.: Stackpole Books, 1972), 143.
2. Mackenzie, Long Island, 26 October [1776], in *Diary of Frederick Mackenzie: Giving a Daily Narrative of his Military Service as an Officer of the Regiment of Royal Welch Fusiliers during the Years 1775–1778 in Massachusetts, Rhode Island and New York* (Cambridge: Harvard University Press, 1930; reprint, New York: Arno Press, n.d.), 89. Hamilton to James Duane, [Liberty Pole, New Jersey, 3 September 1780], in Harold C. Syrett and Jacob E. Cook, eds., *The Papers of Alexander Hamilton,* 26 vols. (New York: Columbia University Press, 1961–1979), 2:411. John Shy in *A People Numerous and Armed: Reflections on the Military Struggle for American Independence,* rev. ed. (Ann Arbor: University of Michigan Press, Ann Arbor Paperbacks, 1990), 177, noted, "Only a pervasive armed organization, in which almost everyone took some part, kept people constantly, year after year, at the hard task of revolution."
3. George Washington to Joseph Reed, Headquarters New Windsor, 5[–7] May 1781, in John C. Fitzpatrick, ed., *The Writings of George Washington, from the Original Manuscript Sources, 1745–1799,* 39 vols. (Washington, D.C.: U.S. Government Printing Office, 1931–1944), 22:46. Hamilton certainly thought that the states had too much say in army matters. As the army was "an essential cement of the union" he believed that only Congress should have control. He also thought that only the personal influence of Washington might hinder the tendency of some lines in the army obeying their states over Congress. Hamilton to James Duane, in another part of 3 September 1780 letter, in Syrett, ed., *Papers of Alexander Hamilton,* 2:402.
4. He began as he meant to go on: Washington to Massachusetts General Court, [c. 1 April 1776], and New York Committee of Safety to Washington, New York, 18 April 1776, in W. W. Abbot, ed., *The Papers of George Washington,* Revolutionary War Series (Charlottesville: University Press of Virginia, 1985–), 4:8, 81. Charles Royster in *A Revolutionary People at War: The Continental Army and American Character, 1775–1783* (1979; reprint, New York: W. W. Norton, 1981), 51, discussed civil authority.
5. Fred Anderson in *A People's Army: Massachusetts Soldiers and Society in the Seven Years' War,* paperback ed. (New York: W. W. Norton, 1985), 27, defined provincial armies. Harold E. Selesky in *War and Society in Colonial Connecticut* (New Ha-

ven, Conn.: Yale University Press, 1990), 144, listed some of the distinctive features of the expeditionary forces. James Kirby Martin and Mark Edward Lender, in *A Respectable Army: The Military Origins of the Republic, 1763–1789* (Arlington Heights, Ill.: Harlan Davidson, 1982) and Royster in *A Revolutionary People* discussed this idea.

6. Robert A. Nisbet in *The Sociological Tradition* (New York: Basic Books, 1966), 48, 74–76, gave a basic definition of community, and then defined and analyzed what Ferdinand Tünnies called Gemeinschaft (essentially a community based on common mission) and Gesellschaft (society constructed via legal, contractual structures).

7. Royster, in *A Revolutionary People,* and Shy, in *A People Numerous and Armed,* among others have noted the rise, fall, and rise again (or at least desire for the rise again) of the *rage militaire* and patriotism during the war.

8. With due respect to John Winthrop's "we shall be a city upon a hill" in his sermon "A Model of Christian Charity," and to Perry Miller's study of declension in *The New England Mind: The Seventeenth Century* and *The New England Mind: From Colony to Province* (Cambridge, Mass.: Harvard University Press, 1939, 1953).

9. John O'Brien, *A Treatise on American Military Laws, and the Practice of Courts Martial; with Suggestions for their Improvement* (Philadelphia: Lea & Blanchard, 1846), 322. Although Article 23 does not itself use the term *camp follower,* various authors (see below) over time have used the term to describe the people listed or have called this the "camp-follower article."

10. Myna Trustram in *Women of the Regiment: Marriage and the Victorian Army* (Cambridge: Cambridge University Press, 1984), 82, 84, quoted *The Lancet* (1861) and the *United States Gazette* (1874) on "the human part of an army's impedimenta" and "the female impedimenta of the regiment."

11. O'Brien, *Treatise on American Military Laws,* 150. There were a few discrepancies in how various authors defined these groups. All of the authors I consulted agreed on the definition of a sutler; however, there was not a consensus on who was a retainer and who a public servant. I used O'Brien's definitions because they most accorded with my own research. His interpretation is supported by William Winthrop, *Military Law and Precedents,* 2nd ed. (Washington, D.C.: Government Printing Office, 1920; reprint, New York: Arno Press, 1979), 98–99. Winthrop describes retainers (for Article 63 in the contemporary articles of war which included sutlers under the heading of retainers) as "camp-followers attending the army but not in the public service," and "persons serving with the armies in the field" as "civilians in the employment and service of the *government* [italics are his]." Giving more support to this argument is Frederick Bernays Wiener's *Civilians Under Military Justice: The British Practice since 1689 Especially in North America* (Chicago & London: University of Chicago Press, 1967), 7. Wiener, in classifying the civilians who accompanied the British army in the field in 1689 and thereafter, stated that retainers included officers' servants, volunteers, women, and children, and he differentiates them from the individuals who served in the civil departments of the army. Reading the article somewhat differently were William C. DeHart, *Observations on Military Law, and the Constitution and Practice of Courts Martial . . .* (New York: Wiley & Putnam, 1846), 24–25, and S. V. Benét, *A Treatise on Military*

Law and the Practice of Courts-Martial (New York: D. Van Nostrand, 1862), 29. Both DeHart and Benét defined retainers as those connected to the military service by pay or fee (Benét appears to have taken his definition directly from DeHart), and "persons serving with the armies" as including all persons who receive their compensation from private sources (such as servants).

12. Barton Hacker, "Women and Military Institutions in Early Modern Europe: A Reconnaissance," *Signs: Journal of Women in Culture and Society* 6, no. 4 (1981): 653.
13. Ibid., pp. 650, 655.
14. Ibid., p. 651, on prostitution. Trustram, *Women of the regiment,* p. 30, on marriage.
15. Ibid., pp. 30–32, 86.
16. Ibid., p. 105, on work legitimizing position. Paul E. Kopperman, "Medical Services in the British Army, 1742–1783," *Journal of the History of Medicine and Allied Sciences* 34 (1979): 436–38. [Charlotte] Browne, "Journal of Mrs. Browne, Braddock's Expedition, 1754–1757," copy in The New-York Historical Society, New York City. Diary printed in full but with variations from this manuscript, from MS. in Library of Congress in Isabel M. Calder, ed., *Colonial Captivities, Marches, and Journeys* (1934; reprint, Port Washington, N.Y.: Kennikat Press, 1967). Thanks to Ross D. Netherton for a copy of Carol C. Deakin's "Support Personnel: Women with General Braddock's Forces," in James Allen Braden, ed., *Proceedings of Northern Virginia Studies Conference, 1983* (Alexandria: Northern Virginia Community College, 1984), in which she discussed Charlotte Browne.
17. Braddock ordered a limit on the number of women at Fort Cumberland, with only four allowed to each of the Virginia and Maryland Ranger companies; in Deakin,"Support Personnel," p. 89. Selesky, *War and Society in Colonial Connecticut,* pp. 182–83, pointed out New Englanders' religious objections to the women. Anderson in *A People's Army,* pp. 118–19, when noting that the women were regulated, used the term *military justice; martial law* is perhaps more precise. Paul E. Kopperman, "The British High Command and Soldiers' Wives in America, 1755–1783," *Journal of the Society for Army Historical Research* 60 (1982): 14–15.
18. *The Royal Gazette* (see *Rivington's New-York Gazetteer*), 25 September 1779, p. 2, cols. 1–2. This is followed by an account about a woman disguised as a male trying to enlist in the British army destined for America so as to join her lover, an officer who had been sent there about two years earlier.
19. Kopperman, "British High Command," pp. 17–19, 24–25.
20. Ibid., pp. 26–27; and "Medical Services," p. 439.
21. Anderson, *People's Army,* p. 88, on sutlers. Wiener, *Civilians Under Military Justice,* pp. 87–88. Wiener gave a quick introduction to the civil departments in the text but more fully discussed personnel in the footnotes.
22. Joseph S. Tiedemann said that the British army was an agent of the Revolution in that it fostered hatred among many Americans, in "Patriots by Default: Queens County, New York, and the British Army, 1776–1783," *William and Mary Quarterly,* 3d ser., 43-1 (1986), reprinted in Peter S. Onuf, ed., *The New American Nation 1775–1820,* Vol. 3: *The Revolution in the States* (New York: Garland, 1991), pp. 295–323. Stephen Conway in "To Subdue America: British Army Officers and the Conduct of the Revolutionary War," *William and Mary Quarterly,* 3d ser., 43-3

(1986), reprinted in Onuf, ed., *The New American Nation*, Vol. 2: *Patriots, Redcoats, and Loyalists* (New York: Garland, 1991), pp. 139–65. Walter Hart Blumenthal, *Women Camp Followers of the American Revolution* (Philadelphia: George MacManus, 1952), p. 58. Blumenthal stated that shortly after Lexington and Concord, many women were left homeless, but that few of them followed the Minutemen; most went to friends and relatives in the countryside. It was only later that more women joined their men in the army. The *Pennsylvania Gazette*, 18 June 1777, p. 3, col. 2, reported on the assembly's resolutions concerning the evacuation of Philadelphia residents.
23. Mackenzie, Rhode Island, 26 November [1777], *Diary*, 215.
24. *The Royal Gazette*, 27 December 1777, p. 2, col. 2. Jonathan Clark's "The Problem of Allegiance in Revolutionary Poughkeepsie" in David D. Hall, John M. Murrin, and Thad W. Tate, eds., *Saints & Revolutionaries: Essays on Early American History* (New York: W. W. Norton, 1984), pp. 285–317, on the retention and coercion of loyalty in one particular community.
25. *Pennsylvania Gazette*, 7 June 1780, p. 2, col. 2.
26. *Pennsylvania Gazette*, 10 November 1779, p. 3, col. 1. Extract of a letter from Charleston about Savannah, dated 9 October 1779; and 23 August 1780, p. 3, col. 2.
27. An "Abstract of the Number of Men, Women, Children and Waggoners Victualed at the Commissary Generals Provision Stores between the 17th and 20th July 1778," in the Clinton Papers, 37:18, at the William L. Clements Library, University of Michigan, Ann Arbor, noted hundreds of women and children with the loyalist as well as British forces in New York and Rhode Island. It also specifically referred to 315 male and 12 female refugees. Mackenzie, on 23 July [1778, New York], in *Diary*, 572, recorded that rebels appeared near Morrissania and had "plundered & burnt the huts of the Refugees" and that the commander in chief ordered "those poor men, who now amount to 490, to be furnished with tents, and to receive pay and provisions as Soldiers during the time they continue under the present circumstances. Most of them have large families." *The Royal Gazette*, 7 November 1778, p. 3, col. 4, ran an ad that refugees in need of assistance should call on Col. Beverley Robinson in King-Street by the 16th. Then on 6 January 1779, p. 1, col. 1, a "PUBLIC NOTICE is hereby given to the distressed Refugees, that the Gentlemen appointed to distribute the money collected by subscription for their relief, attend at the Police Office in Smi[t]h-Street, every Thursday. . . ."
28. Winthrop, *Military Law,* British Articles of War in effect in 1765, Articles I–IV, Section VIII, pp. 935–36; and 1775 American Articles of War, Articles LXIV, LXV, and LXVI, p. 958; O'Brien, *Treatise on American Military Laws*, 1776 American Articles of War, Articles 1–4, Section VIII, pp. 317–18.
29. Advertisements in *The Royal Gazette*, 8 July 1778, p. 1, col. 3, and 29 September 1779, p. 2, col. 3. Petition, Inhabitants of County of Culpeper about sutlers preying on soldiers and other men being willing to sell for less if given access to camp, 16 November 1776, Legislative Petitions, General Assembly, Legislative Department, Archives, The Library of Virginia, Richmond. For other examples, see Chapter III.
30. Headquarters, 15 October 1776, Sir William Howe Orderly Book, 27 January 1776–1 May 1778, at William L. Clements Library.

31. Kopperman, "British High Command," p. 15.
32. Janice E. McKenny, "'Women in Combat': Comment," *Armed Forces and Society* 8 (Summer 1982): 686. Hacker, "Women and Military Institutions," p. 661.
33. Headquarters New York Island, 1 October 1776, Sir William Howe Orderly Book, 27 January 1776–1 May 1778.
34. Kopperman, "British High Command," pp. 29–30.
35. Ibid., p. 28, on Wood Creek incident. *The Royal Gazette,* 21 April 1779, p. 3, col. 1.
36. See *Pennsylvania Gazette,* 11 October 1780, p. 2, col. 1. for a contemporary published account of Lady Harriet. Don Higginbotham, *The War of American Independence: Military Attitudes, Policies, and Practice, 1763–1789* (1971; reprint, Boston: Northeastern University Press, 1983), pp. 188–89.
37. Mackenzie, [Rhode Island], 22 August 1777, *Diary,* p. 169.
38. John F. Stegeman and Janet A. Stegeman, *Caty: A Biography of Catharine Littlefield Greene* (1977; reprint, Athens: University of Georgia Press, Brown Thrasher Books, 1985), pp. 23–24.
39. *The Royal Gazette,* 13 June 1778, p. 4, col. 3, and 19 May 1779, p. 3, col. 4. *Pennsylvania Gazette,* 28 July 1779, p. 2, col. 3. To get a sense of the numbers and distribution of servants, compare the commands in American orderly books ordering waiters back to the line, etc. (see Chapter V), to Sylvia Frey's analysis in *The British Soldier in America: A Social History of Military Life in the Revolutionary Period* (Austin: University of Texas Press, 1981) and *Water from the Rock: Black Resistance in a Revolutionary Age* (Princeton, N.J.: Princeton University Press, 1991). In the latter book, on page 163, Frey pointed out the authorized and perceived numbers of blacks used as servants by British officers, soldiers, and wives in 1780–1781.
40. Benjamin Quarles, "Lord Dunmore as Liberator," in James Kirby Martin and Karen R. Stubaus, eds., *The American Revolution: Whose Revolution?* (Huntington, N.Y.: Robert E. Krieger, 1977), pp. 78–83. Frey, *Water from the Rock,* pp. 121–22. *Pennsylvania Gazette,* 31 January 1781, p. 3, col. 1. An extract of a letter from Petersburg, Virginia, dated 12 January, tells of the burning of houses along the James River and the abduction of a great number of Negroes by the enemy. *The Royal Gazette,* on 6 February 1779, p. 3, col. 4, ad about "Labourers in the service of the Royal Artillery" who deserted from "the Virginia Company of BLACKS."
41. *Pennsylvania Gazette,* 24 November 1779, p. 3, col. 1. In a report coming out of Charleston, 20 October, some reasons were given why the assault on Savannah did not succeed.
42. Higginbotham, *War of American Independence,* p. 396. Philip S. Foner, *Blacks in the American Revolution* (Westport, Conn.: Greenwood Press, 1976), p. 71.
43. Higginbotham, *War of American Independence,* p. 393.
44. McKenny, "Comment," pp. 686–87.
45. Wayne E. Carp, *To Starve the Army at Pleasure: Continental Army Administration and American Political Culture 1775–1783* (Chapel Hill & London: University of North Carolina Press, 1984), p. 65.
46. Royster in *A Revolutionary People,* pp. 25, 114–18, discussed Americans' concept of the army as an organization and its place in the Revolution.

47. Ibid., p. 133. Royster said that by 1777 "the hope for interchangeable citizens and soldiers no longer described the Continental Army," but there was still the belief that soldiers were citizens and would shortly return to civilian life. Therefore I call this a citizen army as opposed to Britain's army of career soldiers. Trustram, *Women of the Regiment*, p. 18: "Until 1847 enlistment in the army was for life or until a discharge on medical grounds was granted." Frey, *The British Soldier*, p. 118: "The average foot soldier had better than ten years of service." Apparently rumors to the effect that Americans wishing to serve with the British would have to enlist for life caused some problems in recruiting. Clinton published a proclamation assuring prospective soldiers of a good bounty and an enlistment of only three years in any provincial regiment of their choice in *The Royal Gazette*, 4 August 1781, p. 3, col. 1.
48. Hacker, "Women and Military Institutions," p. 654. Frey, in *The British Soldier*, pp. 118–19, 132, 137, discussed the bonds between the men—both officers and soldiers—in a regiment and that "the military style of life tended to produce a cohesive community." She noted that this was partly due to the long lengths of service and the fact that the British army tried to unite family members and friends in the same company.
49. *Pennsylvania Gazette*, 30 October 1782, p. 2, cols. 1–3. In this response to the Earl of Shelburne by "Common Sense," a number of points are made about why Americans rebelled and continued to fight. Address from the Massachusetts General Court to Washington, [Watertown], [c. 28 March 1776], in Abbot, ed., *Papers of Washington*, 3:555–56.
50. Higginbotham, *War of American Independence*, pp. 263, 412–13. Higginbotham referred to Charles Stuart, a British officer, who after seeing the determination of American soldiers, felt something new was being added to warfare: that to win, officers and men must be animated by common ideals. Of course shared zeal as an ideological weapon was not entirely new to war. Higginbotham also stated that revolutionary newspapers spurred Americans to call for freedom and into a sense of nationalism. He believed that whereas nationalism was an instigator of revolutions in Europe, Africa, and Asia, it was merely the product, not the cause, of revolution in America. I would say that nationalism was both product and cause. It was produced by the war, yet it in turn caused others to enter the war and prolong the fight, and in the end nationalism led to a constitutional revolution. Conway, in "To Subdue America," pp. 164–65, stated, "The patriot press . . . naturally enhanced the notoriety of the hard-liners by providing a regular diet of tales of destruction, insult, and injury experienced at the hands of the king's troops."
51. Headquarters Valley Forge, 1 March 1778, *Valley Forge Orderly Book of General George Weedon of the Continental Army under Command of Genl. George Washington, in the Campaign of 1777–8* (1902; reprint, New York: Arno Press, 1971), p. 245.
52. Lt. Col. Henry Beekman Livingston to Washington, Ft. Constitution, [NY], 11 [–14] June 1776, in Abbot, *Papers of Washington*, 4:500–501. In his letter, Livingston said, "I Cant Learn that any Provision is made for a Barrack Master or a Conductor of Stores, tho' they are Persons we Can Scarcely do without. . . ." This belief in the

value of their contributions is repeated in pension applications; see, for instance those of Daniel Morris, artificer, and William Burnett, wagoner, in John C. Dann, ed., *The Revolution Remembered: Eyewitness Accounts of the War for Independence* (Chicago: University of Chicago Press, 1980).

53. Linda K. Kerber, *Women of the Republic: Intellect and Ideology in Revolutionary America* (Chapel Hill: University of North Carolina Press, 1980), pp. 73–74. Kerber stated that it is not clear that shared hospital service politicized army nurses the way shared military service widened men's allegiances. She noted that most women who contributed to the patriotic cause did so in an individual rather than institutional context. "They did not change their domestic identity (though they put it to a broader service), and they did not seriously challenge the traditional definition of the woman's domestic domain." Nancy F. Cott, *The Bonds of Womanhood: "Woman's Sphere" in New England, 1780–1835* (New Haven: Yale University Press, 1977), p. 188. The military community certainly serves as an example of what Cott saw in postwar America: "Amidst the weakening of traditional dependency relationships the only hierarchy vociferously maintained (outside of racism) was women's subordination to men, or more specifically, wives' subordination to husbands."

54. *Pennsylvania Gazette,* 16 July 1777, p. 3, col. 1. The young ladies of Amelia County, Virginia, entered into a pact "not to permit the addresses of any person" unless he had proven by valor and length of service in the American army "that he is deserving of their love." Phyllis Lee Levin, *Abigail Adams: A Biography* (New York: St. Martin's Press, 1987), pp. 135–36, 81–87.

55. *Pennsylvania Gazette,* 21 June 1780, p. 1, cols. 1–2. Doctor Thacher thought this noteworthy enough to copy it out, with a few alterations, of one of the newspapers. James Thacher, *Military Journal of the American Revolution* (1862; reprint, New York: Arno Press, 1969), p. 240.

56. Hamilton to Elizabeth Schuyler, [Teaneck, New Jersey, August 1780], in Syrett, ed., *Papers of Hamilton,* 2:397.

57. *Pennsylvania Gazette,* 10 October 1781, p. 3, col. 2. Mrs. Mary Fishbourne, the patriotic widow of William Fishbourne, died suddenly on Tuesday, 2 October, at the age of fifty-five. For comparison: *The Royal Gazette* on 16 January 1779, p. 3, col. 3, lauded loyalist women who were apparently trying to sponsor or equip a privateer with a poem that included: "Whose well-taught minds, in just connection view, / What's to your God, your King, and Country due."

58. Hacker, "Women and Military Institutions," p. 659. Linda Grant DePauw, "Women in Combat: The Revolutionary War Experience," *Armed Forces and Society,* 7 (Winter 1981): 209–10. DePauw in her thought-provoking article overstated that tens of thousands of women were involved in active combat. She divided these women into three groups: those who served in a distinct branch of the Continental Army and were referred to as "women of the army"; those who enlisted in the regular troops; and those women who served as irregular fighters affiliated with local militias. In trying to show the importance of women to the army, a laudable goal, DePauw was a bit extreme in stating "women of the army" formed a distinct branch of service.

59. Robert Fridlington, "A 'Diversion' in Newark: A Letter from the New Jersey Continental Line, 1778," *New Jersey History* 105 (Spring/Summer 1987): 75–78.
60. McKenney, "Comment," p. 688. Both women were discharged as soon as their sex was discovered. McKenny refuted some of DePauw's claims. There is a controversy over the designation of "Molly Pitcher." Common lore has it that Molly Pitcher was Mary Ludwig Hays, but some evidence seems to point to that title being invented years after the war (Thacher in his *Military Journal* does refer to a Molly Pitcher on 4 July 1778, but there are some inaccuracies in his story which may indicate that he added it in for publication later) and may have been used to personalize the heroism of all such women in the war. Perhaps the best way to define this heroine is to say that "Molly Pitcher" is the idealized Mary Ludwig Hays; her tale is based upon the exploits or stories of Hays and is used to illustrate the contributions of camp women in the Revolution.

2

The Army
A Continental Community

> I found a mixed multitude of People here, under very little discipline, order, or Government.
>
> General George Washington
> Cambridge, Massachusetts
> 27 July 1775[1]

General George Washington rode into the army camp at Cambridge on 2 July 1775. The "commander-in-chief of all the troops raised, and to be raised, for the defence of the United colonies"[2] looked around and immediately began to plan for the bitter campaign to come: the campaign to establish a well-regulated and respectable military community. By August he had broken one colonel and five captains for cowardice or embezzlement and arrested two other colonels on the same charges. At the same time he struggled to straighten out the "indifferent" officers, he worked on shaping up the rank and file. Washington fumed that the provincial troops by no means deserved the heroic reputation they had garnered in the press. He found them to be "exceeding dirty & nasty," but, showing a modest amount of optimism, concluded that they would fight well if properly officered.[3] During those frantic first months Washington paid little heed to camp followers unless they were volunteers petitioning him for commissions or sutlers able to provision his troops. Later in the war, however, as he struggled to keep the army intact, supplied, and savory, he devoted more attention to all the people belonging to the army, for they profoundly affected the force he had to make fit to fight.

Common service and common experiences would help forge disparate persons into one people: one community. Assisting that process, with varied results, was the emphasis on subordinating the individual—with his or her personal habits, interests, and desires—to the group so as to ensure the survival of the army and the success of the Revolution. Yet within that community, reflecting the composition of civilian society, there would still be distinctions between persons due to origins, rank, duties, race, and gender.

Furthermore, political and military demands, ideological and regulatory requirements, as well as logistical and humanitarian concerns defined the parameters of the Continental Community. The army had not only to win the war, but the organization and its community were supposed to reflect the image Americans had of themselves and the hopes they had for their country. On a more basic level, the army had to be able to pack up and move its people from post to post as needed, as well as feed, clothe, and shelter them. To do any of this with any sort of effectiveness and efficiency required the implementation of a strong administrative system. The army's leaders tried. They cajoled and they ordered, and then, as appropriate, rewarded and punished the officers, soldiers, and followers. The community, and the system for its administration, evolved over the course of the war. Neither ever became perfect: the same old problems cropped up time and time again during the war, but on the whole progress—tenuous though it was—was made in creating a more effective fighting force and a more orderly community.

The first steps—soon running into a continuing process—in regulating this community were attempts to minimize the need for external regulation or discipline. The Continental Congress, provincial (later state) governments, and military leaders wanted men to pick up their arms, defend their country, and promote the Revolution freely as befitted virtuous, enlightened warriors. Therefore, as they began recruiting, they appealed to the martial spirit in American society and glorified soldiering: soldiers were heroes, and society would heap honors upon its warriors.[4] As long as a rage against injustice and a fever for adventure heated the blood in men's veins, the call to arms worked. But the *rage militaire* soon subsided: men's passions cooled in the winter of 1775–1776, then rekindled a bit with the Declaration of Independence; but then reason, that is, personal interests, tended to prevail. Essentially, too, the revolutionaries were awakening to the difference between that splendid myth of the warrior and the slogging reality of the soldier.

Washington attempted to foster both recruiting and retention by appealing to both the ideological and the material interests of his countrymen. If liberty, independence, equality, and honor could not impel a man to take up arms, then surely property, and the desire to protect or acquire it, would. Nor did Washington ignore the men already in the service. In November of 1775 he bemoaned the lack of public spirit that was leading to a disintegration of the line; he decried the "dirty, mercenary Spirit" that pervaded the army. But on a calmer day, even after receiving depressing regimental returns, Washington realistically recognized that "there must be Some other Stimulus besides, Love for their Country, to make men fond of the Service." He remarked to John Hancock that it would cost the government nothing extra but do much good if soldiers were to receive their pay for October and November and perhaps an advance of a month's pay.[5] Throughout the war the general continued to remind his soldiers of their patriotic duty while he labored to provide them with the necessities not only for battle but for life.

The American military community thus developed around a dichotomous core of duty and self-interest, but while the self-interest was recognized and to some measure satisfied, recruiters continued to expound upon the nobility of the sacrifice. Newspapers, pulpits, and orders bombarded soldiers and civilians with the message that they must persevere in the struggle to maintain American liberties. Camp residents ingested huge amounts of rhetoric detailing the political positions of the warring parties. One of the facets that made this war so revolutionary was this injection of "ideological conflict into warfare."[6] Yet despite all the propaganda and proselytizing, many in the military community still had a difficult time choosing between public or national liberty and personal freedom.

In the extreme, in battle, the virtuous warrior may be called upon to relinquish his liberty and perhaps his life to secure the liberties and lives of others. Even everyday army life demanded that military and associated personnel give up some measure of individual choice and action so as to preserve order and insure combat readiness. This meant that there was a constant struggle to reconcile personal autonomy with national need. Washington recognized these internal conflicts and painfully acknowledged the result: soldiers would not always do their duty; they would not always stand and fight in the face of overwhelming odds. He felt that their lack of discipline reflected the fact that they were free men. The revolutionaries' devotion to freedom and representative government led to their revolt against the crown, but it also made them unreliable soldiers. They were restive under military discipline, and yet that discipline was necessary to the preservation and success of the army.[7] Fortunately for those trying to build an American fighting force, the very insistence on individual rights that sometimes made military life chaotic also served to keep many people in the army. They did not take well to army discipline and duties, but they were determined to fight. A foreign officer serving with the British observed, "what Religion was there [during the Huguenot wars in France], Liberty is here, simply fanaticism, and the effects are the same."[8] Throughout the war Washington and others constantly attempted to rekindle that dedication, or what some would call fanaticism, in order to preserve the army's strength and the community's spirit.

As Dr. James Thacher, a young physician who would soon join the Continental service, recorded in January 1775, "In no country . . . is the love of liberty more deeply rooted, or the knowledge of the rights inherent to freemen more generally diffused, or better understood, than among the British American Colonies." He went on to write, on 21 April, of a burgeoning American patriotism after the battles at Lexington and Concord: "The people of New England have taken the alarm, and their hearts are animated even to enthusiasm. There is an enthusiasm in religion, in politics, in military achievements, and in gallantry and love, and why not an enthusiasm in the love of country? No species of enthusiasm surely can be more laudable, or more honorable. Never was a cause more just, more sacred than ours...."[9]

The legislatures, Congress, and the commander in chief never let nation or army forget that theirs was a sacred endeavor. God's blessings were for this enlightened but beleaguered people. When the Massachusetts legislature decided to make Thursday, 23 November 1775, a day of public thanksgiving to offer praise and prayer to God so that the ultimate patriot would continue "to smile upon our Endeavours, to restore peace, preserve our Rights, and Privileges, to the latest posterity; prosper the American Arms, preserve and strengthen the Harmony of the United Colonies, and avert the Calamities of a civil war," Washington commanded that "all Officers, Soldiers & others" take part.[10] Even though God did not immediately restore peace or divert civil war, Americans continued to make the deity a part of their military strategy. Whenever Congress directed that there be a day of fasting, humiliation, and prayer, as it did, for example, for 15 May 1776, 17 December 1777, and 27 April 1781, Washington encouraged the troops to participate by ordering that no work be done that day and that the chaplains prepare appropriate discourses.[11] God and politics did mix during the American Revolution.

Providence, patriotism, posterity, and property loomed large in all rallying and battle cries. As soldiers of the Pennsylvania Rifle Regiment (or 1st Continental Regiment as it was also then designated) were informed on 2 July 1776: "The time is now near at hand which must probably determine whether Americans are to be freemen or slaves—Whether they are to have any property they can call their own—Whether their houses and farms are to be pillaged and destroyed and they consigned to a state of wretchedness from which no human efforts will probably deliver them. The fate of unborn millions will now depend under God on the courage and conduct of this army."[12] The troops had a duty to fulfill the dreams of those who had died for independence, and a responsibility to ensure freedom for future generations; for as the historian Charles Royster has pointed out, the war had become "one of the obligations of a contract between the living, the dead, and the unborn."[13] A little over a year later, troops were asked, "Who can forbear to Emulate their [the resolute militia to the north] noble Spirit? Who is there without Ambition to Share with them the applauses of their Countrymen & of all Posterity, as the Defenders of liberty & procurers of Peace & Happiness to Millions in the present & future Generations?"[14] Weighed down with their obligations to generations past and present, but uplifted by the promise of being honored by God, nation, and millions of future Americans (the revolutionaries were positive posterity would never forget their triumphs and tribulations), people had strong incentives to join and then remain with the army. Should a soldier's resolve weaken, however, Washington was prepared: "It is a noble Cause we are engaged in, . . . But it may not be amiss for the Troops to know, that if any Man in action shall presume to skulk, hide himself, or retreat for the enemy, without the order of his commanding Officer; he will be *instantly shot down,* as an example of cowardice; . . . Next to the favour of divine providence, nothing is more essentially necessary to give this Army the victory of all its enemies, than Exactness of discipline. . . ."[15]

Washington was determined to provide that ingredient so essential to victory and, incidentally, community cohesion. In 1775, as he handed down order after order relating to rules and discipline, the relative ranks of units and officers, and the requirements for effective military action, the encamped soldiers and civilians coalesced into the Continental Community. It was a community that proved flexible enough to adapt to the reorganizations of 1776, 1777, 1778, 1779, 1781, and 1783.[16] It could do this because it was greater than the individual units that made up the army; if a regiment disbanded, deployed, or reorganized, it often meant only that a superimposed army organizational unit, not the underlying base of people, had changed.

There was continuity because the fundamental mission of the army never changed and the community's government remained consistent throughout the war. The Continental Community was a heavily regulated community, governed by decree. When Washington took charge of the army at Cambridge, he made sure that all inhabitants of the community knew they were subject to orders: "The Adjutant of each Regiment is required to take special care, that all general orders are communicated, as well to the private men, as to the officers—that there may be no Plea of Ignorance." On 17 July 1775 he repeated and clarified the previous order by telling the adjutants to read the orders to the off-duty men every evening; he then pounded home his point on the 20th when he told the aides-de-camp and brigade majors to keep all general and brigade orders recorded in a book, again so that there would be no excuse for ignorance.[17] Commanding officers worried about the dissemination of orders throughout the war and constantly reminded their subordinates that they were duty-bound to know all applicable regulations and orders and to pass them on. After orders (supplementary orders given after general, brigade, or regimental orders) for the 3rd New York Regiment at Fishkill on 6 March 1777 specified that the general orders passed on by Colonel Cortlandt (probably Philip Van Cortlandt of the 2nd New York), who copied them from General Alexander McDougall's orderly book, "be placed in the Main Guard Room" and that the officers acquaint their men with the contents. A month later garrison orders for Fort Constitution included a request that the commander of the artillery send a person daily to the post commander to receive the latter's orders for the garrison, and "if any Commanding Officer of a Company neglect to provide an Orderly Book and appoint an Orderly Sergeant or Corporal to Receive the Daily Orders—It will be Esteemed Disobedience of Orders, Orderly Sergeants or Corporals who Neglect to attend the Adjutant at the Beating of the Sergeants call, The Adjutant must Confine for Disobedience of Orders." Commanders also promised dire punishment for any person found defacing or tearing down orders posted in the guardhouses and continued the general policy of reading orders at the evening parade.[18]

Everyone—officers, soldiers, and camp followers—had to obey the rules that regulated the Continental Community within its own boundaries and in its relationship with the surrounding civilian communities. While orders most commonly dealt with the discipline and duties of the soldiers, officers received plenty of guidance as well. Washington had set the tone as early as August 1775 when, after hearing of unauthorized visits to nearby towns by too many officers, he directed that commanding officers confine any officers who were absent without written permission from their brigade's general. He then authorized commanders to arrest officers who disobeyed the order in the future. Washington gave a reason for his severity: "When Officers set good Examples, it may be expected that the Men will with zeal and alacrity follow them, but it would be a mere phenomenon in nature, to find a well disciplin'd Soldiery, where Officers are relax'd and tardy in their duty; nor can they with any kind of propriety, or good Conscience, set in Judgment upon a Soldier for disobeying an order, which they themselves are every day breaking. . . ."[19]

As for civilians, Washington had already warned the sutlers, tavern owners, and innkeepers in the vicinity of the camp that if they continued to supply soldiers with "immoderate Quantities of Rum, and other spiritous Liquors" without the written permission of the soldiers' captains they could expect severe punishment.[20] Control of military-connected civilians continued over the years; for example, not only sutlers but wagoners and women as well had orders to take proper charge of their horses at Smithes Clove in June 1779. General orders promised retribution to any person who allowed his or her horse to continue to graze and trample the inhabitants' property.[21]

The orderly books also illuminated another way in which the military community was regulated—through returns and rosters. All army units, company level and above, kept written rolls of their personnel. These rolls most commonly took two forms: muster rolls and inspection returns. The former usually had names and ranks followed by remarks columns; the latter divided the unit by rank and then listed the number present for duty, sick, on furlough, held as prisoner, and so on. The army at times also requested returns on special groups of people. For example, when company commanders at Fort Schuyler in 1777 had to submit returns of their men, the post engineer had to submit a list of all the carpenters, artificers, and laborers (except those soldier-artificers belonging to regiment and garrison) he had employed at the time.[22] On 20 August 1778 headquarters personnel at White Plains wanted "Returns of all the Negroes, in the Several Rigements to be made out Immediately[,] Rigementally Digested into Brigade Returns & brought into the Orderly Office Next Satturday."[23] In 1780 the West Point commandant wanted the garrison quartermaster to furnish him with a "Return of all the Sutlers in Garrison, and by whom they are Licensed."[24] As the war progressed, army commanders became increasingly concerned about the number of dependents accompanying their troops and periodically requested information about them. According to general orders of 14 June 1781, "An exact return of all the Women with the Army who draw Provision from the Public is to be given in at the Orderly Office, as soon as may be." The next day the brigades and regiments passed on the order: the commanders were to hand in their returns of the women with each company to the regimental adjutant at the beating of retreat, and the regiments in turn were to deliver their returns to the brigade major at orderly time on the 16th.[25] In this manner army commanders tried to keep track of all the people within the perimeters of their units.

One of the primary difficulties challenging the creation, and certainly the control and success, of the army was insuring its security. It had to be secured against foe and friend. The former, though difficult, was a relatively straightforward task. The latter was trickier because military leaders had to minimize the disruptions and distractions created by civilians and civil society and government, and yet had to do so without alienating those civilian bodies. They also endeavored to make sure that their own people did not jeopardize cordial civil-military relations.

As hard as commanders strived to keep their people within the lines, they tried harder to limit access to camp and garrison to those who belonged or were attached to the army, and to local inhabitants authorized to offer goods and services to military personnel.[26] The Continental Community was a restricted as well as restrictive community, thus providing another angle to the definition of "belonging to the army": belonging denoting access to the lines. This was an important distinction, especially as community members knew that others wanted admittance. The attempt to make it a "closed" community may have given some a feeling of protection against outside forces.

Physical security was necessary both to deny the enemy information and to deny thieves their livelihood. Security may appear to be a matter of common sense, but as Washington learned shortly after taking command, many lacked that sense. When he found soldiers and officers conversing with the enemy around Cambridge that July, the appalled and angry general promised that any officer, noncommissioned officer, soldier, or "any other Person whatever" found conversing or corresponding with enemy officers or sentries would be court-martialed and severely punished.[27] Later that month Washington ordered that all passes be discontinued, and that no one "be admitted into the Lines, unless introduced by an Officer, who can vouch for him, or by Order of the Officer commanding in the Lines."[28] In September 1776, when the American army faced the British in New York, he further intensified camp security. Washington ordered officers not to allow anyone to pass beyond the outer sentries without written permission from the brigadier of the day. Sentries were to fire upon anyone disobeying the directive. Washington added that any person entering the camp from the enemy's lines was to be brought for questioning before that brigadier general. That individual, in turn, was to send a written report along with the person to the commander in chief.[29]

Variations of these directives established security throughout the war. Sentries at West Point in February 1780 had orders not to allow any suspicious person or stranger to enter the works unless that person was acknowledged by an officer.[30] That April, in New Jersey, Washington, after being told that there were suspicious characters lurking around camp, directed that officers, especially those of the guards, examine all strangers "found in camp or in the vicinity," and if they did not have proper credentials "send them to the officers of the day for particular examination who will either dismiss or confine them as circumstances may require. The importance of [suppressing] Spies demands the strictest attention." Over a year later, in 1781, as the army gathered itself together for another campaign, Washington again gave security strict attention. In June he wrote to the Comte de Rochambeau that secrecy was "more than commonly necessary" where the latter was, for "the enemy will have emissaries in your Camp in the Garb of peasants with provisions and other matters and will be attentive to every word which they may hear drop." In his own camp Washington ordered that "no person not belonging to the Army is to be permitted to pass through the Camp without being carried to the General or one of the field Officers of the day who will examine him or her very critically and suffer none to pass of suspicious Character or who does not give a satisfactory Account." Then the commander in chief wrote to Major General Alexander McDougall at West Point, to alert him and urge "particular Caution and Watchfulness" because he had information of a spy—with a mole under one eye, a scar on one temple, and appearing "in the Garb of a common Country man"— sent out to reconnoiter the post.[31]

That the supposedly secure community had holes there was no doubt. Spies gathered information (some of it correct) on the Continental Army both from without and within the camps throughout the war. Perimeters around encampments, those in New York in 1778 serving as prime examples, were as secure as sieves against these particular followers. Some, it is true, did not set out to follow the army for this purpose, but deserters who switched sides and reported to the enemy assisted espionage efforts. When William Miller changed sides that August, he was interviewed by a British intelligence officer. Miller, a Scotsman who had lived thirteen years in the colonies, had served with the Continental Army for eighteen months as a carpenter and then in the army for three months as a soldier. His information included estimates on American magazines, provisions, and wagons.[32]

One of the British army's most effective agents, a woman who mingled with American troops to sell thread and other supplies, loitered around Washington's quarters to record conversations. During one mission, from Tuesday, 11 August, to Saturday, 15 August, she listened to officers debate the possibility of taking Long Island, found out that General Horatio Gates and Colonel Morgan had light infantry troops under their command somewhere near Dobbs Ferry, and discovered that three thousand army troops and two thousand militia under the command of Lafayette had marched for Rhode Island on 3 August (the day after she left the camp on a previous mission). This follower, who obviously did not belong to the American army, also uncovered information about Lord Stirling's (General William Alexander) command, counted the equipment in the park of artillery, and learned from a friend in the camp that Captain James's whole troop was ready to desert. Her report on that mission also detailed the disposition of the troops, including the fact that on Thursday the 13th the whole army was drunk after having received two months pay (she believed that had the British army advanced on that day they could have destroyed the Americans). On her mission from 12 to 17 September, she observed the army at White Plains, marched out with the Pennsylvania troops heading to North Castle on the 15th, reached Washington's headquarters at Peekskill with them on Wednesday, and left them Thursday morning at sunrise when they moved out. Later that month, when she again joined Washington's army, she ascertained not only the strength and position of the American forces but also conversed with a talkative officer who revealed the defenses at Danbury and then gossiped about Washington's low spirits. The woman was unable to fade out of camp on that particular mission. She left the army on Friday night, but being discovered by a person named Smith (a deserter from the 27th Regiment), was detained by General Grant's aide-de-camp from Monday the 28th to Wednesday. Upon her release she made her way back to the British lines and reported in on 30 September.[33] American vigilance proved ineffective in this case; either the female spy's cover as a camp peddler held, or her sex made her questioners lenient. This spy was released; others were not so lucky.

That fall the British intelligence service sent out Joseph Styres to spy on the American army. While returning by way of the heights above Tarrytown, information from a deserter who knew him resulted in his arrest two miles from a Colonel Hammond's (probably Lieutenant Colonel James Hamman of the New York militia) post. He was brought before the colonel and examined, but before anything else could happen he managed to escape from a sentry and make his way back to his own lines to report on the enemy's numbers and movements.[34] Many spies managed to get in and out of the American camp; however, the Continentals did catch—and hold on to—a few of them. A division court-martial at Danbury in October 1778 tried David Farnsworth and John Blair for spying around the "Encampment of the Armies of the United States" and for carrying counterfeit money brought from New York. The court found them guilty of the charges and sentenced them to death. Washington approved the sentence and ordered them to be executed as soon as they arrived at Gates's division.[35] Tory recruiters, trying to steal men as opposed to information, were handled in the same way.[36]

The Continental Army also tried to keep its people and property safe from enemy Indians. After commissioners tried to obtain alliances or, failing that, ensure neutrality, Continental forces attacked the Iroquois in the New York hinterlands. At various times and places in the backcountry, army and militia units also battled other tribes who were either affiliated with the British or attempting to protect their own interests; these included the Shawnee, Delaware, Cherokee, and Creek. The Continental Army did have some native allies among the Oneidas, Tuscaroras, and Catawbas, and those allies sometimes did bring followers into camp, but often the Indians following and watching these troops were not friendly.[37] Fort Schuyler's commander reminded his people of the threat in garrison orders of 12 April 1778: "There being reason to suspect that there is a Scouting party of Enemy Indians skulking about this place no person is to be suffered to Straggle into the Woods or to go any Distance from the Fort except they are on Command. The parties who go out to work, are to have proper Guards."[38] Where fortifications were strong and guards attentive, the Continentals blunted Indian incursions, but where defenses were weak, as along the Ohio frontier, the Indians proved highly destructive.[39]

Thieves struck through the army's defenses as well. On the night of 8–9 November 1779, at an artillery park in New York, someone broke into the shop kept by the field commissary of the Military Stores Department and took a chest containing steel, brass files, and other articles. Samuel Hodgdon, the commissary, promised a reward for the apprehension of the thief. He also provided the information that an inhabitant seen lurking about the shop with a two-horse wagon may have committed the robbery.[40] People stole and pilfered army supplies throughout the war, for although the American army did eventually beat the British, it never did rout the thieves that plagued it in garrison and on the march. Orderly books held numerous advertisements concerning items lost or stolen and offering rewards for the return of goods or bringing in the thieves. These records also made it clear that thievery was not confined to civilians, but that military members engaged in it as well.[41]

As the army struggled to keep some people in camp and others out, and as it endeavored to regulate the actions of all who came in contact with the troops, it extended its authority at times to limit the movement of persons not only through the camps themselves but the American lines as well. Perhaps the widest the military cast its net was in southeastern Pennsylvania in the winter of 1777–1778: it tried to control all movement going in and out of Philadelphia. The army wanted a complete stop of traffic in information and provisions. Sentries already routinely checked out the men who wanted to pass through their posts, but at that time they received specific orders to regulate the movement of women as well. Orders issued from the headquarters at White Marsh stated that "No Women coming out of Philadelphia are to be permitted to pass the First Guards without being told they cannot return again [;] if upon being informed of this they chuse to come out they are to be allowed to pass the Guards into the Country." The order applied not only to guards but to scouting parties as well. Women were again under scrutiny in February of 1778. First the army had to squelch rumors that Mr. Jones, the deputy commissary general of issues, had given a pass to a woman to carry thirty pounds of butter into Philadelphia. Then, having become too lenient over the winter, it clamped down on visitors because of "the most pernicious consequences having arisen from Suffering Persons (Women in particular) to pass and repass from Philadelphia to Camp under a pretence, of coming out to visit their friends in the Army and returning with necessaries to their families, but realy with an intent to entice the soldiers to Desert. . . ." The army threatened to punish both soldiers and civilians caught disregarding the ban. Then to further increase its control, the army that March ordered officers commanding outposts and scouting parties that they were not to issue passes into Philadelphia because such permits defeated the very purpose of their guards and scouts.[42]

The army's actions did have an impact on the civilians living within its realm of influence. Sarah Wister, a young Quaker from Philadelphia staying with relatives outside the occupied city, recorded her encounter with a sentry determined to do his duty. It was a fine May day when Wister and three other young women decided to stroll over to a neighbor's place. They ambled past two picket guards who did not interrupt their excursion, but on their way home a sentry stopped them and said he had orders not to allow anyone to pass without leave by the officer at the guardhouse. The friends faced a dilemma: the officer was surrounded by men, and it was not at all proper for the young women to go to him, but it was also quite stupid to stay there as night fell. Wister tried to talk the sentry into letting them pass, but to no avail. Then one of her friends attempted to walk by the man; that was a mistake, for the guard then presented his weapon, bayonet fixed, and scared them further. Fortunately, at that point the officer came over, sorted out the problem, reprimanded the soldier, and let them go.[43] Sarah Wister and her friends were no threat to the army's security, but the sentry probably did not deserve a reprimand since he was right to be suspicious of women who wandered about the military's perimeter. Women, such as the milliner Margaret Hutchinson, did carry intelligence to the enemy in Philadelphia, just as they did in New York.[44]

Throughout that long season at Valley Forge, the army's authority reached beyond its accompanying community. Whenever it apprehended someone acting suspiciously in camp or out, the military incarcerated the accused and then brought him or her before a military tribunal. A general court-martial in April found three inhabitants of Pennsylvania guilty of attempting to aid the enemy. Philip Culp and John Blooman received fifty lashes and duties in the public service (their work to continue until the enemy left the state) for attempting to transport flour to the British in Philadelphia. The court allowed that they could get out of their enforced employment if they enlisted in the military. John Evans, who attempted to send provisions into the city, did not suffer the lash, but he was sentenced to labor for the public's good at Carlisle as long as the enemy remained in Pennsylvania.[45]

Although the army tried to control civilian actions that aided the enemy and harmed the Continental cause, its focus was always on its own people. In attempting to minimize any friction that might arise between the military and civilian communities, army commanders concentrated on retaining personnel and regulating their behavior. Washington addressed one of the biggest causes of friction between the communities when he issued orders, which included threats of dire punishment, to prevent plundering and destructive disregard of property. He appealed to his soldiers' patriotism as well as their consciences. In the spring of 1776 he told the troops "that we come to protect; not to injure the property of any man," and in the fall he reminded them "that no plundering Army was ever a succesful one."[46] When that lesson did not take, he reminded them again in 1777: "were we in an Enimies Country such Practices wil be unwarrantable but committed against our friends are in the highest degree base Cruel & Injurous to the Cause in which we are Engaged. . . . Such crimes have brought reproach upon the army and Every Officer & Soldier Suffers by the practice of it."[47] Years passed and warnings continued, as in July 1781 when Washington ordered that cattle and horses taken "by volunteers or any other persons (except properly taken in action) shall be restored to the owners of whatever political Character they are. . . ." It pained him "to Reflect how disgraceful and derogatory it would be to the reputation of an Army who are the Assertors of Freedom as well as of the Rights of Humanity and of individuals should they ever be guilty of plundering in the minutest article."[48]

The general continued not only to issue such admonishments throughout the war, but followed his words with action. Offenders suffered the full weight of the law, often by way of the whip, but sometimes in the form of the noose. Washington, often charitable to those found guilty of various other crimes, commuting or lightening sentences handed down by the court, was seldom merciful to those convicted of plundering. He could not condone the subversion of one of the tenets of the Revolution: the protection of property. As teacher as well as commander, Washington was determined that his people would learn this lesson. Many did; as did some—but not all—British commanders who recognized that plundering as a punitive policy would probably alienate rather than generate more possible supporters within the American populace.[49]

To maintain cordial relations between the military and civilian communities, the American army's leaders had not only to prevent miscreants in the Continental Community from abusing their neighbors, but also to protect their own people and property from abuses by outsiders.[50] This was made difficult by the fact that the army and its people were not always well thought of after the first flush of martial spirit in 1775–1776 and after militiamen went home to be replaced by soldiers who enlisted for three years or the duration. Two young officers made observations to this effect in 1780. It was in April when the first officer walked out of religious services in Springfield, Massachusetts, because the minister, a Mr. Brook, in his sermon "cast such severe reflections on the Continental Army & on those Parents who had sons in the Army as obliges me in Justice to myself & the Army to quit a Person so impertinently abusive."[51] That October, Ensign Benjamin Gilbert wrote to his father and stepmother caustically describing citizens who despised and slighted the soldiers only to turn around and adore those same soldiers when their communities were threatened by enemy attack or occupation.[52]

Soldiers, generally being the young and less well-to-do, which was translated by some contemporaries as the more irresponsible, irreverent, and indigent members of American society, were induced into its service but not always welcomed (in contrast to the more socially acceptable officers) into its communities. Americans who wanted to believe that the army was a patriotic band of solid citizens did not like being confronted with what appeared to be mercenaries and an increasingly professional army. It suggested something about themselves—namely, a diminution of virtue and equality—that they did not want to know.[53] So when the enemy had already disrupted local life, the army's presence was accepted with relief; but when the army itself proved disruptive, when it created problems rather than peace and profits, then the civilian communities took no pleasure in its company. Washington and his commanders worked throughout the war to change that attitude by trying to create respectable soldiers and an acceptable army. They sometimes had help from the civilian authorities.

The Continental Congress and state governments occasionally acted as mediators in troublesome situations by passing resolutions that controlled local government and resident transactions with the soldiers. For example, in 1777 the General Assembly of Delaware passed a resolution stating that it was unlawful to arrest a soldier in the American army for debt, unless the plaintiff swore before the proper witnesses that the soldier owed more than fifty dollars. It also declared that "no inn-keeper, tavern-keeper or public house-keeper, shall demand, take or receive from any recruit or soldier, whilst upon a march, any more than One-sixth of a Dollar for any one meal," nor could such persons demand or accept recompense for lodging these recruits or soldiers.[54] The governments passed such resolutions not only to regulate the contact between civilians and soldiers, but also to help keep the soldiers in the ranks where they belonged. Furthermore, to keep the army in the field, and its worrisome people in the military community as opposed to in their own communities, these governments had to arrange for pay and provisions. All too often they did a poor job of it, so perhaps it was not surprising that members of the military came back to haunt them.

***

Constituents of the Continental Community needed more than a national objective and a secure camp to keep them there; they required physical sustenance. Both the states and the Continental Congress intermittently provided food, shelter, and clothing (in varying quantities and quality) for military and associated personnel, but that was never enough: they also had to pay their servants. Those who labored in or with the army expected their "customary due" both in recognition of the work itself and its importance to the cause.[55] As such, the payment of wages was vital not only to an individual's survival but to his or her sense of self-worth. This, in turn, affected a person's commitment to and cooperation in the war effort. As the survival of the army rested upon the continued participation of officers, soldiers, and civilian workers, as well as the support of their families, the importance of material reward and assistance was manifest. On a more mundane level, officers and soldiers needed money because they had to supplement their government issues with items bought from camp sutlers and in civilian marketplaces. Army employees and other followers received little in the way of government issue to begin with (they often did receive rations), and so they too needed funds with which to purchase other necessities. Wages were even more essential to the many people who supported not only themselves but families. To fight for an ideal was recognizably virtuous; to stay because it was honorable to do so was laudable; but to many practical Americans it was pay (or at least the promise thereof) that made soldiering endurable.

Doctor Thacher noted in July of 1778 that many officers were dissatisfied and then went on to explain why. He commented that officers generally joined the army for one or a combination of three reasons: patriotism, monetary reward, or the "novelty of the employment." Whatever the category they fell into, all believed the contest would be short. They were wrong. As the fight continued over the years, patriotism dissipated, money depreciated, and the military commission lost its appeal. Many officers had left lucrative employment to serve their country, only to contemplate the possibility of destitution by war's end. As a result of these ruminations, many officers resigned. Washington, worried about losing too many of his experienced officers, approached Congress about a solution in 1778. Upon his recommendation, Congress decided to award all commissioned officers who served to the end of the war an annual pension of half-pay that would commence at the war's conclusion and continue for a total of seven years. Congress also resolved that the noncommissioned officers and soldiers who served to the end of the war would receive a bonus of eighty dollars at that time.[56] That was not the first solution nor was it the last. Officers and soldiers wrangled with their representatives in Congress over the financial rewards of service throughout the war and after.

After the first flush of excitement that accompanied rebellion faded, most men contemplating service took time to weigh patriotism and adventure against monetary recompense. The scale often tipped in favor of civilian security over military glory. After strolling around the camp at Cambridge in December 1775, Thacher noted that many of the Connecticut troops could not be persuaded to remain in the army; they quickly left camp after their enlistments expired. Thacher also reported that recruiters were distributed throughout New England but voluntary enlistments proceeded slowly. He seemed to subscribe the desire for higher wages to a subsiding of the patriotic spirit.[57] His observation was basically sound. When nobler impulses failed to induce a man to join the army, bounties, pay hikes, and pensions that offered land as well as money sometimes succeeded. The problem was that "sometimes" was not good enough.

To counter the problem of diminishing ranks, the army occasionally resorted to the impressment of vagrants, and recruiters (much to Washington's displeasure) enlisted British deserters and prisoners of war into the American service.[58] Also, although Washington and other officers voted against the enlistment of African Americans in October 1775, by December the commander in chief supported it. He needed men, and there were free blacks who wanted to enlist; furthermore, if their service was not accepted, he feared they would apply to the British army.[59] As Washington continued to have difficulty filling the lines, he proposed that men be drafted into the army. Congress, after pondering the proposal for a while, finally consented to a military draft that would be essentially controlled by the states. Congress gave the states quotas to fill, which the states in turn usually divided among their militia regiments. Thus a militiaman might find himself conscripted to serve with the Continental forces. Being drafted, however, did not always mean one was left without alternatives. Sometimes a draftee could avoid such military service by paying a fine or by getting a substitute to go in his place.[60] Actually, some other enlistees apparently also had that option in times of sickness, disability, and approved leaves of absence: as long as they received permission from their commanders and gave money to their substitutes. John Beach, for example, turned to a substitute when he became ill in the fall of 1777. He gave Michael Linch his enlistment bounty and returned his clothing issues to his captain. Linch then enlisted in Beach's place as a matross, or gunner's assistant, in Captain Mansfield's company of the 2nd Continental Artillery.[61]

Other members of the Continental Community—the civilians with the army—did not face the necessity of providing substitutes when they wanted to leave their jobs, but then they rarely received bounties or pensions as recompense either. They did, however, have as much, or more, difficulty in receiving their wages and rations. Joseph Trumbull, commissary of stores and provisions, employed many people in his department. On 20 January 1776 he petitioned Congress to accept and then direct that his people be paid agreeable to the amounts he proposed on his annexed list. Apparently his employees "had no pryor allowance for their Services, nor has any pryor All[ow]ance therefor been established for them."[62] Some of Trumbull's people may have been officers or soldiers of the line detailed for special duty, and as such they would have received military pay, but Trumbull's list indicates that most were not. His clerks, laborers, coopers, and cooks all started work without a guaranteed rate of pay and rations. Problems in acquiring, paying, and rationing staff department personnel (commissary, quartermaster, adjutant general, hospital) continued throughout the war. Part of the difficulty lay in the constant vacillating between using military (specifically, line or combat) or civilian personnel in these departments.[63] Generally, as the military system developed, the army preferred to put uniformed members into these positions. The practice not only saved money, it helped to maintain military control and order in the staff departments. For example, by 1782, according to a congressional resolution, the adjutant general, his deputies, and his assistants all came out of the military line, but clerks could be either subalterns (lieutenants) or volunteers.[64] Other departments also generally became more militarized over time. One big exception was the quartermaster department; during the last years of the war that department turned over many of its duties to civilian contractors.

The quartermaster department serves as a fine example of the incorporation of civilians into a military organization, for besides contractors, that department also hired artificers to supplement both the soldiers detailed to it and the volunteers who had enlisted to serve specifically in artificer companies. The civilian artificers in the army community usually received higher pay than their enlisted colleagues, but the army had ways of getting some of that back. In January 1781 there was a problem in getting money to pay the artificers employed in the department, so Quartermaster General Timothy Pickering decided to provide them with clothing. Pickering told Joseph King, the clothier of the quartermaster department, that enlisted men were entitled to bounty clothing, but "Cloathing issued to any other persons employed by Colonel [Hugh] Hughes [deputy quartermaster for New York], is to be charged to him at their just Value in specie, as the same Articles would have sold on the 19th. of April 1775—Colonel Hughes in setling with the persons receiving Cloathing as above mentioned will either charge them at the same prices or higher according to the nature of his Contracts with them."[65] All of the artificers continued to receive their rations, but whereas the enlisted artificers could comfortably (relatively speaking) await their pay in their new clothing, the hired ones not only were stuck waiting for their wages, but then also owed for the new clothes they wore. They were not free to quit the community until they paid their bills.

Quite a number of other civilians found work in the hospital department. A few civilian physicians assisted in the military hospitals from time to time, but most doctors and surgeons' mates were commissioned officers in the hospital department or in the regiments. They directed personnel, such as apothecaries and their mates, stewards, orderlies, and nurses, who joined the army to serve in medical positions or who were drafted from their regiments into them. Most commanders, however, were not happy to have their soldiers detailed out of the line. Thus the medical department suffered a chronic lack of service personnel. It tried to counter the problem by hiring civilians—both male and female. In the fall of 1780 Dr. William Eustis had some trouble organizing the hospital in the vicinity of West Point. He wrote to Colonel John Lamb at that post on 12 October and asked if he could "recommend some poor honest refugee or other person suitable for a steward to the Hospital. The pay is too trivial to induce any person to accept the place who has any other business; at the same time it is a place of decent maintenance for a poor man. If there is any one on the point or near whom you think suitable. [I] shall esteem it a favor if you would send him over as we are in want of such assistance."[66] The army not only looked for a few good, but poor, men, to staff its hospitals, it also recruited women to serve as matrons and nurses. Their work was hard, the tasks menial, and the pay paltry, but nurses also received rations to sustain themselves and their families.[67]

Other women in the camps became entrepreneurs, most commonly engaged in the laundry business. The task of washing clothing was sometimes imposed upon women followers by company commanders, for it served to justify the rations given to these women, but other women set up shop on their own, charging as much as the market could bear. As with everything else, however, the army did regulate their business practices at various times and places to benefit the soldiers but still allow for what its officers deemed to be fair wages. In June of 1780, for instance, company commanders at West Point reported that in their opinion "the following Prices be paid for Washing; to the Women, who draw provisions, with their respective Companies; For a Shirt two Shillings; Woolen Breeches, Vest, and Overalls, two Shillings, each; Linen Vest, & Breeches, one Shilling, each; Linen Overalls, one Shilling & Six Pence, each; Stock, Stockings, & Handkerchief, Six Pence, each; The Women who wash for the Companies, will observe these regulations."[68]

Other entrepreneurs, in particular the camp sutlers, also had to heed military authority. Washington made that quite clear early in the war when he established the rules of camp commerce in August of 1775. He had no objection to the appointment of one sutler to each regiment as long as the appointment cost the public nothing, and provided the colonel of each regiment "doth become answerable for the Conduct of the Sutler so appointed, and taking care, that he conform strictly to all Orders given for the regulation of the Army, and that he does not in any Instance attempt to impose upon the Soldiers in the price of their goods."[69]

The Continental Community was a company town. It had one major employer—to a greater or lesser extent, just about everyone within it worked for or with the army—that set the rules for not only working but living in the community. Besides providing jobs and promising pay, the army decided where its people would stay (both the community as a whole and the individuals within it as well), determined the social and legal hierarchy, and legislated as well as executed its own regulations. Yet within this controlled and rather peculiar American community people tried to live as ordinarily as possible in the most extraordinary of circumstances.

The very nature of the Continental Community made the pursuit of ordinary life an interesting and difficult challenge: it was both mobile and segmented. Each of the many cells that made up the whole could at any one time be in garrison, battle, or on the move. Army life therefore meant dislocation and disruption. When soldiers marched out of their garrisons and encampments, the civilians with them either had to stay put, leave for their own chosen destinations, or follow behind.

Many chose to follow—or had no choice but to follow—and the army constantly made allowances for them. When word came down on the night of 5 July 1777 to abandon Ticonderoga and Mount Independence, Doctor Thacher received orders "to collect the sick and wounded, and as much of the hospital stores as possible, and assist in embarking them on board the batteaux and boats at the shore." Thacher moved his people out, making note that "Having with all possible despatch completed our embarkation, at three o'clock in the morning of the 6th, we commenced our voyage up the South bay to Skeensboro,' about thirty miles. Our fleet consisted of five armed gallies and two hundred batteaux and boats deeply laden with cannon, tents, provisions, invalids and women."[70] Further to the south, and a month and a half later on 23 August, General George Weedon at Stanton near Germantown relayed Washington's orders that the army was to march through Philadelphia and that no women belonging to the army were to be seen with the troops on their march through the city. The men were excused from carrying their camp kettles that day as well. Washington had two reasons. The first he stated: he wanted his soldiers to be unencumbered. The second was implied: he wanted his troops to look sharp as well as move sharply. The commander in chief could not ban all female followers, but he obviously believed it would be best to keep them as invisible as possible. Five days later at Wilmington, Washington and Weedon ordered their people to prepare for an active campaign. They wanted officers and men to store nonessential baggage, to deliver the sick to the director general of the hospital, and to limit the number of female followers to those "absolutely necessary & such as are actually useful."[71] Then on 13 September the orders read, "no Women under any pretence what ever to go with the Army but to follow the Baggage, The Soldiers are to Carry their Camp Kettles which, if the Army should come to Action are to be put into the Waggons with their Tents."[72] Action came at Paoli, Pennsylvania, on 20 September, and, following the British occupation of Philadelphia on the 26th, at Germantown on 4 October.

Women figured in the marching orders of later campaigns as well. If plans called for a rigorous march or an immediate engagement, commanders would order women to remain behind. If the regiment to which they belonged was not returning to that place, they could be directed to go to another garrison. Most of the time, however, they were permitted to follow the troops as long as they also followed orders. One of the duties of the Marechaussee Corps, a special provost unit of light dragoons, in 1778 was "to Remain on the old Ground till the Colems & Baggage have Marched off in order to secure all such Soldiers as have loitered in Camp and the Officers are to see that the soldiers and women who march with the Baggage do not Transgress the Genl. Orders made for their Goverment."[73] Nevertheless, the women did tend to ignore orders, especially ones that infringed on their comfort. Most women rode on the wagons at every opportunity, and virtually every time officers ordered them off; and sometimes the officers ordered them out of the line altogether.[74] On 19 June 1781 the posted order read, "No Women will be suffered to ride in Waggons, or Walk in the ranks this Campaign, Unless there are very Perticular reasons for it, of which the Genl. officer, or officer commanding the Division or Brigade to which they belong, is to be the Judge. A written Permission *only* will avail, without this the officers of the Day, or Police, are not only authorized to turn them out, but requested to inflict Inst. Punnishment upon those who shall Be found transgressors of this order."[75]

Washington was particularly stringent in 1781 because he wanted to engage in some bold operations. He prepared for the summer's campaign by sending some troops down to the southern theater and then gathering his main army for an offensive against the British in New York. But by mid-August Washington had committed himself to a major offensive in Virginia. Upon receiving word of Admiral Francois, Comte de Grasse's movements on 14 August, Washington informed subordinates to ready their commands for movement.[76] General Henry Knox's efficiency was just one example of the speedy response exhibited by all the commanders. By the 18th Lamb's artillery had its orders: "All the Park, except the four light three pounders, which were ordered today, are to march, under your directions, tomorrow morning 7 oClock in the manner that will hereafter be directed. The spare ammunition and everything belonging to the Park, are included in this order, and the artificers belonging to your own regiment, with travelling forges and a proportion of the necessary tools." Colonel John Crane's 3rd Continental Artillery Regiment was to be left behind, but commissaries and quartermasters, wagon masters, and forage masters were expected to accompany the troops.[77] The women and children able to travel with the troops received the usual order to keep off the wagons. They were also forbidden to mix with the men on the march, and told to keep to the rear of the baggage.[78]

Washington's main army crossed the Delaware River on the 1st of September and marched through Philadelphia on the 2nd. The

> line of march, including appendages and attendants, extended nearly two miles. The general officers and their aids, in rich military uniform, mounted on noble steeds elegantly caparisoned, were followed by their servants and baggage. In the rear of every brigade were several field-pieces, accompanied by ammunition carriages. The soldiers marched in slow and solemn step, regulated by the drum and fife. In the rear followed a great number of wagons, loaded with tents, provisions and other baggage, such as a few soldiers' wives and children; though a very small number of these are allowed to encumber us on this occasion.[79]

Then, after either sailing down from the Head of Elk or marching down through Virginia, these troops reached the banks of the James River. On the 25th the troops marched from their encampment through Williamsburg. They arrived at Yorktown on the 26th and settled down within a mile of the enemy's redoubts. On the 27th other units, which had been waiting for those from the North, marched to join them. The whole army, French and American, then marched on the 28th to their assigned positions facing the enemy's line of defense. On the 29th the American army moved in closer. On the 30th the British abandoned their outer works, the Americans closed in, and the siege was on.[80]

The siege of Yorktown was a prime example, despite the crowds of spectators who impeded operations,[81] of the military performing its mission. It was also an example of how this mission, the fight for independence, also disrupted the very community formed to perform it. Death was the ultimate disrupter in terms of weakening military units and fragmenting families, but preparation for engagement was a prime contributor to community disorder. Sometimes the disorder was slight, at other times substantial. When the combined army marched on Yorktown, a detachment of two hundred men stayed in Williamsburg to guard the provisions, stores, and hospitals.[82] Many noncombatants remained behind with the baggage as well. Indeed, Washington and other commanders had tried to trim the Continental Community of any excess personnel at the beginning of the campaign, long before the first bombardment. Washington had advised the troops who were supposed to be fit for action and free from incumbrances to deposit at West Point "such of their Women, as are not able to undergo the fatigue of frequent Marches; and also of every Article of Baggage which they can in any wise dispense with."[83] The sentiment that women were so much baggage, to be dispensed with as the men saw fit, was not unusual. Lieutenant William Feltman of the 1st Pennsylvania noted on 16 August that Lieutenant Crawford of his regiment left the encampment near Bottoms Bridge in New Kent County, Virginia, that morning to escort some soldiers' wives back to Pennsylvania.[84]

Shucking followers before a campaign was common. A year earlier, in August 1780, Doctor Thacher had recorded Washington's orders that the army "disencumber itself of all heavy baggage, which, with the women and children," were to be sent to West Point, and then to hold itself ready to march at a moment's notice. Yet Thacher also noted instances when women would not be shunted aside. Some women followed their spouses into battle, and when enemy fire killed their husbands, a few of them stepped into the breach and fired back. Thacher specifically commented on two women who replaced their husbands at artillery pieces: Margaret Corbin, who received a pension for her services at Fort Washington in 1776; and a woman called Molly Pitcher at Monmouth in 1778.[85] These women showed how far outside their prescribed places some followers would go to support their army and its mission.

This focus on mission by followers as well as by military members helped the community survive the stress of warfare. The mission served as both an excuse and an explanation for the disruptions inherent to army life. Yet life with the army was not one of constant alarms and excursions. There was the intense period of planning and training before a campaign began, and then the period of reevaluation and recuperation at campaign's end, in order, as Henry Knox wrote, "to put the army in all its branches on such a footing as to be able to take the field next Campaign with the greatest probability of success."[86] It was at these times, when the army was in garrison between campaigns, or even when it was encamped between battles, that this community's governmental and social organization most clearly developed. Those were the times and places when service members and civilians returned to the more mundane issues, duties, and irritations associated with life in the Continental Community.

***

The Continental Community, similar to any community where a large number of people are brought together in close confines, suffered from disturbances and disruptions. They ranged from small interpersonal squalls to soldier-driven cyclones. The former could usually be handled by commissioned or noncommissioned officers low in the chain of command without ever having to resort to the military courts, but when matters escalated into the latter, a formal procedure was necessary. The most extreme disputes, represented by riots and mutinies, often resulted in trials, hangings, and dismissals, but occasionally they opened a dialogue for renegotiation between army management and labor. This rather distinctive American twist to command-rank relations was not allowed to go too far, however. The Pennsylvania line mutiny, over lack of pay and disagreements about the soldiers' terms of enlistments, in January of 1781 did result in few of the mutineers being punished and both plaintiffs and defendants submitting to the arbitration of their dispute; but when the New Jersey troops attempted to follow Pennsylvania's example, the army clamped down before a pattern could be established. Some of the mutiny's leaders were immediately tried, and two were executed.[87] General Anthony Wayne followed the latter example when mutiny once again reared its head among the Pennsylvania troops that May. Six men accused of disorderly and seditious behavior were condemned to death. Wayne pardoned two; the other four were shot.[88]

Massive disputes were rare compared to the daily contretemps and arguments that were part of camp life. The participants resolved most of these contests by themselves or had them handled summarily by the most senior person present, but sometimes formal application to the law was required. Such was the case at Fort Schuyler early in 1778 when Nancy Weedon and Sergeant Dean of the artillery squared off. The angry sergeant confined Weedon for "impeaching his Character" but was in turn imprisoned on the accusation of "Defrauding Mrs. Weedon of her provision." As neither could think straight, the court took over, studied the charges, found both not guilty, and ordered them released from confinement.[89] The records do not say whether the combatants then shook hands and reconciled their differences or merely entered into a smoldering cease-fire.

Such contentiousness was not confined to the lower ranks of the army: officers regularly battled among themselves. They became agitated and argued over seniority, leadership, orders, privileges, and honor, among other things. There were simple disputes, such as that between a few junior officers encamped near Morristown in June 1780, which ended in name-calling and the aggrieved parties lodging "out doors in the open Air—not chusing to sleep with a person of such a disposition." And there were exchanges that ended in bruised egos: as happened that August when one young gent in the army decided Colonel Crane was not much of a gentleman because he reprimanded the former publicly.[90] Other disputes—especially those over rank and seniority, perhaps indicating how close the perceived connection was between rank in the army and rank in society—escalated to the point that officers threatened resignation due to perceived slights to their honesty, abilities, or honor.[91]

When the issue was truly grievous, and when denied the satisfaction of resolving their problems by duels (Articles 2 and 3, Section VII of the 1776 Articles of War outlawed dueling), some officers, attesting to the developing litigious nature of American society, challenged their adversaries in court. Others, reflecting perhaps a certain violent streak in the American nature, dueled anyway and then ended up in court. Washington was, by turns, enraged, dismayed, and sorrowed by such activities. When a court-martial in early 1778 sentenced Ensign John Foster of the 6th Pennsylvania Regiment to be discharged for challenging Captain Walter Cruise to a duel and for behavior unbecoming an officer, Washington approved the sentence but upon considering the circumstances restored Foster to his former rank. Washington, however, took the opportunity to observe how sorry he was that a dispute between officers was conducted in such a manner.[92] His sorrow was not enough to end the dueling. Two years later Doctor Thacher recorded a number of his fellow officers' encounters in his journal. He was contemptuous of a practice that wasted lives for mistaken points of honor.[93]

This contentiousness among officers resulted in many, ranking both high and low, finding themselves in court. The more senior the officer, the more likely the charges would stem from his conduct in battle or during a campaign. Generals brought up on charges included Charles Lee, Philip Schuyler, and Arthur St. Clair. Junior officers were more often brought up on charges of insubordination. Such was the case at Valley Forge in December 1777. A court-martial found Ensign Benjamin Arnold of Colonel Israel Angell's 2nd Rhode Island Regiment guilty of "behaving in a disorderly unsoldier like manner in Camp on the 6th. of December, with refusing to retire to his Quarters when ordered by the Colonel, sending him for answer that he would go when he pleased and not before, & also with refusing to do his duty when regularly warn'd and threatning to leave the Service, whether he could a discharge or not." The court sentenced him to be cashiered with infamy with the commander in chief's full approval.[94]

The friction between officers (which was certainly seen in the ranks as well) was due at least in part to cultural differences and changes. Products of the local cultures from whence they came, these men interacted with others based on slightly different rules of engagement. For the most part these were not major differences, but they were enough to cause misperceptions and miscommunication at times. For instance, the egalitarianism of some northerners did not sit well with southern gentlemen, including Washington, who preferred more deferential behavior. On the other hand, the individualism of some southern planters may have been seen as excessive self-assertion by northern townsmen. That did not stop northerners from exerting themselves against southerners, however. Indeed, it could be that this close contact and the resulting conflicts between the men of different areas helped ensure that assertive individualism would be part of the American definition of masculinity. Contributing to this was the fact that many officers were intent on not only creating a new nation but on making a name and place for themselves in it. In the army a man had somewhat greater opportunities to achieve a higher social status than he may have had at home.[95]

An officer's commission bestowed immediate status on a man, for an officer's rank was equated with the social rank of gentleman. In practice, it was not a simple equation. As illustrated in the cases described above, there were some problems establishing not only proper military behavior but proper gentlemanly behavior as well. Many American officers were not of gentle birth or occupation, and thus had not been raised into the role. While that made some uneasy, others embraced the change in status and quickly adopted the form if not the substance of their new social rank. To the discomfort of both groups, some observers did not accept the transformation. As a correspondent snickered to General Henry Clinton in 1776, "I must tell you, the Col. of a New York Regt. is a Butcher & the Major a Chimney Sweeper. Quelle Canaille!"[96] A German officer held by the Americans in Cambridge in 1777 wrote that the officers from the two opposing armies did not associate with one another. There was more than just a touch of snobbery in his comment that "the regiments here are militia and nearly all their officers are artisans. It cost a lot of pains to get the idea into the heads of the inhabitants here that our officers have no [civil] occupation; it was thought that they simply refused to ply their trade from caprice."[97] In the European tradition, gentlemen interested in pursuing a military career became officers; in the American interpretation, men interested in achieving a gentleman's status and privileges pursued officers' positions. Yet because they were not raised to assume them, they did not always perceive, understand, or adopt the appropriate gentlemanly behaviors or responsibilities. Washington, however, had no choice but to open the officer's ranks to the eager and the ambitious, as well as the truly able and dedicated (and thus open up an avenue for social mobility). He could not depend on getting officers only from the small pool of distinguished planters, merchants, and professional men; there were not enough of them to lead the army through the almost eight years of war. Although the senior officers generally came from the upper echelons of American society, junior-grade officers represented a more democratic mix. Some people may have deplored the necessity, but they accepted the army's policy to recognize all officers, regardless of origins, as gentlemen with all the rights and privileges that accompanied that social station.[98] It would, however, become the additional duty of the gentlemen officers to train the officers-cum-gentlemen.

Many of the latter made it difficult by focusing on the privileges, as opposed to the duties, in an active social life. Lewis Beebe, a physician with the army, thought the activities of the officers did them no credit. He scathingly noted at Crown Point on 4 July 1776 that although the army had been encamped there for several days and feared an enemy attack, no moves to fortify the garrison were being undertaken. Instead of preparing to meet the foe, the generals occupied themselves with riding their gaily accoutred horses about the camp, the field officers spent most of their time sitting on courts-martial, and the captains and subalterns congregated at grog shops.[99] Two years later, in November 1778, Doctor Thacher expressed his own mixed feelings about camp amusements. He offered a partial excuse for himself and his fellow officers by saying that the campaign was drawing to a close and they were stationed far (in the Highlands) from the enemy in New York City. Feeling secure "and military duty not being very urgent, our officers appear disposed to relax in their discipline, and contract a habit approaching to dissipation. They have adopted the practice of giving suppers alternately, with music and dancing through half the night. These are the favorite amusements of the Virginia and Maryland officers, but they do not accord precisely with my own views of time well spent, though I am frequently enticed to a participation in their banqueting revels."[100]

Officers at all levels of command filled their social calendars with dinners, dances, teas, and numerous other engagements. Generals and regimental commanders, especially when their wives visited them, frequently issued formal dinner invitations to one another.[101] These senior officers also often invited junior officers to dine. General Washington was known for his wide hospitality, as was General Nathanael Greene. Lieutenant Francis Brooke of the 1st Continental Artillery reminisced after the war about Greene's graciousness. Brooke had been at the headquarters outside Charleston to have a requisition endorsed by the general. After doing so, Greene commented to Brooke that he kept a roster of the officers and invited them to dinner in rotation. Greene told Brooke that he would be invited in time, but mentioned that whenever he was off-duty Mrs. Greene would be happy to see him. Brooke believed he received the extra invitation because his family in Virginia had shown Catharine Greene hospitality when she passed by their home on her journey south to join her husband. Thereafter Brooke was often at headquarters and, according to him, became something of a "pet" of the general's.[102] Another young officer recorded numerous instances of breakfasting and dining with senior officers.[103] Actually, the breakfasts, dinners, and soirees given by the senior officers were not merely pleasant diversions (and some subalterns would probably have questioned the appellation *pleasant*); they also served as training forums for the junior officers and furthered their indoctrination as members of the military brotherhood.

The officers further strengthened this brotherhood by presenting and attending military reviews and celebrations. A visit by the French minister Monsieur Conrad Alexandre Gérard and the Spanish agent, or observer as the Americans called him, Don Juan de Miralles, in May of 1779 spurred the army into a grand display. "At the signal of thirteen cannon, the great and splendid cavalcade appoached in martial pomp and style. . . . Having arrived on the field of parade, the commander-in-chief, with the foreign ministers and general officers, passed in front of the line of the army, from right to left, in review, and received the military honors due to their rank." After that the gentlemen dismounted and took seats next to the visiting ladies in order comfortably to watch the army go through some field maneuvers. International relations served as an excuse for many other celebrations and parties as well. In July 1781 a few American officers received an invitation to dine with some of their allies. The

French received their guests under an elegant marquee and offered them an excellent meal of roast beef served in the French style. The only difficulty, according to Doctor Thacher, who was at the meal, was language. As each group was ignorant of the other's language, conversation lagged.[104] That did not stop the allies from continuing to trade invitations over the course of that campaign and after. A year later, on 31 May, the American army at West Point celebrated the birth of the dauphin of France with a most elegant entertainment. General Washington hosted a dinner for his officers and honored guests—over five hundred people.[105]

Such engagements formed only a small part of an officer's social life. If an officer enjoyed seeing new things or was intent on bettering himself, he could act as Lieutenant Isaac Bangs did and explore out of camp or engage an instructor. After the American army arrived in New York in 1776, Bangs made a grand tour of the city, including a trip to a synagogue to "observe the Method of the Jewish Worship," and hired a "gentleman" to teach him and a few of his fellows French.[106] More often these officers visited back and forth among themselves, shared in afternoon teas, or passed around the grog upon the conclusion of the day's labors. Occasionally they became very merry men indeed, as when a group of about thirty officers got "pretty high drinking Milk Punch till almost one o/ clock."[107] At other, perhaps more sober, times a few would get together to play cricket or some other sport. Some enjoyed playing cards, although Washington frowned on games of chance. And when not carousing among themselves, they enjoyed the company of women at the many dinners, dances, and teas held in garrison and on the road.[108] Washington saw such pursuits as suitable entertainment for gentlemen; indeed, he enjoyed the ladies and dancing so much that he, along with the other leading figures at Morristown in early 1780, was willing to pay a subscription to support a dance assembly there.[109]

Women figured prominently in the social lives of most officers. The officers not only courted and called upon the female relations accompanying their colleagues but mixed with the women in the communities through which they passed. Baron Ludwig von Closen of the French army, being a visitor to the United States, both enjoyed and studied American women. In the course of a year, from December 1780 to December 1781, he recorded his opinion of the "fair sex" from Boston to Williamsburg. The former, he decided were not only pleasant but were distinguished for their education and fine figures. As for the latter, he felt that they were most hospitable. They were not among the prettiest he had seen, an observation echoed by Ensign Benjamin Gilbert (another close observer of the female form), but they were generally agreeable and well-bred. Closen preened over his observation that the women there found French manners much to their taste.[110] One young woman from Yorktown was so bewitched by the visitors that she succumbed to temptation and soon found herself, as the French would say, *enceinte*.[111]

Just as the officers looked forward to female company, so too did women, in a grand display of cordial civil-military relations, welcome their arrival. Sarah Wister filled her journal with her excitement and pleasure at having military visitors. In October 1777 "two genteel men of the military order" rode up to the Foulke farmhouse and asked if General William Smallwood could be quartered there. Wister's aunt consented, and by evening the general was in residence with his military family and the farm was surrounded by a large guard of soldiers, horses, and baggage wagons. A delighted Sarah Wister went to bed that night to dream "of bayonets and swords, sashes, guns, and epaulets." Smallwood and his officers remained there for approximately two weeks, enlivening the ladies' teas and evenings with much reading, talking, and laughter. Wister mentioned dining with some of the officers and walking out with a few of them. When the army marched out, Wister wrote of her dismay: "for when you have been with agreable people tis impossible not to feel regret when they bid you adieu perhaps for ever. [W]hen they leve us we shall be immur'd in solitude."[112]

When officers felt in need of some of that solitude, they sometimes took leave of the army for short periods of time. At the end of a campaign, once the army was in its winter quarters, many officers requested and were granted leave to visit their homes and families, although it must be noted there was a bit of a struggle between the officers and their commander in chief on this issue. Washington, leading by example, never took leave and generally would have preferred that his officers did the same. Many officers, however, wanted to visit their families and see to their private affairs. Washington tried to make it policy to refuse furloughs early in 1778 at Valley Forge, saying the officers needed to concentrate on preparing the army for the next campaign. The result was the resignation of many officers. Months later, at the end of the 1778 campaign, when there was a window of opportunity before everyone had to focus again on spring training, and showing an attitude of "if you cannot beat them, regulate them," Washington condoned furloughs but only under certain restrictions, which essentially boiled down to limiting the number allowed to go at any one time and keeping enough around to take care of and train the troops.[113] This certainly suggests why families, troublesome though they were at times, were welcome in the winter garrisons: they kept the officers there. Unfortunately, not all wives or families were able to visit, and thus some officers felt they had to go home.

Although commanders expected a prompt return, they resignedly accepted excuses and delays when circumstances changed their subordinates' travel plans. In April 1778 Lieutenant Colonel Eleazer Oswald of the 2nd Continental Artillery wrote Colonel Lamb that he had not proceeded to camp in accordance with his orders because his daughter, Polly, had been ill; but after her death he set out to join his unit. Oswald also serves as an example of how officers had the freedom to resign their commissions and leave the army when they were discontented in camp, distracted by troubles at home, or just desirous of change. Oswald had threatened to resign in 1777 after clashing with the officer commanding the post at which he was stationed.[114] Lamb convinced him to stay in then, but Oswald did eventually resign for other reasons later in 1778. In 1780 a Lieutenant Hubbell passed word to Lamb that he would have to resign if he was not allowed to stay with his wife until she recovered from her illness. Lieutenant William Hubbell of the 2nd Continental Artillery resigned that year on 1 October.[115] The social life and relative freedom of movement enjoyed by officers reflected their status as the gentlemen of the army.

Just as the officers, by their origins, represented the egalitarian nature of American society in comparison to their European allies and foes, so too did the soldiers. It appears, however, that the egalitarianism was more evident in the composition of the officer corps than in the companies of men, for although soldiers came from all ranks in American society, a good many, if not the majority, especially after 1776, came from the lower orders—and certainly looked it. Many were quite young, and some were black. A British officer at the capitulation of Charleston described the American troops as a "ragged dirty looking set of People," but gave them credit for having acquired some discipline over the course of the war.[116] Baron von Closen, an ally more disposed to think well of American soldiers, expressed his admiration for them on at least two occasions in July of 1781. He first commented that although ill-clothed in "only some trousers and little linen jackets," the troops were "very cheerful and healthy" in appearance. Later he exclaimed that it was "incredible that soldiers composed of men of every age, even of children of fifteen, of whites and blacks, almost naked, unpaid, and rather poorly fed, can march so well and withstand fire so steadfastly."[117]

Although the army preferred to have free white adult males filling the ranks, it did accept some African Americans, young adolescents, and indentured servants. Then it had to decide what to do with them. Many people feared giving weapons to blacks (whether free or slave) and protested the enlistment of African Americans. The army initially tried to accommodate the protesters by barring the enlistment of blacks, but it soon reversed itself when faced with a manpower shortage. By December 1777 so many blacks had joined the service that an outside observer, a German officer who was a prisoner in Cambridge (and so was not fully impartial and was commenting only on New England troops) was able to say, "You never see a regiment in which there are not a lot of negroes." He reasoned that the numbers resulted from masters sending their blacks to serve in their place, not because African Americans freely chose to fight.[118] His reasoning was faulty; many African Americans independently made the decision to join the army. The military, however, remained ambivalent about black troops throughout the war and thus diverted many into supporting roles as wagoners and waiters.[119]

The army also often channeled into noncombat positions the boys who enlisted. It commonly placed them in the drum and fife corps or had them serving as waiters to the officers. Officers actively recruited boys for the former. Brigadier General Henry Knox had directed Colonel Crane to do so in April of 1777. Over a year later, in October 1778, Captain-Lieutenant Jacob Reed of the 2nd Continental Artillery wrote to Colonel Lamb about a lad he had sent over to his quarters the day before: he had enlisted the boy with the drum major. The new drummer or fifer told Reed he was indentured to a Mr. Keating but had his master's permission to join the army.[120] But by 1781 Brigadier General Edward Hand, the adjutant general of the army, grumbled to a colleague (after complaining about some recruits, black and white, who were mentally and physically unfit for service) about the many boys in every brigade who were too small and young for the army. It was time to do something more creative and constructive with the lads. In 1782 Baron Frederick von Steuben, the army's inspector general, created a special guard or company of boys who were too young and small to serve in the line but were to continue with the army for the campaign. He put them in the charge of a sergeant from the 2nd Connecticut Regiment and assigned the detachment to Hand. The adjutant general then undertook the task of finding a sober and steady corporal who would keep the boys in order and perhaps instruct them in reading and writing.[121] Steuben's and Hand's experiment, essentially an apprenticeship program, was unusual in that other officers often kept the boys in their units in an attempt to maintain unit strength.

Rhode Island, New Jersey, Maryland, and Delaware (due to their desire to fill quotas, but with limits) permitted servants and apprentices to enlist without their masters' permission but monetarily compensated the masters for their loss. Other states required such enlistees to have permission from their masters and usually did not provide compensation.[122] With or without permission, numerous indentured laborers and slaves enlisted in the army, leaving their masters to place advertisements in newspapers promising rewards for the runaways.[123] Both state governments and senior commanders ordered officers not to accept such people into their companies, but many refused to look too deeply into their recruits' antecedents: they needed soldiers to fill the ranks.

Soldiers lacked the freedom of movement granted the officers; nor were they as readily accepted by the communities around which they camped. Many enlisted men and noncommissioned officers became as tired of or disgusted with army life as their officers did. Some suffering from an indisposition diagnosed as homesickness became weak and melancholy.[124] Others worried about their families and their farms or businesses. For all of these men, finding relief was a problem. As their officers seldom granted them leaves (although it was not unknown[125]), and resignation was not an option, quite a number of them resorted to desertion. Newspapers and orderly books contained numerous notices and trial accounts of deserters. Company and regimental commanders advertised in local papers for the return of their runaways. They included descriptions of their errant troopers and promised rewards to anyone who would restore the soldiers to the army.[126] Once captured, men accused of desertion were brought to trial and, if convicted of the offense, punished. Repeated desertions could result in a sentence of death, but generally punishment was the lash.[127]

Instead of always promising retribution, Washington sometimes offered pardons to deserters if they turned themselves in. This generally happened when there was a profound escalation in desertions and Washington believed it wise to refill his line without overloading the courts, or when there was an occasion to celebrate (such as when France became an official ally in 1778). At those times Washington published a proclamation in the newspapers offering full pardon to all deserters who rejoined their corps by a prescribed time. Those who did not take the opportunity offered them were assured that they would be pursued and punished.[128] Some came back after resolving their problems; others did not. Solomon Bans was one who wanted to rejoin his artillery unit if he could return without punishment and at his previous rank. He wrote to Colonel Lamb to explain why he had deserted and to ask the favor of reinstatement. His explanation could serve for many of his fellow deserters. Bans believed he had enlisted for only three years but then did not receive the discharge he thought he deserved. Not only was his discharge withheld, but he had received next to nothing for all his years of service. Finally, he had a young growing family and a small patrimony at home which demanded his care. He felt these reasons at least partially excused his conduct.[129] Washington and his officers deplored and despised desertion, but they could understand the temptation and occasionally made allowances. Over the course of the war Washington issued many general pardons for deserters who returned to the army on their own accord. The courts-martial sentenced others, as they did those captured, to corporal punishment and then sent them back to join their comrades.

It was in the company of those companions that soldiers also tried to find relief from their problems. Their activities did not always sit well with their officers or their civilian neighbors. Soldiers drank and swore, gambled and whored, and engaged in a number of other diversions. Much to the dismay of officers, soldiers had a habit of rambling (as opposed to an officer's exploring?). The men found New York City particularly enticing when they were there in 1776, much to the detriment of military readiness.[130] Some of the soldiers also undermined the military's relationship with the civilian populace by another off-duty activity: swimming. General Greene dressed down his troops after hearing Long Island inhabitants complain "that Some of the Soldiers Come there [the Mill Pond] to swim In Open View of the Women and that they Come out of the Water and Run up Naked to the Houses with a Design to Insult and Wound the Modesty of female Decency." He did not prohibit the soldiers from bathing—in the proper places—but he questioned the absence of the modesty, virtue, and sobriety for which the New Englanders were renowned.[131] Soldiers engaged in other forms of rowdy behavior in camp and out as they celebrated their patriotism, from destroying symbols of the old order to—despite numerous prohibitions and threats of dire punishment—firing off their weapons within their own lines. Official celebrations often set off the barrages, but sometimes it was just high spirits.[132] High spirits, but more likely empty stomachs and pockets, caused soldiers to engage in some less acceptable pursuits. The inhabitants around Fishkill, New York, complained to Major General Benedict Arnold in September 1780 that some of the troops stationed at that post were not kept under proper military discipline: the soldiers had plundered their property.[133]

The soldiers' entertainments, however, generally mirrored the activities of the officers: they played ball, drank grog, and danced and talked with a number of "fine Girls" (which in a few cases led to marriage).[134] Their active and colorful social life occasionally tempted an officer out of gentlemanly behavior: the result was often ruinous for the officer. A court-martial in 1780 found Lieutenant Anthony Wright of the Artillery Artificers guilty of refusing to pay his debts to some matrosses (gunners' assistants), drinking with private soldiers in public houses at their own expense, going to one of their dances without having first been invited, playing cards that same night with some of the privates, beating and abusing two matrosses, and borrowing a pair of shoes from a matross and not giving them back.[135]

Wright would not have gotten into trouble if he had followed the guideline published in October 1778 that stated that officers should encourage "purity of morals" by way of example, influence, and penalties. The particular impetus for that advice, which was really only a reiteration of earlier counsel, was the continuing rise of a common kind of licentiousness: swearing had "risen to a most disgusting height; A regard to decency should conspire, with a Sense of Morality to banish a vice productive of neither Advantage or Pleasure."[136] Doctor Beebe had commented on the problem earlier in the war, in the spring of 1776. As he dealt with the sick and dying of his regiment, he contemptuously wrote that "Death is a Subject not to be attended to by Soldiers; Hell & Damnation is in allmost every ones mouth from the time they awake till they fall asleep again, the Stupidity of mankind in this situation is beyond all Description." He found it incredible that the troops always found some duty to do so that they could not attend to daily prayers or even the preaching on Sunday. He noted that it was "esteemed very unpopular, and unbecoming a Gentlemen, in the Camps to attend upon any religious exercises, and happy would it be, did not many officers endeavour to inculcate, & establish this principle in the minds of others." Beebe was still muttering in October of that year: "Our chaplain does not yet return, the Regt. is extremely happy in his absence, as they can bear to hear Edwardeanism preached with the same degree of pleasure as a Living animal can b[e]ar hot burning coals."[137]

Observers outside the camps became aware of such behavior and sentiments and expressed their dismay as well. "A True Patriot" inserted an article in the *Pennsylvania Gazette* about the evils of libertinism. He said he admired the gentlemen of the army for their bravery in defending the country, but was sorry to see by their actions that they obviously felt that religious precepts should offer no restraint upon men. He deplored their frequent balls, their excessive drinking, the cursing and swearing, their disregard for public worship, and their neglect of the laws passed by Congress to restrain vice in the army. He stated that the chaplains were probably as unprincipled as the other officers.[138] John Adams wrote General Greene that the public's perceptions of army life hindered its recruiting efforts. "The Prevalence of Dissipation, Debauchery, Gaming, Profaneness, and Blasphemy, terrifies the best people upon the Continent from trusting their Sons and other Relations among so many dangerous snares and Temptations. Multitudes of People who would with cheerfull Resignation submit their Families to the Dangers of the sword shudder at the Thought of exposing them to what appears to them, the more destructive Effects of Vice and Impiety."[139]

Observations such as these showed that the Continental Congress and General Washington were not entirely succesful in their endeavors to create a godly or pious army. Both Congress and commanders certainly tried. The Continental Congress passed a resolution in 1776 allowing one chaplain to each regiment and suggested that the regimental commanders pick exemplary persons to fill the positions and then see to it that the officers and soldiers accord the chaplains the proper respect and attend religious exercises. Congress reminded everyone that "the blessing and protection of heaven are at all times necessary but especially so in times of public distress and danger." Washington compounded the directive by stating that he hoped each one of his people would "live and act as becomes a christian soldier defending the dearest rights and liberties of his country."[140] Throughout the war Congress, Washington, and other army commanders set aside days for religious observances and promoted attendance at religious services. Their efforts were not in vain, for many people in the army did attend to their ministers and attempt to live moral lives. One young soldier wrote his parents that he was constantly visited by a chaplain while in the hospital at Greenwich, New York. Then he passed on the observation that "Yorkers" were very profane people; he had heard women swear as many bad oaths as the old soldiers, and thus, although a sinner, he was not tempted by them at all.[141] Although critics such as Beebe and "The True Patriot" were never satisfied, the Continental Community scarcely equaled Sodom and Gomorrah. Indeed, sometimes civilian inhabitants expressed happiness with their army neighbors. The citizens of Burlington, New Jersey, thanked Colonel Lamb and his officers for their attention and care in maintaining order among their troops while they were stationed in the vicinity. They wished the army well and offered their hope that the war would soon end so that all could enjoy domestic life once again.[142]

As the residents of Burlington discovered, the army was not constantly engaged in amusements. Most officers worked hard to fulfill the demands of their positions, and some even followed Washington's recommendation to spend their leisure moments furthering their military education. Washington always advocated study for his officers, but he made a point of promoting it in May 1777 after forbidding play at cards, dice, or any other games except those involving exercise at Morristown. He figured officers could find enough to do in training, disciplining, and caring for their men. If they had any spare moments, he suggested they study military authors, for that would reflect well on them and improve their performance.[143] Some took him to heart; others needed prodding time and again. Major Sebastian Bauman, in a letter to Knox in December 1779, puzzled over his junior officers who, immured by bad weather, complained they did not know what to do with their time: "I tell them to study if they do not like mathematic the Humanities which would give the[m] work enough. Strange, they should not know how to pass their time; when I cannot find time to be alone."[144]

Generally, most officers and soldiers found their days filled with numerous duties. Their primary tasks were purely military in nature: they drilled to improve their maneuvering and fighting skills; they stood guard, went out on patrols, and, ultimately, engaged the enemy. Of secondary, but no less vital, importance were the chores they performed to keep the army fed, fired, and nailed down. Valley Forge over the winter of 1777–1778 was the scene of great and continuous activity. It provided a prime example of the army's life in camp. Only when the weather was bitterly severe did the officers release the soldiers from their duties to go huddle in their huts. Days began with brigade parades. Then details of men would split off to march out and relieve outposts and guards, or perform labor such as foraging, fortifying, and building. Some helped the artificers who repaired the wagons, weapons, and other equipment. Those not otherwise engaged hauled firewood or visited the camp markets.[145]

Soldiers often laid down their arms to pick up reins, hammers, and ladles. Commanders commonly assigned a few of their men to handle their units' wagons and horses and, when pressed, to drive the quartermaster department's wagons. Even soldiers who were unfit, due to injury or illness, for other supposedly more strenuous or specialized camp duties received assignments as wagoners.[146] The army was not about to waste manpower. This was evident in the way it utilized the many skilled craftsman who filled its ranks. Artisans could be pulled from the line if campaign preparations demanded it, such as in New York in the spring of 1776 when the quartermaster general needed more armorers and smiths, but usually it was when the army went into winter quarters that orders went out to pull all the carpenters, wheelwrights, joiners, and other artisans from their companies and set them to work plying their trades. The other men received assignments that required less skill—such as knocking together their barracks.[147] At other times regiments and companies received orders to release just a few men for special duties that ranged from carpentry to cooking.

The soldiers generally prepared their own provisions, but they did not always cook them. Sometimes women served as cooks, but often commanders designated one or more men, some of whom may have been invalided, to do the cooking for a prescribed number of soldiers.[148] As with just about everything else, this task was regulated. Officers (at times this job was given to the quartermasters) determined where the camp kitchens were to be placed. Company commanders were then supposed to inspect regularly these cooking facilities and the soldiers preparing food in them to make sure everything was in accordance with the health standards of the day.[149] At the end of the war the soldiers settled in garrisons not only dressed their provisions but grew some of them as well—Washington encouraged the troops to create regimental vegetable gardens.[150]

Washington could encourage gardening by 1783 because the war was winding down and most of the soldiers were well versed in their camp and combat roles. It had been another story at the beginning of the war. At that time Washington tried to cut out all nonessential chores so as to focus his soldiers' energies on fighting and surviving. At first fighting took a backseat to survival when sickness in camp proved more deadly than enemy shells. Washington found he first had to train his people in elementary camp hygiene before he could concentrate on military drills. The Massachusetts Provincial Congress warned him upon his arrival at Cambridge that although the soldiers were brave and intelligent, they had "but little knowledge of divers things most essential to the preservation of Health and even of life [in the military]. The Youth in the Army are not possess'd of the absolute Necessity of Cleanliness in their Dress, and Lodging, continual Exercise, and strict Temperance to preserve them from Diseases frequently prevailing in Camps...."[151]

To clean things up, the commander in chief laid down some rules, and his subordinates proceeded to enforce them. At the simplest and most intimate level, officers reminded soldiers (especially when they went on guard duty or parade) to attend to their personal hygiene: to wash their hands and faces, shave their beards, and comb their hair.[152] Then they concentrated on getting their people to dig and use latrines. Instructions quickly changed to orders, with threats of dire punishment for noncompliance, when the soldiers or their followers disregarded proper procedures.

In August 1775 Washington ordered that every company appoint a camp color man (someone detailed to do camp maintenance), who, with others so chosen and under the direction of a quartermaster, would sweep the streets, fill up the latrines and dig new ones, and bury all the filth that could affect the health of the troops. The quartermasters, in turn, were responsible for seeing that their people persevered in the battle to "remove that odious reputation, which (with but too much reason) has stigmatized the Character of American Troops."[153] Unfortunately, that reputation still wafted after the army years later. General Greene had to order a fatigue party out in August of 1777 to bury all the filth in and around the camp at Germantown. He ordered the camp color men to fill up the old vaults and dig new ones, and then to gather up all the human waste outside the vaults and bury it. Greene complained that "such a stench arises on every side of it [camp] now as threatens the passengers [passers-by] with immediate Pestilence."[154] The hygiene battle continued into 1779 when brigade quartermasters had to supervise the removal of all the rubbish in camp and then see to it that every hole in the streets was filled upon the completion of the proper necessary houses. They also had to make sure that no one relieved (they used the term *eased*) himself anywhere other than in the proper facilities. Published orders gave due warning that soldiers detected in the crime would not only be punished but would also be fined one dollar, which would be paid to the informer; women and children caught in the act would be turned out of the encampment.[155]

In the fall of 1781 Washington, surprised by the "quantity of Offal and other offensive matter at the different slaughter yards about Camp remaining unburied," threatened arrest for any commissary who allowed this to continue, but in the meantime he wanted a detail established to clean everything up, including the "dead Horses and other putrid bodies about the Camp."[156] That December the commandant of Burlington Barracks, New Jersey, promised confinement for trial by court-martial to "Any persons who should be Detected in Easing themselves About the Baracks yard or fence which Enclose the yard—Excepting the Little house for that purpos—or any non Commissioned Officer or private who shall be Detected in easing themselvs in the Little house Now building for the Officers." The commandant then found it necessary to expand his orders in April of 1782: throwing filth and waste water out of the back windows of the barracks, as well as out of the doors and off the galleries (balconies), was also a court-martial offense.[157]

In the never-ending struggle to maintain a more aromatically reputable army, officers gave both men and women plenty of opportunities to wash their clothes. For some reason, however, perhaps because they did most of the laundry, women got into trouble more often for illegal or unsafe washing procedures. At Fort Schuyler in May 1778 garrison orders forbade women to wash clothing within the fort or in its ditch.[158] That October, at Fredericksburg, the camp commandant ordered his officers and men to police the women. He had heard that the women of the brigade continued in the practice of washing their dirty clothes in the run upon which the men depended for drinking water. Any woman found washing in it, unless she was below the brigade's encampment, was to be immediately placed in the guardhouse.¹⁵⁹ In July of 1779 the 1st Pennsylvania's regimental orders included a stricture against women washing in front of the tents or throwing soapsuds and any other filth onto the regimental parade ground.¹⁶⁰

Public health suffered because of private abuses. Disease struck officers, soldiers, and camp followers alike. Although busy after battles dressing wounds, boring (trepanning) and binding fractured skulls, and amputating appendages, army surgeons and their mates spent most of their time treating assorted fevers (inflammatory, intermittent, remittent, bilious, putrid, etc.), dysentery, scurvy, rheumatism, venereal disease, numerous other disorders, and occasionally the pregnancies of camp women.¹⁶¹ They also isolated and treated small pox victims and carried out the army's inoculation program (which encompassed everyone in camp, women and children included) against that disease.¹⁶² Regimental surgeons and mates tried to deal with most of the complaints within the perimeters of their own units, but when the number of patients multiplied too rapidly or an illness became too severe, they sent the sick into hospitals.

Many times headquarters would send down orders that the sick were to be removed from the camp and sent to the nearest Continental hospital.¹⁶³ The hospital department set up both temporary and permanent hospitals in churches, government buildings, and private residences. It established these medical centers in centralized locations such as Yellow Springs, Philadelphia, Sunbury, Trenton, Pluckemin, Baskenridge, Fishkill, and Albany.¹⁶⁴ When it had the chance, the army also set up smaller brigade hospitals. At Valley Forge the officers commanding brigades received orders to set aside some ground near their units, preferably in the center rear of the brigade area, where hospitals could be erected. These hospitals were huts: plans called for them to be fifteen feet wide and twenty-five feet long and at least nine feet high, with a window on each side and a chimney at one end.¹⁶⁵ Once hustled into these hospitals, the sick received not only medical treatment but the attention of line officers as well. Washington ordered each of his brigade commanders at Valley Forge to appoint daily a captain to visit that unit's sick in or near the camp. Those captains had to make sure that the patients were well attended and had everything they needed (as much as circumstances permitted) to regain their health. In almost the same breath, Washington practiced preventive medicine by commanding that an officer be appointed every day to inspect the soldiers' huts to see that they were clean and their roofs weatherproof.¹⁶⁶

Commanders struggled to get their people under cover for most of the war. The housing problem was less acute during the summer campaigns when the army was on the move and the troops could sleep under the stars if necessary, but when the amount of precipitation rose and the temperatures dropped, the Continental Community needed to move out of its tent cities and into sturdier housing. In December 1779 Doctor Thacher eloquently described a situation the army had faced in previous years and would face again. Suffering from the deep snow and freezing temperatures, the troops had reached the wilderness area near Morristown where they were to build winter quarters with no wagons, baggage, tents, or blankets.

> Our only defence against the inclemency of the weather, consists of brushwood thrown together. Our lodging . . . was on the frozen ground. Those officers who have . . . a horse, can always have a blanket at hand. Having removed the snow, we wrapped ourselves in great-coats, spread our blankets on the ground, and lay down by the side of each other five or six together, with large fires at our feet, leaving orders with the waiters to keep it well supplied with fuel during the night.[167]

When the baggage finally did arrive, the soldiers found it difficult to pitch their tents on that frozen ground. The tents were only a temporary solution, however, for the officers moved quickly to warm their soldiers by putting them to work building log cabins.

Many of those rough huts not only housed the troops in the winter of 1779–1780 but again served the needs of the army the following winter. Although some had been demolished over the course of the year, when Pennsylvania soldiers returned in November 1780 they found enough cabins left, with only minor repairs required before habitation, to house them all. Those durable huts showed what lessons had been learned at Valley Forge: they had been built and laid out according to the regulations issued at that encampment. Each hut, complete with fireplace, was about sixteen feet long by fourteen wide and generally housed ten to twelve men who slept in bunks built up along the walls. The common layout of an encampment placed the officers' quarters directly to the rear of their soldiers' lodgings. Officers' huts, although not always uniform in design, usually had two rooms that were occupied by three or four men.[168] Regimental hutments also included kitchens and sometimes huts designated solely for the women who belonged with the troops. At one time the New Hampshire line had thirty-six soldiers' huts, ten officers' cabins, three kitchens, and twelve women's huts. The 1st and 3rd Massachusetts brigades recorded that they had the sum of ninety-four soldiers' huts, fifty-four quarters for officers, twenty-eight kitchens, but only ten huts for women.[169]

The army built barracks where it was more permanently garrisoned, as in Boston, Massachusetts; West Point, New York; and Burlington, New Jersey. Elsewhere, when it could, it placed its people in public houses and government buildings, and when it could not, it put them in tents.[170] The quartermaster general was responsible for the issue and care of the tents and marquees that housed the army for most of the war. He handed them out at the beginning of each campaign and then demanded their return as the soldiers marched into their barracks or huts at the end of the season.[171] His was not an easy job. The quartermaster general would mutter about the misuse or misappropriation of his tents, only to have the officers and soldiers retort that his tents were ill-made and ill-suited to their needs. Timothy Pickering encountered this problem in 1781 when everyone complained that the new tents were too small to hold the proper number of men.[172]

The quartermaster general was not the butt of all complaints: everyone had a lot to say to the commissary general (and later the civilian contractors who took on the job of provisioning the troops) about the food as well. They complained about both quantity and quality. The soldiers often did not receive the full rations to which they were entitled. Sometimes there was a dearth of certain items, perhaps due to a poor harvest or the hoarding of supplies by civilians; sometimes the transport system broke down and there was no way to get the goods to camp. In the fall of 1777 there were recurring shortages of salt, whiskey, and flour. Thomas Jones, the issuing commissary, often had no bread or flour to issue to the troops, but he was able to stave off starvation because of the almost regular arrival of cattle—another species of camp follower—from New England that were tended to and then butchered in camp.[173] The supply situation worsened over that winter at Valley Forge. When some members of the Continental Congress heard about the hungry troops, they urged Washington to seize whatever food his people needed. Although he sometimes had to resort to such measures, Washington resisted such suggestions then and at other times. He realized that relieving his soldiers through the seizure or impressment of civilian supplies would undermine the principles for which they were fighting and destroy the political support of the people.[174] Washington, instead, tried to work through the system to ensure the delivery and distribution of provisions.

According to a 1775 resolution by the Continental Congress, daily provisions for a soldier included a pound of beef or fish, or three-quarters of a pound of pork, a pound of bread or flour, and a pint of milk when available. Each man was also to get a quart of spruce beer, or share in the gallons of molasses distributed among a company of one hundred men. In addition to the above, the army was supposed to provide him with three pints of peas or beans each week, or an equivalent ration of vegetables, along with one-half pint of rice or a pint of Indian (corn) meal.[175] In the course of the war, Congress and the general officers would fiddle with the proportions as the availability of foodstuffs waxed and waned. They often waned. During the starving time at Morristown in January 1780, some soldiers roasted their old shoes, and a few officers supposedly "killed and ate a favorite little dog that belonged to one of them."[176]

Throughout the Revolution soldiers were supposed to receive one ration per day unless on a special work detail, but the number of rations allowed officers changed over the years. In 1775 officers were allocated rations in proportion to their rank. For example, a surgeon drew three rations per day, but his mate could take only two.[177] Then in 1778 Congress resolved that officers were entitled to only one ration per day, but that they would also receive a subsistence allowance "that they may live in a manner becoming their Stations."[178] After officers protested against such meanness, Congress changed their allowances once again to include graduated rations according to rank as well as subsistence money. According to that 1782 resolution, surgeons then received one and one-half rations per day and over four dollars subsistence pay a month. A surgeon's mate received only one ration and a bit over three dollars.[179] Women, children, and volunteers also drew rations; they could receive anywhere from a quarter to a full ration depending on what services they provided. Sometimes the army even placed civilian clerks and artisans on the ration rolls.[180]

By February 1783 the American army was better fed, covered, and clothed than it ever had been before in winter quarters. It was also better disciplined—a matter simply proven by sight and smell. Washington was agreeably affected by the view of the "present comfortable and beautiful situation of the troops." He was pleased to remind them "of a circumstance which will be remembered to their immortal reputation; that during the whole time the army was encamped the last Campaign on Verplanks Point, there never was any filth or trash to be seen on the parade nor any thing offensive to the sight or smell, in the invirons of the encampment. . . ." It had taken him over seven years to do it, but Washington finally had an army fully fit to fight.[181] As it turned out, however, his troops were all dressed up to go nowhere except home. While Congress examined the provisions of the preliminary peace treaty, Washington began to disband the Continental Army. When peace was officially proclaimed that fall, the remaining soldiers and followers broke ranks and left camp, leaving behind a small cadre that continued to serve as the United States Army but taking with them the memories, lessons, and connections forged in the Continental Community.

They would remember bad or no food, the stench, the itch, building huts, and sharing blankets. They could swap stories, in which the names changed but the events were the same, about guard duty, parade drills, marches, and battles. Furthermore, they would mourn the fallen, scorn the turncoats, discuss their officers, and demand recognition and recompense from their states and nation. These people, especially those who had served for years, had left their homes, given up civilian freedom for military discipline, and become the symbols as well as soldiers of the Revolution. Washington had told them that, as had their officers, and during the war they concentrated on what their commanders told them, not on the civilians who denigrated them. And lo and behold, after the war was over they found their hardships celebrated, the rough edges of their characters smoothed, and their poverty ignored.[182]

That most of those who served in or with the army did so for money was conveniently forgotten. So too was the fact that some joined more out of a sense of adventure than patriotism. Although the desire for both acquisition and adventure had long been part of American history and built into what could be called the American character, the new American nation wanted to concentrate on patriotism—to establish itself upon an ideal. That was acceptable to most veterans—until it really hurt their pocketbooks—because it hallowed their labor and lives, and because they had been indoctrinated in that image of themselves over the course of their service. Such a belief was necessary for the civilians because the creation of the army and the development of its community had resulted in an authoritarian subsociety that dismayed and was distrusted by many Americans. Instead of reflecting American society, it seemed antithetical to it. That was not actually the case. There was a growing number of poor in American society at that time, and many young men in search of opportunity away from home. But the growing age and economic stratification was not something Americans wanted to see. Nor did they want to acknowledge that authoritarian structures were part of the Revolution, not just in the military but in the local governments that had policed their people. So the issue became one of instilling and institutionalizing virtue both during and after the war: creating a respectable and successful army and nation.

Washington, as commander in chief of the army, concentrated on the former task. He needed an army that would persevere and fight well. To do that he had to transform undisciplined men into soldiers. That meant not only having them trained in the manual of arms but educated in the definition of citizenship. It was a challenge to take these former subjects, who had declared themselves free men, that next step into the demands and costs of citizenship. It was a long process, and not wholly successful all the time among all the people, as seen in the desertions, mutinies, and even in the start, though not the conclusion, of the Newburgh affair. Washington had to get the officers and soldiers, and, yes, the followers, to equate personal desires with national interest, and even if he could not get that, to at least subordinate personal interest to that of the nation's and modify personal behavior for the public good. To do the first, he reminded his people of the Revolution's goals and ideology; to do the latter two, he applied discipline and regulation. That it worked is shown in the survival of the army.

The Continental Army, born of necessity, fostered by ideology, and held together by sheer cussedness, as well as camaraderie and its commanders, was the core of a military community. This military community included civilian personnel and dependents. Some of these civilians joined the community in order to contribute to the American cause; others were there only to make a living. Washington managed them all: officers and soldiers, government servants, families, and camp merchants. With the advice and intermittent assistance of the Continental Congress and state governments, Washington determined who was allowed into the Continental Community, where it would be located, and how it would operate. He and his subordinate commanders had a say in everything from religion and justice to cooking and outhouses. Sometimes community inhabitants disobeyed orders, which meant that the army had to minimize the damage they caused and maximize the punishment they felt. Most got the message: life in this community was predicated on "doing good," not doing well.

Notes

1. George Washington to John Augustine Washington, Cambridge, 27 July 1775, in W. W. Abbot, ed., *The Papers of George Washington*, Revolutionary War Series (Charlottesville: University Press of Virginia, 1985–), 1:183.
2. Thacher, Cambridge, July 1775, James Thacher, *Military Journal of the American Revolution* (1862; reprint, New York: Arno Press, 1969), p. 29.
3. Washington to Lund Washington, Cambridge, 20 August 1775, in Abbot, *Papers of Washington*, 1:335–36.
4. John E. Ferling, "'Oh That I was a Soldier': John Adams and the Anguish of War," *American Quarterly* 36, no. 2 (1984), reprinted in Peter S. Onuf, ed., *The New American Nation 1775-1820*, Vol. 2: *Patriots, Redcoats, and Loyalists* (New York: Garland, 1991), p. 22.
5. Washington to John Hancock, Cambridge, 28 November 1775; Washington to Lt. Col. Joseph Reed, Cambridge, 28 November 1775; Washington to Hancock, Cambridge, 19 November 1775, Abbot, *Papers of Washington*, 2:446, 449, 399.
6. Don Higginbotham, *The War of American Independence: Military Attitudes, Policies, and Practice, 1763–1789* (1971; reprint, Boston: Northeastern University Press, 1983), p. 262.
7. Robert Middlekauff, *The Glorious Cause: The American Revolution, 1763–1789* (New York & Oxford: Oxford University Press, 1982), pp. 334–35, 509. Middlekauff pointed out that public responsibility vs. private desires is one of the classic dilemmas all free people face at one time or another.
8. Lieutenant Hinrichs to Professor Schlüzer, Harlem, New York, 18 September 1776, in Ray W. Pettengill, trans., *Letters from America 1776–1779: Being Letters of Brunswick, Hessian, and Waldeck Officers with the British Armies During the Revolution* (1924; reprint, Port Washington, N.Y.: Kennikat Press, 1964), p. 181.
9. Thacher, 8 January 1775, *Military Journal*, p. 8. On 21 April 1775, p. 13, Thacher beautifully illustrates what Charles Royster in *A Revolutionary People at War: The Continental Army and American Character, 1775–1783* (1979; reprint, New York: W. W. Norton, 1981) called the *rage militaire*.
10. General Orders, Headquarters Cambridge, 18 November 1775, in Abbot, *Papers of Washington*, 2:393.
11. General Orders, Headquarters New York, 15 May 1776, in Abbot, *Papers of Washington*, 4:305. General Orders, Headquarters at the Gulph, 17 December 1777, in John C. Fitzpatrick, ed., *The Writings of George Washington, from the Original Manuscript Sources, 1745–1799* (Washington, D.C.: U.S. Government Printing Office, 1931–1944), 10:168. General Orders, Headquarters New Windsor, 27 April 1781, Ibid., 22:2.
12. Headquarters, 2 July 1776, Orderly Book of the Pennsylvania Rifle Regiment under Col. Edward Hand, vol. 1, copy at Historical Society of Pennsylvania, Philadelphia (hereafter cited as Hand's Pennsylvania Rifle Regiment Book).
13. Royster, *A Revolutionary People at War,* p. 102.
14. General Orders, Headquarters Wilmington, 5 September 1777, *Valley Forge Orderly Book of General George Weedon of the Continental Army under Command of Genl. George Washington, in the Campaign of 1777–8* (1902; reprint, New York: Arno Press, 1971), pp. 34–35.

15. General Orders, Headquarters Cambridge, 27 February 1776, in Abbot, *Papers of Washington,* 3:379–80.
16. Robert K. Wright, *The Continental Army* (Washington, D.C.: Center of Military History, United States Army, 1983), passim. Wright gave a clear overview of the many changes tried by both line and staff as the army tried to increase its effectiveness.
17. General Orders, Headquarters Cambridge, 5, 17, and 20 July 1775, in Abbot, *Papers of Washington,* 1:62–63, 123, 133–34.
18. After Orders, Fishkill, 6 March 1777; Garrison Orders, Fort Constitution, 5 April and 7 May 1777; Garrison Orders, Fort Schuyler, 20 December 1777, in Mss. Orderly Book kept at the Headquarters of LTC Marinus Willett of the 3rd New York Regt., from 17 February 1777 to 21 May 1778, The New-York Historical Society (microfilm; hereafter cited as Mss. 3 New York Orderly Book).
19. General Orders, Headquarters Cambridge, 22 August 1775, in Abbot, *Papers of Washington,* 1:347.
20. General Orders, Headquarters Cambridge, 11 July 1775, in Ibid., 1:106.
21. General Orders, for the right wing at Smithes Clove, 29 (or possibly 30) June 1779, Orderly Book of the 1st Pennsylvania Regiment (hereafter cited as 1PA Orderly Book with appropriate date), 24 May–25 August 1779, Historical Society of Pennsylvania, Philadelphia.
22. Garrison Orders, Fort Schuyler, 13 June 1777, Mss. 3 New York Orderly Book.
23. Headquarters White Plains, 20 August 1778, 1PA Orderly Book, 26 July–20 December 1778.
24. Garrison Orders, West Point, 21 August 1780, Orderly Book, Col. John Lamb's 2nd Regiment of Continental Artillery, New York, 26 June 1780–30 December 1780, The New-York Historical Society's Collection of Early American Orderly Books (microfilm, David Library of the American Revolution, Washington Crossing, Pennsylvania). Lamb's regimental orderly books (all listed under the same title) in The New-York Historical Society's Collection will hereafter be referred to as Lamb's 2CA Orderly Book and differentiated by date.
25. General Orders, [New York], 14 June 1781, Brigade & Regimental Orders, 15 June 1781, Lamb's 2CA Orderly Book, 29 May–22 June 1781.
26. Headquarters near Dobb's Ferry, 5 August 1781, in Fitzpatrick, *Writings of Washington,* 22:461–62. Orders were quite specific about limiting access to camp to people "belonging to the Army" and those with special authorization.
27. Headquarters [Cambridge], 15 July 1775, Orderly Book of the Pennsylvania Rifle Battalion, June–4 December 1775, Historical Society of Pennsylvania.
28. General Orders, Headquarters Cambridge, 26 July 1775, in Abbot, *Papers of Washington,* 1:172.
29. Headquarters [New York], 22 September 1776, George Washington's HQ Orderly Book, New York, 31 August–4 October 1776, War Department Collection of Revolutionary War Records, Record Group 93 (overall collection referred to hereafter as RG 93), Revolutionary War Miscellaneous Manuscript Collections, National Archives, Washington, D.C.
30. Orders for West Point area, Headquarters Robinson's Farm, 7 February 1780, Lamb's 2CA Orderly Book, 30 November 1778–4 February 1779 and 11 January–18 February 1780.

31. General Orders, Headquarters Morristown, 10 April 1780; Washington to Comte de Rochambeau, Headquarters near Peekskill, 30 June 1781; General Orders, Headquarters Tarrytown, 2 July 1781; Washington to Maj. Gen. Alexander McDougall, Headquarters, 4 August 1781; in Fitzpatrick, *Writings of Washington,* 18:241; 22:293–94; 22:323; 22:459.
32. New York, 12 August 1778, British Intelligence Journal, New York, 1778, 2248, Manuscript Division, Library of Congress.
33. New York, 19 August 1778, 19 and 30 September 1778, Ibid.
34. New York, 1 October 1778, Ibid.
35. General Orders, Headquarters Fredericksburgh, 23 October 1778, in Fitzpatrick, *Writings of Washington,* 13:139–40.
36. Thacher, Upstate New York (possibly Ticonderoga), 30 January 1777, *Military Journal,* p. 73. Daniel Strong, found lurking about with enlistment orders for loyalist regiments, was tried and executed as a spy.
37. Mention of Indian alliances in Higginbotham, *War of American Independence,* pp. 328–29; more specific information in such entries as "Delaware Indians" and "Iroquois Indians" by Colin G. Calloway in *The American Revolution, 1775–1783: An Encyclopedia,* ed. Richard L. Blanco. (New York: Garland, 1993), 1:454–55, 809–12.
38. Garrison Orders, Fort Schuyler, 12 April 1778, Mss. 3 New York Orderly Book.
39. *Pennsylvania Gazette,* 14 May 1777, p. 2, col. 2–3.
40. Artillery park (East Chester below White Plains?), 9 November 1779, Lamb's 2CA Orderly Book, 24 August 1779–20 February 1780.
41. There are numerous advertisements concerning items lost or stolen in Headquarters Valley Forge Orderly Book, 1–31 January 1778, RG 93, Revolutionary War Miscellaneous Manuscript Collections, National Archives, and in *Valley Forge Orderly Book;* an example in the latter (p. 72) was General Orders, Headquarters [Skippack?], 7 October 1777.
42. Orders, Headquarters White Marsh, 21 November 1777; Report, Headquarters Valley Forge, 3 February 1778; Orders, Headquarters Valley Forge, 4 February 1778 (Walter Hart Blumenthal, *Women Camp Followers of the American Revolution* (Philadelphia: George MacManus, 1952) showed this on pages 66–67); Orders, Valley Forge, 26 March 1778, in *Valley Forge Orderly Book,* pp. 136, 220, 221, 270.
43. Wister, 11 May 1778, in Kathryn Zabelle Derounian, ed., *The Journal and Occasional Writings of Sarah Wister* (London & Toronto: Associated University Presses, 1987), p. 59.
44. Mary Beth Norton, *Liberty's Daughters: The Revolutionary Experience of American Women, 1750–1800* (Boston & Toronto: Little, Brown and Company, 1980), p. 175.
45. Headquarters Valley Forge, 13 April 1778, Maj. Gen. Heath's Headquarters Orderly Book, from Boston to Providence, 23 May 1777–20 October 1778 (hereafter cited as Heath's HQ Book), RG 93, Revolutionary War Miscellaneous Manuscript Collections, National Archives.
46. General Orders, Headquarters New York, 25 April 1776, in Abbot, *Papers of Washington,* 4:123. Headquarters, 6 September 1776, George Washington's HQ Orderly

Book, New York, 31 [record misprint says 21] August–4 October 1776, RG 93, Revolutionary War Miscellaneous Manuscript Collections, National Archives.
47. General Orders, 26 December 1777, Copy of Orderly Book, 1st Virginia State Infantry Regiment, 1777–1778, Virginia Historical Society, Richmond.
48. General Orders, Headquarters near Dobb's Ferry, 4 July 1781, in Fitzpatrick, *Writings of Washington*, 22:327–28.
49. Higginbotham, *War of American Independence*, p. 414. For British policy, see Stephen Conway's "To Subdue America: British Army Officers and the Conduct of the Revolutionary War," *William and Mary Quarterly*, 3d ser., 43 (1986), reprinted in Onuf, ed., *The New American Nation*, Vol. 2: *Patriots, Redcoats, and Loyalists* (New York: Garland, 1991), pp. 139–65. British General Orders, from on board HMS *Greyhound*, Sandyhook, 29 June 1776, Sir William Howe Orderly Book, 27 January 1776–1 May 1778, stated "any person belonging to the Army or Transports found guilty of Plundering... will be Executed on the Spot." In William L. Clements Library, University of Michigan, Ann Arbor.
50. General Orders, Headquarters New Windsor, 1 June 1781, in Fitzpatrick, *Writings of Washington*, 22:151.
51. On March (Springfield), 26 April 1780, in Continental Army-Military Life, Diary by U/I Author, 21 April–25 September 1780, in Virginia Historical Society, Richmond. From noting names, units, and dates it appears that the author is possibly Lt. Elias J. Parker.
52. Benjamin Gilbert to his father and stepmother, Totoway, 15 October 1780, in John Shy, ed., *Winding Down: The Revolutionary War Letters of Lieutenant Benjamin Gilbert of Massachusetts, 1780–1783* (Ann Arbor: University of Michigan Press, 1989), p. 26.
53. John Shy in *A People Numerous and Armed: Reflections on the Military Struggle for American Independence*, rev. ed. (Michigan: University of Michigan Press, Ann Arbor Paperbacks, 1990), p. 173. Harold E. Selesky in *War and Society in Colonial Connecticut* (New Haven: Yale University Press, 1990), pp. 82, 154, 162–63, showed the onset of this with earlier colonial expeditionary forces.
54. *Pennsylvania Gazette*, 28 May 1777, p. 4, col. 1.
55. Charles Neimeyer in "America Goes to War: Race, Class, and Ethnicity in the Continental Army" (draft of the manuscript to be published by New York University Press), noted the tenacity with which soldiers defended their "customary dues'" or social wages on pages 313–14. These wages, although they depreciated over the war, showed that they were freemen and volunteers, not slaves.
56. Thacher, Highlands, opposite West Point, 3 July 1778, *Military Journal*, pp. 136–37. Washington announced the Congressional Resolutions on pensions in General Orders, Headquarters Valley Forge, 18 May 1778, in Fitzpatrick, *Writings of Washington*, 11:412. Thacher later recorded in May 1780 (pp. 193–95) that after officers continued to harp on the same old grievances, and Washington supported them, Congress offered more compensation.
57. Thacher, Cambridge, December 1775, Ibid., p. 34.
58. Higginbotham, *War of American Independence*, p. 394.
59. The issue of enlisting African Americans into the army troubled many officers, and they brought it before the committee Congress appointed to look into army matters

in the fall of 1775. At that time [Cambridge, c. 18 October 1775] the question was raised, "Ought not Negroes to be excluded in the New Inlistment? especially such as are Slaves—By a Council of Officers both are." Footnote 24 (p. 189) refers to the answer given by the Council of War on 8 October: "agst them altog[e]ther." In December Washington lifted the ban on enlisting blacks; he gave some of his reasons in the General Orders of 30 December and in a letter to John Hancock on 31 December, in Abbot, *Papers of Washington*, 2:188, 189, 620, 623.

60. Higginbotham, *War of American Independence*, pp. 392–93. In compiler John Frederick Dorman's *Virginia's Revolutionary Pension Applications, Abstracted*, 3 vols. (Washington, D.C., 1958–1959) there are a number of references to hiring a substitute or being one. For example, check, James Aiken, Archibald Allen, Benjamin Allen, Charles Allen, and Nathan Anderson.
61. Lt. Col. Eleazer Oswald to Lamb, Fishkill, 12 November 1777, John Lamb Papers, The New-York Historical Society (microfilm), reel 1. Although perhaps not strictly enforced, Article 7, Section XIII, of the 1776 Articles of War imposed limits on hiring substitutes: "No soldier belonging to any regiment, troop or company, shall hire another to do his duty for him, or be excused from duty, but in case of sickness, disability or leave of absence."
62. "A list of persons employed in the Commissary General Department," and petition to Continental Congress by Joseph Trumbull, Cambridge, 20 January 1776, Sol Feinstone Collection, no. 1395, David Library of the American Revolution, Washington Crossing, Pennsylvania (microfilm).
63. It is difficult at times to determine who was civilian and who was military in the staff departments. The use of a rank or title only sometimes helped—at the beginning of the war many persons in these departments received rank as part of their compensation, most later "staffers" were not authorized line ranks (such as captain or major) but used them anyway. Adding to the difficulty is the ambivalence of some Continentals as to whether staff department personnel were really members of the military. Checking rank and unit affiliation helps place some people; for others it is more a matter of extrapolating their condition from the positions they held.
64. Congressional Resolution of 1 August 1782 on the composition and compensation of personnel in the adjutant general's department published in General Orders, Headquarters Newburgh, 26 December 1782, Lamb's 2CA Orderly Book, 27 November 1782–5 January 1783.
65. Timothy Pickering to Joseph King, Clothier in quartermaster department, Newburgh, 26 January 1781, Numbered Record Books Concerning Military Operations and Service, Pay and Settlement of Accounts, and Supplies in the War Department Collection of Revolutionary War Records (hereafter referred to as Numbered Record Books), M853, roll 25, vol. 124, National Archives, Washington, D.C. (microfilm, David Library).
66. Dr. William Eustis to Lamb, [Robinson's near West Point, New York], 12 October 1780, John Lamb Papers (microfilm), reel 2.
67. Linda K. Kerber, *Women of the Republic: Intellect and Ideology in Revolutionary America* (Chapel Hill: University of North Carolina Press, 1980), pp. 58–60.
68. Artillery (Garrison?) Orders, West Point, 29 June 1780, Lamb's 2CA Orderly Book, 26 June–30 December 1780, 4 August–13 October 1781. Another example of

washerwomen charges being regulated (along with those of barbers, tailors, and shoemakers) is found in Regimental Orders, [New York], 19 August 1782, Almon W. Lauber, ed., *Orderly Books of the Fourth New York Regiment, 1778–1780 [&] the Second New York Regiment, 1780–1783 by Samuel Tallmadge and Others with Diaries of Samuel Tallmadge, 1780–1782 and John Barr, 1779–1782* (Albany: University of the State of New York, 1932), p. 610.
69. General Orders, Headquarters Cambridge, 7 August 1775, in Abbot, *Papers of Washington,* 1:260.
70. Thacher, 14 July 1777, *Military Journal,* pp. 82–83. Thacher then noted that they reached "Skeensboro" at 3:00 P.M. but had to flee again within two hours after a surprise attack from Burgoyne's troops, in the process all their cannon, provisions, much of the baggage, and several invalids fell into enemy hands.
71. General Orders, Headquarters St[e]nton near Germantown, 23 August 1777, and General Orders, Headquarters Wilmington, 28 August 1777, *Valley Forge Orderly Book,* pp. 19–20, 24–25.
72. General After Orders, Headquarters Germantown, 13 September 1777, Ibid., p. 49.
73. Summary of duties for Marechaussee Corps, published for edification of army at large, recorded on 11 October 1778, in Lamb's 2CA Orderly Book, 26 September–27 November 1778.
74. Two examples of orders pertaining to women riding in the wagons are: Headquarters Smithes Clove, 7 June 1779, 1 PA Orderly Book, 24 May–25 August 1779, and Major General Greene's Orders, Headquarters Steerapia, 19 September 1780, Lamb's 2CA Orderly Book, 7 September–2 November 1780.
75. Headquarters, 19 June 1781, Lamb's 2CA Orderly Book, 29 May–22 June 1781. The word *only* was underlined in the book.
76. Middlekauff, *The Glorious Cause,* p. 563.
77. Brig. Gen. Henry Knox to Lamb, Camp near Dobb's Ferry, 18 August 1781, John Lamb Papers (microfilm), reel 2.
78. Regimental Orders, Haverstraw, 23 August 1781, Lamb's 2CA Orderly Book, 26 June–30 December 1780.
79. Thacher, marching south, 8 September 1781, *Military Journal,* pp. 271–72.
80. Thacher, Virginia, 22–28 September 1781, Ibid., pp. 278–79. Feltman essentially picks up on the chronology of events in Virginia, 27–30 September 1781, William Feltman Military Journal, 1781–1782, Historical Society of Pennsylvania (hereafter cited as Journal, 1781–1782).
81. War was a spectator sport. On 9 October 1781 people indulging their curiosity on the siege lines were told to walk on the surface of the trenches so as not to interrupt the works (in Orderly Book of the 1st Virginia Battalion of 1781, kept by Col. Christian Febiger?, 9 October 1781–2 May 1782, at Historical Society of Pennsylvania). On 16 October 1781 "The commander in chief having observ'd that the trenches are constantly crowded with spectators, who . . . greatly impede the opperations of the Siege, He therefore orders that no officer who is not on duty shall hereafter enter the trenches, except Genl. Officers & their Aids, and that no inhabitant or person not belonging to the army be suffer'd to enter the trenches at any time without permission from the Maj. Genl. of the trenches." In Orderly Book of Brigadier General Anthony Wayne, Combined Pennsylvania Battalions, 1781, in Wayne Papers, Historical Society of Pennsylvania.

82. Closen, Virginia, 28 September 1781, Evelyn M. Acomb, trans. and ed., *The Revolutionary Journal of Baron Ludwig Von Closen 1780–1783* (Chapel Hill: University of North Carolina Press, 1958), p. 138.
83. General Orders, Headquarters King's Ferry, 22 August 1781, in Fitzpatrick, *Writings of Washington*, 23:37–38.
84. Feltman, [Near Bottoms Bridge, New Kent County, Virginia], 16 August 1781, Journal, 1781–1782. Feltman was probably referring to Edward Crawford who had served with the 1st Pennsylvania earlier, but had, according to Heitman in the *Historical Register of Officers of the Continental Army*, transferred to the 3rd Pennsylvania on 1 January 1781.
85. Thacher, marching from New Jersey to New York, August 1780, and at Providence, Rhode Island, 30 July 1779, and Highlands, 4 July 1778, *Military Journal*, pp. 206–7, 169, 138.
86. Knox to Washington, Artillery Park, 1 December 1777, in The Henry Knox Papers, IV, 76, GLC 2437, The Gilder Lehrman Collection, on deposit at The Pierpont Morgan Library (microfilm, David Library).
87. Thacher, from West Point to Pompton, 4 January 1781 and after, *Military Journal*, pp. 246–53. Thacher discussed the mutinies and the army's responses. See also Carl Van Doren, *Mutiny in January: The Story of a Crisis in the Continental Army now for the first time fully told from many hitherto unknown or neglected sources* (New York: Viking Press, 1943).
88. *Pennsylvania Gazette*, 30 May 1781, p. 3, col. 2.
89. Garrison Orders, Fort Schuyler, 5 March 1778, Mss. 3 New York Orderly Book. Nancy Weedon is not to be confused with General Weedon's wife, Catharine.
90. [Near Morristown, New Jersey], 19 June 1780 and 7 August 1780, Continental Army Life, Diary by U/I Author (Parker?).
91. Sebastian Bauman of the 2nd Continental Artillery was apparently a rather prickly sort, who threatened resignation over a number of issues, including promotion and command accountability. See, for example, Knox to Bauman, 28 December 1777, and Bauman to Lamb, West Point, 8 December 1779, in Sebastian Bauman Papers, Vol. 1, 1775–1779, in New-York Historical Society. Louis Clinton Hatch, in *The Administration of the American Revolutionary Army* (1904; reprint, New York: Burt Franklin, Lenox Hill, 1971), pp. 36–37, discussed the quarrels over rank. Rhys Isaac noted how military authority and rank was connected to social authority and status in one of the colonies/states in *The Transformation of Virginia, 1740–1790* (1982; New York: W. W. Norton, 1988), pp. 105, 109.
92. Headquarters Valley Forge, 18 January 1778, *Valley Forge Orderly Book*, p. 195.
93. Thacher, 29 and 30 August 1780, *Military Journal*, pp. 209–10.
94. Headquarters Valley Forge, 6 January 1778, *Valley Forge Orderly Book*, pp. 183–84.
95. E. Anthony Rotundo, *American Manhood: Transformations in Masculinity from the Revolution to the Modern Era* (New York: Basic Books, 1993), pp. 3, 13–15, 19. Rotundo noted a shift from "communal manhood" to "self-made manhood" in New England in the late colonial and early republic periods. Among the authors who have discussed the competitiveness and assertiveness of southern men are Rhys Isaac, in *Transformation of Virginia*, p. 95, and Allan Kulikoff, in *Tobacco and Slaves: The Development of Southern Cultures in the Chesapeake, 1680–1800* (Chapel Hill: University of North Carolina Press, 1986), pp. 220–29. Nancy F.

Cott, in *The Bonds of Womanhood: "Women's Sphere" in New England, 1780–1835* (New Haven: Yale University Press, 1977), pp. 11f, proposed that by the mid nineteenth century the southern image of the lady influenced northern ideas on women's roles more than the reverse. Along that line, I suggest that southern and western individualism as perceived by northerners in the army may have had something to do with the shift Rotundo perceives.

96. Charles Mellish to Clinton, Grosvenor Place, 2 February 1776, 13:32 in Clinton Papers, William L. Clements Library.
97. Letter from a German Officer, Cambridge, 18 December 1777, in Pettengill, *Letters from America*, p. 132.
98. Higginbotham, *War of American Independence*, pp. 101–2. Royster in *Revolutionary People at War*, pp. 43, 87, 94, and Shy in *People Numerous and Armed*, p. 251, also discussed officer status.
99. Beebe, Crown Point, 4 July 1776, in Frederick R. Kirkland, ed., *Journal of Lewis Beebe: A Physician on the Campaign Against Canada, 1776* (Philadelphia: Historical Society of Pennsylvania, 1935), p. 15.
100. Thacher, Highlands, 23 November 1778, *Military Journal*, p. 55.
101. Examples of invitations include: Nathanael and Catharine Greene to Henry and Lucy Knox, Long Island, a Thursday evening in June 1776, in Robert E. McCarthy, ed., *The Papers of General Nathanael Greene*, Part I: 1766–July 1780 (Scholarly Resources, Inc., microfilm); and Major Shaw (for Gen. and Mrs. Henry Knox) to Lamb, a Sunday morning in 1778, John Lamb Papers (microfilm), reel 1.
102. Francis J. Brooke, *A Family Narrative of a Revolutionary Officer* (1849, 1921; reprint, New York: Arno Press, 1971), pp. 94–95. These events took place in 1781–1782.
103. 22, 24, 27, 28 May and 9 June 1780, in Continental Army Life, Diary by U/I Author (Parker?). This counters Royster's contention in *Revolutionary People at War*, p. 91, that senior officers held aloof from junior ones (perhaps such behavior indicated who felt secure in both official and social rank). Rebecca D. Symmes, editor of *A Citizen-Soldier in the American Revolution: The Diary of Benjamin Gilbert in Massachusetts and New York* (Cooperstown: New York State Historical Association, 1980) pointed out on page 13, that Washington, who certainly did not promote officer-enlisted familiarity, did support the formation of Freemason lodges in the army in hopes of countering low morale. Within such lodges there was a mingling of men from all ranks.
104. Thacher, New Jersey, 2 May 1779, and near Kingsbridge, New York, 13 July 1781, *Military Journal*, pp. 162, 265. A short essay by Light Townsend Cummins explaining Juan de Miralles's role can be found in Blanco, ed., *The American Revolution: An Encyclopedia*, 2:1077–78.
105. *Pennsylvania Gazette*, 12 June 1782, p. 3, col. 1.
106. New York City, 19 April, 8 June, 9 July 1776, in Edward Bangs, ed., *Journal of Lieutenant Isaac Bangs, April 1 to July 29, 1776* (1890; reprint, New York: Arno Press, 1968), pp. 23–24, 40–42, 57.
107. [Tappan], 25 September 1780, Continental Army Life, Diary by U/I Author (Parker?).
108. Thacher, Orangetown, New Jersey, 14 August 1780, *Military Journal*, pp. 208–9. Feltman, [Jacksonburgh, South Carolina?], 22–24 February 1782, Journal, 1781–1782. Bloomfield, Albany, 11 May 1776, in Mark E. Lender and James Kirby Mar-

tin, eds., *Citizen Soldier: The Revolutionary War Journal of Joseph Bloomfield* (Newark: New Jersey Historical Society, 1982), p. 45. Journal Entry, New Kent County, Virginia, 22 June 1781, Itinerary of the Pennsylvania Line, 1781, Historical Society of Pennsylvania. Thacher mentioned visiting Doctor [John] Cochran and then having tea with Major [Lemuel?] Trescott and Captain [Nathaniel?] Cushing. Feltman recorded going to a dance at Major [James?] Moore's bowery on the 22d, playing cricket on the 23rd, and having guests to dinner on the 24th followed by "grogg" drinking with a number of assembly men. Bloomfield wrote of drinking tea in the evening with a number of officers and ladies. In terms of gaming, see Washington forbidding it in General Orders, Headquarters Cambridge, 26 February 1776, Abbot, *Papers of Washington,* 3:362, and at Headquarters Valley Forge, 8 January 1778, Fitzpatrick, *Writings of Washington,* 10:276, but Gilbert playing cards anyway on 28 December 1779, Symmes, ed., *Citizen-Soldier in the American Revolution,* p. 62.

109. Subscription for Dancing Assembly, [Morristown, New Jersey, January–February 1780], in Harold C. Syrett, ed., *The Papers of Alexander Hamilton* (New York: Columbia University Press, 1961), 2:263.

110. Closen, Headquarters Rhode Island, 25 December 1780; Boston, 18 March 1781; Winter Quarters in Virginia, 24 November 1781; 15 December 1781; in Acomb, *Revolutionary Journal,* pp. 48–49, 66, 166, 168–69. Gilbert to Lt. Park Holland, [August 1781], in Shy, ed., *Winding Down,* p. 47.

111. In correspondence between Elizabeth Ambler and Mildred Smith, 1780–1782, Elizabeth Jacquelin Ambler Papers, 1780–1823, Manuscript Division, Library of Congress (photostats).

112. Wister, Foulke Farm, Pennsylvania, 19, 26, 31(?) October, and 1 November 1777, Derounian, *The Journal and Occasional Writings of Sarah Wister,* pp. 44–49.

113. See Washington's displeasure in orders and correspondence. General Orders, Headquarters Valley Forge, 2 January, GW to Col. William Malcom, 6 January, to Brig. Gen. John Glover, 8 January, to Brig. Gen. George Weedon, 10 February, to Maj. Gen. John Sullivan, 14 February 1778, in Fitzpatrick, *Writings of Washington,* 10:247–48, 269–70, 280–81, 448–49, 460–61. See acquiescence with restrictions in GW to Brig. Gen. Peter Muhlenberg, 15 October 1778, and General Orders, Headquarters Fredericksburg, 2 November 1778, in Fitzpatrick, *Writings of Washington,* 13:82–83, 196–97. Examples of officers receiving leave include Capt. Gershom Mott and Col. John Lamb in 1779. Mott to Lamb, Pluckemin, 13 January 1779, and order of Major General McDougall, 1 February 1779, in John Lamb Papers (microfilm), reel 1. That Washington continued to dislike furloughs is seen in Hamilton's note to his fiancee Elizabeth Schuyler, [Teaneck, New Jersey, 31 August 1780], in Syrett, ed., *Papers of Hamilton,* 2:388. "I could not with decency or honor leave the army during the campaign. Besides this my Betsey, The General is peculiarly averse to the practice in question."

114. Lt. Col. Eleazer Oswald to Lamb, New Haven, 1 April 1778, and "On a dirty, filthy Hill behind the Church" [Peekskill?], 1 July 1777, John Lamb Papers (microfilm), reel 1.

115. Capt.-Lt. [Isaac] Hubbell about [William?] Hubbell to Lamb, Middle Redoubt, 25 July 1780, Ibid., reel 2.

116. John S. Salmon, "A British View of the Siege of Charleston: From the Diary of Captain John Peebles, February 11–June 2, 1780." Master's thesis, College of William and Mary, 1975, p. 85.
117. Closen, White Plains, 4 July 1781, and as he passed through New York, 23 July 1781, in Acomb, *Revolutionary Journal,* pp. 89, 102.
118. Letter from a German Officer, Cambridge, 18 December 1777, in Pettengill, *Letters from America,* p. 119.
119. Example in Timothy Pickering to Major General Heath, New Windsor, 27 December 1781, Numbered Record Books, M853, roll 26, vol. 82.
120. Knox to Lamb, Morristown, 13 April 1777, about recruiting drummers and fifers and keeping them in school, and Capt.-Lt. [Jacob] Reed to Lamb, 8 October 1778, John Lamb Papers (microfilm), reel 1.
121. Hand to Brigadier General Patterson [prob. John Paterson], New Windsor, 21 May 1781, and Hand to Col. Walter Stewart, Inspector for the main army, Orderly Office at Newburgh, 16 July 1782, Numbered Record Books, M853, roll 17, vol. 162.
122. Higginbotham, *War of American Independence,* pp. 394–95. *Pennsylvania Gazette,* 28 May 1777, p. 1, col. 3, published resolve of Delaware Assembly to allow officers of the state's Continental battalion to enlist apprentices or servants whose terms of servitude did not exceed two years (with the payment of an appropriate amount of money to the master/mistress). Randolph W. Church, comp., *Virginia Legislative Petitions: Bibliography, Calendar, and Abstracts from Original Sources 6 May 1776–21 June 1782* (Richmond: Virginia State Library, 1984). This has a number of petitions from masters for compensation for servants who enlisted; most petitions were rejected. Examples are Lewis Lee's and John Aimes's petitions (recorded 21 November 1777) asking for compensation for indentured mulatto servants who enlisted in the military service; both requests were denied (pp. 146–47, no. 478, 480).
123. *Pennsylvania Gazette,* 20 August 1777, p. 1, col. 2: two young gunsmith's apprentices ran away from Michael Witner; Witner hoped that if they approached a recruiting officer that officer would send them back. That same day (same page and column of *Gazette*) Isaac Budd advertised for the return of his Dutch servant man, promising a reward even to a recruiting officer who may have enlisted him. The 5 September 1781 issue, p. 3, col. 3, carried an ad for the return of a "NEGROE MAN, named CAESAR," who was believed to have gone to Philadelphia with the intention of enlisting or serving aboard a ship.
124. Thacher, around Springfield [New Jersey?], 19 June 1780, *Military Journal,* pp. 202–3. Thacher mentioned the "perplexing instances of indisposition, occasioned by absence from home, called by Dr. Cullen nostalgia, or home-sickness" and noted it seemed most frequent among New Englanders.
125. Washington protested to the President of Congress, from Headquarters near Fredericksburg, 24 October 1778, against giving furloughs to the Carolina troops because they lived too far away. In a letter to Col. Theodorick Bland on 5 November, about Bland's upcoming cantonment in either Frederick Town, Maryland, or Winchester, Virginia, he permitted furloughs to those willing to reenlist if so rewarded. In Fitzpatrick, *Writings of Washington,* 13:145–46, 207. Gilbert, while a sergeant in Albany, got a furlough on 27 January 1778; see Symmes, ed., *Citizen-*

Soldier in the American Revolution, p. 23. Joseph Plumb Martin in *Private Yankee Doodle: Being a Narrative of some of the Adventures, Dangers and Sufferings of a Revolutionary Soldier,* ed. George F. Scheer (1830; New York: Little, Brown, Popular Library ed., 1963), p. 135, mentioned soldiers, including himself, getting furloughs in the early months of 1779. It appears that soldiers in regiments away from the main army and relatively close to their homes found it easier to obtain leave.

126. *Pennsylvania Gazette,* 30 July 1777, p. 3, col. 3.
127. Headquarters White Marsh, 11 November 1777, Copy of Orderly Book, 1st Virginia State Infantry Regiment, 1777–1778, Virginia Historical Society, and Headquarters Moore's House, 15 August 1779, 1 PA Orderly Book, 24 May–25 August 1779. In the first instance the court found Ensign Saunders of the Virginia State Regiment guilty of being absent and neglecting his duty and sentenced him to be reprimanded (officers did not receive corporal punishment). In the second case a division court-martial found Thomas Martin and James McKrady of the 1st Pennsylvania guilty of desertion and attempting to go to the enemy; the court sentenced them to receive 100 lashes each. Repeated desertions could result in a sentence of death, while mitigating circumstances, such as youth, could result in a reduced sentence, as shown in General Orders, Headquarters Valley Forge, 19 and 28 January 1778, in Fitzpatrick, *Writings of Washington,* 10:320, 358–60.
128. *Pennsylvania Gazette,* 24 March 1779, p. 3, col. 1.
129. Solomon Bans [or Bams] to Lamb at West Point, New Haven, 4 November 1782, John Lamb Papers (microfilm), reel 2.
130. Headquarters New York, 13 July 1776, in *Order Book Kept By Peter Kinnan July 7–September 4, 1776,* intro. by M. E. Kinnan (Privately printed, New Jersey: Princeton University Press, 1931), p. 8. Headquarters, 4 September 1776, Hand's Pennsylvania Rifle Regiment Book. Order repeated on 10 September.
131. Orders, [Long Island], 18 May 1776, McCarthy, *Papers of General Nathanael Greene* (microfilm), pt. 1, no. 00421. There is an earlier example of the same problem: General Orders, Headquarters Cambridge, 22 August 1775, in Abbot, *Papers of Washington,* 1:346. "The General does not mean to discourage the practice of bathing, whilst the weather is warm enough to continue it; but he expressly forbids, any persons doing it, at or near the Bridge in Cambridge, where it has been observed and complained of, that many Men, lost to all sense of decency and common modesty, are running about naked upon the Bridge, whilst passengers, and even Ladies of the first fashion in the neighbourhood, are passing over it, as if they meant to glory in their shame: The Guards and Centries at the Bridge, are to put a stop to this practice for the future."
132. Disapproval of pulling down statue in Broadway, Headquarters, 10 July 1776, *Order Book Kept By Peter Kinnan,* p. 6. Brigade Orders, 26 December 1777, Copy of Orderly Book, 1st Virginia State Infantry Regiment, 1777–1778. Note that the shooting occurred the day after Christmas; although most Americans did not celebrate the holiday as richly as the Germans, they did recognize it as a special day.
133. Gen. Benedict Arnold to Lamb, Headquarters Robinson's House, 8 September 1780, John Lamb Papers (microfilm), reel 2.
134. Gilbert's social life in the last months before being promoted to ensign illustrates that of the noncommissioned officer (NCO), March through October 1779, in

Symmes, ed., *Citizen-Soldier in the American Revolution,* pp. 48–59. Betsey Foot Hewes met her future husband at a ball where locals and soldiers mingled in Newtown, Connecticut, in January 1779. She married Samuel Hewes of the New Hampshire Regiment in December but did not become a camp follower. In John C. Dann and John Harriman, eds., "The Revolution Remembered—By the Ladies," *American Magazine and Historical Chronicle* 3 (Autumn–Winter 1987–1988): 72.

135. Headquarters Morristown, 26 March 1780, in Orderly Book: American Headquarters, Morristown, New Jersey, 21 February–17 May 1780, The New-York Historical Society's Collection of Early American Orderly Books (microfilm, David Library).
136. Headquarters Fredericksburgh, 21 October 1778, in Fitzpatrick, *Writings of Washington,* 13:118–19.
137. Beebe, St. Johns, 4 June 1776; Crown Point, 27 June 1776; Ticonderoga/Mt. Independence, 25 October 1776, in Kirkland, *Journal of Lewis Beebe,* pp. 8, 13–14, 32.
138. *Pennsylvania Gazette,* 7 April 1779, p. 1, col. 1–2.
139. John Adams to Greene, Philadelphia, 9 May 1777, in McCarthy, *Papers of General Nathanael Greene* (microfilm), pt. 1, no. 00835.
140. Headquarters, 9 July 1776, Hand's Pennsylvania Rifle Regiment Book.
141. Thomas Hale to his parents, Greenwich [New York], 13 September 1776, Sol Feinstone Collection (microfilm).
142. Joseph Bloomfield, chairman, city of Burlington, to Lamb, Burlington [New Jersey], 28 August 1782, John Lamb Papers (microfilm), reel 2.
143. *Pennsylvania Gazette,* 14 May 1777, p. 3, col. 1. The paper published the general orders Washington issued on 8 May from Morristown.
144. Bauman to Knox, West Point, 30 December 1779, in Sebastian Bauman Papers, Vol. 1.
145. Barbara MacDonald Powell, "The Most Celebrated Encampment: Valley Forge in American Culture, 1777–1983," Ph.D. dissertation, Cornell University, 1983, pp. 14–15. Orderly books support Powell's description of a very active army at Valley Forge; see Headquarters Valley Forge Orderly Book, 1–31 January 1778, RG 93, Revolutionary War Miscellaneous Manuscript Collections, National Archives.
146. Headquarters Fredericksburgh, 12 November 1778, in Fitzpatrick, *Writings of Washington,* 13:248.
147. Headquarters New York, 5 May and 14 June 1776, in Abbot, *Papers of Washington,* 4:204, 521. Brigade Orders, Pluckemin, New Jersey, 9 December 1778, Lamb's 2CA Orderly Book, 30 November 1778–4 February 1779 and 11 January–18 February 1780.
148. Headquarters [Peekskill, New York], 13 October 1776, Orderly Book [Continental Army] 6 October–December 1776, Sol Feinstone Collection (microfilm). Martin in *Private Yankee Doodle,* p. 88, wrote that while in New Jersey in the fall of 1777 their meager provisions were cooked by invalids.
149. Brigade Orders, [Artillery Park near Fredericksburg, New York?], 26 September 1778, Lamb's 2CA Orderly Book, 26 September–27 November 1778. General Orders, Headquarters Cambridge, 14 July 1775, Abbot, *Papers of Washington,* 1:114.
150. Orders, Headquarters Newburgh, 24 March 1783, in Edward C. Boynton, ed., *General Orders of George Washington Commander-in-Chief of the Army of the Revo-*

lution Issued at Newburgh on the Hudson 1782–1783 (1909; reprint, Harrison, N.Y.: Harbor Hill Books, 1973), pp. 72–73. Gardening was also conducted at New York frontier forts and by the British Army. John William Krueger, "Troop Life at the Champlain Valley Forts During the American Revolution," Ph.D. dissertation, State University of New York at Albany, 1981, p. 113. Sylvia Frey, *The British Soldier in America: A Social History of Military Life in the Revolutionary Period* (Austin: University of Texas Press, 1981), p. 30.

151. "Address from the Massachusetts Provincial Congress," Watertown, 3 July 1775, in Abbot, *Papers of Washington,* 1:53.
152. Headquarters White Plains, 1 August 1778, and Division Orders, Paramus, 4 December 1778, 1 PA Orderly Book, 26 July–20 December 1778.
153. General Orders, Headquarters Cambridge, 1 August 1775, in Abbot, *Papers of Washington,* 1:206–7.
154. Greene's orders, Germantown, 6 August 1777, in McCarthy, *Papers of General Nathanael Greene* (microfilm), pt. 1.
155. Orders, 12 February 1779, Sgt. John O'Neill Orderly Book, February–September 1779, Military Manuscripts Collection (MG7), Pennsylvania State Archives, Harrisburg.
156. General Orders, Headquarters before York, 5 October 1781, in Fitzpatrick, *Writings of Washington,* 23:175–77.
157. Regimental Orders, Burlington Barracks, New Jersey, 12 December 1781, Lamb's 2CA Orderly Book, 7 December 1781–4 February 1782, and Regimental Orders, 26 April 1782, Orderly Book, Lamb's 2CA Orderly Book, 7 February–7 August 1782. General Orders, Headquarters near Dobb's Ferry, 5 July 1781, touched on the issue of privacy by recommending that bushes surround the vaults, in Fitzpatrick, *Writings of Washington,* 22:329.
158. Garrison Orders, Fort Schuyler, 21 May 1778, Mss. 3 New York Orderly Book. Relating back to earlier issue, these orders also said, "The Qr. Mr. Sergeant will have Tubs placed at the Several Corners of the Barricks for the Men to make Water in which are to be Emptied and washed every Morning."
159. Brigade Orders, Fredericksburg, 25 October 1778, 1 PA Orderly Book, 26 July–20 December 1778.
160. Regimental Orders, 13 July 1779, 1PA Orderly Book, 24 May–25 August 1779.
161. Thacher, Albany, 24 October 1777, *Military Journal,* pp. 112–13, and various returns of the sick and wounded in camps and military hospitals, 1778–1780, Revolutionary War Rolls, 1775–1783, M246, roll 135, National Archives (microfilm, David Library). Two pregnant patients are listed in the return from the hospital at Danbury for the period 20 October–7 November 1778.
162. Orderly books and journals mention inoculation often (pros, cons, efficacy, etc.). Examples include: Beebe, 19 May 1776, in Kirkland, *Journal of Lewis Beebe,* p. 4, and General Orders, Headquarters Valley Forge, 18 March 1778, *Valley Forge Orderly Book,* p. 263, and General Orders, New Windsor, 19 April 1781, Lamb's 2CA Orderly Book, 21 February–28 March 1781, and Thacher, Highlands, January 1782, *Military Journal,* pp. 307–8.
163. See this in the orders, Headquarters White Marsh, 15 November 1777, Copy of Orderly Book, 1st Virginia State Infantry Regiment, 1777–1778.

164. "A General Return of the Sick and Wounded in the Military Hospitals, belonging to the army . . . ," from 1 February to 1 March 1780, Revolutionary War Rolls, 1775–1783, M246, roll 135, National Archives (microfilm, David Library). This return listed "Places where Military hospitals are open."
165. Orders, Headquarters Valley Forge, 9, 13 January 1778, Copy of Orderly Book, 1st Virginia State Infantry Regiment, 1777–1778.
166. Orders, Headquarters Valley Forge, 29 January 1778, HQ Valley Forge Orderly Book, 1–31 January 1778.
167. Thacher, near Morristown, December 1779, *Military Journal,* pp. 180–81.
168. Van Doren, *Mutiny in January,* pp. 29–31. At Valley Forge: Capt. [John] Doughty to Lamb, Park of Artillery [Valley Forge], 27 January 1778, John Lamb Papers (microfilm), reel 1, wrote, "We are all Happily seated for the Winter in our Logg Houses, which prove very comforta[ble] & shall enjoy much Happiness if Mr British don't Disturb us."
169. "Return of Quarters for the New Hampshire Line & the 1st and 3d Massachusetts Brigades," no date or place, RG 93, Letters, Returns, Accounts, and Estimates of the Quartermaster General's Department, 1776–1783, M926, National Archives (microfilm, David Library).
170. Col. Timothy Danielson to Washington, Roxbury Camp, 31 July 1775, in Abbot, *Papers of George Washington,* 1:200. Danielson wrote Washington that he had received his orders (via General Thomas) to remove Captain Ball and company from quarters in order to "accommodate one Mr Waters with a convenient House of Entertainment." He protested Ball's removal to "gratify a Dram Seller," especially when there were too many of them in camp already, and hoped that the order would be repealed. In footnote 1: Joseph Reed wrote to Thomas on 15 July saying that Col. [Joseph] Trumbull had applied to Washington on behalf of a person who wanted a house occupied by some soldiers in order to keep a tavern. Reed said Washington left the matter up to Thomas. If Thomas agreed, arrangements could be made. If needed, Trumbull would furnish tents for the men.
171. General Orders, Headquarters Cambridge, 22 November 1775, Ibid., 2:416, and Headquarters Valley Forge, 4 January 1778, HQ Valley Forge Orderly Book, 1–31 January 1778.
172. Pickering to Col. Jabez Hatch, Camp Phillipsburg, 12 July 1781, Numbered Record Books, M853, roll 26, vol. 127. Pickering told Hatch to remind the tent makers of the proper dimensions for their product.
173. Powell, "The Most Celebrated Encampment," pp. 10–11. Washington to Peter Waggoner, Mount Vernon, [9] September 1781, in Fitzpatrick, *Writings of Washington,* 23:109, about the route south the cavalry, wagons, and cattle were to take. There were numerous animals following the army, from the cattle driven into encampments and with the troops on the march, to the horses and oxen that served as transportation. Occasionally one also sees reference to dogs, such as "old Bose" who had traveled down from West Point to Yorktown with the Sappers and Miners and liked to hunt shoats with them. Martin, *Private Yankee Doodle,* p. 199.
174. Middlekauff, *The Glorious Cause,* pp. 413–14.
175. General Orders, Headquarters Cambridge, 8 August 1775, in Abbot, *Papers of George Washington,* 1:269.

176. Martin, *Private Yankee Doodle*, p. 150.
177. Thacher, [upstate New York], September 1776, *Military Journal*, pp. 60–61. Thacher listed the monthly pay of officers and soldiers and mentioned how rations were allotted.
178. Copy of congressional resolution, Headquarters [Valley Forge?], 2 June 1778, Heath's HQ Book.
179. Knox to Lamb, Camp Prakenis, 12 July 1780, John Lamb Papers (microfilm), reel 2. Knox commiserated with Lamb on having to subsist on only one ration while his duty (command at West Point) put him to much greater expense than any colonel commanding a brigade. He mentioned it to Washington, but Washington would not do anything about it for fear of setting a bad precedent. Knox told Lamb that the general officers had urged Congress to allow officers to draw the number of rations as originally established. Congress heard, but it took it awhile to act: change came in 1782. Resolve of Congress (22 April) published in orders, 1 May 1782, Lamb's 2CA Orderly Book, 7 February–7 August 1782.
180. See chapters 4–6 for more information.
181. General Orders, [Newburgh], 10 February 1783, in Fitzpatrick, *Writings of Washington,* 26:111–13. Wayne E. Carp, *To Starve the Army at Pleasure: Continental Army Administration and American Political Culture 1775–1783* (Chapel Hill & London: University of North Carolina Press, 1984), p. 216.
182. Joseph Plumb Martin's *Private Yankee Doodle* serves as a testimonial. Especially note the last pages of the book when he answers critics of the army and of the pensions being awarded to veterans.

3

The Mercantile Community
Sutlers and Other Suppliers

To Mr . . . . . of . . . .

You are hereby permitted to exercise the functions of a sutler in the American army now laying before York; conforming yourself to the rules & regulations of the army; & particularly to such as are or shall be made respecting sutlers. Given under my hand in camp before York the . . . day of . . . 1781

T. Pickering QMG
License Form, 8–9 October 1781[1]

Sutlers, contractors, and other merchants who did business in or with the Continental Community wanted to do well—some hoped to do extremely well. Focused on the pursuit of economic happiness, they tended to equate private gain and public service instead of seeing them as conflicting interests. Members of the Continental Congress and Army, on the other hand, wanted them to minimize or even forego profit in favor of public service. These differing perceptions of economic patriotism led to skirmishes between the forces of commerce and the leaders of the army. Throughout these struggles, even though they never achieved full or lasting victory, the latter were able to control the former, first through a continuing barrage of regulation and second by accepting and exploiting the connection between private interest and public virtue: that as long as suppliers were guaranteed a profit, even though it might not be as large as they would want, most would operate within regulations.

Sutlers, contractors, and other sellers of goods to the army and its community were not unpatriotic. On the contrary, although some were simply opportunists, others—as demonstrated by their affiliation with the American military—wanted the Revolution to succeed and provided services and products to help both the people and institution that served the cause.[2] Some just had a problem accepting sacrifice as part of the definition of patriotism. That was common enough, for soldiers and officers had the same problem; however, by operating within the community but not actually serving in the military, these people had somewhat more control over the extent of their sacrifice (or losses) and, at least in the case of contractors, more of a chance to manipulate the ties between national and personal fortunes. During the war such opportunism could be, and often was, interpreted as a lack of virtue. Therefore it was up to the army to instill virtue—and thus guarantee success—in its suppliers, as it did in its soldiers, through regulation and discipline.

The Continental Army was a market: a characteristic and function shared by armies both before and after the American Revolution. Merchants and tradesmen determined to exploit this market closely affiliated themselves with the army by becoming sutlers and contractors. The former became some of the first civilian residents of the developing Continental Community when they followed the New England militias and expeditionary forces into the camp around Cambridge in the spring and summer of 1775. Sutlers attached themselves to the ranks in order to supply soldiers with the goods required to make army life bearable: generally liquor, soap, and extra provisions. The Continental Army, in turn, adopted sutlers and placed them under orders. Unlike the resident sutlers, contractors were often merely visitors for much of the war as they moved in and out of camps to fulfill their business obligations. Only after the army switched to a new system of provisioning by contract in 1781–1782 did some contractors and their agents become relatively permanent members of the military community. Then the contractors' increased contact and closer affiliation with the troops resulted in their receiving more army supervision. The first set of suppliers worked primarily at the personal level, the second at the institutional, but both were necessary to the Continental Community.

The army also attracted and thus attempted to regulate (and in some cases discourage) other entrepreneurs who sold goods and services just outside its encampments. Most of these vendors were local people who saw the presence of a military unit in their neighborhood as a serendipitous business opportunity: a market to be exploited only so long as it remained in the area. Army commanders accepted, even welcomed, the presence of honest vendors but tried to make sure that military personnel did not suffer from illegal or unhealthy (a service such as prostitution was often both) business practices. Although only some of these sellers became members of the Continental Community, all of them helped to create it. Their businesses, the goods and services they offered, attracted other people into the military domain. Civilians who wished or needed to follow the army found it easier to do so when there were marketplaces and merchants, such as sutlers, available to supply them with the necessities of life.

A sutler was a person with military authorization "to reside in or follow the camp with food, liquors, and small articles of military equipment, or others, for general use or consumption." That was the most precise definition, but, unfortunately for clarity, not the one always adhered to during the Revolution. The army sometimes used the noun *sutler* to describe any person who sold "provisions or drinks, or other commodities or merchandise whatsoever."[3] It often used the verb, *suttling,* to describe vending, authorized or not, in and around camp. Such broad interpretations gave the army legal leeway when regulating all those who engaged in trade within its lines.

As it did with everyone else within its jurisdiction, the army regulated sutlers and other merchants in accordance with the Articles of War. The articles gave the army the authority to issue orders and demand compliance. If vendors did not follow orders, or if someone accused them of malfeasance, they could be court-martialed and driven from camp. The Continental Congress deemed it desirable to adopt the British and other European precedents of placing sutlers and other retailers under direct military control because they were adjuncts often integral to camp operations and soldier morale. In 1775 Congress used the British Articles of War as a guide when it created its own rules; however, the British articles and those first American articles were not identical. Whereas British Article 23, Section XIV, stated that sutlers, retainers, and others serving with the army were subject to orders "according to the Rules and Discipline of War," American Article 32 stated that they were "subject to the articles, rules, and regulations of the continental army."[4] The American version was more restrictive of the exercise of military authority over civilians. In effect it said that the American army had to govern its followers according to published orders and regulations instead of the more flexible "Discipline of War." The American Articles of War of 1775 differed from the British ones in another way as well. They did not include an article that permitted all officers, soldiers, and sutlers to bring into garrison "any Quantity or Species of Provisions, eatable or drinkable, except where any Contract or Contracts are or shall be entered into by Us, or by Our Order, for furnishing such Provisions."[5] American entrepreneurs, however, did not wait for permission; they assumed the privilege and practice.

In 1776 Congress discarded the old rules and enacted the second Continental Articles of War, which were much closer to the original British model. Article 23, Section XIII, placed sutlers and others under orders "according to the rules and discipline of war." A possible legal loophole was thereby closed and military authority—the discipline of war—strengthened. Articles 1 through 4 in Section VIII of the American legislation echoed the same articles and section of the British version, including the second article that allowed officers, soldiers, and sutlers to bring into army forts any "eatable or drinkable" provisions not already contracted for by the government or army (this was amended in April 1777 to include only eatable provisions because of problems with intoxicated soldiers in camp). The first article stated that sutlers were not allowed to sell liquor or food, or keep their shops open "for the entertainment of soldiers, after nine at night, or before the beating of the reveilles, or upon Sundays, during divine service, or sermon." The penalty for doing so was dismissal from all future suttling. Article 3 required all commanding officers in American forts, barracks, or garrisons to see to it that all sutlers supplied the troops "with good and wholesome provisions at the market-price." Failure to do so could result in charges of neglect of duty. This article thereby insured that these officers paid as close attention to their sutlers as to their soldiers. The final article forbade commanders to charge "exorbitant prices for houses or stalls, let out to sutlers," or allow others to do so. Nor could these commanders, for their own advantage (profit), lay duties upon "or be intrusted in the sale of such victuals, liquors, or other necessaries of life, which are brought into the garrison, fort, or barracks, for the use of the soldiers, on the penalty of being discharged from the service."[6] Thus Section VIII broadly outlined what was expected of both sutlers and the officers who were to supervise them.

The Articles of War provided the army with the ways and means to maintain order in soldier-sutler relations and to exercise quality control. Under the aegis and within the guidelines established by the articles, commanders issued orders to control the actions of all sellers, but they directed most of their orders to those people who could properly be called sutlers, the traders who had the closest continuing contact with the troops. Other merchants came and went and thus merited less attention. If they were contractors, abuses were generally dealt with at higher echelons—by the state governments or the Continental Congress. If they were local people selling goods in a camp market, complaints could be brought before local magistrates. Such outside jurisdiction was often not feasible or desirable in the case of sutlers, however. Sutlers were always with the army; they belonged to the army in ways the others did not. Therefore the army regulated their conduct.

On 11 July 1775, just over a week after assuming command in Cambridge, Washington began to curb the liberties taken by sutlers. He noted, "Notwithstanding the orders of the provincial Congress [meaning the Massachusetts government], some persons are so daring as to supply the Soldiers with immoderate Quantities of Rum, and other spiritous Liquors." The general tried to eliminate the problem by informing sutlers, tavern keepers, and inn holders that they risked severe punishment if found selling liquor to any noncommissioned officer or soldier without written permission from that soldier's company commander.[7] Then on 7 August Washington gave qualified approval for military, rather than governmental, appointment of sutlers. After reviewing the applications that had been made in favor of sutlers supplying regiments with necessities, he stated that he had no objection to each regimental commander appointing one sutler to serve his own troops, "provided the publick is not to be taxed with any Expence in his Appointment—and Provided also that each Colo. be answerable for the Conduct of the Sutler so Appointed—And taking Care that he Conforms Stricktly to all orders Given for the Regulations of the Army and that he does not intend on any Impose on the Soldier in the price of his goods."[8] Although the appointment of sutlers at the regimental level changed over the course of the war, the rest of the order remained in effect as general policy.

Throughout the war Washington and his subordinate commanders tinkered with the general regulations in order to sharpen their applicability at certain places and in particular situations. The tinkering began almost immediately. Washington issued another order to regulate suttling further on 6 September after a growing proliferation of "pretended Sutlers," as he called the unauthorized vendors, produced such a traffic in liquor that the troops were constantly debauched. He forbade anyone to sell liquor or other stores to the troops unless appointed to a regiment by that unit's commanding officer or by the government. When that order, in turn, caused confusion and consternation among commanding officers dealing with sutlers who rather creatively construed the order over the following months, Washington stepped in and on 14 November stated that people had incorrectly interpreted the order to mean that sutlers could sell liquor to soldiers belonging to other regiments without the permission of the soldiers' commanders. Therefore he issued a new order stating "that no Commanding Officer of a Regiment, shall authorize more than one Sutler to a Regiment, and such appointment shall be notified in Regimental Orders, and no person being authorised, shall presume to sell spiritous Liquors to any Soldiers belonging to any other regiment, without leave in writing under the hand of the Commanding Officer to which such Soldier belongs." In February 1776 Washington reiterated the order of only one sutler per regiment, promised severe punishment to unlicensed vendors, and, so as to ensure compliance, asked that the names of licensed sutlers be sent in to headquarters.[9]

Two years later, as the army settled into Valley Forge in the winter of 1777–1778, a board of general officers convened to develop new guidelines on suttling. Their deliberations resulted in a recommendation that "a Sutler be appointed to each Brigade whose Liquors shall be inspected by two Officers Appointed by the Brigadier for that purpose and those Liquors sold under those restrictions as shall be thought reasonable." Washington simultaneously published and implemented their suggestions on 26 January by ordering that brigade sutlers be appointed and that they sell their stock of liquor at the sanctioned prices which he then listed. He also directed that "any Sutler who shall be convicted before a Brigade Court Martial of having demanded more than the above rates or of having adulterated his Liquors or made use of Deficient Measures shall forfeit any Quantity of his Liquors not Exceeding Thirty Gall[ons] or the value thereof at the foregoing rates[.]" One part of the forfeited stock or money would be given to the informer and the rest used to the benefit of the soldiers. Washington then concluded by giving the sutlers permission to sell leaf and "Pigg Tail" tobacco and hard soap at designated prices, and reminding them that neither they nor any person acting under them could sell articles that were reserved for the public market.[10]

Washington added to the preceding orders in April. After reiterating that only one sutler could be appointed to each brigade, he ordered the brigade commanders to submit the names of their sutlers to the adjutant general and then report any change in the situation thereafter. He also stated that these authorized tradesmen were to have only one suttling booth within the limits of their respective brigades where they could sell liquor and other merchandise; he forbade them to sell their alcoholic stock anywhere else. The commander in chief expected sutlers to sell their alcoholic beverages solely to members of the brigades to which they belonged, thus continuing the practice he had established for regimental sutlers in 1775, but at newly prescribed prices. He lowered January's prices in an action undoubtedly appreciated by soldiers and cursed by sutlers. After limiting the sutlers' trading practices, however, Washington then moved to protect their interests while the army remained at Valley Forge. He forbade anyone, besides licensed sutlers and commissaries sent by the states, to sell liquor in camp or within seven miles of the camp. Persons found violating this directive would have their stock seized (without payment) for the army's use. There were exceptions to this rule. Washington authorized the quartermaster general to permit one or more houses of entertainment to operate near camp in order to accommodate any travelers in the vicinity. Persons receiving an operating license for that purpose, however, had to promise not to sell liquor to anyone belonging to the army.[11] Apparently some people believed Washington could not or would not follow through on these restrictions. They were mistaken. On 26 May he sent out a detachment to seize the liquors in unlicensed tipling houses; in this case he did authorize receipts for stock taken, but receipts given with the warning that seizure would be absolute the next time.[12]

The quartermaster general exercised more and more authority over merchants in and around camps as time passed. In 1781, as the army dug in before Yorktown, headquarters notified commanders that "permission may be granted to the sutlers to sell liquors and refreshments to the Army under such regulations as the Quarter Master General shall establish: upon complyence with which they will meet with due encouragement, and protection in their persons and property." Although commanders continued to control the sutlers belonging to their units by demanding that they comply with brigade and regimental orders, by the end of the war licensing was generally finalized through the quartermaster general's office, and the quartermaster general served as arbitrator in establishing general army regulations.[13]

As the war wound down in 1783, some generals, brigade commanders, and officers commanding regiments met with the quartermaster general at Newburgh to establish more specific regulations "respecting the Sutlers and Markets of the Army." They delivered the results of their collaboration to the commander in chief who, on 2 March, ordered the army to observe ten new regulations, some of which merely repeated previous ones. The first rule was an old one: only one sutler per brigade. The second stiffened up licensing requirements: a license to suttle could be provided "only on the Joint recommendation of the Commanding Officers of the corps in a Brigade" and when approved by the brigade's commander. The third regulation required brigade commanders to appoint weekly, or more often if needed, a committee of officers to look into the quality of their sutler's stores and the prices being charged for the merchandise. These officers had to report their findings to their commander so that he could compare their notes and then correct any abuses practiced by the affiliated sutler. The fourth requirement closely followed the third: policing officers had to visit the sutler's quarters daily in order "to Discover and report any Disorderly practices." The commanders refused to give sutlers permission to sell mixed liquors in the fifth regulation. In the sixth they warned that any sutlers not licensed in the approved manner must leave the army within twenty days after publication of these regulations or find their stores forfeit, but the sutlers could try to sell off their stock within those twenty days. The seventh regulation appears to have forbidden regimental paymasters to pay off noncommissioned officer and soldier accounts held by sutlers unless approved by the service members' commanding officer. The eighth ruled "That there shall be two market places, one near the interval between the York and Jersey Brigades, and one near the public Building." The ninth regulation set aside Wednesdays and Saturdays as market days, while the tenth conveniently established Friday as payday.[14]

The 1783 rules reflected the problems confronted and lessons learned over the course of the war; they also tied together regulations established at army as well as subordinate unit levels. In his first year of command and thereafter, Washington established that he would not accept sutlers who encouraged disorder in his army. It was difficult to maintain order in the face of the liquid spirits, high spirits (which could be manifested in fine bouts of boxing, especially—according to one observer—among Irishmen), and possible spies and subversives who loitered around sutlers' huts, but Washington not only assigned the provost marshall the job of policing the sutlers' establishments, he also informed all officers that it was their job to aid the provost in this.[15]

The commanding officers of both garrisons and individual units supplemented general regulations with ones pertinent to their own situations, either as preventive measures or to counter corruption already present. Sometimes they merely emphasized or fine-tuned a rule already stated in the Articles of War or in general regulations. That happened at Crown Point in July of 1776 when orders forbade sutlers to sell liquor to the soldiers after sunset or allow the soldiers to linger about their huts after that time. It was a twofold order: sutlers were required to shoo soldiers off their premises, and the soldiers were to "Repair to their Respective tents at tattoo Beating & not to bee Stroaling About the Camp after that time." At other times leaders responded to more specific problems within their commands. When there was too much intemperate suttling at Ticonderoga that same July, Major General Horatio Gates recommended that the commanding officers of the corps exert themselves to suppress it. He strongly suggested that they seize all rum and other liquors from sutlers who were not officially attached to the units and deliver the goods to the commissary. Two weeks later one of Gates's subordinate commanders clamped down on a sutler in his specific brigade. Colonel Arthur St. Clair, after hearing that a sutler had been passing his own private "Notes of hand" among the soldiers as cash, requested that his regimental commanders collect the notes held by their soldiers. He planned to compel the sutler to pay the full amount of the notes' declared worth as a punishment for "so Infamous and Pernitisus a Practice."[16] These officers took action after a problem developed. Orders to and about sutlers often were a reaction to events, but officers also issued preventive commands in the hopes of forestalling abuses.

All of these orders circumscribed sutler transactions, for commanders generally did not allow free enterprise in their camps. Commanding officers commonly fixed prices, especially for liquor. As previously noted, Washington set some prices in January and then again in April of 1778. At those times he was primarily concerned with establishing the cost of peach and apple brandy, whiskey, and a few other beverages, but Washington stipulated prices for other liquors, such as rum, French brandy, and gin that spring as well, primarily because vendors had taken advantage of the fact that they had not been listed in the January orders. Disgusted with exorbitant rates, Washington called for a council of all the officers commanding brigades to meet and determine the proper prices to be charged. They published the authorized prices on 28 March.[17] Officers met many times during the war to fix prices according to current currency values. Although the cost of liquor remained of paramount interest, they determined the prices of other goods as well. When Lieutenant Chilion Ford, regimental adjutant for the 2nd Continental Artillery, posted the authorized prices for goods offered by Mr. Freeman, the brigade sutler, on 24 June 1779, the regulated merchandise included tobacco, paper, ham, bacon, coffee, sugar, as well as rum and claret.[18]

Other brigade and garrison orders, in line with general regulations, determined what sutlers could sell, when they could sell, and how they could sell. Accordingly, the 1st Pennsylvania Brigade, which was part of the main army, in August 1778 informed its subordinate regiments that no one was allowed to sell for the brigade "except Such as will Govern himself as follows—To provide as much Mutton [,] Fowls and Vegatables as Shall be apply'd for by the Officers—every Monday & Thursday—Officers are to Bespeak what they want on Satturdays & Wednsday mornings all at moderate prices." Besides insisting on those requirements, the brigadier also prohibited sutler sales of liquor to soldiers without a written permit from an officer or for any reason after the beating of retreat.[19] The last part of that order was echoed in a 1780 orderly book of the 2nd Continental Artillery. Recorded therein were West Point garrison orders that on 16 September required soldiers to retire to their quarters at the beating of tattoo and warned that any sutlers found harboring or entertaining soldiers "after that time, may depend on having their Liquor seized;—and themselves sent from the Point." One week later the garrison commandant again threatened confiscation and banishment for another offense. After being informed that some sutlers had refused to accept Continental currency in their transactions, the commandant gave a firm response: "Any Sutler who shall hereafter refuse to Sell for Continental Money may depend on having his Effects Seized, and be obliged to quit the Point."[20]

Eventually certain orders that were repeated time and time again by regimental, brigade, and garrison commanders were reiterated in general orders and became army policy. After various post and unit commanders prohibited sutlers to sell alcohol to soldiers without written permission from a commissioned officer (a slight shift in policy from previous orders that demanded the permission come from a commanding officer), Washington, in May 1783, finally ordered that all "contractors and sutlers of the army" were to observe the same restriction. He also asked that "any instances which shall be discovered of fraud or unfairness in the dealings of sutlers or traders might be reported in writing to the orderly office, in order that measures should be taken to remedy all abuses of that kind." It appears that contractors, whose main purpose was to feed the army as a whole, were also allowed to do a bit of suttling on the side by the end of the war, but in doing so had to observe the same regulations.[21]

As mentioned before, to help it limit the numbers of sutlers allowed with the military and regulate their actions within the camps, the army insisted that sutlers be licensed. Much of the onus for that was placed upon the commanders who appointed them, but the responsibility was that of the sutlers as well. They had to register with the commands they served. On 3 July 1776 all the sutlers at Crown Point had to submit their names to the deputy quartermaster generals (or quartermasters as they came to be called) of the regiments to which they belonged. Noncompliance would result in dismissal from the grounds; but to insure compliance and prevent excuses, commanding officers received orders to send their orderly sergeants to notify sutlers personally of the requirement. The commanding general also felt obliged, due to sutler extravagance and extortion, to ask that the officers send him the prices their soldiers paid for certain goods along with the sutlers' names.[22] Garrison orders at Fort Constitution in March 1777 instructed: "The Commanding Officer of the Artillery to make a Return of the Strength of that Corps in the Garrison. The Commissary & Quarter Master to make a Return of the Provisions, and Stores of the Garrison. The Armourers and other Artificers[,] Bakers[,] Sutlers[,] Retailers and every other Person belonging to, or residing in this Garrison are to report themselves to the Commanding Officer immediately."[23] In that particular case, sutler registration was simply added into regular camp administration. By late 1778 there was an attempt to centralize sutler registration in the main army. A summary of the duties of the Marechausee Corps, which, as part of its duties, assisted the provost marshall, included a requirement that Captain Bartholomew Von Heer, its commander, keep lists of all licensed sutlers and confine followers of the army who suttled without permission. To aid Von Heer, every newly authorized sutler, in the artillery park at least, was ordered to signify his appointment to the captain and produce a certificate from his unit's commanding officer proving it.[24] Such registration helped strengthen the affiliation between sutler and unit and destroyed any future pleas of ignorance on either side when a misdeed was discovered. Commanders thereby knew that they had sutlers, and knew them by name, and sutlers became familiar with the command and staff members who could issue them orders.

The governments and commanders who appointed sutlers were supposed to be discriminating in their choices: they were expected to weed out knaves, charlatans, and officers. The Continental Congress, first through the Articles of War and then by way of a supplemental resolve, wanted to prevent the last group from making a profit from its association with soldiers. The 1775 Articles of War stated that commanding officers could not be interested in the sale of provisions and liquors to the soldiers; involvement could result in discharge from the service. When officers who were not commanders began to engage in such commerce, Congress moved to close the gap in the legal code. On 17 June 1776 Congress resolved that "no Officers Shall Settle or sell to the Soldiers under penalty of being Fined one months Pay and Dismissed [from] the Service with Infamy on Conviction before a Court Martial." The resolution then passed among the brigades and regiments; and when it was published at Ticonderoga it included what appeared to be a caveat from either that post's commanding officer or the commander in chief: "The Gen. Earnestly Hopes that no Officer High or Low will be Guilty of a Breach of the Above Resolve. When an Officer Desends to be mean enough to Turn a Huxter to his men he cannot expect any due Obeydiance from them. Soldiers will ever esteem a man of Honour as much as they will Dispise a Contray Caractor."[25] The resolution continued in force as a supplemental measure after Congress passed the 1776 Articles of War without the appropriate change in Article 4, Section VIII. It took a while, however, for the resolution to be put into effect in all the army camps spread out over the states: on 1 September a Lieutenant Colonel Belinger was still selling at German-Flatts in the Mohawk Valley of New York.[26]

Although Congress and command prohibited such peddling by gentleman officers, both legislators and commanders preferred to have gentlemanly sutlers, or, more precisely, solid middle-class tradesmen in the camps. A few candidates for the posts apparently fit the bill. General Henry Knox in August of 1778 informed his brigade at White Plains that "Messrs Piercy & Marvin" had appointments as sutlers to the park of artillery, adding that "They will conform to the Rules, establish'd for their Conduct." He also, however, safeguarded their territory by commanding the brigade quartermaster to check around from time to time to see that no sutlers, except those with his permission, entered or remained in the vicinity of the park.[27] The artillery often divided up into smaller tactical units that were then attached to various infantry brigades or sent off to different posts. That could explain why less than five months after Messieurs Piercy and Marvin became authorized sutlers another vendor was appointed to the corps. Piercy and Marvin may have already left the brigade or been found wanting, but, more likely, they stayed with one part of the corps as it entered winter quarters and thus left the 2nd Continental Artillery stationed at Pluckemin, New Jersey, in the winter of 1778–1779 in need of its own sutler. That unit soon filled the position with a worthy applicant: "Silvanus Seeley Esqr." received the appointment of sutler to the corps on 9 January.[28]

In May 1782 Washington saw Mr. Nathaniel Sackett as a proper candidate for a sutler position. He gave him permission to sell to the army until there were orders to the contrary and as long as he conformed "to the regulations for conducting that business." The quartermaster general was to instruct him in the latter.[29] Although Mr. Sackett appeared to be a trustworthy merchant and may even have been a gentleman, Washington wanted to make sure he knew the rules. All too many sutlers, with or without the "mister" before their names or "esquire" after, had undermined army order and discipline throughout the war by disregarding regulations. The problem could be traced back to sutlers who mislaid gentlemanly behavior in their pursuit of profit and to hucksters with no pretense to honor. The army dealt with them all by informing them of regulations, giving them orders, and punishing transgressors.

On 30 August 1782 the army's headquarters at Newburgh issued orders for the movement of troops, women, and baggage to Verplanck's Point. Supplementary orders directed the behavior of sutlers. As the army gathered itself together, Major General Knox moved to control not the sutlers' selling but their buying practices. The order was a bit unusual, but its promises of retribution were not. Knox directed that all the boards used as beds by the officers and soldiers, as well as other things which had been taken out of the barracks, be collected and stored. Then he said, "If any sutler or trader is found purchasing any of the foregoing articles from the soldiers, they may depend upon not only having their licenses taken from them, but also be otherwise punished."[30] That other punishment could include, as it did throughout the war, summary confiscation of stores and banishment from post, as well as court-martial and a variety of sentences from fines to whipping to imprisonment.

Commanders were not at all loathe to drag sutlers before military tribunals. John McClure discovered that in December of 1777 when a general court-martial tried him "for suttling in Camp contrary to Genl. orders." McClure pleaded guilty. After hearing his plea and reviewing the evidence, the court rather leniently concluded that his suffering in the provost jail had sufficiently punished him for his crime and ordered his release.[31] A general brigade court-martial was not as lenient to another sutler in November of 1778, but then his crime was considered more heinous. The court found John McGraugh guilty of abusing and defrauding a local inhabitant. It sentenced him to receive one hundred lashes on his bare back, "well Laid on," and to return the ill-gotten money. The court also ordered that he be drummed along the line and then confined until he revealed his accomplices.[32]

Sometimes sutlers suffered at the hands of the army not because of their own misdeeds but because of the necessities of a campaign or the problems, such as incompetence and interrupted supply lines, that often arise in war. When Major General John Sullivan prepared for the 1779 summer campaign, he tried to divest his troops of all nonessential personnel; he included sutlers within that designation. He would allow none to accompany his troops on the expedition into New York, nor would he allow any to stay at the Wyoming post. Sullivan ordered the commissary to accept what liquor the sutlers had on hand and to pay a reasonable price for it; he also promised that any sutler trying to sell his stock after that time could expect to have his liquor seized without hope of recompense. The general did not want to be bothered by sutlers while on campaign, but he wanted their stock because he found the commissary's liquor stores to be inadequate.[33] Although they rarely resorted to it (the army did not want to alienate its dependent merchants any more than it wished to disturb other civilian suppliers), commanders did occasionally seize sutlers' stores, usually with promises of payment, to supplement inadequate rations. Greene confiscated rum from sutlers and other followers of the army when his troops ran out of the spirit in September 1780; but he, like Washington and many other officers, preferred not to impress goods. Commanders did it only when there was no other choice left to them: they had to either impress what was needed or see the army dissolve—and the latter was unacceptable, for if there was no army there would be no independence.[34]

***

Impressment of sutler or other civilian supplies was always a last resort; commanders used it only when the army's current supply system proved inadequate or broke down, which was actually rather often. As the army struggled to avoid Draconian measures to ensure supplies, Congress tried to help by reorganizing, several times, the military's logistics services. In the early years of the war, congressional and military leaders focused on closely incorporating all supply functions under the commissary and quartermaster departments. It was a way of maintaining public supervision over military affairs and controlling private profiteering at this critical time of national birth. This could also be seen as an innovation in this branch of the military sciences, for European armies had been relying on private contractors for over a century.[35] Wartime, however, proved to be an inauspicious time for such experimentation: disrupted trade, bad markets, depreciating currency, and some able but inexperienced administrators for this size of an operation added up to starvation in the Continental Community. Ultimately, Congress and the army decided to relinquish some administrative control within the logistics system in return for better products and more efficient delivery. They turned much of the problem of supply over to contractors in 1781. The army, however, maintained external control by inspecting products and procedures, supervising payments, and otherwise regulating contractors in the camps. Contractor personnel may not have been paid directly by the army, but like the civilians in the logistics branches, they were working in the Continental Community, and commanders made sure they worked to the benefit, not detriment, of the army. Actually, the use of contractors in 1781 was not entirely new to the Continental Army; what was different was the extent to which the army then began to utilize them.

In the first months of the war, many state units employed contractors to procure and deliver their provisions. One such contractor, Richard Backhouse, supplied Thompson's Pennsylvania Rifle Regiment for part of the summer of 1775. As a middleman in the supply, specifically procurement, chain he bought goods from his contacts (both men and women: they included John Hendershot, who supplied him with beef; Ann Snook, who sold him mutton, and Jane Allen, who baked bread for him) in nearby civilian communities, hired people to haul the provisions to camp, and then, upon completion of these transactions, presented his accounts to the army for recompense.[36] Most of these early contractors or independent agents operated on a small scale, working for one or more military units, although a few (especially in New England) operated at the state level. Later, when the Continental Congress incorporated all the state units into the Continental Army, it built supply departments around merchants with even greater contacts so as to develop a more extensive and somewhat more centralized supply network.

Congress organized and then reorganized the agencies or departments that supplied the army, eventually settling on a bifurcated design for them. It established field units to handle the receipt and issue of supplies to the troops and departmental units to procure and deliver the supplies. The field detachments were supervised by both the military commanders they served and their respective quartermaster and commissary departments. The procurement units, on the other hand, were initially little more than groups of merchants who obtained the materials needed by the chiefs in the respective supply departments. The latter units eventually expanded to include production, repair, and storage of military items, developing into fixed subordinate branches of the supply departments that were administered by deputies.[37] The deputies were at first called purchasing agents. They not only bought necessary equipment and provisions themselves, but established contracts with other merchants and tradesmen for supplies as well. For example, Abraham Livingston put the butcher Daniel Hinslee of New York City under contract to supply the Continental troops in that city with fresh beef in March of 1776.[38]

Most of the deputies' subordinate contractors cannot properly be called camp followers, for they were too far removed from the military realm. These contractors made their arrangements with purchasing agents or other supply department personnel and then fulfilled their contracts by delivering the goods to a deputy, a magazine, or, if near the proposed recipient, a designated quartermaster or commissary within a military camp. They did not issue the provisions to the troops themselves, nor did they generally follow the army on campaign. They commonly carried out their contracts in their own shops or territories. Some operated close to the army, others distant from it; some worked on a large scale, others small. A few of these people had appointments as county contractors: they supplied the military with various wares and provisions collected from within their designated areas. Other contractors operated at a more elementary level, offering only one product or service, such as providing firewood, to a nearby garrison or encampment.[39] The military's supply system relied heavily on these people.

Even as Congress established commissary operations in 1775, some of its members, especially after looking at the cost and complications of furnishing rations, seriously considered the possibility of supplying the army wholly by contract without the intervention of staff departments. Although Congress decided to continue the departmental supply system, it did approve ration contracting for the troops in Virginia and permitted other supply contracts elsewhere. Such contracts usually applied to small units separated from the main army.[40] Most of the contractors involved also operated efficiently enough to provide an uncomplimentary contrast when the commissariat ran into problems.

When the commissary department was unable to buy or otherwise acquire enough provisions in December 1779, Congress asked the states to provide the army with certain supplies. It promised that each state's contribution would be credited toward the money each was required to raise in taxes for the United States. After reviewing this measure, Congress came to believe that if the needed supplies could thereby be procured, it could dismiss many commissary department purchasing agents; thus, what had initially been an emergency maneuver became a new system of supply in 1780. The specific supply system required that each state collect, and deliver to designated places within their boundaries, the quotas of meat, flour, rum, salt, forage, and tobacco that Congress apportioned to them according to their resources. Congress would then give them credit for all items that passed inspection and were accepted by the army.[41]

Many supply officers criticized the new system. Quartermaster General Nathanael Greene said it was more convenient for the states than good for the army. He complained that not only were the quantities ordered inadequate but the supply conduit itself was not adequately set up. Congress tried to correct the latter problem in July 1780 when it gave the quartermaster department the tasks of transporting and storing all public property, including the specific supplies gathered by the states. Greene did not have to bother with the new duties; late that month he resigned his staff appointment and joyously resumed his line duties. He left the new quartermaster general, Timothy Pickering, and the commissary general of purchases, Ephraim Blaine, with the problem of trying to make the system work. They tried, but both found it inefficient and inadequate.[42] By the spring of 1781 the army had to resort to impressment once more, and Congress began to study the idea of contracting for supplies.

In May Congress completed its preliminary study and initiated operation of the contract system. After having the Board of War provide an estimate on the rations required by the main and southern armies, and after deciding that rations were to be contracted at an agreed-upon price for the period from 1 July to 1 January of the next year, it opened the bidding to interested parties. The interested parties were ready. Companies, such as Duer and Parker, had been newly set up to take advantage of this business opportunity. Others, such as Comfort Sands and Company, moved quickly to undercut other bidders and grab a major share of this market. On the government's side, there was a bit of confusion at this point over who could make these contracts. Congress did not initially assign the responsibility to any one department, but the Board of War assumed that the contracts would be made by the chiefs of the regional military and staff departments under the direction of the superintendent of finance, Robert Morris, since he was supposed to supervise everyone employed in procuring public supplies and spending public money. Congress formally gave Morris the power to contract for all supplies needed by the army that July and, in doing so, essentially closed out the commissariat system. Blaine remained in office until the conclusion of the 1781 campaign, but after helping provision the troops on the journey north after Yorktown, he retired from the service.[43] Contractors then took over both the procurement and issuing of supplies.

While the contractors were supplying much of the army over the second half of 1781, Congress and the army evaluated the value of the switch. That the reviewers saw it as an essentially positive change was seen when, midway through that initial contract term, Morris validated the new system by advertising for proposals "for supplying by contract, the rations deliverable by the public at the post of Wyoming, to such Officers, Soldiers and others, as are or may be entitled to them, from a certain time to be fixed in the contract until the expiration of twelve months thereafter."[44] After that time the army at Wyoming and elsewhere renewed some old contracts and made new ones.

Even when productive, relations between the army and its contractors were not always harmonious. They squabbled over bills and payment, the method of issuing supplies, and the quantity, quality, and nature of the provisions. Soldiers noted that while they did do better under the new system, there were problems with it by the winter of 1782–1783.[45] After the honeymoon period in late 1781 and early 1782, the army did find itself doing battle against avarice among contractors: in particular, Comfort Sands and Company. It disturbed contractor-camp relations on the Hudson for a while, but by January 1783 harmony was restored. As Washington put it, "Sure I am, the Army will ask no more of the Contractors than their indubitable rights, and I am perswaded there is too much liberality and good sense in the latter to descend to the *low dirty* tricks which were practiced in the time of Comfort Sands whose want of liberality, I will go further, and say lack of common honesty, defeated his favourite scheme of making money which appears to be the only object he had in view."[46] Yet, even as they complained about the inadequacies and avarice of contractors, most staff and line officers believed contracting to be more efficient and economical than the previous supply systems. The new system did eliminate many staff or middlemen positions in the procurement, transportation, and issuing of supplies. As Pickering wrote to Ralph Pomeroy, one of his deputies, in December 1781: "All the commissaries will shortly be superseded by the contractors; & with the dissolution of the commissariates many quarter masters at posts will become unnecessary." Another factor, more easily seen now than at the time, also contributed to the new system's efficient operations: the contract system operated under more stable conditions. After Yorktown there were no major campaigns; instead of provisioning troops on the move, contractors supplied garrisons.[47]

The army maintained supervisory control over contractor operations in camp. When Morris or his designated deputies signed agreements with contractors, they did not give them autonomy. The army regulated contractors, especially their agents in camp, in a way similar, although not identical, to how it regulated other camp civilians. The military exerted somewhat less control over contractors' everyday behavior; it did not reprimand them in the orderly books or bring them before courts-martial as it did other followers. This difference could be attributed to the more peaceful conditions under which the army was operating at the end of the war (there appear to have been fewer courts-martial of other civilians at that time as well) and to the willingness of Morris to break contracts, as with Comfort Sands and Company, on account of contractor malfeasance and thereby rid the army of a few unwanted adjuncts.[48] Actually, the nonappearance of contractors before the courts may merely indicate that they engaged in a smart business practice: adhering, or appearing to adhere, to the guidelines established by the army, their business partner. There were still times when these new "citizens" in and suppliers to the Continental Community went a little too far in making themselves at home in camp. Brigadier General Hand was certainly peeved that they were using soldiers as butchers at Norfolk, Saratoga, Albany, Nine Partners, Little Brittain, New Windsor, and Poughkeepsie.[49]

The military concentrated on regulating the contacts between contractors and military personnel. It established what each party had to do in order to make the supply system operate; and when problems developed, its quartermaster general tried to devise solutions. Earlier in the war, when the army employed smaller-scale contractors, they could be dealt with at subordinate levels in the staff departments or at the smaller unit level, but the big contractors at war's end needed to be handled more centrally. Pickering became a, if not the, central point of contact, for he appears to have acted not only as the middleman between the army, or more precisely Morris, and the contractors but served well as the mediator in military-contractor disputes at more subordinate levels for the first year of the contract system.[50] Then, in September 1782, Morris lightened Pickering's load somewhat by appointing Ezekiel Cornell as inspector of contracts. Under Morris's aegis, Cornell negotiated contracts and arbitrated disputes arising from them.[51]

Quartermaster General Pickering was particularly interested in maintaining accurate provisioning rolls. Correct returns helped minimize waste and greed by facilitating both the planning and reviewing stages of the system. Unit quartermasters had to compile rosters of both military and authorized dependent personnel so as to request sufficient supplies. Contractors needed personnel numbers in order to figure out the quantity of supplies they had to provide and thus needed to buy from their own subcontractors or other tradesmen. Pickering wanted to see the lists so as to study the accounting methods on both sides and make sure costs remained as low as possible. The result was more paperwork. Line and staff personnel submitted lists to various offices at all levels in their chains of command. A number of letters and orders illustrated the administration process. For example, on 18 December 1781 Pickering wrote Colonel Hugh Hughes, his deputy in New York, that he required a return of all the people employed in his department. Pickering especially wanted to have the names of those employed at all the posts from Wappings Creek to Kings Ferry listed along with their pay and the number of rations drawn for each worker and his family. He had to have the information in a hurry because he had promised to give the data by the end of the week to the contractors who were to supply those posts with provisions.[52] This method of checks and balances was seen on a smaller scale a little over a month later when the commandant of Burlington Barracks in New Jersey wanted Dr. Garret Tunison, the 2nd Continental Artillery's surgeon, to report to him the number and state of the sick every Saturday morning. Determined to prevent double rationing due to men being provisioned both by their units and the hospital, he commanded that "All Orders upon the Contractor, for Provision for the Sick, must be sent to the Commandant to be countersigned," and stated that the surgeon would issue stores and provisions to all patients except those in the hospital or recuperating in the Sappers and Miners quarters.[53]

Contractors did not figure in regulations the way sutlers did because sutlers belonged to the army in a way contractors did not. Contractors belonged perhaps not so much to the army as with it: they acted essentially as partners rather than dependents or subordinates. When sutlers lobbied for and accepted appointments from line commanders, they agreed to be controlled by them. Contractors, on the other hand, bargained with staff department chiefs before reaching an agreement or contract that included instructions concerning their operations with and services for the army. When their preliminary instructions proved insufficient, contractors usually contacted the secretary at war, or Morris, Pickering, and later Cornell, not local commanders, for clarification. Lincoln, in December 1781, referred the contractor firm Smith and Lawrence to Pickering for directions relative to the issuing of firewood and forage to the posts north of Poughkeepsie. So Pickering sent them, with recommended modifications, the "plan for conducting the quarter master general's department" that Congress had passed in July of 1780 and an order regulating the issue of wood published by the Board of War in January 1781 to serve as guidelines. Pickering mentioned that they should not religiously dispense just the specified quantities when "necessity, humanity, & the good of the service" required extra allotments; they could change the rules in such cases. A month later Pickering also clarified matters for Comfort Sands and Company. After receiving letters of instruction from the superintendent of finance and the secretary at war, the contractors had difficulty determining whether or not they were to provision Colonel Hughes and his assistants. Pickering said that although the plan for his department did not assign them public provisions, circumstances required that they be supplied. If Congress did not sanction this, the rations could be charged to their pay, "hardly a shilling of which have they received to this day; and without their rations they could not possibly have existed. It is also true that near a year [has passed] since I reported this matter to Congress, who have not to my knowledge made any objection. It is impossible for me to furnish money for their subsistence, and if provisions be denied them the department in this state will be dissolved. I have therefore to request that their usual rations be allowed them until I get the affair settled at Philadelphia."[54]

After the contract system had been fully implemented, the army did try to get such affairs settled by formally establishing the new standard operating procedures whereby provisions were to be issued. The secretary at war published the rules in May 1782. They spelled out the actions commanders and quartermasters had to take in order to receive supplies. Both line units and staff departments had to establish the rations allowed to each individual and then hand in returns which "must specify the number, stations, or occupations of the persons, the number of days to be drawn for, the commencing and ending of the time, both days included, and the number of rations in the whole; this return, with proper receipts, will be sufficient voucher for the Contractors." Building upon those rules were those established in December for the new contract of the coming year. Naturally, the amount of paperwork involved increased again. There were forms for drawing rations in the civil departments, for the sick, and for prisoners. And while the army allowed regiments to draw sixteen rations for every fifteen men in order to have food for their accompanying women, it denied rations to unarmed (nonmilitary) servants who were to be paid by their masters (to whom subsistence money was given for that purpose).[55] The army wrote these regulations to give uniform guidance to and maintain uniform practice on the military side of the military/contractor equation.

The army regulated contractors via operating orders as well. In March 1783 the headquarters at Newburgh issued the command that officers drawing provisions for fatigue men, or other parties not able to draw supplies with the rest of their regiment, must sign separate returns for them. The second part of that command ordered contractors to issue provisions to soldiers away from their regiments only when such a separate return was signed and submitted, except in cases where the commander in chief directed otherwise. Later that same month a general order encompassed more than military personnel when it included the request that contractors acquire an ample supply of vinegar so that it could be regularly issued once the weather warmed up.[56]

Contractors, however, were seldom merely recipients of orders. Just as they had a say in formulating their contracts, they often helped to make subsequent rules. On 27 December 1782 Washington ordered brigade and regimental commanders to meet with the contractors who were scheduled to start supplying the army from 1 January. They were to assemble at Major General Robert Howe's quarters on the coming Sunday. The officers and contractors who met that day, the 29th, "agreed that to accommodate service, the officers will for the present apply to their respective Commissaries on the after-noons of Tuesday, thursday and saturday in every Week, commencing their draught for the first of January on tuesday the 31st instant, which rule will be observed, except on special occasions, when for the convenience of officers in that situation the Contractors have agreed to dispence with it." The contractors, having made that concession, soon asked for one on the part of the army. On 25 February in the new year general orders noted that the contractors for the army having requested, agreeable to their contracts, that a person be appointed to inspect the cattle reserved for the military, one Henry Wykoff of Fishkill was appointed for that purpose "untill the pleasure of the Superintendent of Finance shall be known."[57]

Besides inviting contractors to participate in certain conferences, the army provided them with military guards for their stores as well. Sutlers were important to troop morale, but if necessary the army could operate without them. As welcome, but not always essential, auxiliaries, it offered them the security of the camp and protection or recompense from thieves and vandals under the articles of war. Contractors, on the other hand, were vital to military operations;

therefore the army took extra precautions to safeguard their services and supplies. Regiments stationed at posts where contractors were located rotated guard details among themselves.[58] It was not really a new duty: they had done the same for earlier quartermaster and commissary stores and continued to provide the service for all remaining stock in those departments (upon the closure of the commissary department the quartermaster department assumed the duties and stores that were not taken by the contractors).

Quartermaster stores, and soldiers to guard them, were still necessary because contractors did not provide everything everywhere at all times. On 1 May 1782 Pickering received a letter from Colonel Lamb at Burlington informing him that the contractors at that post were no longer furnishing the artillery there with forage. After getting Morris's approval, Pickering wrote Colonel John Neilson, the deputy quartermaster general of New Jersey, to send the necessary supplies on to the artillery. He said that Morris would provide the money and that the bearer of the letter, Abraham Rand, forage master, would receive and issue the forage. Pickering explained his choice of Rand by telling Neilson that the forage master had purchased "most of the hay for the contractors, at from three to four pounds per ton; and has as much as seven tons engaged, which will be about a months supply." Pickering concluded with the instructions that Rand should "give his certificates of the quantities, qualities & prices agreed on, to the sellers," whom Neilson must then pay.[59] Pickering had to make such arrangements for other units as well.

***

Contractors replaced the commissariat and worked in tandem with the quartermaster department; but, like the army's supply departments, they could not supply the troops with everything they needed, much less wanted. Sutlers continued to benefit from the army's struggle with logistics as they opened their stalls and peddled their wares. Other entrepreneurs too found the army a lucrative market throughout the war. Sutlers usually had a corner on that market inside camp boundaries, but sometimes commanders allowed soldiers and dependents to engage in trade or welcomed outside civilians in to sell on designated days.

The army generally strictly limited trade within its camps when it was on the move, but commanders were often more permissive, as long as sellers followed orders, when settled into garrison. Fort Schuyler in New York fit the latter model. After Colonel Peter Gansevoort and his 3rd New York Regiment bravely defended the post in the 1777 campaign, Congress officially appointed Gansevoort colonel-commandant of the fort on 4 October. Gansevoort's duties as commandant included the government of the military and civilian entrepreneurs in his community—something he had engaged in even before he received his official appointment. On 23 September he reminded the people who pastured cows at the post that they received their feed "from the Publick"; therefore "Six Pence pr. Quart is the highest price that they may Receive for Milk." Any person found charging more than that would find his or her cows confiscated and "delivered over for the Use of the Sick of the Hospital." Not everyone heeded the warning. On 2 May 1778 a court-martial found Private James Patterson of Captain Henry Tiebout's company guilty of selling milk for nine pence per quart even though he had received public fodder; it ruled that his cows be given to the hospital. Gansevoort approved the sentence, ordered that the cows be delivered, and had the prisoner released. The story did not end there, however, for a contrite Patterson asked for forgiveness and the restoration of his livestock (and, coincidentally, a vital part of his livelihood). On 5 May Gansevoort magnanimously accepted Patterson's promise of future good behavior and returned the cows, but he took the opportunity to assure Patterson "and all others who may be posses'd of Cows at this Garrison that this is not to be a precedent for any future Offence of this Kind." When not engaged with cows and milk peddlers, Gansevoort focused on other economic enterprises. On 5 April 1778 he ordered all persons (be they soldiers, camp followers, or neighboring civilians) with hogs running about the garrison immediately to ring them or see them slaughtered; the hogs in their rooting had injured the fortifications. Earlier, on 14 December 1777, he commanded the garrison's bakers (who could be either civilian or military) to charge no more than one shilling for a loaf of bread, and each loaf, in turn, had to weigh six pounds.[60]

The Continental Community as a whole, not just Fort Schuyler in particular, was the scene of great economic activity. Officers and soldiers could and did write home for the goods or money that they needed to help them survive,[61] but generally they had to find other ways to live on or supplement their usually nonexistent wages. Raising livestock was one way, but another, at least in the garrisons, was to go out and find work. In the fall of 1782 at West Point the sergeants of the Sappers and Miners allowed one of their soldiers, who sometimes acted as their waiter, to go off and work for a nearby farmer. The soldier received his wages in milk, butter, and other eatables, which he always shared with the mess.[62] In January 1783 soldier-entrepreneurs cut wood around the Newburgh area and then transported it on hand-drawn sleds to New Windsor where they sold it. Washington had to put a stop to that. But then in February the quartermaster general advertised a recompense "of six pence, or half a ration per cord" to those who would cut wood for the use of the hospitals.[63]

Members of the community also found other ways to transform military promises into "pay," and not all of them were legal. Officers at and around West Point used a Comfort Sands and Company courier in 1782 to trade their "Pierce's notes" in Philadelphia for cash. They got a better return on these promissory notes there. Speculators snapped up such notes from officers and soldiers around the camps, but at such a detrimental rate to the latter that Washington felt compelled to warn his people against it in May 1783.⁶⁴ The community was always cash poor, and for most of the war the soldiers did not even have the government's notes to sell. Instead they sold or "swopt" its property. They sold or traded plunder that they picked up, whether it came from their own army or the enemy's. They sold the shirts off their backs, the guns out of their hands, and the food out of their mouths, if doing so got them something they wanted more. All that, plus their occasional pay or a friendly loan, gave them the wherewithal to patronize the sutlers and markets.⁶⁵

Sutlers encountered competition, and commanders more trouble, right outside garrison gates, primarily on market days but at other times as well. The military community's neighbors operated market stalls and grog shops, engaged in major wholesale transactions and minor retail sales, and tried just about everything, legal and illegal, to make a profit off the army's people. Commanders tried to control profiteering by extending their authority over all markets and marketers serving the Continental Community. Besides supervising the tradespeople who lived and operated within camp and garrison lines, as Gansevoort did with his cowherds and bakers, commanders regulated businesses brought into the lines temporarily and those operating outside the lines that were readily available to their people. Washington, for example, in February 1783, when setting up regular markets around Newburgh, set up measures to stop the evil and improper commerce in public property between inhabitants and soldiers.⁶⁶ Even though most of the marketers were local people who did not belong to the army (although at certain times and places such civilians were subject to martial law), the army determined what they could legally sell to service members, where they could sell their wares, and what prices they could charge.

The army established its control over marketers early in the war. In September 1775 General Greene noted that inhabitants were gouging soldiers' pocketbooks by demanding exorbitant prices for their produce. To combat that practice, he appointed Mr. Asa Minor clerk to the market and instructed him to establish a marketplace in front of Colonel Brewer's regiment. He then informed everyone that "No ma[r]keting what Ever is to Be allowed in any oather part of the Camp but at that place So appointed by the Clark. He is allso to Regulate the Prises of all produce Brought into Camp and no Parson to Exseed the prices on penalty of having thair Porduce Saized and taken From them for the Benefit of the armey."⁶⁷ Gansevoort later followed that precedent at Fort Schuyler. On 31 December 1777 he said he would fix the prices on articles brought in for sale "so as to prevent any Imposition on this Garrison." The next February he delegated this authority to a "Court of Regulation" which established prices for cider, vegetables, fowl, dairy products, tobacco, and other items. This court ordered, "That for the future, No Farmer[,] Officer[,] Soldier or other shall be allowed to sell any of the above Articles at a higher price...."⁶⁸ There may have been a problem with this development: the passage was crossed out of the orderly book.

There was no such problem or question at Valley Forge. The orderly books in that command recorded numerous directions for markets and marketers. On 20 January 1778 Washington ordered his generals and other brigade commanders to meet at General Sullivan's quarters the next morning so as to decide whether or not a public market should be opened in the camp. If they decided in the affirmative, he wanted them to determine where and when the market should be held as well as what regulations and how many guards would be necessary to preserve good order. They also had to settle upon (after seeking the advice of "some of the most Intelligent Country Men") appropriate prices for the items that would be offered for sale.[69] These officers did not follow the first part of the order but did meet the remaining conditions. Instead of meeting on the 21st, they met a few days later on the 24th and at that time agreed to the establishment of a public market. Washington had the results of the committee's deliberations published in his orders of 8 February. In accordance with their recommendations, he declared that starting the next day, Monday the 9th, the market would be held at the Stone Chimney picket post on the east side of the Schuylkill River every Monday and Thursday, set up near the North Bridge every Tuesday and Friday, and placed near the adjutant general's office every Wednesday and Saturday. He also mentioned that they had fixed the prices on much of the merchandise and that handbills printed with the regulations would be delivered to the brigades so that the rules could be disseminated to the troops. As they had not yet settled upon a "clerk of the Market," Washington ordered the officer commanding the Stone Chimney picket detail to see to it that the regulations were followed and "to distribute the Handbills amongst the market people who attend."[70]

When Washington was comfortable with his three established and regulated modes of supply—commissariat, sutlers, and markets—at Valley Forge, he shut down other ways to buy goods. On 17 April he ordered regimental quartermasters to travel out into the countryside and contract with people for milk and other necessities for the sick. He wanted them to complete these transactions by the 21st, for after that date no one would have permission to leave the camp in order to purchase provisions: "henceforward no Officer[,] Soldier or other Person belonging to the Army shall go or send out to purchase any of those Articles which are usually brought to Market or bargain for them any where else."[71] The markets had adequately and efficiently (although, as it turned out, temporarily) filled the remaining gap in the supply system.

Marketers filled the gap, or at least part of it, from Cambridge to Newburgh, and the army welcomed their trade even as it suspiciously scrutinized their business practices and politics. When West Point's commandant in August 1780 ordered inhabitants bringing in items for sale to have their names and business reported to him first and then to set up their wares at Elderkin's Wharf near the commissary's store and nowhere else, he was following well-established procedures forged in previous years and at other posts.[72] Eleven months later Washington advertised, "For the Benefit of the Army, and the Encouragement of the Inhabitants," that two marketplaces would be set up at Dobbs Ferry, one in the American and one in the French camp. All sellers would be "protected in their Persons and Property, and shall have full and free Liberty to dispose of their Produce, without Molestation or Imposition," but it was expected that "every Person on his or her first coming to the above Markets will be furnished with a Certificate of Recommendation shewg their Attachment to the American Cause and Interest, . . . that no Injury may arrive to the Army from the Arts of Designing and evil minded Persons."[73]

Even as they regulated the outsiders, commanders had to make sure their own people did not interfere or discourage civilian enterprise. Soldiers established a bad reputation in 1776 for abusing market people and taking their things, so Washington had to promise punishment for offenders and protection to the marketers.[74] As soldiers became more creative in their methods of acquiring goods and money, officers had to guard against other abuses besides simple assault and theft. After hearing that soldiers attending the ferry had exacted tribute or tolls from people using the ferry to transport their products to the garrison, the commandant of West Point in 1780 strictly prohibited the practice and guaranteed severe punishment for transgressors.[75] The army wanted no one to interfere in the exchange of goods once it had established regulations and sellers were abiding by them.

When or where the army found it difficult to control sellers, it tried to regulate buyers. In the summer of 1779 a board of officers established a price ceiling for produce and other items purchased by army personnel in the right wing of the army. Noncommissioned officers or soldiers found acceding to and paying higher prices were threatened with court-martial. After Washington recommended that other units abide by the newly established prices, the field officers and captains of the 2nd Continental Artillery encamped near Chester, New York, decided to adopt the new regulations within the artillery park with one temporary exception: as Mr. Freeman, sutler to the park, had already stocked up on certain items and arranged for more to be delivered as a result of an agreement with the corps, he could charge more and soldiers could, without penalty (except to their purses), pay his prices. The officers did not want Freeman to suffer from a change inaugurated after their original agreement, but they granted this dispensation only for products brought into camp within a certain period. Colonel Lamb approved their recommendations and enjoined his officers "to secure & bring to punishment, any soldier who may be found acting contrary thereto." He also extended the order to include "women belonging to the park and should any one of them be found guilty of a breach of these Orders will be dismissed from the park with disgrace."[76] Gansevoort had enacted a similar measure at Fort Schuyler in 1777. After ordering that no one be allowed to sell liquor or any other article to a soldier without first receiving permission from the man's commanding officer, Gansevoort commanded that "no Soldier shall buy Spiritous Liquor or Articles of any other Specious at the present Exorbitant price upon penalty of being punish'd for Disobedience of Orders."[77]

Given the relative infrequent appearance of such orders in the books, commanders apparently preferred to regulate sources rather than recipients, especially where liquor was involved. Drunkenness was a continuing problem throughout the war. General Greene attempted to combat the problem on Long Island in August of 1776 by forbidding gin shops to sell their stock to soldiers and threatening soldiers found "disguis'd with Liquor as has been too much the practice heretofore" with dire punishment, "as no Soldier in such situation can be either fit for defence or Attack." He also ordered sutlers to sell soldiers no more than one-half pint of spirits per day. Greene warned everyone that if his orders were not complied with he would see to it that no more liquor would be retailed at all.[78] Years later Washington was still fighting the problem. In May 1782 he tried exerting control at Newburgh via the liquor rations; he suggested that each corps maintain a liquor roll, "from which the name of every soldier shall be struck off who addicts himself to drunkeness or injures his constitution by intemperance." He also condemned the "evil practice of swallowing the whole ration of liquor at a single draught" and suggested that it could be prevented if sergeants would "see it duly distributed daily and mixed with water at stated times; in which case instead of being pernicious, it will become very refreshing and salutary."[79] A year later the 2nd Continental Artillery was battling inebriation at West Point: "It has been observed that some of the Non-commissioned officers, and many of the Soldier[s], have (of late) been frequently seen Drunk on the Parade—As such conduct is not only destructive of all Order and Discipline, but disgracefull to the regiment; the Officers, are earnestly requested, streniously to exert themselves, to prevent, if possible, a practice, so extreemly injurious to the service; and ruinous to the Soldiers: as it totally unfits them for either Military, or, Civil Life."[80]

The army attempted to prevent alcohol abuse by carefully distributing liquor rations and, more particularly, curbing the sale and sellers of the substance. In August 1775 Greene requested that officers in each regiment at Prospect Hill submit lists of the names and business places of persons retailing liquor without a sutler's license so that steps could be taken to "Supress impositions of this kind and the offendars brought to Due punishment." Early the next month Greene dispatched a fatigue party out to "Plowd Hill" to put "Benjman [P]iper and [P]encan" out of business for retailing sutler's (liquor) stores without a license within the brigade's boundaries, whereby "the Throops are much Debauched [and] the Soldiers rendred Undutiful." Greene wanted Piper and Pencan imprisoned in the main guardhouse until further orders and their property confiscated.[81] Other commanders at other times and places tried to rout out the problem as well. Four years later, in August of 1779, unlicensed people were selling liquor to soldiers in West Point and on boats docked in nearby rivers, much to the subversion of good order and discipline. Major General Alexander McDougall decided to put a halt to it by having their liquor stocks seized and deposited with the commissary.[82]

When the alcohol problem became especially bad, commanders would not merely force unlicensed people out of business, they would also revoke suttling licenses and demand that those vendors leave camp. The army at White Marsh banished sutlers in the fall of 1777, but the measure proved ineffective when some of the sutlers and neighboring inhabitants opened "tipling Houses within and adjacent to the encampment." As a result the deputy quartermaster received orders to discover such houses and suppress them and to warn everyone engaging in "this pernicious trade that if continued any longer their liquors shall be seized and they expelled from the Neighbourhood of the Army on pain of the severest punishment if they return."[83]

The alcohol problem followed the troops wherever they went, often under the aegis of the soldiers and women followers who participated in the liquor trade. The 2nd Continental Artillery's commander, Colonel Lamb, strictly prohibited the practice at West Point in July 1780 after hearing that soldiers and their wives were selling rum to the men of the corps. He promised that men caught transgressing the directive would be severely punished and women offenders sent from the garrison. He then sent out the sergeant major to seize whatever illegal rum stock he could find and report back with the names of the delinquents. He essentially repeated the order for the corps (for his units at West Point and probably for those stationed elsewhere) three months later: "No Soldier, or Soldier's Wife to be permitted to sell any kind of Liquor, on pain of having it Seized, and the Soldier punished for disobedience of Orders."[84] John Flagley, a matross in Captain George Fleming's company, almost experienced how painful the punishment could be. A court-martial found Flagley guilty of disobedience of orders for selling liquor and sentenced him to receive fifty lashes on his bare back. Before Flagley had to strip, however, Lamb or a detachment commander overturned the conviction by saying the charge was not supported.[85] Apparently it was extremely difficult to keep some artillerymen and their wives out of the liquor business; for a year later, as the corps was bombarding Yorktown, an irritated Lamb again addressed the issue: "The Commanding officer is astonished, that altho' he has repeatedly issued orders, to prevent the Soldiers Wives selling Rum, the practice is still continued. He earnestly calls on each officer, to exert himself, in preventing it in future, as it is not only injurious to the Service, but disreputable to the Regiment."[86]

Sexual misconduct and its results were as injurious to the service as alcohol abuse. Promiscuity and prostitution not only revealed a certain lack of virtue that boded ill for the army's image, they fostered disease that ravaged the army's body. In October 1778 Dr. John Cochran reported 20 men down with venereal disease at Fredericksburg, New York. A colleague, George Draper, reported 42 cases at Smiths Clove on 13 July and 25 cases at West Point on 2 August, a number that rose to 33 on 10 August 1779. William Brown, a physician and director-general of hospitals, in his "General Return of the Sick and Wounded in the Military Hospitals, belonging to the Army . . ." for the month of February 1780, recorded that 115 venereal patients remained in the hospitals as of 1 March.[87] Commanders tried to prevent the spread of social diseases and, more important to some, social and military disorder by banning prostitutes from their camps.

Early in the war, in June 1775, General Artemas Ward ordered that no lewd women be allowed in camp. Anyone knowing of such people was to report them so that the "nuisances" could be dealt with.[88] In May a year later, while encamped in New York City, the 1st New York regimental commander, Colonel (later General) McDougall, ordered, "No Woman of Ill Fame Shall be permitted to Come into the Barricks on pain of Being well Watred under a pump, and Every Officer or Soldier who Shall Bring in Any Such woman will be tryd and Punished by a Court Martial."[89] Unfortunately for McDougall and other commanders, New York City offered a variety of other locations in which the pleasure trade could be pursued. An area called the Holy Ground (it was owned by Trinity Church) was known as a prime location for prostitution. The intrepid Lieutenant Isaac Bangs, who set out to explore all the wonders of New York City in the spring of 1776, not only checked out a synagogue, the Dutch Church, and the Church of England, but the misnamed Holy Ground as well. He found the residents there to be impudent, immodest, and brutal. He could not understand how any man could want to intimate with the creatures, and yet had to admit that many of the officers and soldiers had done so—with dire results. Bangs worried that "unless there is some care taken of these horrid Wretches by the Genl., he will soon have his Army greatly impaired, for they not only destroy Men by Sickness, but they sometimes inhumanly Murther them; for since Monday last two Men were found inhumanly Murthered & concealed, besides one who was castrated in a barbarous Manner."[90] Some soldiers rioted and tore down buildings after the discovery of the murder and mutilation of their comrades. But otherwise, the military tried to defend itself by having guards police the area and its inhabitants.

Prostitution was apparently more often practiced, and thus more of a problem, when the army was encamped in or near more densely populated areas. Washington got his troops away from the dangers of New York City only to have to warn his subordinate commanders a year later to "prevent an inundation of bad women from Philadelphia."[91] They may have obeyed orders then, but some officers were certainly not averse to the introduction of "bad women" elsewhere. When the army was settled in around Newburgh in early 1783, a few of the officers established a seraglio, or brothel, nearby where they could have "super fine Kippen Issued immediately on application."[92]

On the whole, orders guarding against prostitutes were rare and courts-martial against women accused of the crime even more so, though the latter did occur. Sergeant Gilbert recorded that on 29 May 1778 Polly Robinson came into the 5th Massachusetts Regiment. A day later she and another women named Marcy were put under guard and court-martialed. Then on 5 June Robinson and a woman named Nel Tidrey were drummed out of the regiment.[93] Prostitutes were generally outsiders, not members of the Continental Community (and drumming them out was one way of ensuring that). Women formally engaged in the trade apparently thought twice about following the often impoverished American soldiers. Smart businesswomen would have preferred British officers, who had more disposable income, although the association could be dangerous if their client happened to be on parole, as a couple of women learned at Prospect Hill in June 1778. An American sentry mortally wounded Lieutenant Brown, of the 21st British Regiment, when he insisted on passing the sentry's position while "riding in a chaise between two women of (easy) virtue." As it was contrary to general orders to allow women to pass the lines, it was the sentry's duty to stop him. "The unfortunate officer treated the sentry with contempt, insisted on passing, without giving any reason for so doing; upon which the sentry, after repeated orders to the officer to stop, shot him through the head."[94]

A few female followers of the American army may have turned to prostitution when desperate, but the evidence suggests that the majority of women accepted as belonging to the army never practiced the profession. On the other hand, as hospital returns indicated, men and women of the army were by no means celibate. An occasional letter illustrates the point as well. Samuel McKenzie, a surgeon in the hospital department, wrote to his superior and friend, Dr. Jonathan Potts, from Bennington about his social life: "I want Doctr. Treat here very much to prescribe Rules for the Doctrs as they [s]eem very fond of Bundling and the Tory Girls seem to have no Objection to that kind of amusemt. I assure you tho' our room is not 12 feet square we had no less than three females last night and expect more this [evening]." He went on to say that he intended to take a room at the Parrons; the added attraction there was Mr. Parron's daughter, a "Delicious fine Girl" who could not be debauched for that had happened some months ago. Benjamin Gilbert, too, first as soldier and then as officer, recorded a number of lusty times with the women of town and camp.[95]

A few other army neighbors and followers endeavored to offer other special—and legal—services. When Dr. James Thacher returned from his furlough to resume his duties at the hospital in Albany in February 1778, he found that some "gentlemen belonging to the hospital[,] being desirous of improving in the accomplishment of dancing," had convinced a Mr. John Trotter to instruct them in that art every afternoon. Trotter had taught dancing in New York City for many years and was considered an accomplished master.[96] Thacher did not explain why Trotter was in Albany, but it is possible that the aging Trotter (at approximately fifty-eight years of age) was a refugee from British-occupied New York City. The 2nd Continental Artillery instituted another sort of school when it was quartered at Pluckemin, New Jersey, in February 1779. The artillery had been using the local schoolhouse or academy for courts-martial, officers' meetings, and other official functions, but then it went a step further and engaged Mr. Colles, the preceptor, to teach the officers of the corps mathematics and other pertinent subjects that would better qualify them for their duties.[97]

Sutlers, contractors, and other entrepreneurs provided the army with the services and supplies it needed (although frequently not at the time or in the quantity required), and some it desired but did not necessarily need. Some of these sellers belonged to the army, such as those followers who engaged in trade, or those engaged in trade who became camp followers. Sutlers, by the very nature of their appointment, lived and operated under military control. Other suppliers might more properly be defined as belonging with the army. Contractors accepted military supervision but enjoyed certain legislative as well as mercantile prerogatives within the Continental Community. Finally, there were the other sellers who certainly attached themselves to the camps at various times but who as unaffiliated civilians did not belong to or, according to some observers, even with the army. Some of these people were seen and treated as guests, others as pests. Whether or not they actually belonged to the army, all of these people found themselves subject to military intervention whenever they pursued their trades in or close to the Continental Community. Their goods, services, and even their persons were scrutinized and regulated so that they benefited the army and did not disrupt the community.

Notes

1. Timothy Pickering, blank copy of the "Form of a lisence for Sutlers," Yorktown, Virginia, 8–9 October 1781, War Department Collection of Revolutionary War Records, Record Group 93 (overall collection referred to hereafter as RG 93), Numbered Record Books Concerning Military Operations and Service, Pay and Settlement of Accounts, and Supplies (hereafter referred to as Numbered Record Books), M853, roll 26, vol. 82, National Archives, Washington, D.C. (microfilm, David Library of the American Revolution, Washington Crossing, Pennsylvania).
2. Thomas M. Doerflinger, *A Vigorous Spirit of Enterprise: Merchants and Economic Development in Revolutionary Philadelphia* (Chapel Hill: University of North Carolina Press, 1986), p. 212 and ch. 5, especially 236–40: about traders whose passions were "getting and spending" instead of virtue and patriotism" but who contributed to the Revolution as they worked both for themselves and the army. Other authors who addressed this issue, in varying degrees, in their examinations of army logistics are: E. Wayne Carp, *To Starve the Army at Pleasure: Continental Army Administration and American Political Culture, 1775–1783* (Chapel Hill: University of North Carolina Press, 1984); Erna Risch, *Supplying Washington's Army* (Washing-

ton, D.C.: U.S. Army Center of Military History, 1981); and James A. Huston, *Logistics of Liberty: American Services of Supply in the Revolutionary War and After* (Newark: University of Delaware Press, 1991).

3. William C. DeHart, *Observations on Military Law, and the Constitution and Practice of Courts Martial* (New York: Wiley & Putnam, 1846), pp. 24–25. This is a later interpretation of a later set of articles, but the camp follower article did not change much in the seventy years after the 1776 Articles of War, nor did the military's definition of sutlers/traders and their liability.

4. British Article XXIII in the British Articles of War of 1765 and American Article XXXII in the American Articles of War of 1775, in William Winthrop, *Military Law and Precedents,* 2d ed. (Washington, D.C.: Government Printing Office, 1920; reprint, New York: Arno Press, 1979), pp. 941, 956.

5. British Article II, Section VIII, Ibid., p. 935.

6. Articles 1–4, Section VIII, American Articles of War of 1776, with 14 April 1777 revision of Article 2, in John O'Brien, *A Treatise on American Military Laws, and the Practice of Courts Martial; with Suggestions for their Improvement* (Philadelphia: Lea & Blanchard, 1846), pp. 317–18, 328–29. Articles I–IV, Section VIII, British Articles of War, in Winthrop, *Military Law,* pp. 935–36.

7. General Orders, Headquarters Cambridge, 11 July 1775, in W. W. Abbot, ed., *The Papers of George Washington,* Revolutionary War Series (Charlottesville: University Press of Virginia, 1985–), 1:106.

8. General Orders, Headquarters Cambridge, 7 August 1775, in Orderly Book, Gen. George Washington, Headquarters Massachusetts, 31 August–24 September 1775, The New-York Historical Society's Collection of Early American Orderly Books (microfilm, David Library).

9. General Orders, Headquarters Cambridge, 6 September and 14 November 1775, 9 and 21 February 1776, in Abbot, *Papers of George Washington,* 1:418–19; 2:369–70; 3:272–73, 350.

10. Headquarters Valley Forge, 26 January 1778, *Valley Forge Orderly Book of General George Weedon of the Continental Army under Command of Genl. George Washington, in the Campaign of 1777–78* (1902; reprint, New York: Arno Press, 1971), pp. 209–10.

11. Headquarters Valley Forge, 16 April 1778, Major General Heath's Headquarters Orderly Book, from Boston to Providence, 23 May 1777–20 October 1778, RG 93, Revolutionary War Miscellaneous Manuscript Collection.

12. General Orders, Headquarters Valley Forge, 26 May 1778, in John C. Fitzpatrick, ed., *The Writings of George Washington from the Original Manuscript Sources, 1745–1799* (Washington, D.C.: U.S. Printing Office, 1931–1944), 11:455.

13. Headquarters, before York, 4 October 1781, and General Orders, Headquarters Newburgh, 23 November 1782, Ibid., 23:173; 25:369.

14. General Orders, Headquarters Newburgh, 28 February 1783 and 2 March 1783, Ibid., 26:172, 175–77.

15. General Orders directing that provost marshall and other officers keep an eye on sutlers and their customers, Headquarters Cambridge, 14 February 1776, in Abbot, *Papers of Washington,* 3:305–6. Joseph Plumb Martin, as he recounted in *Private Yankee Doodle: Being a Narrative of Some of the Adventures, Dangers and Suffer-*

ings of a Revolutionary Soldier, ed. George F. Scheer (1830; New York: Little, Brown, Popular Library ed., 1963), p. 129, saw what he described to be the sport of "lowbred" Europeans indulged in by two Irishmen at a sutler's tent or hut. Washington's Instructions to Capt. Bartholomew von Heer, Headquarters, 11 October 1778, noted that "booths of unlicensed Sutlers, are great Sources of disorder and Riot." General Orders, Headquarters near Dobbs Ferry, 7 July 1781, included demand that sutlers send persons not belonging to the army to authorities for questioning, in Fitzpatrick, *Writings of Washington,* 13:68–69; 22:334–35.

16. Crown Point, 4 July 1776, Headquarters [Ticonderoga], 27 July 1776, and Brigade Orders, [Ticonderoga], 9 August 1776, Orderly Book of the 4th Pennsylvania Battalion, 10 April–30 April 1776 and 21 June–20 September 1776, Historical Society of Pennsylvania (hereafter referred to as 4 PA Bn Orderly Book). The brigade orders referred to Colonel St. Clair so I called him such in the text; however, St. Clair was promoted to brigadier general effective that same day—9 August.

17. Headquarters Valley Forge, 20 and 28 March 1778, *Valley Forge Orderly Book of General George Weedon,* pp. 266, 273.

18. Camp near Chester, New York, 24 June 1779, Col. John Lamb's 2nd Regiment of Continental Artillery, 8 June, 14 June–19 August 1779 (kept by Chilian Ford), The New-York Historical Society's Collection of Early American Orderly Books (microfilm, David Library). All of Lamb's regimental orderly books in The New-York Historical Society's collection will hereafter be referred to as Lamb's 2CA Orderly Book and differentiated by date. Entry mentioned the price of "flitch"; as in a flitch of bacon.

19. Brigade Orders, 19 August 1778, Orderly Book of the 1st Pennsylvania Regiment under Col. James Chambers, 26 July–20 December 1778, Historical Society of Pennsylvania.

20. Garrison Orders, West Point, 16 and 24 September 1780, Lamb's 2CA Orderly Book, 26 June–30 December 1780, and 4 August–13 October 1781.

21. Examples of brigade and garrison orders forbidding sutlers to sell liquor to soldiers without their customers having written permission include that already stated in note 14 and then the orders at West Point, 1 March 1783, in Lamb's 2CA Orderly Book, 20 February–28 March 1783. The transformation into a general order came at Headquarters Newburgh, 21 May 1783, as seen in Edward C. Boynton, ed., *General Orders of George Washington Commander-in-Chief of the Army of the Revolution issued at Newburgh on the Hudson 1782-1783* (1909; reprint, Harrison, N.Y.: Harbor Hill Books, 1973), pp. 82–83.

22. Crown Point, 3 July 1776, 4 PA Bn Orderly Book.

23. Garrison Orders, Fort Constitution, 13 March 1777, Mss. Orderly Book kept at the Headquarters of LTC Marinus Willett of the 3rd New York Regt., from 17 February 1777 to 21 May 1778, The New-York Historical Society (microfilm).

24. Summary of duties of Marechaussee Corps, 11 October 1778, Lamb's 2CA Orderly Book, 26 September–27 November 1778. The order to the sutlers to report in to Von Heer was added to this orderly book's distillation of the more extensive instructions to Capt. Bartholomew Von Heer, 11 October 1778, in Fitzpatrick, *Writings of Washington,* 131:68–69. The latter ordered Von Heer to keep a list of licensed sutlers.

25. Headquarters [Ticonderoga], 5 September 1776, 4 PA Bn Orderly Book. It is some-

times difficult to determine to which general these books are referring—at times they mean Washington and at others their local commanding general; in this case it appears that Washington sent on a comment to be delivered with the resolve.

26. The above copy of the resolve reached Ticonderoga on 5 September, and another copy had reached the 1st Pennsylvania Regiment by 21 June (with caveat: "The Genl. expects a strict obedience will be paid thereto), in Orderly Book of the Pennsylvania Rifle Regiment, 16 June–4 October 1776, Historical Society of Pennsylvania. "Lt. Col. Belinger" was mentioned in *Citizen Soldier: The Revolutionary War Journal of Joseph Bloomfield,* ed. Mark E. Lender and James Kirby Martin (Newark: New Jersey Historical Society, 1982), p. 103. No Belinger or Balinger is listed in Heitman's *Historical Register of Officers of the Continental Army,* but he lists a Lt. Col. Fred Ballinger of the New York Militia and a Col. Peter Bellinger also of the New York Militia.

27. Brigade Orders, White Plains, 26 August 1778, Orderly Book, Brigade of Artillery with Washington's Main Army, 23 July–31 December 1778, The New-York Historical Society's Collection of Early American Orderly Books (microfilm, David Library).

28. Pluckemin, New Jersey, 9 January 1779, Lamb's 2CA Orderly Book, 30 November 1778–4 February 1779 and 11 January–18 February 1780.

29. Headquarters Newburgh, 13 May 1782, in Boynton, *General Orders of George Washington . . . at Newburgh,* p. 18.

30. Headquarters Newburgh, 30 August 1782, Ibid., p. 57.

31. Headquarters Valley Forge, 3 January 1778, in *Valley Forge Orderly Book of General George Weedon,* pp. 177–78.

32. Brigade Orders, 10 November 1778, Orderly Book of the 1st Pennsylvania Regiment (hereafter referred to as 1 PA Orderly Book), 26 July–20 December 1778, Historical Society of Pennsylvania.

33. Orders, Headquarters Wyoming, 29 and 30 July 1779, in Capt. Christian Myers's German Regiment of Pennsylvania Orderly Book, 25 June 1779–29 March 1780, Manuscript Division, Library of Congress. Heitman in his *Historical Register* spells Myers as Meyers.

34. Greene to Washington, Camp Tappen, 23 September 1780, Sol Feinstone Collection (microfilm), David Library of the American Revolution; E. Wayne Carp, *To Starve the Army at Pleasure,* pp. 87–88.

35. Carp, Ibid., p. 83, on Washington's aversion to impressment and desire to maintain good civil-military relations. An example of supervision at work can be seen in the scrutiny of Quartermaster General Thomas Mifflin as revealed in Washington and Joseph Reed correspondence (especially the P.S. in letter from Cambridge, 25 March 1776, in Abbot, *Papers of Washington,* 3:538). Huston, *Logistics of Liberty,* p. 264.

36. The Richard Backhouse Account Book, 1775, at the Historical Society of Pennsylvania, contains statements from suppliers on the amount of money they received for their goods, certificates from company commanders that Backhouse supplied their riflemen with provisions, notes by Backhouse on what he was paid by Captains Chambers, Hendricks, and Miller of Thompson's regiment for delivering their supplies, and a mileage count from Pennsylvania to Massachusetts among other things.

37. Risch, *Supplying Washington's Army,* p. 15.

Sutlers and Other Suppliers 117

38. John McKesson, In Committee of Safety ... New York, 30 March 1776—a pass issued to Daniel Hinslee, butcher, allowing him to travel into different areas of New York and into Connecticut in order to procure cattle. The Abraham Livingston referred to in the pass may have been the same man who became a captain in the 1st Canadian regiment that December. Sol Feinstone Collection (microfilm). As Huston, *Logistics of Liberty,* p. 67, points out, before 1780 purchasing agents were generally civilians.
39. Pickering to David Matthews, Wagon Conductor, Newburgh, 21 December 1780, about procuring forage for horses, etc.; mentions that Mr. Hoops, contractor for "Sussex Country," can winter any horses Matthews leaves with him. Pickering to Aaron Forman, Assistant Deputy Quartermaster, Newburgh, 30 January 1781, about stockpiling wood—he disliked employing soldiers for cutting and hauling wood for it cost too much, so he advertised for persons willing to contract to supply the troops with wood and received some responses. In Numbered Record Books, M853, roll 25, vol. 124.
40. Risch, *Supplying Washington's Army,* pp. 165–66.
41. Ibid., pp. 230–31.
42. Ibid., pp. 232–33, 238–39.
43. Ibid., pp. 244–45, 187; Huston, *Logistics of Liberty,* pp. 279–80.
44. *Pennsylvania Gazette,* 26 September 1781, p. 1, col. 1.
45. Martin, *Private Yankee Doodle,* p. 228.
46. Washington to Superintendent of Finance, Newburgh, 8 January 1783, in Fitzpatrick, *Writings of Washington,* 16:20–21.
47. Risch, *Supplying Washington's Army,* pp. 252–58 passim. Support for Risch's analysis can be found in the Pickering papers, Numbered Record Books, M853. Examples include Pickering's letter to Ralph Pomeroy, New Windsor, 19 December 1781, roll 26, vol. 82 (quoted in part); Pickering to Col. Jabez Hatch, New Windsor, 15 December 1781, roll 26, vol. 127; Pickering to Colonel Hughes, New Windsor, 28 December 1781, roll 26, vol. 82; and Pickering to Comfort Sands, Esqr. & Co. (contractors), New Windsor, 4 January 1782, roll 26, vol. 83.
48. Risch, *Supplying Washington's Army,* pp. 256–57.
49. Hand to Col. P. Cortland (probably Philip Van Cortlandt), Orderly Office Newburgh, 24 July 1782, Numbered Record Books, M853, roll 17, vol. 162.
50. One can see Pickering's role develop in the correspondence referred to in footnote 47.
51. Risch, *Supplying Washington's Army,* p. 255.
52. Pickering to Col. Hugh Hughes, Deputy Quartermaster General, New Windsor, 18 December 1781, Numbered Record Books, M853, roll 26, vol. 82.
53. Garrison Orders, Burlington Barracks, 29 January 1782, Lamb's 2CA Orderly Book, 7 December 1781–4 February 1782.
54. Pickering to Smith & Lawrence, Contractors, New Windsor, 26 December 1781, and to Comfort Sands, Esqr., & Co., Contractors, New Windsor, 31 January 1782, Numbered Record Books, M853, roll 26, vols. 82 and 83.
55. Copies of Benjamin Lincoln's "A System on which Provisions are to be issued," 1 May 1782, are in Lamb's 2CA Orderly Book, 7 February–7 August 1782 (and in the Orderly Book, Col. John Crane's Third Regiment of Continental Artillery, 12 March–18 May 1782, in The New-York Historical Society's Collection of Early

American Orderly Books). Officers did not receive ration allowances under the contract system as they had under the old method; they received a subsistence allowance which they could use to purchase rations for themselves and their families. Regimental Orders, Burlington Barracks, 10 January 178[2], Lamb's 2CA Orderly Book, 7 December 1781–4 February 1782. "Regulations for drawing Provisions on the New Contract," in General Orders, Headquarters Newburgh, 28 December 1782, Lamb's 2CA Orderly Book, 27 November 1782–5 January 1783. "Monthly Abstract of Provision for the Quarter Master General's Department, under the Contract for the States of New York [and] New Jersey In the Month of January 1783" is an example of a provision return found in Record Group 93, Letters, Returns, Accounts, and Estimates of the Quartermaster General's Department, 1776–1783, M926, National Archives (microfilm, David Library).

56. General Orders, Headquarters Newburgh, 12 and 19 March 1783, Lamb's 2CA Orderly Book, 20 February–28 March 1783 version of orders, others in Fitzpatrick, *Writings of Washington,* 26:209, 247.
57. General Orders, Headquarters Newburgh, 27 and 31 December 1782 and 24 February 1783, in Fitzpatrick, *Writings of Washington,* 25:477, 496; 26:159–60.
58. G[arrison] Orders, Burlington Barracks, 19 and 20 January 1782, Lamb's 2CA Orderly Book, 7 December 1781–4 February 1782.
59. Pickering to Colonel Neilson, Philadelphia, 1 May 1782, Numbered Record Books, M853, roll 26, vol. 83.
60. Garrison Orders, Fort Schuyler, 23 September 1777, 2 and 5 May 1778, 5 April 1778, 14 December 1777, Mss. Orderly Book kept at the Headquarters of LTC Marinus Willett of the 3rd New York Regiment, 17 February 1777–21 May 1778, The New-York Historical Society (microfilm). Heitman's entry on Gansevoort in his *Historical Register* gives a record of the congressional resolution making him colonel-commandant. To ring a hog is to put a ring through the nose—my thanks to the Andersons for this clarification.
61. See Benjamin Gilbert's letters home, especially that to his father on 21 January 1781 from West Point, in John Shy, ed., *Winding Down: The Revolutionary War Letters of Lieutenant Benjamin Gilbert of Massachusetts, 1780–1783* (Ann Arbor: University of Michigan Press, 1989), p. 34.
62. Martin, *Private Yankee Doodle,* p. 221.
63. General Orders, Headquarters Newburgh, 8 January and 11 February 1783, in Fitzpatrick, *Writings of Washington,* 16:23, 120.
64. Account by Henry Seymour, who had been employed by Comfort Sands and Company, in John C. Dann, ed., *The Revolution Remembered: Eyewitness Accounts of the War for Independence* (Chicago: University of Chicago Press, 1980), pp. 376–78. General Orders, [Newburgh], 21 May 1783, in Fitzpatrick, *Writings of Washington,* 26:446–47. The promissory notes were probably given that nickname in "honor" of John Pierce, the paymaster-general.
65. See examples of all this in Gilbert, 10 and 13 March 1778, [Albany, New York], in Rebecca D. Symmes, ed., *A Citizen-Soldier in the American Revolution: The Diary of Benjamin Gilbert in Massachusetts and New York* (Cooperstown: New York State Historical Association, 1980), p. 27. See also Martin in New York, September 1776, outside of Valley Forge, December 1777, and near Williamsburg, September 1781, in Martin, *Private Yankee Doodle,* pp. 48, 98, 191–92.

66. Washington to Gov. George Clinton, Headquarters Newburgh, 17 February 1783, in Fitzpatrick, *Writings of Washington,* 26:139.
67. Greene's Orders, [Prospect Hill], 19 September 1775, in Robert E. McCarthy, ed., *The Papers of General Nathanael Greene* (Scholarly Resources, Inc., microfilm edition), Part I; part of Hitchcock Orderly Book no. 2 (with its extremely poor spelling and punctuation, this book records Greene's orders but not his writing). Asa Minor is not mentioned in Heitman's *Register* as an officer in the army. There was both a Col. Jonathan Brewer and a Col. David Brewer of the Massachusetts Regiment.
68. Garrison Orders, Fort Schuyler, 31 December 1777, and an entry that was addended to or just followed 7 February 1778 orders, Mss. Orderly Book kept at the Headquarters of LTC Marinus Willett of the 3rd New York Regiment, 17 February 1777–21 May 1778.
69. Headquarters Valley Forge, 20 January 1778, Headquarters Valley Forge Orderly Book, 1–31 January 1778, RG 93, Revolutionary War Miscellaneous Manuscript Collection.
70. Headquarters Valley Forge, 8 February 1778, in *Valley Forge Orderly Book,* pp. 228–29. John Trussell examined the establishment of markets via Weedon's orderly book in *Birthplace of an Army: A Study of the Valley Forge Encampment* (Harrisburg: Pennsylvania Historical and Museum Commission, 1979), pp. 31–32.
71. Headquarters Valley Forge, 17 April 1778, Heath's Headquarters Orderly Book, from Boston to Providence, 23 May 1777–20 October 1778, RG 93, Revolutionary War Miscellaneous Manuscript Collection.
72. Garrison Orders, West Point, 13 August 1780, Lamb's 2CA Orderly Book, 26 June–30 December 1780.
73. Washington to Samuel Loudon, Headquarters near Dobbs Ferry, 10 July 1781, in Fitzpatrick, *Writings of Washington,* 22:351–52.
74. Headquarters [New York], 26 July and 16 August 1776, in Peter Kinnan, *Order Book Kept By Peter Kinnan July 7–September 4, 1776,* introduction by M. E. Kinnan (Privately printed, Princeton, N.J.: Princeton University Press, 1931), pp. 32–33, 68.
75. Garrison Orders, West Point, 16 August 1780, Lamb's 2CA Orderly Book, 26 June–30 December 1780.
76. Camp near Chester, New York, 1 July 1779, Lamb's 2CA Orderly Book, 8 June and 14 June–19 August 1779.
77. Garrison Orders, Fort Schuyler, 30 October 1777, Mss. Orderly Book kept at the HQ of LTC Marinus Willett of the 3rd New York Regt., 17 February 1777–21 May 1778.
78. Orders, Long Island, 16 August 1776, in McCarthy, *Papers of General Nathanael Greene* (microfilm), Pt. I, from Henshaw Orderly Book.
79. Headquarters Newburgh, 16 May 1782, in Boynton, *General Orders of George Washington . . . at Newburgh,* p. 20.
80. Regimental Orders, West Point, 2 May 1783, Lamb's 2CA Orderly Book, 28 March–25 June 1783.
81. Orders, [Prospect Hill, Massachusetts], 19 August and 2 September 1775, in McCarthy, *Papers of General Nathanael Greene* (microfilm), Pt. I, from Hitchcock Orderly Book.

82. Headquarters at Moor[e']s House, 12 August 1779, 1 PA Orderly Book, 24 May–25 August 1779.
83. Headquarters White Marsh, 24 November 1777, Major General Heath's Headquarters Orderly Book, from Boston to Providence, 23 May 1777–20 October 1778, RG 93, Revolutionary War Miscellaneous Manuscript Collection.
84. Artillery Orders, West Point, 27 July and 26 October 1780, Lamb's 2CA Orderly Book, 26 June–30 December 1780.
85. No date or place but placed before the 7 September 1780 entry in microfilm, Lamb's 2CA Orderly Book, 7 September–2 November 1780. For another example of the crime and punishment of unlicensed liquor sellers see Gilbert's diary entries for 9, 10, and 11 May 1778, when Sergeant Cook at Fort Putnam brought home some whiskey (which Gilbert certainly enjoyed) but then was court-martialed and sentenced to have his liquor confiscated and be reduced in rank (latter soon restored), Symmes, ed., *Citizen-Soldier*, p. 31.
86. Regimental Orders, before Yorktown, 12 October 1781, Lamb's 2CA Orderly Book, 20 June–21 October 1781.
87. "A Return of the sick &c in Camp at Fredricksburg," 25 October 1778; "A Return of the Sick in Camp [Smiths Clove]," 13 July 1779; "A Return of the Sick in Camp [West Point]," 2 August 1779; "A Return of the Sick in Camp [West Point]," 10 August 1779; and "A General Return of the Sick and Wounded in the Military Hospitals, belonging to the Army, commanded by his Excellency General Washington, from Feb. 1. to March 1. 1780," in Revolutionary War Rolls, M246, roll 135, National Archives (microfilm).
88. Walter Hart Blumenthal, *Women Camp Followers of the American Revolution* (Philadelphia: George MacManus, 1952), p. 59.
89. Headquarters New York City, 7 May 1776, Orderly Book, Col. Alexander McDougall's 1st New York Regiment, 25 March–15 June 1776, The New-York Historical Society's Collection of Early American Orderly Books (microfilm, David Library).
90. James C. Neagles, *Summer Soldiers: A Survey & Index of Revolutionary War Courts-Martial* (Salt Lake City, Utah: Ancestry Inc., 1986), p. 22. Bangs, New York, 25 April 1776, in Edward Bangs, ed., *Journal of Lieutenant Isaac Bangs, April 1 to July 29, 1776* (1890; reprint, New York: Arno Press, 1968), pp. 29–31. Thanks to Stuart Goldman for sending me a copy of a letter from Lt. John Noyes in New York on 12 May 1776 to his wife, in which the officer deplores the wicked city in general and whores of the Holy Ground in particular, who for the price of a dollar "are Seven times as open as man & Wife."
91. As mentioned in Blumenthal, *Women Camp Followers,* p. 66, and recorded as General Orders, Headquarters at Derby, 24 August 1777, in Fitzpatrick, *Writings of Washington,* 9:129–30.
92. Gilbert to Capt. Jonathan Stone, Cantonment New Windsor, 1 March 1783, and Shy's editorial notes in his *Winding Down,* pp. 86–87.
93. Shy introduction, Ibid., p. 15; and Gilbert, [Fort Putnam near West Point], 29 and 30 May, and 5 June 1778, in Symmes, ed., *Citizen-Soldier,* p. 32. There were not many references to courts-martial of alleged prostitutes in Neagle, *Summer Soldiers,* or in the orderly books. While such courts-martial were rare (or rarely re-

corded), civilian court proceedings might tell another story. Linda Grant DePauw discussed the issue of prostitution in "Women in Combat: The Revolutionary War Experience," *Armed Forces and Society* 7 (Winter 1981): 211. Her analysis that prostitution in the American camp was rare and army women generally respectable appears sound—though I will add that they were respectable in the way that the army and its soldiers were respectable, which means that, depending on the observer, this was debatable.

94. Brown's story was published in *The REMEMBRANCER; or, Impartial Repository of Public Events. For the Year 1778,* vol. 6 (London, 1778), p. 346, and followed up in vol. 6 (. . . For the Year 1778, and Beginning of 1779), 2. Rare book room, U.S. Army Military History Institute, Carlisle Barracks, Pennsylvania.
95. Samual McKenzie to Potts, Bennington, 27 August 1777, Dr. Jonathan Potts Papers, 1766–1780, Historical Society of Pennsylvania. Benjamin Gilbert in Symmes, ed., *Citizen-Soldier,* and Shy, ed., *Winding Down.*
96. Journal entry, Albany, 4 February 1778, James Thacher, *Military Journal of the American Revolution* (1862; reprint, New York: Arno Press, 1969), p. 122. Trussell in *Birthplace of an Army* places Thacher and Trotter at Valley Forge when they were actually at Albany. Thacher accompanied sick soldiers to Albany in July 1777 and remained there, except for his furlough, until the hospital was ordered to move to the Highlands in June 1778. Trussell may have been misled by Thacher's general December entry in which he recorded news of Valley Forge. (He also entered the page as 146 instead of 122; perhaps he had a different edition.)
97. Artillery Park, Pluckemin, New Jersey, 23 February 1779, Lamb's 2CA Orderly Book, 5 February–30 May 1779.

4

Retainers to the Camp
The Conjugal Family

> ... she drew her rations as other soldiers did.
>
> Mary Cockron, follower
> Pension information, 1837

Mary Cockron, an old and needy widow in 1837, was in the process of applying for a pension when her advocate wrote to Pennsylvania's secretary of state requesting service information on her late husband. William Cockron had enlisted in Captain Robert Kirkwood's company of the Delaware Regiment in the Pennsylvania line and had served for over five years. His wife, with her name enrolled on the company roster so that she could draw rations, had essentially soldiered along with him.[1] Many other women, also sharing the rigors of soldiering but not called soldiers, belonged to the army. In legal parlance they could be called retainers to the camp. Many of the diverse peoples who flocked to the army could be so categorized. While sutlers and other vendors followed the army in order to pursue profit, commerce was rarely the primary motivating reason for most of the other civilians who accompanied the troops, although some of them did engage in mercantile activities after they settled within the Continental Community. Retainers to the camp included dependent family members, servants, and volunteers: a varied group in terms of positions and power, they all had the same legal status under military law because they were people who followed the army on account of personal attachments and private intentions or loyalties. Some of them expressed patriotic sentiments and aided army operations, but their attention was generally focused first on the private and then on the public arena.

Women were ineligible for military service but not for service to the military. Sometimes welcomed, oftentimes denigrated, they were a highly visible, vocal, and patriotic part of the Continental Community. Their positions within that community reflected both the sphere of women in society as a whole and the respective social ranks from which they came. The majority of women with the army represented the poorer elements of American society. When people talked about "women of the army," they were referring to the low-status women who lived and worked among the troops. The association of these followers with the military contrasted sharply with that of the senior officers' wives, the next most visible class of women. The wives, or "ladies" as they were also called, of the senior officers visited the military's ranking personnel to give domestic cheer and comfort. Both groups followed the army to remain close to loved ones, but whereas the first also operated under the necessity to find sustenance, the second entered the camps prepared for an active social life. A third group, junior officers' wives, appears to have been quite small and composed of a socially and economically mixed membership. Some members demonstrated attitudes and activities that mirrored the first category of women, and others, the second.

Most of these women, along with the other family members that appeared in the camps, were dependent on their men in service. Not only did they rely on these men for material support, they were essentially controlled or at least heavily influenced by the demands and wishes of their related officers and soldiers. Such dependency certainly reflected the familial and legal structures of the age and society, but now it created a problem for the military. A man was supposed to provide for and protect his family; now however, it was his duty to secure his nation. Many, if not most, military men found it difficult to do both well. Somehow the army had to resolve or at least ameliorate this conflict so that the men could focus on the national fight and so that the families could support them in this.

The army, somewhat grudgingly, endeavored to provide for its female dependents. Officers put soldiers' wives to work and allocated rations for them while squiring their own wives to dinners and dances in both the military and civilian communities. Then, when the army readied itself for a campaign, most officers sent their own wives home and ordered the soldiers' dependents who would continue with the army to stay out of the way and obey all regulations applying to their conduct. Sometimes these retainers obeyed, and sometimes they did not, as they juggled their jobs, domestic obligations, and personal desires within the military framework. Obedience was contingent upon a variety of factors: external ones included the situations back in their home communities and the strength of the army's coercive mechanisms in its own community; while internal ones included the strength of the desire to remain with the army, the acceptance of the primacy of the military mission, and, for a few, an identification with the army and a belief that they could contribute to its efforts to achieve national independence.

Although a few of these camp followers did pick up arms on occasion, they entered the Continental Community not to fight but to be with male kin, sustain their families, and generally to serve themselves. Most women with the army remained focused on their own domestic circles and chores throughout their association with the military, or more accurately, their association with military personnel. They remained within the feminine sphere even as they entered the military one. This feminine sphere, already having shown some flexibility throughout the colonial period as people defined women's work according to time, place, and circumstance, did appear to expand in this crisis as the revolutionaries applied women's work to the public sphere. Nevertheless it remained distinct. Both women's attitudes and actions in camp, as did men's, reflected those held by their counterparts in civilian communities. Indeed, visits to and residence within the Continental Community reinforced their beliefs (and those of the soldiers) on femininity and female roles as they were juxtaposed against the military as a masculine preserve and war as a manly pursuit.[2]

Exposed as they were to the horrors of war and the harshness of life on campaign, the men and women of the army may have clung all the more tenaciously to an image of peaceful domesticity. They tried to maintain a facsimile of it when *en famille* with the army and looked forward to re-creating it at home when the war was won. The romanticizing of domesticity appears to have begun in the camps where single and separated soldiers were removed from the reality of it and where those with families present had so little chance of preserving it. It began as patriarchalism was both challenged and reinforced by the exigencies of war and military life.[3]

The very nature of the military community and way of life reinforced female dependence at the same time it demanded female fortitude and, occasionally, supported female initiative. Whereas women left alone at home when husbands or other male family members joined the army learned to exercise and often to like autonomy,[4] women with the army remained heavily dominated by males. That domination was twofold: on a primary level they were controlled by their male family members; on a secondary level by that most male of institutions, the military. Although repeatedly, if not daily, exposed to a revolutionary rhetoric that denounced enforced dependence, and although they called themselves patriots as they labored to support their soldiers and the war effort, most camp women did not or could not use the Revolution's precepts to revolutionize their personal lives. They instead accepted the growing glorification of their domestic position.

The women of the army, as did their sisters elsewhere, saw their domestic roles become politically and even militarily significant. Women's roles within household and society did not fundamentally change; what did change was the perception of the importance of those roles. A woman could display her patriotism through her actions as consumer, household manager, producer, wife, and mother. She could strike at the enemy by boycotting British merchandise, and then curtail household consumption and step up home industries such as spinning so that she not only helped sustain her family but also cast her "mite into the Treasury of the public good." That included providing her army with needed provisions such as lint, linen, and bandages. Finally, in her most patriotic act, one demonstrating that women, no less then men, were capable of public virtue, a woman could subordinate her needs to those of the nation and send her father, husband, brothers, and sons to war.[5]

This growing recognition of the importance of the role of women to the commonwealth was a result of the American rebellion and a part of the American Revolution. Perhaps reveling in that recognition, women did not take this opportunity to rebel against their position in society; instead, they used their position to aid the efforts of the United States. Their utilization of that position, however, and their contributions through it, as well as the accolades by male Americans established its place within the new political environment. "Republican motherhood" was the most visible and long-lasting result.[6] Both men and women came to believe that the future and security of the new republic rested upon the ability of the nation's mothers to educate their sons to be responsible citizens. That proved to be a momentous step, for after women established the importance of their influence within the household they set out to prove that the intelligence and capability required there could and should be applied outside the home as well. Their part in what was essentially a political revolution would engender later social and cultural changes.

Camp women differed from their sisters at home in that instead of sending their men off to war, they followed them into camp. That made their patriotism suspect to some people who believed that by entering the camps these women displayed neither public nor private virtue. At a time when female virtue was defined as chastity and public virtue as self-sacrifice, these women were perceived as being deficient in both. The perception was both true and false. In terms of chastity, while it was true that some did not meet the standards set by those arbiters of American social and sexual behavior—the upper and middling orders—others were respectable wives forced to conduct married life in the open but crowded conditions of camp. As for public virtue, certainly some female followers were not patriotic: they did put their own needs first. But other followers may have thought that their actions revealed a high level of patriotism: to allow the family's principal laborer to join the army and then to follow him was a form of abnegation—a renouncing of what could possibly have been a more stable and prosperous way of life for a risky one with the service. Actually, patriotism was a secondary issue, and the critics' arguments had value. Most families with the military were there simply because they had no alternative means of support; because of poverty or British occupation, they had no property or business to maintain them at home while the father or husband was away. They relied on their uniformed family members to support them on a soldier's wages and rations, and they attempted to supplement that meager fare with rations allocated to dependents and by obtaining work within the Continental Community.[7]

Washington did not like to see his army laden with women and other family members. They distracted his soldiers, disrupted operations, diverted scarce resources, and prevented the army from presenting a neat, uniform appearance. He accepted their presence, however, because he knew that he would lose a good portion of his army if he did not. Men with families in trouble would desert or ask for hardship furloughs or discharges, as Private Ralph Morgan did in December 1775. Colonel James Mitchell Varnum wrote Washington that Morgan, whose wife and two children were without a roof to cover them, had requested an eight-day furlough to deal with the problem. Varnum could not oblige on his own authority because of general orders that forbade furloughs for men who had not reenlisted (Morgan had declined the honor), so he asked Washington to make an exception in this case. This early in the war, before the manpower shortage so straitened the army, Morgan received more than a furlough; he got a discharge.[8] In the process of trying to deal with such petitions and desertions due to family problems, Washington came to accept the fact that in order to keep his army together he had to allow his soldiers the opportunity to keep their families together. After making that concession, Washington endeavored to make such retainers assets rather than liabilities; he wanted them to earn their keep, and he hoped to prevent their embarrassing him and the army.[9]

Washington never achieved the latter goal; female camp followers continued to embarrass him and distress other observers throughout the war. While there were occasional references to the heroism of individual followers, comments about the aggregate tended to be rather negative. Two men, one a soldier and one an officer, noted the appearance and behavior of these women, and their children, while on the way to Tappan in 1780. Joseph Martin, while watching the baggage of the army pass by, was amused to see the number and clothing of those followers accompanying the baggage of the middle states: "of all specimens of human beings, this group capped the whole. A caravan of wild beasts could bear no comparison with it. There was 'Tag, Rag and Bobtail'; 'some in rags and some in jags,' but none 'in velvet gowns.' Some with two eyes, some with one, and some, I believe, with none at all." He thought their dialects, from "the Irish and Scotch brogue, murdered, English, flat insipid Dutch," to the other puzzling lingoes, were "as confused as their bodily appearance was odd and disgusting."[10] The officer, too, was struck by the army's human baggage. The women, he began,

> were the ugliest in the world to be collected . . . their Visage dress etc every way concordant to each other—some with two others with three & four children & few with none—I could not help pitying the poor innocent Creatures—their way of living and treatment with the many low & Scandalous examples ev'ry day shown them will make them imitate their Parents vices; and make many who have naturally good dispositions as vicious as the worst of them—the furies who inhabit the infernal Regions can never be painted half so hideous as these women.

He continued with the observation that their "deformity of Aspect & Shape" offered such a great contrast to "those of the Sex who possess the delicacy that is naturally great in them," that men were left with the notion that the latter were "no way inferior to Angels."[11]

The majority of the fallen angels refused to display the decorum that Washington—and other gentleman officers—desired of their sex; nor did they readily obey his orders. The problem was ultimately one of class roles and expectations. Washington associated with women of his own social order. He welcomed the presence of his wife when in winter garrison and enjoyed the company of his senior officers' wives when they visited the camps, but he was uncomfortable with women of the lower orders. In that society, where a person's place and behavior were defined both by rank (civilian and military[12]) and gender, Washington was used to dealing with ladies (the term then and herein used to denote women of high social status), courteous to women from the middling orders, but dismayed by white women in the lower ranks of society who seemed to follow a totally different social code. All of these women, regardless of social standing, occupied domestic positions and displayed so-called feminine behavior, but the duties inherent to their positions and the behavior acceptable to their peers differed according to that ranking.

Most female camp followers lacked the polish and graces that were so much a part of the eighteenth-century lady (especially the southern lady with whom Washington was most familiar). They did not retire from public view when pregnant and then give birth within the confines of their homes; instead, they followed the army even when big with child and then gave birth in camp or military hospital. They did not accept the concept of a genteel poverty; they would rather steal than starve. Finally, some of these women could match their men curse by curse and drink after drink.[13] In other words, they practiced the domestic, economic, and social skills they needed to survive in their particular environment. Yet, to so generalize about these women is to ignore their diversity. Among the rank and file were both foreign and native women converging on camp from all points on the compass, single women and married women, women with children and others without. Some women had a great sense or need of family; others had none. Greater difficulties faced the former as they tried to care for their children in this harsh world of limited pay and long marches. On one occasion a Presbyterian minister "suggested to the wife of the grenadier, *Gabel,* of the Royal Deux-Ponts [an allied force], that she leave him one of her daughters, whom he would adopt as his own child, in return for some thirty louis to ease the campaign for her. The grenadier and his wife, who were very much attached to this child of four, steadily refused [his] offer."[14] Furthermore, while some women wished to escape the confines of camp, others saw camp life as an escape. An Irish servant woman by the name of Mary Montgomery ran away from her master, John Heap, in 1777. When he advertised for the return of the runaway, Heap mentioned that he suspected that "she went after Captain Matthew Irvine's company, in General Weedon's brigade."[15] Whatever their origins, these women were hardy people.

The army could neither rid itself of these family followers nor ignore them, so it decided to provide rations; but it also—to facilitate order and efficiency, and perhaps, incidentally, instill virtue—imposed regulations and set some to work. In the British army a soldier's wife, one who had been married with the permission of the soldier's commanding officer, became part of the regiment. She was entitled to certain privileges which were denied the wives who were married without leave. The British army created this system of military marriage in order to control the rate and number of marriages among the troops, and to establish a means of absorbing the women and children into the hierarchy of the regiment. It minimized the threat to a man's military loyalty and efficiency by making the family indebted to the benevolence of the regimental officers and by subjecting everyone to military discipline. The family's allegiance thus belonged to the regiment rather than solely within and to itself.[16] The American army could not establish a system of approved military marriages, especially since many men were already married before they signed on, but it could decide how many family members it would carry "on the strength" of its regiments. It also determined that retainers to the camp, especially those receiving army provisions, were subject to orders. If a person accepted the army's food and hospitality, then that person also had to accept regulation by the army. As in the British army, the American army implemented these measures in order to minimize the demands a family would place upon an individual soldier and to insure the allegiance of the family to the army.

Either the following of retainers at the beginning of the war was less substantial than at the end or the army initially did not see them as a great problem, for it made few requests for official returns of the women and children in the early years.[17] It may be, however, that officers dealt with the problem rather informally at first but later—when the main army spent more time in garrisons and its supply system became more established (and, in particular, when contractors took over the provisioning for the army)—required a more formal accounting to allocate resources. As the army moved into Valley Forge in December of 1777, an account of rations drawn by the infantry there included rations for women.[18] In August 1779 at the Tioga stockade that was called Fort Sullivan, the officer left in command as the expedition moved out against the Iroquois, probably Colonel Israel Shreve of the 2nd New Jersey, informed his subordinates that he wanted returns of all the troops of every regiment left in garrison along with the women and children there. He said that no rations would be issued to anyone except those included in the returns.[19] Captain Aaron Aaron of the 3rd New York complied with the order by submitting "A Return of the Women & Children Left in Charge of Baggage, Necessary to wash for Genl.

Clintons Brigade." He counted the women and children belonging to the New York regiments. The 2nd New York had two women, a Mrs. Lambertson and a Miss Smith with two children. The 3rd New York included a Mrs. Parker and the misses Sherlock, Haburn, and Jackson on its rolls. The 4th listed Mrs. Cothal, Mrs. Penojer, Miss Smith and child, plus Mrs. Canby and child, while the 5th had Miss Weymyre, Miss Clinton, and Miss Austin.[20]

By 1780 requests for information on families in camp had multiplied and marriage ties had become a method whereby to determine priorities in rationing. Provisioning problems in the Highlands led to orders denying rations to sutlers and other men, or their wives, not in the public service, as well as unmarried women (who were, incidentally, ordered to leave the garrison). Commanding officers of the corps garrisoned there were to ascertain the characters of the women who drew rations and hand in the names of those married to the noncommissioned officers, soldiers, and artificers. They were also to give these women certificates. Commissaries were only to issue rations to those married women whose names were noted on the backs of the returns.[21] Then on 17 November 1780, while at West Point, the 2nd Continental Artillery, in accordance with that day's general orders, asked its company commanders "to furnish immediate Returns, of the Women, & Children, in their respective Companies, who draw Provisions; distinguishing those that are married; and those that are not." At another time, 19 August 1781, and place, "Cinksing," the army again asked for returns, this time "of all the Women and Children in Camp, distinguishing those that have Husbands, and also Returns of the Husband's Names, & whether they be in this Division of the Army or not." It wanted the returns delivered to headquarters by noon the next day. The 2nd Continental Artillery jumped right to it and ordered the returns made up and then delivered to its own brigade major at ten o'clock the next morning. This artillery unit continued to keep tabs on its women even when there were no general orders specifically demanding returns. In May 1782 it asked that returns of the women in the companies, "specifying the Time they have been in the Regt.," be delivered to the adjutant. Then on 17 December it ordered that company returns of the women drawing provisions be given to the regimental quartermaster.[22]

As the army entered the new year, and the last year of the war, it attempted to establish a new way to provision its families. The transition began with two orders: in the first Washington decreed that sixteen rations would be issued for every fifteen men in a regiment or corps, thus fixing that for every fifteen men one ration would be set aside for the women accompanying them.[23] In the second he ordered "A return of the number of Women in the several Regiments, which compose the Army, Certified by the Commanding Officer of the Corps, they respectively belong to; is to be given at the Orderly Office on the Second Day of Janua[r]y next." Then on 5 January more figures were requested. Washington wanted to make a comparison between "the number of Women and Children, that would have drawn Rations, in the several Corps under the late regulations" and "the number of Extra Rations daily drawn in the Corps, agreeable to the present regulations."[24] The army's administrators and supply managers included the 15:1 ratio in their new system of issuing rations under contract in an attempt to depersonalize the provisioning of families and to prevent abuses and overdrafts on the supplies. Washington, however, (even though he began implementation of the new regulation for provisioning families) did not like the new rule and set out to discredit or circumvent it. He believed it increased the number of rations set aside for followers above what was actually needed even as it decreased the flexibility of commanders to provide for them: some regiments had more followers than others, and the system should account for that.

The new system was in actuality not new. The British army had utilized ratios to determine the supplying of women, generally accepting six or fewer women per company of one hundred men, both before and during the war. American commanders, lacking guidance from their own headquarters, had used that ratio as an informal guideline when apportioning rations for their companies or regiments.[25] By 1781, however, the army's administrators were clamoring for a formal regulation. General Hand, the army's adjutant general, in a report to the Board of War that May, wrote, "I wish it could be determined what number of women should draw rations in a regiment or rather what proportion their number should bear to that of the men; and whether Children be allowed Rations."[26] A month later Benjamin Lincoln, the secretary at war, and Robert Morris, the superintendent of finance, told Washington that they thought women's rations should be limited to a fifteenth of the rations issued to noncommissioned officers and privates. Washington disagreed at that time and continued to disagree almost two years later after that ration plan was finally (although, as it turned out, temporarily) implemented. In January 1783 Washington explained to Morris that he thought the new regulation implied that an abuse had existed which needed correction, and that he believed that was an incorrect reading of the situation. After consulting his orderly book, Washington concluded that "upon every return of the number of Women called for (at different periods) when compared with the totality of the Army, it has been found, that no general Rule consistent with American, or British Customs, could be established that would not encrease the agregate amount of the Issues and therefore that it was better to submit to a surplusage in some Corps than to render the expence greater and the evil more extensive by adopting a limitation whh. would pervade the whole Army. especially too, as some of those Corps were, and still are, under particular circumstances." He gave as his example the New York regiments that carried Long Islanders and others on their rolls who had fled British occupation. After seeing the suffering children, and hearing the cries of the women and the complaints of the husbands, Washington took action. He said that the latter had justly remarked that their wives "'could earn their Rations [wages with which to buy their own food], but the Soldier, nay the Officer, for whom they Wash has naught to pay them.'" Washington felt the army had to provide for soldiers' dependents "or lose by Desertion, perhaps to the Enemy, some of the oldest and best Soldiers in the Service."[27]

Washington always focused on the welfare, mental as well as physical, of his men rather than their dependents; but because the latter affected the former, he made concessions. Officially Washington, as commander in chief and a public servant, stated (and associates such as Joseph Reed repeated) that families could not be supported on the public's or military's stock of provisions unless an emergency warranted it.[28] In practice, as a commander of and among troops, he took care of their (and thus his) retainers. After expressing his disapproval of the new regulation to Morris and telling him that he thought it "a right inherent, with Command to limit (as circumstances and the nature of Service may require) the proportion of Women to the Men of an Army," Washington decided to exercise that right. On 8 March he wrote Knox that because there were so many women and children with the New York infantry regiments he had been left with the options of either circumventing the new ration system or driving the excess dependents out of camp. The latter, he believed, would probably have resulted in men leaving to follow their families. He had therefore directed that all of the women and children then present with those troops could continue to draw rations as before. He then went on to add that as the artillery regiment was in the same situation, he would allow it, too, to proceed as before; "but as that indulgence was to remedy, and not to create, an evil, I would by no means extend it to Women who on the prospect of it, have since been brought into Camp; and I would wish you to see that no such do draw Provisions."[29] Proof that Knox passed the word down to his artillery regiments appeared on 11 March when the regimental orders for the 2nd Continental Artillery stated, "The women who drew Rations from the publick previous to the General Orders of the 28th Decem[] last, will again be entitled to recieve provisions for themselves and Children."[30]

Washington's direct intervention in that case was somewhat unusual. He usually tried to stay above the problem, especially in the early years of the war, and thus avoid taking a stand that contradicted official policy. Instead, he permitted his subordinates to take care of their retainers as long as they did so prudently and accepted responsibility for their own actions. In effect, Washington recognized that a state of emergency often existed but left it to his subordinates to make the decision to help in individual cases and to find their own solutions.

Pickering encountered the problem of reconciling policy with practice in a particularly difficult case early in 1781. That February he wrote to Colonel Alexander Hamilton, one of Washington's aides-de-camp, for advice on provisioning the destitute families of two men, Moses Dean and Hezekiah Gibson (or Gillson), in Colonel Baldwin's Regiment of Artificers. Pickering filled pages with his distress:

> A daughter of Gillson Lives with Mrs. Pickering; a little wanderer, a perfect stranger. Some time since she came unasked[;] when told by one of the Servants to go home, she replied "her mother had nothing for her to eat." Dean informs me that he has two other Sons (besides those now in the Artillery) who have served as Soldiers for three years. I enquired of both how they had subsisted their families in time past. [T]hey replied, that they had sold every thing they had brought with them ... even to their very Clothes: and that during the last summer, & untill Arnold's Flight, they had been allowed to draw three Rations each for their families. They said that Genl. Poor at first, afterwards Genl. Arnold, gave orders for those Issues, which the Commissary had stopp'd since Arnold's flight. Dean first requested a similar order: but it appeared to me highly improper that public Officers ... should at their option become discretionary Almoners for the public. It would open a Door for innumerable Abuses. Too many irregularities of the Kind have already been practised. Yet the forlorn Condition of these poor men demands Relief. But they are not alone. Hundreds of Soldiers Families are also distress'd. What is granted to one should not be denied to another in like Circumstances: ... I am clear it will be better to discharge Dean & Gibson than give them four daily Rations. But if we begin to discharge Soldiers to relieve their distress'd families, where shall we stop? ... As Cases similar to the above must frequently have fallen under your Notice, I beg you will inform me what order has usually been taken concerning them.[31]

Hamilton replied that "the situation of the two artificers can only be pitied not redressed. The families of men in the service cannot be the object of military provision, and it will be impossible to discriminate. This is the General's sentiment and has governed in all former application of the same kind."[32] Pickering apparently did not accept that as the only way to deal with the problem. In a letter to an assistant commissary of issues at Fishkill Landing, Richard Platt, a deputy quartermaster, wrote, "The Q MGenl. having agreed, in consideration of the Wives of Hezekiah Gibson & Elihu Cary, cooking each, for a mess of Artificiers, which superseded the necessity of two men being employed on that Business, that one Ration should be allow'd, daily, to each of those Women."[33] There was no mention of Dean and his family, but Pickering probably found a way to help them too.

Later that year, on 11 August, Pickering noted that the number of rations to be given to the families of the boatwrights serving the army in the Highlands was left to his judgment. He asked his deputy in New York, Colonel Hugh

Hughes, to determine how many adult and juvenile dependents he would have to provision and how much each should be allowed. Pickering was anxious not to give them too much, for he feared that they would sell or trade surplus and thus give "general offence." Hughes quickly responded, for just one week after his initial request Pickering wrote that he agreed to the ration allowance that Hughes had fixed upon.[34]

Army personnel confronted rationing problems, including those resulting from retainers following prisoners, at every level in the chain of command. Lieutenant Garret H. Van Wagenen, a deputy commissary of prisoners at West Point, wrote Lamb at Fishkill on 13 September 1779 that he would willingly supply a Mrs. McCarty with provisions as soon as it was determined that her husband was a prisoner of war. Van Wagenen said the delay resulted from the fact that Mr. McCarty had changed his story: he had first declared that American troops had captured him just before Burgoyne's surrender but later asserted that he was actually a deserter from the British army. Van Wagenen asked Lamb to question the woman for her side of the story. A day later he again had to write to Lamb because Mrs. McCarty had taken matters into her own hands and visited him that morning. She declared that her husband was a deserter from the British, so Van Wagenen told her that if that proved true her husband would be released, and if it was not, he would supply her with provisions.[35] Van Wagenen was the logical person to apply to in that case, but many dependents did not personally approach officers with their supply problems; they instead asked the noncommissioned officers for help. An example of this occurred in February 1780. Sergeant John Mnthorn [sic] certified that the bearer of his note, Robert Blowers, and Blowers's wife were each entitled to a two-weeks supply of state stores. Blowers delivered the note to Captain Mead of the 1st New Jersey, who, in turn, added his authorization and sent it on to a Lieutenant Darby, issuer of state stores.[36]

The number and condition of families with the troops varied considerably by time, place, and military unit. The Valley Forge return of December 1777 listed 400 rations for women. A provision return from New Windsor in June 1781 indicated that 137 women received rations, while another return in January 1783 showed that 405 women and 302 children were provisioned at or in the vicinity of West Point and New Windsor with, in what probably was the common practice during the war, a full ration for women and half ration for children.[37] Given the probable number of noncommissioned officers and soldiers at these places, the ratio between men and women at New Windsor appeared to have been approximately 26:1, and that at Valley Forge closer to 44:1. Over the course of the war, and acknowledging that some units may have had many more followers and others none, it has been estimated that the number of camp women equaled approximately three percent of the number of men.[38] Unfortunately, an inadequate number of returns and the unequal distribution of followers made an accurate accounting of these people difficult then and now, but they did indicate that they numbered in the thousands over the course of the war. Various notes and orders gave a better indication of the quality of camp life than of the number of those who participated in it.

The army's assistance to followers extended beyond rationing. It quartered them within barracks, huts, and tents; and it gave them both medical and legal aid. When the troops settled into barracks, space was allocated for their families. In winter cantonments such as Valley Forge and Morristown, commanders assigned camp women to the few huts set aside specifically for them. The army also occasionally provided tents for retainers when on the march or in more temporary encampments. On 17 August 1777 Captain Robert Kirkwood recorded his division's instructions for determining the number of tents needed. Brigade majors had to consult with the quartermaster on the availability of tents and then turn to their adjutants to receive a count of the men and women in their respective regiments. After that they were supposed to calculate the number of tents needed by figuring one tent for every two commissioned or staff officers, one tent for four sergeants, and one tent to six privates or corporals, as well as wagoners and women and others. Circumstances, namely, not enough tents, caused the ratio to be altered by 13 September. Each field officer received his own tent, but other officers had to share four to a tent, and everyone else lived intimately at eight to a tent.[39]

Followers in need of medical assistance received care at the military hospitals or were attended to by regimental surgeons. Occasionally medical attention was forced upon them, as when commanders desiring to halt the spread of venereal disease ordered that the women be examined and a report made of those found infected.[40] Usually, however, they sought care for other reasons. Mary Beaches was laid up with a fractured femur in the hospital at Albany in August 1777, Jane Herrin was in an unnamed hospital during August 1778 because of childbed fever, while the hospital at Danbury took care of two pregnant patients in the period from 20 October to 7 November 1778.[41] Military hospitals and surgeons treated numerous retainers, but an accurate count of the number of such patients and the nature of their illnesses cannot be determined because the doctors and institutions did not always indicate their patients' status in their returns. Although many returns did give names and unit attachments as well as reasons for treatment, others only listed disorders with the number of people treated, released, convalescing, or dead. In the latter returns, unless the condition was sex-specific such as pregnancy or inflammation of the testes, there was no way to determine how many of the patients may have been women.

Camp women who had been victimized sometimes had access, when their complaints touched on such issues as the order of and discipline in camp, to the military legal system in their search for justice and redress. A garrison court-martial at Fort Sullivan on 1 September 1779 found a soldier, John Emersly, guilty of "Stealing & Selling Clothing belonging to Catharina Castner." The garrison court sentenced Emersly to receive a hundred lashes, the punishment to be carried out in front of the troops, and ordered that half his pay be held back or diverted each month until he had reimbursed Castner.[42] The stockade's commandant approved the sentence, and thus this follower, Castner likely being one of the nurses or washerwomen allowed to remain at this forward post after all nonessential women were ordered back to Wyoming, received not only provisions but justice. Up at Fort Schuyler in 1781 a soldier in one of the New York regiments, Isaac Mott, pleaded guilty to abusing a Mrs. Moody and her daughter (possibly the dependents of Captain Andrew Moodie of the 2nd Continental Artillery) and for leaving his fatigue without permission. The court sentenced him to suffer fifty lashes on his bare back.[43] Female plaintiffs appeared to have been quite unusual; women more commonly appeared as defendants, although that too was relatively rare, accused of having violated officers' orders and army regulations.

Under Article 23, Section 13, of the 1776 Articles of War, retainers to the camp were subject to orders according to the rules and discipline of war. Noncompliance could result in the follower facing charges before a court-martial or, more customarily, facing summary punishment within the unit; officers frequently tacked on reminders of these possible consequences when they issued orders to followers. The army resorted to these orders in an attempt to prevent or ameliorate any negative impact the retainers may have had on civilian-military contacts, camp life, and army operations. The orders, with or without threats of dire punishment, served as a constant reminder of the army's jurisdiction over civilian dependents.

Army commanders strove diligently to maintain good relations with the civilian communities in which they encamped or through which they passed. They most especially did not wish to be embarrassed by the actions of their accompanying women, nor did they wish to be embroiled in quarrels or legal complaints that resulted from followers' misdeeds. Unfortunately, they frequently found their wishes ignored. On 16 July 1778 a general, either Washington or a division commander, expressed his indignation that some villain had dared to perpetrate horrible depredations in the neighboring friendly countryside. To prevent further abuses, the general ordered that no soldier or woman be permitted to leave camp except when accompanied by a noncommissioned officer, both of whom had to have a pass from the commander of their regiment specifying the time they left and the hour by which they must return. The general warned, "any Soldier or Camp woman found out of Camp, without such a pass to receave Immediately 50 Lashes, and 100 if found Plundering."[44] Almost one year later the army again received numerous complaints from neighboring inhabitants. Horses belonging to the army had cropped the harvest. As the army preferred to believe that horses "of them that are not allowed By the Regalation of Congress to keep any" were responsible for most of the destruction, the commanding general at Smithes Clove requested regimental commanders "to order from the Camp all those Belonging To women[,] soldiers and others not Inlisted within thir Respective Commds."[45] In August 1782 a garrison commandant, who may have been at Burlington, New Jersey, but was most likely at West Point, ordered stricter measures after hearing complaints that some soldiers and their wives had been plundering the neighboring cornfields. He declared, "As they can have no occasion to pass through the Corn Fields, they are strictly forbiden to do it in future: and such of the Soldiers as shall be detected in stealing Corn, may depend on being severly punished. The Women who are found guilty of the like, shall be drummed out of the Corps."[46]

The same commander ten days later "thought proper to direct that any Women who may be found with the Regiment after this information [order], that has not belonged to the Regiment prior to their arrival at this Post; and who cannot produce Permission in writing from the Commandant for his approbation of their continuance—may depend on being drummed Out of the Corps."[47] Quite a few officers believed that the best defense against problems was good riddance (to launch an offensive against the women and children in camp). Washington had tried years earlier to implement such a policy in August 1777: when the army was encamped near Philadelphia, he prohibited the admission of new female followers in the camp and endeavored to get rid of some of those already in place.[48] Such orders seldom resulted in a permanent reduction in the female force. Women ordered out of camp often returned.

As the army could not beat, either by drum or cat-o-nine-tails, all female retainers out of camp, it focused on preventive as opposed to punitive measures to regulate their conduct within its perimeters. It assigned them places and supervised their conduct both on the march and in garrison. Washington repeatedly ordered the women to remain with the baggage instead of marching alongside the troops when the army was on the move, and then constantly reminded them that they were to walk with, not ride in, the wagons carrying the baggage.[49] These orders were passed down the line. Kirkwood recorded orders on both 26 July and 13 September 1777 that forbade women to accompany the troops and told them to stay with the baggage. The former order added that none were to ride the wagons except those judged really sick.[50] It was not only a matter of image, important as that was to most Continental officers; there was a tactical reason for this as well. Baggage wagons encumbered the army's movements and were a major liability in battle. In the latter case the wagons, and supposedly the women, could be driven off the field and out of action's and harm's way.

The army saw the soldiers' women and children as ambulatory baggage and ordered them about accordingly. The army did, however, occasionally allow its followers to ride, on both horses and boats, instead of walk. In August

1779 the headquarters at "Quiletimank" (in or near the Wyoming Valley in Pennsylvania) issued orders to units leaving there by water commanding that excess passengers on the boats be returned to shore unless they had a certificate from their commanding officer that stated they were unable to march. Headquarters also informed regimental commanders to order such women as could ride to disembark from the boats and proceed on horseback. Women riding the spare horses would "Diminish the Number of Drivers taken from the army."[51] As it turned out, many of these same women would soon find themselves riding the river back down again. In another situation, Sarah Osborn was not that concerned about what the army wanted when she made riding privileges a prerequisite to her following her husband into the army in 1780. The next year, with her access assured by her husband's position with the commissary guard, she rode in the wagons or on horseback from West Point through Philadelphia, followed, after a short Chesapeake voyage (again receiving preferential treatment, for other women—for instance, the women of Washington's guard—were ordered to go round by land from the Head of Elk), by her alternating between horseback and foot on the march to Yorktown.[52]

Osborn was certainly one of the favored few, for officers also ordered women either to remain in a certain camp or to go to a different one when they felt their units were too heavily encumbered with women. They were most likely to order this when preparing for movement or action. When he recommended such disposal and dispersal prior to and then on the march to Yorktown in 1781, Washington was following the precedents he and other subordinate commanders had set earlier. Orders telling the Delaware regiment on 18 June 1777 to ready itself for the march also directed that the women left on the other side of Connell's ferry and the men left to guard the baggage be brought immediately into camp.[53] They would wait there until the troops returned or until they received orders to move out and join them elsewhere. The commander of Fort Sullivan tried to strip his garrison of all superfluous personnel in August and September of 1779. On 27 August he ordered all the women (who had just marched or, if fortunate, ridden up by horseback and boat from Wyoming) except those employed as nurses and those "Absolutely Necessary to wash for the Troops" to get ready to move again. He planned to ship them back to Wyoming where they would draw provisions until the troops returned to that post. Women who could produce certificates from officers stating that they were to remain behind "to take Charge of Baggage or for any other Necessary Purpose" were allowed to stay. The commander warned that no provisions would be issued to women who presumed to stay without certificates or proper employment. On the 28th he gave the word that two large and fifty-three small boats would set out that evening. After reminding the women to embark in accordance with his previous orders, he added to his earlier warning: women who endeavored to stay without permits would not only receive no rations but would be sent out in a later party of boats. After a few weeks, still feeling weighed down by excess personnel, the commander ordered, "The Invalids & all supernumery Officers that have no Charge of Baggage are to go to Wyoming as soon as Conveneant, all Woemen that are Not Absolutely Necessary as Nurses in the Hospital, or to Wash for the troops, are Also to Go Down to that Post."[54]

The one thing that could guarantee a retainer a place and provisions with the army was her or his labor. As one set of orders for West Point put it, "No wemen [though married and certified] Shall Draw provisions Unless they will wash at Such a Reasonable Rate as the Commanding officer of the Corps in which they Draw Shall fix."[55] This also illustrated what kind of labor they were expected to perform. Most eighteenth-century Americans preferred to see women working within the domestic economy, which could include not only the home but the family's fields or shop; however, they understood when economic necessity forced women to seek employment elsewhere. But such understanding seldom translated into more job opportunities or placement of women in well-paying, responsible positions. Women who did obtain the latter positions generally did so upon the death of their spouses: they managed the family business to support their children and then often handed it over to a son when he was of age to handle it. Most jobs available to women were simply extensions of the work they did at home: they cooked, sewed, cleaned, laundered, and nursed. And, if necessary, they or their husbands also put their children to work. Boys and girls, especially those of the poorer or middling economic classes, helped their parents in the home and at work, each within his or her gender-related sphere.[56]

The Continental Community mirrored the rest of American society in its utilization of female and, when using boys as waiters and girls as mothers' helpers, child labor. The army would have preferred to have done without women's help but found it could not. These people were dependent on the military, but the army in many ways also depended on them, though it offered little thanks for such support services. There was no glory in such work; because it belonged within camp and baggage train and off the battlefield, army and society awarded it little recognition.[57] Such work belonged to women, and men wanted no part of it. Nevertheless, when women were not available to assume these chores, or if they refused to have the entire burden shifted to their shoulders, men did learn to perform some of these tasks. Soldiers learned to cook and wash and nurse. In doing so they became part of a new military trend: from the eighteenth century on, armies first assumed greater control over and then internalized (or militarized) their support services. The role of followers and the importance of their labor declined accordingly.[58] Perhaps Washington's attitude against retainers was not a personal or instinctive reaction: it may have reflected his preference for a new, more military (as in controlled and professional) approach to support services. Unfortunately for Washington, he did not have enough manpower to perform these duties; he had to resort to woman power. As it turned out, the employment of camp women helped resolve a dilemma: as they had to ration most of these followers anyway, leaders found they could better justify their largesse if the women were actually working for their companies and regiments.

American commanders set their female retainers to work at a variety of domestic chores and domestic manufactures. Although it appears that it was not common, women did on occasion sew and mend military apparel and equipment for the army in addition to doing so for individuals. On 11 January 1781 a pleased Lieutenant Colonel Ebenezer Stevens of the 2nd Continental Artillery informed his company commanders that he had procured cloth that could be made into coats for the regiment. Interestingly, on the 16th a regimental order asked for an immediate return "of all the Taylors, and Women in the Regiment." The women were probably asked to help in the endeavor, but orders on the 22nd only mentioned that "those Taylors that have been returned, are to get ready to work upon the Mens Coats tomorrow morning." It was quite possible, for this procedure had been followed at other times, that the women cut out the patterns and left the actual tailoring to the men.[59] In April 1782 Pickering wrote to Peter Anspach (there was a clerk and paymaster of this name in the quartermaster department) telling him that he wanted Mr. Meng (probably Christopher Meng, a storekeeper with the main army) to examine the bolts of oznaburg cloth that had arrived from Virginia and pick out what was best for knapsacks and get as many made as possible. Pickering suggested that if Meng cut out one in the proper shape, "he could get some careful woman to cut out the residue; & employ other women to make them up."[60] Meng may have turned to camp women to get the job done.

A few women entered domestic service in Continental Community households. Washington had housekeepers, as did a number of other general officers. These senior officers, and their wives, hired camp women to attend to their household needs. Just eleven days before Arnold's desertion, his aide, Lieutenant Colonel Richard Varick, wrote Lamb, "The Genl. begs me to ask you if you can recommend a trusty industrious & decent Woman, now at the Point, to him, to be employed as an Assistant to his Housekeeper." The new employee's duties would include washing and other domestic chores. The laundry must have been piling up in the Arnold household; the general appeared quite eager to have her services as soon as possible. Lamb was asked to facilitate domestic matters again in December, this time for General and Mrs. Knox. A Major T. Shaw wrote, "I shall be much obliged if you will give orders for Chas. Proud of Lymond's company, and Wm. Sinnex of mine, to repair immediately to this place. The former is husband to Mrs. Knox's woman, and is intended to be annexed to the Artificers in the Park, *pour convenience de la femme*. The other is wanted by the General."[61] Domestic harmony reigned when both household mistress and help were happy.

Positions within a household were rare because there were not many true households in the Continental Community; the more commonly available jobs were those of cook, laundress, and nurse. Such positions were often of a more temporary nature as well; army units and hospitals hired women for varying periods of time: from a few days to months. Some of these employees were local women paid to perform these duties while the army was in their area; others were actually camp followers. Hannah Thomas, who may or may not have been a retainer, received fifty-eight pounds, two shillings, and sixpence in payment for cooking for twelve men in the quartermaster general's department during the month of October 1780. When some artificers gathered at Fishkill in 1782 to work for the army, they brought female relations with them. The quartermaster department paid a few of them to cook for the men. Sarah Parsell cooked for the wheelwrights, Mrs. Cregier performed the same service for the blacksmiths, and Mrs. Lloyd served up meals to the express riders. Parsell and Cregier received twelve days pay, at two shillings per day, for work done that January, while Lloyd worked from May through September at ten dollars in New York currency per month. Parsell and Cregier received considerably less than their artisan relations, but Lloyd's monthly pay as a cook equaled that of her hostler husband. There did not appear to be any discrimination in the wages of women cooks as opposed to those of men in the same position. Thomas Wright, a cook for the tent makers at Fishkill, also received two shillings per day for his twelve days of work in January, while Andrew Wear, a quartermaster department cook at West Point, was paid over six New York dollars per month for his services that year.[62]

Most women were not officially employed as cooks, though they certainly performed that function. Jacob Nagle recalled his anticipation of a fine breakfast that one of the soldiers' wives was cooking in "the camp kittle on a small fier about 100 yards in the rear of the Grand Artilery," and his dismay when an enemy cannonball, that September day at Brandywine, bowled through the kettle and its contents.[63] Sarah Osborn recollected setting up in back of the American tents at Yorktown and, along with other women, doing some "washing, mending, and cooking for the soldiers." When the food was ready, she carried the "beef, and bread, and coffee (in a gallon pot) to the soldiers in the entrenchment." Indeed, she heard about the British surrender when she was preparing to carry breakfast down to the entrenchments to the four soldiers for whom she commonly cooked. Despite her emphasis on her cooking adventures at Yorktown, however, Osborn usually was employed in sewing and washing for the soldiers.[64]

More female retainers found paid work as washerwomen than as cooks. They were a familiar sight in the military community from war's onset to its end, and commanders often mentioned them in orderly books and letters when they hired them, provided for them, and tried to regulate them. On 20 June 1776

Captain Joseph Bloomfield delivered a return to his colonel that included three washerwomen among the seventy-two soldiers, two officers, and at least one volunteer who were present and accounted for in his company.[65] Years later, in September 1780, another captain, George Fleming wrote his superior, Colonel Lamb, that

> I have been unfortunate in loosing Peter Young, by his taking a hearty draught of cold Water. I propose continuing her still a Washerwoman belonging to the Company, as a small recompense for her long Service & late Husband's, in case she chooses.
>
> David Cornwall tells me you will admit his Wife to draw Provisions, provided I certify she is a Washerwoman to the Company; if that will be sufficient, I willingly certify it, as the Man behaves exceeding well, and it gives me pain to think a Woman should want Victuals, when her Husband is faithfully doing his Duty with me, & it out of his power to help her.[66]

That November Fleming consulted Lamb about washerwomen once again. The army's experimentation with a new supply system had left Fleming perplexed as to how to provide for his laundresses. He had not known that they were to be included when the company drew provisions from state stores until Lieutenant Colonel Stevens had informed him, when he noticed Fleming's omission, that he had added two washerwomen to his return so that he could get the extra supplies. Fleming was happy to know he could get his women provisioned but said Stevens's estimate was too few by half. "As the proportion one Woman to Wash for ten, makes four the Compliment," he requested that Lamb change the number of his women to four.[67]

Officers and soldiers could pay these laundresses by the piece or they could attempt to hire women to do their washing for a set wage. There were problems inherent to each method. Overcharging was a common one when it came to piecework. The 2nd Pennsylvania Regiment tried to prevent it in the fall of 1778 by setting the rates that could be charged the soldiers (others made their own arrangements). Colonel Walter Stewart warned that women who did not abide by these regulations or refused to do the laundry at the set rates would be turned out of the regiment, and if they attempted to remain, drummed out, for he was determined that "no women shall draw rations from the continent in his regiment unless they make use of their endeavours to keep the men clean."[68] The problem was still prevalent elsewhere, however, as when Sergeant John O'Neill noted in February 1779 that "wash women belonging to y army" made a practice of charging the officers and soldiers extravagant prices for the work they performed in camp. Officers in O'Neill's camp also attempted to halt the practice by stipulating the prices to be charged. Laundresses, when soap was provided for them, could ask only one-half dollar per dozen (a dozen of what,

O'Neill did not specify); those "who will presume to Charge more than y price afore mentioned will immediately be ordered out of Camp & not to be sufferd to return."[69] In June a year later, after the commander at West Point ordered that no woman could draw provisions unless she did laundry at a reasonable rate as determined by her corps' commanding officer, the 4th New York determined what prices its women could charge. The regiment then revised those rates on 19 August 1782, while at Newburgh: the women could charge two shillings per dozen (large and small) articles if they used their own soap but only one and sixpence if the army provided it.[70]

Washerwomen may have sometimes outrageously overcharged for piecework, but if a man tried to circumvent that by making a woman a personal employee, people were liable to wonder why he needed private laundry service and perhaps wonder what else the woman was doing for him. A few officers attempted to avoid ruinous laundry bills by putting washerwomen on their own payrolls. Colonel Ebenezer Huntington exclaimed in January 1780 that because Continental money was so worthless, his wash bill exceeded his wages. He decided that it would be best to hire a woman to live in the camp to do the laundry for him and some of his officers. He knew that some people would misconstrue his actions, but he was determined to do it because it was cheaper to hire a woman than to pay by the piece.[71]

Although some civilians, male and female, nursed individual soldiers and then asked for recompense, the army generally did not pay for "piecework" nursing. It preferred to hire women and men, whether retainers or local inhabitants, to serve as nurses in the hospital department; and it preferred to employ volunteers over draftees, but, when there were too few nurses or orderly men readily available, it did resort to impressment. The Pennsylvania battalions at Ticonderoga in July 1776 received orders that one woman was to be chosen from each of their companies and sent to the general hospital at Fort George to nurse the sick. The draftees would receive the customary allowance and provisions from the hospital's director. Washington offered the same assurance at Valley Forge in May 1778 when he ordered regimental commanders to assist their regimental surgeons in acquiring as many women of the army as could be convinced to serve as nurses. The army did convince a number of camp women to become nurses, both temporarily, such as after battles, and for longer periods, as when the hospital department was especially short of personnel. One retainer, Jane Norton, the wife of Drum Major William Norton, recounted years after the Revolution, when trying to obtain a pension, that she had not only followed her husband throughout his service during the war, but had nursed sick and wounded American soldiers as well.[72] A distinction has to be made, however, between camp women who temporarily or intermittently cared for the sick and wounded with their companies or regiments and nurses who served in the hospital department. The former were retainers; the latter should be classified as part of that contingent of persons who served with the army.

Most female nurses who served with the army did so for money or rations, but some hoped also to contribute to the effort for independence. The latter had counterparts among the many retainers who did see themselves as patriots, even though their endeavors in that direction tended to be quite different from the idealized female patriotism promoted by many men, George Washington included. Although men appreciated women's domestic contributions to the war effort, many thought women should express their patriotism in relatively passive ways: by admiring the actions of the revolutionaries and by quietly enduring the suffering that attended war. Many women, however, preferred to express their patriotism more actively. Patriotic women not only practiced their civil faith in their domestic economies, they publicly stated their opinions in various gatherings and broadsides. A few women, whose actions later earned them the sobriquet of "Heroines of the Revolution," exercised their patriotism by acting as couriers and spies.[73] Camp women could and did participate in all of the above activities. Furthermore, like the men they followed, many felt that their very presence in camp was a patriotic statement. While they admired their soldiers when the latter did something praiseworthy, they too suffered and endured, but rarely quietly or passively.

Patriotic camp women alerted authorities when they found threats to the army's security. Some informed officers when troop unrest and dissatisfaction reached dangerous levels, and others thwarted outright conspiracies. A woman, acting on her own initiative, successfully frustrated a conspiracy in the southern army in 1782. That spring, as the army was encamped outside Charleston, the British bribed a Sergeant Peters of the Maryland line, who was also Greene's cook, to "corrupt" other American sergeants and soldiers. Peters and the British developed a plan whereby the conspirators would first secure all the officers and then signal a troop of British horsemen to come in and take custody of the officers while the sergeants marched the army out to where the British desired it. Peters then laid the plan before his conspirators. Unbeknownst to him, however, one of the sergeants' wives had followed the men and listened in on their discussion. She reported the plan to the general the next morning. The response was quick: "A Serjeant of the Pennsylvania line (who was at the head of the revolt in the Jerseys, in 1780) was immediately shot," and Peters was "condemned to be hanged."[74]

Women had played important roles as informants in those earlier January 1781 revolts as well. After hearing of the mutiny in the Pennsylvania line, General Heath had a camp woman mingle with some of the troops at West Point and then report back on their state of mind. Her information was inaccurate, but that of a retainer with the mutinous New Jersey troops was not. She disclosed their plans to one of the New Jersey commanders on 20 January, but the information came too late to stop the revolt.[75] Sometimes commanders employed retainers as spies, but it appears that most of the time women acted of their own volition.

Although it certainly did not fit within Washington's concept of female patriotism, some camp women chose to demonstrate their allegiance by assuming combat roles. Their doing so caused both admiration and consternation. Men lauded their patriotism when such women performed well, but then they generally tried to discourage other women from emulating their actions. The women themselves had mixed reactions: some of these women may have felt the need to apologize or at least explain away reservations about the propriety of such service; others may not have seen the actions as being so far out of the female sphere. There were times and places when gender role divisions in colonial society blurred.[76] Women in farming families sometimes labored in the fields, and women on the frontier occasionally took up a weapon to defend life and property from marauders. When armies maneuvered around each other and then positioned themselves for battle, they operated in what became essentially a temporary frontier (an area where different countries or societies—or in this case, armies—converged), and a troubled frontier at that. The women in that environment acted accordingly: they either fled, stood fast, or fought. When they chose to engage in battle, they did so to help themselves, their loved ones, the cause, and their country.

It may be impossible to determine whether most women following the army did so only for economic or family reasons, or whether they did so also to make a political statement; but the few who actually fought in battle did make a profound declaration of their commitment to the army's survival and success. Mary Ludwig Hays became the most famous of these women. Commonly referred to as "Molly Pitcher" in folktales years later, she became celebrated for her alleged actions at Monmouth on 28 June 1778. On that day Hays, the wife of Sergeant John Casper Hays, supposedly hauled pails or "pitchers" of water up to the soldiers manning their battle positions. When Hays found her husband lying wounded next to his cannon, she took his place and helped load the cannon throughout the remainder of the battle. Another camp follower known for her actions under fire was Margaret Corbin, who became known as "Captain Molly." When her husband, the matross John Corbin, was killed at his cannon in the battle of Fort Washington in November 1776, Corbin took over his duties of swabbing and loading the gun until she, too, was hit. Corbin, hit by grape shot in arm and chest, was partially disabled for the rest of her life.[77]

Anna Maria Lane never received the widespread accolades accorded the two Mollys, perhaps because she never recounted the exact details of her exploits in battle. Lane appears to have been with the army both as camp follower and as soldier. When her husband, John, enlisted in the Continental Army in 1776, Lane may have enlisted at the same time or else accompanied him as a retainer. Whatever the case, Anna Maria Lane, dressed as a soldier, first fought and then was wounded in the battle of Germantown on 4 October 1777. Her sex may have been revealed when she received treatment for her injury, but, if so, it did not result in banishment from the army. Lane, either as soldier or as retainer, followed her husband for the rest of the war.[78] The exact nature of her status remains vague: if she officially enlisted in the army, then her story is that of a soldier; if she did not, then her exploits illustrate the diversity of a female follower's experiences.

The experiences of female retainers were as varied as the women themselves. The majority of such retainers, and those of utmost concern to the army, were women destitute of home and funds. Their actions in camp and on battlefield reflected their desire, first, to survive and, second, to assist the organization that supported them and served their country. Few of the remaining women retainers to be discussed followed the army as a matter of survival or because of a need to help cause and country. Although a few officers' wives may have been with the army for the same reasons as those following noncommissioned officers and enlisted men, especially if they were refugees, most were there to enhance or express family solidarity and to create and take part in a variety of social activities. They were generally seasonal camp followers.

Most officers left their wives and families at home and then invited them to visit in camp during periods of low military activity. These men depended on their wives to maintain house, farm, and business while they were away and to report back everything that occurred on the home front. Some of these women administered everything themselves; others, with extensive holdings, supervised estate managers and overseers. When a woman could not do the job, whether because of accident or incompetence, the army invariably lost an officer. That was the cause of Lieutenant David Perry's resignation in September 1775: his wife had fallen from a horse and broken both her arms, thus rendering herself incapable of caring for the couple's "small & helpless Children."[79]

Even when their families were forced from their homes, officers generally preferred to have them find temporary lodgings with friends or in rented houses rather than have them follow the army from camp to camp. Lamb's wife and daughters became refugees when the British occupied New York City and some of the surrounding area in 1776. By February 1777 Lamb had them settled in Captain Robert Walker's Stratford, Connecticut, home. Walker, one of Lamb's junior officers, had graciously offered the use of his house as he had little need of it at the time. A few months later Lamb moved his family into rented lodgings in Southington, a town approximately twenty-one miles to the north of New Haven and esteemed for the fact that "there is not a single Tory in the whole Parish." Lamb had to move his family again early in 1779, but by October 1782, when Baron von Closen mentioned seeing Lamb's "several very pretty young girls" there, the family was again in Southington.[80] Considering that Lamb expended a great deal of time in getting his family settled and was away from camp on numerous occasions to visit them, they may have been less of a distraction if they had become camp followers. Walker, too, later spent some time away from his army duties in order to put his personal affairs in order. In April 1779 he wrote Lamb that he had married a Mrs. Peggy Brashier and would soon be setting out to Redbook (possibly Red Hook, New York) where he had left her so as to escort her to Stratford. He ventured the opinion that he did not like "keeping a wife at such a distance especially at the first going off."[81]

Other officers probably came to agree with Walker's sentiments about keeping wives at such a distance. Although Hester Hicks could have been in camp, it was more likely that she was at home when she engaged in the "infidelity and infamous conduct" that caused her husband, Captain-Lieutenant Giles Hicks of the 10th Pennsylvania, to seek a divorce.[82] Yet others may have preferred to keep their wives away. Captain Andrew Moodie may have wished that his wife were anywhere but in camp; Lieutenant Henry Williams certainly would have liked to see Moodie's wife elsewhere. On 30 June 1781 Williams asked Lamb for a transfer from Moodie's company due to the "eternal discord" within that unit. On 1 August he again tendered his request and elaborated on his reason:

> I am sorry to say I am Commanded by Mrs. Moodie & not him as whatever She says is Intirely a law with him. . . . the Other evening a Small debate happened between Capn. Moodie and me Concerning Cadets in hearing of her[,] who [L]ays in next Marquee to me[;] we both parted friends[,] and I went to my bed. [S]oon after He and Mrs. Moodie [had] High Words. . . . Curiosity prompted me to listen to ye discourse which was this. that Capn. Moodie was not the Man he used to be or he would never take such discourse from me and advised him to make use of his pistols which he ought to have done Long before this. . . . Since that he has been indeavouring in A Manner far below that of a Gentleman to Injure my Character.[83]

Economics and social rank defined which officers' wives were in camp, when, and for how long. The wives of junior officers with property generally stayed home. Although a few had resources to hire help to look after things while they were gone (or had an understanding family to do so) and to afford transportation and lodgings for a visit, most did not. The wives of junior officers without property either stayed with friends and relations who could keep them or followed the family's top earner just as some of the enlisted men's wives did. The latter case would have included wives of men who had been in the ranks until awarded commissions as officers. Even though there is not enough information to indicate whether Mrs. Brown was a permanent or seasonal follower, she and her husband, Captain W. Brown (probably William Brown of the 1st Continental Artillery), appear to have had sufficient financial resources to allow them some leeway in their accommodations. While stationed at Fort

Schuyler in September 1780, Brown wrote Lamb at Fishkill that his wife wished to lodge in or around that place until his company was relieved from its present post, and so he asked Lamb to assist and advise his wife as she settled in there.[84] In contrast, Captain Painter (apparently Gamaliel Painter of Baldwin's Artillery Artificer Regiment) needed to rely on the army's hospitality to house his family. Richard Platt, a deputy quartermaster, asked Baldwin "to remo[v]e Capt Painter & family to the Barracks as speedily as may be, in Case there is a Room vacant & no better provision can otherwise be made."[85]

The quartermaster department helped move officers' families in and out of the camps and elsewhere. Pickering personally ordered transportation assistance for a number of junior officers in the spring and summer of 1781. In April, after receiving orders from Washington, Pickering provided wagons and other conveyances to move the family and baggage of a Lieutenant Pepin, described as a Canadian refugee (there was a Lieutenant Andrew Peppin in the 1st Canadian Regiment), from Newburgh to Philadelphia. A few months later Pickering directed one of his assistants to help a Captain Bolter, who had been directing the artificers at Springfield, move his family from that post to Boston. Then, in August, Lieutenant Hoey (probably Benjamin Hoey of Flower's Artillery Artificer Regiment), who directed the laboratory at Philadelphia, wanted to bring his family down from Springfield. Pickering, obviously wanting to keep the supervisors of his various manufacturing units happy, obliged.[86] If only Captain Gershem Mott of the 2nd Continental Artillery had known of Pickering's helpfulness, he could have applied to him instead of asking Knox for help when the superintendent of the general-hospital refused to give him a covered wagon to transport himself, his wife, and their baggage to New Windsor from New Jersey that same summer.[87]

Senior officers, especially colonels and above, commonly came from prominent social and financial backgrounds and could better arrange for and afford to have their wives visit them in camp. The operative word was *visit*. These men issued invitations to their wives when they had settled into a winter garrison, when they believed they would not shortly decamp on campaign, or when they could find them lodgings close enough to the theater of operations for quick calls but far enough away to be safe. The importance of timing was made clear in New York in the spring and summer of 1776. Among the officers' wives who joined their husbands in the city that spring were Martha Washington, Catharine Greene, Lucy Knox, and Mary Morgan (Dr. John Morgan's spouse). But at the beginning of July they all had to be shipped off in a hurry because of news of the enemy's approach. When the attack did not immediately materialize (it did not come until the end of August), the women wanted to return. The whole episode led to a continuing argument between Henry and Lucy Knox that summer, which escalated when Catharine Greene did return and Knox continued to refuse to let his wife do the same. The general, in support of his position, was able to report that General Greene "told her & told me that he never was sorry to see her before but that he now was most heartily." Furthermore, Mrs. Greene had been sent off again. Actually, Lucy and Henry Knox had a number of polite but acrimonious discussions on the issue of visitation throughout the war.[88] Sometimes Lucy Knox lost the battle, as in the spring and summer of 1777, but she won quite a few others; she not only made some long visits when the army was in garrison, she became one of the few senior officers' wives who got to accompany their husbands during active campaigns.

The first thing an officer generally did if he wanted his wife with him was to determine whether the army was to stay in one place for a while; then he had to discover whether acceptable accommodations were available. Dr. Samuel Adams, surgeon to the 3rd Continental Artillery, made no mention of a visit to or from his wife, Sally, when he wrote her in October 1778. There could be no thought of such a treat in those uncertain and uncomfortable days: "Where the *Park* will Winter is unknown to me, should the enemy leave N.York we shall move immediately and I have it from so good Athority as *Genl. Knox's Lady* that if that event should happen, the Park will winter in *N.York:* but if they remain, the Genl. will *endeavour* to carry the *Park* to *Springfield* or *Farmingtown:* but if *Mr. British* does not go off we shall remain where we are, to wait their motions 'til very late, if not Winter here. [M]y mode of life is the same as when I wrote you last, my *house* a *tent,* the *gr[ou]nd,* my *bed.*" The next spring Adams wrote Sally, "Nothing on earth could afford me so much happiness as to have you & my little darling, with me, in cas[e] I could provide you with quarters in which you could be comfortable (and which I could easily do while we remain here) but how soon we may be ordered from here I know not, and the operations of the ensuing campaign are exceeding uncertain." He was afraid he would have to move out and leave her with strangers; nor was he sure he could support her in camp, be he "ever so prudent," in the manner to which she was accustomed.[89]

Other officers, refusing to be so long apart from their wives, managed to find suitable housing or, on occasion, allowed their ladies to join them even when the accommodations were not the most comfortable. Martha Washington, Lucy Knox, Catharine Greene, and "Lady" Stirling (joined on occasion by her daughter Kitty) were all at Valley Forge, where they got a taste of life in the huts, either for themselves or friends, until their husbands settled into better quarters. General Greene was quite good at ferreting out more suitable lodgings for his wife; before that winter was over he had moved his wife (and himself) out of a hut and into Moore Hall down the road.[90] He had done even better the year before when he invited Catharine to summer in New Jersey while the army campaigned in that state and adjacent ones: Greene arranged for his wife to stay at Beverwyck, the home of Mr. and Mrs. Abraham Lott, nine miles from Morristown and twenty-two to twenty-three miles from where the army was to encamp.⁹¹ Then in January 1780 Greene provided better housing for his wife than for his commander in chief. Washington was rather upset about it: there was not enough room to lodge comfortably the numerous members of his military family and the Ford family on whom they had descended. "Eighteen belonging in my family, & all Mrs Fords are crowded together in her Kitchen, & hardly one of them able to speak for the colds they have caught." Washington preferred not to burden Greene with the question of his accommodations beyond having his subordinate issue the appropriate orders and materials, but something had to be done. Washington said he did not blame Greene for the fiasco; indeed, he was satisfied that it was the person to whom Greene had delegated the task who was at fault; but he could not resist a sharp comment: "Far, very far is it from me, to censure any measures you have adopted for your own accomodation [sic], or for the more immediate convenience of Mrs. Greene—at times I think you are entitled to as good, as circumstances will afford; and in the present condition of your Lady [she gave birth on 31 January] conceive that no delay could be admitted—I should therefore with great willingness have made my convenience yield to hers, if the point had lain there."⁹² That was an unusual situation. Washington generally saw the ladies as adding to, rather than subtracting from, the meager comforts of army life.

The ladies did establish a semblance of domestic comfort and routine. At times, instead of sending the foodstuffs, clothes, and furniture that could make their husbands' lives more comfortable—everything from chocolate and coffee to candlesticks and curtains—they brought the goods with them, and they borrowed what they could not bring so as "to keep house in some taste."⁹³ Furthermore, they not only kept house in or near the camps, but a few bore and raised their families there as well. As mentioned above, Catharine Greene was brought to bed at Morristown in 1780. Lucy Knox preceded her by giving birth while with her husband in New Jersey in the spring of 1779. The prattle of these and the other children in the families could add to the other amusements already to be found in the Continental Community.⁹⁴

Besides cementing the family ties, these women initiated a social whirl as they visited among themselves and helped their husbands entertain. Senior officers' wives created a social, as opposed to purely military, circle of the ranking army couples. They attended and hosted numerous teas, dinners, and dances. These could be large, formal events or smaller, more intimate gatherings, and they by no means excluded the multitudes of bachelor (whether by lack of marriage or due to geography or other circumstances) officers. For example, Doctor Thacher recorded on 27 July 1778 that a Colonel Malcome (probably William Malcolm) from West Point, "with his much-admired lady, and several other officers, favored us [the gentlemen of the hospital across the river from West Point] with their company to dine." Then on the 28th the gentlemen of the hospital returned the visit "and were entertained in the most genteel manner."⁹⁵

Bachelors were invited not only because it was the proper thing to do, and because the hosts and hostesses enjoyed their company, but because camp was also a prime place to do a bit of matchmaking. Eligible daughters and young friends of the wives who lived in or visited the camps helped fill out the social scene. Alexander Hamilton found his future wife, Elizabeth Schuyler, at camp, married her in December 1780, and then took her back to his military family at New Windsor in January.[96]

Hundreds of gatherings enlivened camp life throughout the war and up and down the social chain of command: Greene sponsored a little dance in March of 1779; the new Mrs. Alexander Hamilton served tea at the New Windsor headquarters on 1 March 1781; and Martha Washington proved her hostess skills at the formal dinners given at the Hasbrouck House headquarters in Newburgh in 1782–1783.[97] Officers seemed to feel that the ladies, as they called them, added graciousness, gaiety, and color to whatever they attended and thus made sure to include them in all their planned fetes. As Washington put it when he ordered a *feu de joie* for 30 May 1782 in honor of the birth of the dauphin of France: "The Commander-in-Chief desires his compliments may be presented to the officers' ladies with and in the neighborhood of the army, together with a request that they will favor him with their company at dinner on Thursday next, at West Point. The General will be happy to see any other ladies of his own or friends' acquaintances on the occasion, without the formality of a particular invitation."[98] Military life offered the ladies with the army many pleasant occasions and social obligations.

Visiting camp also gave officers' wives the chance to meet and support one another. Martha Washington not only dispensed hospitality in her parlors at the various headquarters but facilitated group efforts and camaraderie as well. As they sewed, knitted, and darned items needed by their husbands and sometimes their husbands' soldiers, officers' wives could discuss the war, the army, and their homes and families as well as how each affected everything else. They needed that camaraderie. As part of the military community but apart from the military itself, they could feel included but excluded at the same time; as their husbands rode off with their comrades to their duties, the women met with theirs to perform their own. The support and sympathy that a woman received within that circle were particularly welcome when neither husband nor neighbors with husbands still at home could understand her sacrifices.[99]

The sisterhood continued beyond the confines of camp or garrison. When a woman was away from the army, she was likely to keep in touch with one or more of the women that remained. If that communication ceased, as it did for Anna M. Parker in 1779, the woman could become concerned and feel cut off. Anna Parker refused to accept silence. When she heard that Colonel John Brooks was in Philadelphia, she seized the opportunity to get a message to him. She asked him about the health of his wife and daughter and then explained why she even had to ask: "I have not been favour'd with a line from Mrs Brooks since I parted with her tho' I have repeatedly wrote to her; indeed I have not received a letter from any o[f] my friends at West Point since September.... tell me how you left Mrs. Brooks and where you left them that I may know where to direct my [letters?]." Mrs. Brooks was still at West Point in August 1780, where she had to take comfort in the company of other women whose husbands had left them there while they officered their troops elsewhere.[100]

All of these women and other dependent family members, whether accompanying privates or generals, were camp followers. The differences between them were a matter of degree, based on the magnitude of their dependency, social rank, and the nature of their time and services in camp. For some, following the army was a matter of family loyalty or social obligations; for others, it was a matter of survival. They were all part of the Continental Community, but those who looked from their spouses or fathers to the army for quarters and provisions were also retainers to the camp.

Most of those deemed to be retainers, the women of the army, were from the lower orders of American society and filled the lower ranks of this military community. Other dependent followers, however, represented the middle and upper segments of society. The ladies with the army were not retainers to the camp the same way the others were: they did not have the same economic and, as a result, administrative ties. The first group was more directly controlled by the army itself. The contrast in what was expected of both sets of women, and in the treatment accorded them, provides a clear illustration of some of the differences between the upper and lower ranks in American society. The contrast is heightened somewhat by the lack of a strong middling majority in this community: there is not the ameliorating aura of the numerically and culturally dominant middle class as found in the culture at large. On the other hand, a certain similarity is highlighted: in both cases the gender hierarchy was most definitely maintained.

Officers welcomed their ladies as diversions; they distrusted the other women as disorderly distractions. The former was a small group and rather easily controlled, but the latter group, numbering in the thousands over the course of the war, required considerable direction because they were potentially more disruptive and certainly more draining on resources. As it proved difficult to ban the women, and then virtually impossible to live without them, they were allowed to remain with the army, but only so long as they provided comfort and encouragement. The officers' ladies did this almost wholly within the private, domestic sphere through their homemaking and entertaining skills, but the women of the army were expected to give a great deal more and contribute to institutional comfort. They had to earn the right to quarters and rations through service not only to their families but to the army.

They did it. Men stayed in the service when they, or the army, could support (however meagerly) their families, and their families, in turn, supported them. It was not simply a matter of maintaining both a sense and structure of family and community in the midst of war. Family and community were dependent upon one another. Wives and mothers, endeavoring to care for their spouses and children, depended on the army for food, shelter, clothing, and, yes, ultimately country. The army depended on them, in turn, to help cook the food, clean the shelters and clothing, and act for the good of their country.

Notes

1. Thomas Hord, Winchester, Virginia, to Pennsylvania Secretary of State, Harrisburg 15 September 1837, Schoff Revolutionary War Collection at William L. Clements Library, University of Michigan.
2. Jan Lewis in *The Pursuit of Happiness: Family and Values in Jefferson's Virginia* (New York: Cambridge University Press, 1983), p. 188, noted how public life in pre-Revolutionary Virginia was almost exclusively a male world and it was only when the private sphere was glorified that women acquired a more significant role. With that in mind, it is interesting to contemplate how those in the military—a public, male world—promoted such a separation between that sphere and the one managed by women at home, and how, at times, they longed to leave the former for the latter. Allan Kulikoff in *Tobacco and Slaves: The Development of Southern Cultures in the Chesapeake, 1680–1800* (Chapel Hill: University of North Carolina Press, 1986), pp. 166, 178, 182, discussed patriarchialism and the duties of husbands and wives. Men were to perform civic duties and provide for their families; women, in return, were to manage the households. Men and women had these same duties in camp. For comparison, to see how another war affected gender roles, see *Divided Houses: Gender and the Civil War,* edited by Catherine Clinton and Nina Silber (New York: Oxford University Press, 1992). Of particular note is the essay by David W. Blight, whose subject, Charles Harvey Brewster, noted how camp and war separate men from women, and the one by Drew Gilpin Faust, who wrote, "Like every war before and since, the American Civil War served as an occasion for both reassertion and reconsideration of gender assumptions."
3. Linda K. Kerber, *Women of the Republic: Intellect and Ideology in Revolutionary America* (Chapel Hill: University of North Carolina Press, 1980), p. 47. Kerber, looking primarily at the home front, suggested that the cult of domesticity may have been a response to the war's disruption of family life. John Todd White in his essay "The Truth About Molly Pitcher," in James Kirby Martin's and Karen R. Stubaus's *The American Revolution: Whose Revolution?* (Huntington, N.Y.: Robert E. Krieger, 1977), pp. 99–105, disagreed with the concept of a battlefield domesticity; he said there was little distinction between male and female roles in the lower socio-economic strata, especially in the military environment. I agree that gender roles sometimes appeared indistinct there, but the attempts at domesticity maintained a separation.
4. Mary Beth Norton, *Liberty's Daughters: The Revolutionary Experience of American Women, 1750–1800* (Boston: Little, Brown, 1980), p. 147. Norton mentioned that widowhood and independent wage earning could alter a woman's perception of self and role, particularly as she came to embrace autonomy and dislike dependence.

5. Kerber, *Women of the Republic*, pp. 8–9, 19, 42–43, 85; and Norton, *Liberty's Daughters*, pp. 155–56, 167–68. Also see Ruth H. Bloch, "The Gendered Meanings of Virtue in Revolutionary America," *Signs*, 13, no. 1 (1987), reprinted in Peter S. Onuf, ed., *The New American Nation 1775–1820*, Vol. 1: *The Revolution in American Thought* (New York: Garland, 1991), p. 262. Contributing to "the public good," in *Pennsylvania Gazette*, 9 August 1775, p. 4, col. 2. Other examples of appeals to female patriotic contributions in the *Gazette:* on 19 July 1775 Philadelphia's Committee of Safety asked for "scraped Lint and old Linen for Bandages"; on 28 June 1780 the paper noted the patriotic subscription for the relief of American soldiers that was raised by Philadelphia women; while on 15 November 1780 and 24 October 1781 it again appealed for lint, linen, and bandages. On women subordinating their needs to the country's, the *Gazette* noted on 31 July 1776 that women in New Jersey and Connecticut managed to get most of the harvest in and that "many of them have declared, that they will take the farming business upon themselves, so long as the rights and liberties of their country require the presence of their sons, husbands, and lovers in the field." In John Frederick Dorman's *Virginia Revolutionary Pension Applications, Abstracted* (Washington, D.C., 1958–1959), vol. 1, there is a pension request from Elizabeth Adkins, the widow of James Adkins, a man who was drafted in Culpeper County in the spring of 1775. According to her application, "He was gone all summer and she had to plough and hoe his corn to raise bread for his children."
6. Kerber, *Women of the Republic*, p. 11.
7. Bloch, "The Gendered Meanings of Virtue," pp. 52–53, in Onuf, ed., *The New American Nation*, pp. 272–73; Kerber, *Women of the Republic*, p. 55; and White, "The Truth About Molly Pitcher," p. 101.
8. Varnum to Washington, Prospect Hill, 5 December 1775, in W. W. Abbot, ed., *The Papers of George Washington*, Revolutionary War Series (Charlottesville: University of Virginia Press, 1985–), 2:499.
9. Carl Van Doren, *Mutiny in January: The Story of a Crisis in the Continental Army* (New York: Viking Press, 1943), pp. 31–32; and White, "The Truth About Molly Pitcher," p. 103.
10. Joseph Plumb Martin, *Private Yankee Doodle: Being a Narrative of some of the Adventures, Dangers and Sufferings of a Revolutionary Soldier*, ed. George F. Scheer (1830; New York: Little, Brown, 1962; Popular Library ed., 1963), p. 169.
11. 20 September 1780, in Continental Army, Military Life, Diary by U/I Author, 21 April–25 September 1780, in Virginia Historical Society, Richmond. Author may have been Elias Parker.
12. Betty Sowers Alt and Bonnie Domrose Stone, *Campfollowing; A History of the Military Wife* (Westport, Conn.: Greenwood Press, 1991), pp. 2–3. They noted a military "caste system," and pointed out that a military wife did not stand on her own merit.
13. White, "The Truth About Molly Pitcher," p. 104. Benjamin Gilbert in recording his drinking and sexual habits pointed out those not only of other men, but of women too. Examples in Rebecca D. Symmes, ed., *A Citizen-Soldier in the American Revolution: The Diary of Benjamin Gilbert in Massachusetts and New York* (Cooperstown: New York State Historical Association, 1980), pp. 30–33.

14. Closen, 22 June 1781, in Evelyn M. Acomb, trans. & ed., *The Revolutionary Journal of Baron Ludwig Von Closen, 1780–1783* (Chapel Hill: University of North Carolina Press, 1958), p. 85.
15. *Pennsylvania Gazette,* 3 September 1777, p. 1, col. 1.
16. Myna Trustram, *Women of the Regiment: Marriage and the Victorian Army* (Cambridge: Cambridge University Press, 1984), p. 190. Although Trustram concentrated on the Victorian army, she did outline the earlier precedents for its military marriage system.
17. Walter Hart Blumenthal, *Women Camp Followers of the American Revolution* (Philadelphia: George MacManus, 1952), p. 60. Erna Risch, in *Supplying Washington's Army* (Washington, D.C.: Government Printing Office, 1981), p. 189, stated that when the war wound down and the main army declined in size, the number of camp followers also declined. I tend to agree with Blumenthal that there were more followers at the end than at the beginning; but Risch is correct in that when soldiers went home their followers did too.
18. John Rees, "'. . . the multitude of women,' An Examination of the Numbers of Female Camp Followers with the Continental Army," Part 1 of 3, *The Brigade Dispatch* 23 (Autumn 1992): 5.
19. Garrison Orders, Fort Sullivan, 26 August 1779, in Captain Christian Myers's German Regiment of Pennsylvania Orderly Book, 25 June 1779–29 March 1780, Manuscript Division, Library of Congress (hereafter cited as Myers's German Regiment Orderly Book). Heitman in his *Historical Register of Officers* records Myers as Meyers.
20. Rees, "'. . . the multitude of women,'" Part 1, p. 6.
21. Garrison Orders, Headquarters Highlands, 25 June 1780, Almon W. Lauber, ed., *Orderly Books of the Fourth New York Regiment, 1778–1780, the Second New York Regiment, 1780–1783 by Samuel Tallmadge and Others with Diaries of Samuel Tallmadge, 1780–1782, and John Barr, 1779–1782* (Albany: University of State of New York, 1932), p. 381.
22. Artillery Orders, West Point, 17 November 1780; Headquarters and Brigade Orders, "Cinksing," 19 August 1781; Regimental Orders, probably at Burlington Barracks, New Jersey, 22 May 1782, and Regimental Orders, West Point, 17 December 1782. These are in the Orderly Books, Colonel John Lamb's 2nd Regiment, Continental Artillery, 26 June–30 December 1780, 20 June–21 October 1781, 7 February–7 August 1782, and 27 November 1782–5 January 1783 in The New-York Historical Society's Collection of Early American Orderly Books (microfilm, David Library). Lamb's orderly books (with same title) in The New-York Historical Society's Collection will hereafter be referred to as Lamb's 2CA Orderly Book and differentiated by date.
23. General Orders, Headquarters Newburgh, 28 December 1782, in John C. Fitzpatrick, ed., *The Writings of George Washington, from the Original Manuscript Sources, 1745–1799* (Washington, D.C.: U.S. Government Printing Office, 1931–1944), 25:478, 480.
24. General Orders, Headquarters Newburgh, 31 December 1782 and 5 January 1783; in Lamb's 2CA Orderly Books, 27 November 1782–5 January 1783, 6 January–19 February 1783.

25. Paul E. Kopperman, "The British High Command and Soldiers' Wives in America, 1755–1783," *Journal of the Society for Army Historical Research* 60 (1982): 27; Orders issued by Headquarters White Plains, 25 July 1778, and Headquarters Fort Sullivan, 15 September 1779, as recorded in Myers German Regiment Orderly Book, mention supernumeries, men and women; the former put their number at 1 in 12 while the latter permitted them to draw provisions for a journey.
26. Hand to the Board of War, New Windsor, 29 May 1781, Numbered Record Books Concerning Military Operations and Service, Pay and Settlement of Accounts, and Supplies in the War Department Collection of Revolutionary War Records (hereafter referred to as Numbered Record Books), M853, roll 17, vol. 162, National Archives (microfilm, David Library).
27. Blumenthal examined the ration ratio problem and Washington's response in *Women Camp Followers,* pp. 79–80. Washington discussed it in a letter to Morris on 29 January 1783 in Fitzpatrick, *Writings of Washington,* 26:78–80.
28. Joseph Reed to Frederick Antis, Philadelphia, 26 May 1780, in Sol Feinstone Collection, David Library of the American Revolution, Washington Crossing, Pennsylvania. Reed said, "it cannot be presumed that Women & Children are supported out of the publick Stock unless on some special Emergency—in which the Necessity of the Care would palliate & even justify the Measure."
29. Washington to Morris, Newburgh, 29 January 1783, and to Knox, Headquarters, 8 March 1783, in Fitzpatrick, *Writings of Washington,* 26:78, 199–200.
30. Regimental Orders, West Point, 11 March 1783, Lamb's 2CA Orderly Book, 20 February–28 March 1783.
31. Pickering to Hamilton, Newburgh, 2 February 1781, in Numbered Record Books, M853, roll 25, vol. 124.
32. Hamilton to Pickering, New Windsor, 9 February 1781, in Harold C. Syrett, ed., *The Papers of Alexander Hamilton* (New York & London: Columbia University Press, 1961–1979), 2:555.
33. Platt to Mr. Else, Newburgh, 1 April 1781, in Numbered Record Books, M853, roll 25, vol. 125.
34. Pickering to Hughes, Camp [near Dobbs Ferry?], 11 and 18 August 1781, in Numbered Record Books, M853, roll 26, vols. 82 and 127.
35. G. H. Van Wagenen to Lamb, West Point, 13 and 14 September 1779, in John Lamb Papers, The New-York Historical Society (microfilm), reel 1.
36. Mead (noted as George on document file note, but name was probably Giles) to E. (probably Ephraim) Darby, 3 February 1780, in Sol Feinstone Collection (microfilm).
37. Most of the follower returns asked for in the orderly books did not survive; those that did sometimes appear incomplete or vague. These accounts and returns are analyzed in Rees, "'. . . the multitude of women,'" Parts 1 through 3, *The Brigade Dispatch* (Autumn 1992, Winter 1993, Spring 1993). The 1777 account is in Part 1, p. 5; 1781 return in Part 2, p. 9; 1783 return in Part 3, p. 2. Rees in footnote 2 of part 1, p. 15, shows evidence of women receiving a whole ration instead of the half ration commonly given British followers in garrison. As for children, orders for 2 July 1780, Headquarters Highlands, in Lauber, ed., *Orderly Books of the Fourth New York Regiment,* p. 389, command that "The Children of the non Commisd

offrs and privates will Draw but half A Ration sucking one to Draw no publick provision." For comparison to the main army, and computed based on one full ration per woman, approximately eighteen to nineteen women (perhaps less, depending on the number of children) were provisioned at Winchester Barracks in Virginia between April and July 1783. Given the possible number of noncommissioned officers, soldiers, and artificers there, the ratio between men and women may have been very close to the 15:1 ratio established by the 1783 regulations. First Virginia Regiment Provision Returns, 1783, Military Records Collection, Accession 24823, Archives, The Library of Virginia, Richmond.

38. Rees, "'... multitudes of women,'" Part 3, p. 3.
39. Division Orders, Headquarters Hanover, 17 August 1777, in Capt. Robert Kirkwood's Delaware Regiment Orderly Book, 1 March–21 December 1777, Force Manuscripts, 7E, Recl. 16, Entry 67, Manuscript Division, Library of Congress (hereafter cited as Kirkwood's Delaware Regiment Orderly Book).
40. Camp at Trenton, 23 July 1777, in Sixth Battalion of North Carolina, Continental Army, Orderly Book, 1777–1778, from The Collection of the Filson Club Historical Society, Louisville, Kentucky.
41. "A Return of the Present State of the General Hospital at A[l]bany," 20 August 1777, in Dr. Jonathan Potts Papers, 1766–1780, 4 vols., Historical Society of Pennsylvania; "Return of Patients in General Hospital," 20–27 August 1778, and "Return of the Sick and Wounded in the American Military Hospital at Danbury Eastern Department," for 20 October–7 November 1778, in Record Group 93, Revolutionary War Rolls, 1775–1783, M246, roll 135, National Archives (microfilm, David Library).
42. Garrison Orders, Fort Sullivan, 1 September 1779, Myers's German Regiment Orderly Book. Lewis S. Shimmell in *Border Warfare in Pennsylvania during the Revolution* (Harrisburg, Pa.: R. L. Myers, 1901), p. 106, mentioned the German regiment under Hand and its hooking up with Sullivan's expedition in July 1779. He noted that a stockade was built at Tioga that August and that a garrison remained there until 5 October when everyone started south for Wyoming again.
43. Garrison Orders, Fort Schuyler, 22 March 1781, in Lauber, ed., *Orderly Books of the Fourth New York Regiment* ..., p. 570.
44. Headquarters (no specific place given), 16 July 1778, Myers's German Regiment Orderly Book.
45. Headquarters Smithes Clove, 13 July 1779, Orderly Book of the 1st Pennsylvania Regiment, 24 May–25 August 1779, Historical Society of Pennsylvania, Philadelphia.
46. Garrison Orders, probably West Point but may be Burlington, New Jersey, 16 August 1782, Lamb's 2CA Orderly Book, 9 August–27 November 1782.
47. After Orders, West Point or Burlington, 26 August 1782, Ibid. The following spring Washington gave a similar order restricting provisions to followers already with the army, not to those who came in since the new system of issues on the expectation of receiving rations; at Headquarters Newburgh, 8 March 1783, Fitzpatrick, *Writings of Washington,* 26:199–200.
48. General Orders, Roxborough farm, 4 August 1777, Ibid., 9:17. Blumenthal mentioned this in *Women Camp Followers,* p. 64.

49. Fitzpatrick's *Writings of Washington* has numerous examples, as do other orderly books, of orders telling women to march with the baggage and stay off the wagons.
50. Headquarters King's Ferry, 26 July 1777, and After Orders, Headquarters Germantown, 13 September 1777, Kirkwood's Delaware Regiment Orderly Book.
51. After Orders, Headquarters "Quiletimank," 2 August 1779, Myers's German Regiment Orderly Book.
52. John C. Dann, ed., *The Revolution Remembered: Eyewitness Accounts of the War for Independence* (Chicago: University of Chicago Press, 1980), pp. 242–44. Washington to Lt. William Colfax, 7 September 1781, Fitzpatrick, *Writings of Washington,* 23:105–6.
53. Hemington (army on move from Princeton), 18 June 1777, Kirkwood's Delaware Regiment Orderly Book. On Washington disposing of women before march, see chapter 2, footnotes 83, 84, and 85.
54. Garrison Orders, Fort Sullivan, 27 and 28 August and 13 September 1779, Myers's German Regiment Orderly Book.
55. Garrison Orders, [West Point], 27 June 1780, in Lauber, ed., *Orderly Books of the Fourth New York Regiment . . . ,* p. 384.
56. Norton, *Liberty's Daughters,* pp. 137–39, children on p. 12.
57. Barton Hacker mentioned how women's work was both necessary yet taken for granted in European armies in "Women and Military Institutions in Early Modern Europe: A Reconnaissance," *Signs: Journal of Women in Culture and Society* 6, no. 4 (1981): 644. Although children probably had to work at times, there has been some evidence unearthed that they certainly played as well. Check Michael Cohn, "Evidence of Children at Revolutionary War Sites," *Northeast Historical Archaeology* 12 (1983): 40–42; with thanks to Lana Eisenbraun for passing this on.
58. Trustram, *Women of the Regiment,* p. 2.
59. Regimental Orders, New Windsor, 11, 16, and 22 January 1781, Lamb's 2CA Orderly Book, 17 December 1780–20 February 1781.
60. Pickering to Mr. Peter Anspach, Philadelphia, 23 April 1782, in Numbered Record Books, M853, roll 26, vol. 83. Anspach and Meng are noted in a listing of Quartermaster department personnel, 1780–1781, in roll 25, vol. 126 of the Numbered Record Books.
61. Varick to Lamb, Headquarters Rob[inson] House, 14 September 1780, and Shaw to Lamb, Ellison's (?), 1 December 1780, in John Lamb Papers (microfilm), reel 2. No Major T. Shaw is listed in Heitman's *Historical Register.* The emphasis on *la femme* is Shaw's.
62. Voucher for Thomas's cooking services by Sgt. Mark "Rodes," Philadelphia, 3 November 1780, in Letters, Orders for Pay, Accounts, Receipts, and Other Supply Records Concerning Weapons and Military Stores, 1776–1801, M927, National Archives (microfilm, David Library). Cooks and artificers are noted in Compiled Service Records of American Naval Personnel and Members of the Departments of the Quartermaster General and the Commissary General of Military Stores Who Served During the Revolutionary War, M880, National Archives (microfilm, David Library), rolls 1 and 2, and listed on "Pay Roll of sundry Persons employed in the publick Service . . ." in Revolutionary War Rolls, 1775–1783, M246, National Ar-

chives (microfilm, David Library), roll 135. Kerber in *Women of the Republic* mentioned a few of these people on pages 56–57.

63. John C. Dann, ed., *The Nagle Journal: A Diary of the Life of Jacob Nagle, Sailor, From the Year 1775 to 1841* (New York: Weidenfeld & Nicolson, 1988), p. 7.

64. Dann, ed., *The Revolution Remembered*, pp. 244–45.

65. Bloomfield, 20 June 1776, in Mark E. Lender and James Kirby Martin, eds., *Citizen Soldier: The Revolutionary War Journal of Joseph Bloomfield* (Newark: New Jersey Historical Society, 1982), p. 87.

66. Fleming to Lamb, with Light Infantry in "Engl. Neighbourhood," 1 September 1780, in John Lamb Papers (microfilm), reel 2.

67. Fleming to Lamb, with Brigade of Infantry near the Great Falls, 19 November 1780, Ibid.

68. Regimental Orders, Fredricksburg, 30 September, Headquarters Fredricksburg, 1 October, and Regimental Orders, Fredricksburg, 7 October 1778, in an orderly book of the 2nd Pennsylvania Regiment, in private collection and published in the *Journal of the First Continental Regiment of Foot,* IVth issue (October–November 1990): 8.

69. Orders, Milstone [near Middlebrook?], 12 February 1779, Sgt. John O'Neill Orderly Book, February–September 1779, Military Manuscripts Collection (MG7), Pennsylvania State Archives, Harrisburg.

70. Garrison Orders, Headquarters Highlands, 25 and 27 June 1780; Regimental Orders, Highlands, 29 June 1780; and Regimental Orders, [Newburgh], 19 August 1782, in Lauber, ed., *Orderly Books of the Fourth New York Regiment . . . ,* pp. 381, 384, 386, 610. Kerber, *Women of the Republic,* p. 56.

71. Blumenthal, *Women Camp Followers,* p. 63.

72. There are numerous examples of people petitioning the Virginia state government for recompense for expenses and labor incurred while nursing soldiers left in their care in Church's Virginia Legislative Petitions and confirmed in the Legislative Petitions themselves in the Virginia State Archives, Richmond. Drafting of women for nursing duties shown in: Orders, Headquarters Ticonderoga, 13 July 1776, Orderly Book of the 4th Pennsylvania Battalion, 10–30 April 1776 and 21 June–20 September 1776, Historical Society of Pennsylvania; Order of the Day, Valley Forge, 31 May 1778, in Sally Smith Booth, *The Women of '76* (New York: Hastings House, 1973), p. 171. A copy of Jane Norton pension application, dated December 1836, is in the Molly Pitcher Papers, U.S. Army Military History Institute, Carlisle Barracks, Pennsylvania.

73. Kerber, *Women of the Republic,* chap. 3, specifically pages 106 and 110. One such heroine was Deborah Champion of Westchester, Connecticut. In September of 1775 her father asked her to carry intelligence to Washington at Boston. Champion, accompanied by the slave Aristarchus, rode for two days, had a tight moment with a British sentry, but managed to complete the mission. Champion to friend Patience, 2 October 1775, Deborah Champion Papers, Manuscripts Division, Library of Congress.

74. *Pennsylvania Gazette,* 5 June 1782, p. 2, cols. 2–3.

75. Van Doren, *Mutiny in January,* pp. 190–91, 210.

76. A later but very clear example of the conflicting male reaction appears in Herman Mann's *The Female Review: Life of Deborah Sampson*, intro. and notes by John Adams Vinton (Mann's original, 1797; Vinton's, 1866; reprint, New York: Arno Press, 1972), pp. 118–19. Mann wrote this book to publicize Sampson's (dressed as a male, she had enlisted as Robert Shurtleff) military service. After extolling his heroine's virtues and resolution in particular, and women's in general, Mann said, "I cannot desire you to adopt the example of our Heroine, should the like occasion again offer; yet, we must do her justice." Sandra M. Gustafson discussed Sampson's struggle to resolve the personal and social tension caused by her straying from the accepted feminine role to assume the masculine in her paper "The Genders of Nationalism: Patriotic Violence, Patriotic Sentiment in the Performances of Deborah Sampson Gannett," at the conference, Possible Pasts: Critical Encounters in Early America, Philadelphia, 3–5 June 1994. Norton discussed the blurring of gender roles on the frontier on page 13 in *Liberty's Daughters*.
77. Norton, *Liberty's Daughters*, p. 174. She mentions how impossible it is to differentiate the motives compelling women to follow the army. For information on Mary Ludwig Hays (later McCauley) look at John B. Landis's "Investigation into American Tradition of Woman Known as 'Molly Pitcher,'" *Journal of American History* 5 (January 1911): 83–95, and William Davison Perrine's *Molly Pitcher of Monmouth County, New Jersey, and Captain Molly of Fort Washington, New York, 1778–1937* (Princeton Junction, N.J., 1937). For information on Margaret Corbin, see Perrine (above) and Edward Hagaman Hall's *Margaret Corbin: Heroine of the Battle of Fort Washington, 16 November 1776* (New York: American Scenic and Historic Preservation Society, 1932).
78. Sandra Gioia Treadway, "Anna Maria Lane: An Uncommon Common Soldier of the American Revolution," *Virginia Cavalcade* 37 (Winter 1988): 134–43.
79. Lt. David Perry to Washington, [Cambridge, circa 6 September 1775], Abbot, *Papers of George Washington*, 1:422.
80. Samuel Broome to Lamb, New Haven, 14 November 1776; Walker to Lamb, Fort Schuyler, 11 February 1777; Lieutenant Colonel Oswald to Lamb, New Haven, 8 April 1777; Maj. James Hughes to Lamb, Windsor, 13 July 1778; McDougall Orders, Peekskill, 2 February 1779; John Harrison to Lamb, Fishkill, 21 March 1779; these and others showed Lamb family movements in John Lamb Papers (microfilm), reels 1–3; Closen, 27 October 1782, *Revolutionary Journal*, p. 262.
81. Walker to Lamb, Greenfield, 16 April 1779, John Lamb Papers (microfilm), reel 1.
82. *Pennsylvania Gazette*, 29 November 1780, p. 3, col. 2.
83. Williams to Lamb, Fort Harkimer, 1 August 1781, John Lamb Papers (microfilm), reel 2.
84. Brown to Lamb, Fort Schuyler, 6 September 1780, Ibid., reel 2.
85. Platt to Baldwin, Newburgh, 19 December 1780, Numbered Record Books, M853, roll 25, vol. 123.
86. Pickering to Thomas Anderson, ADQM, Newburgh, 20 April 1781; to Pepin, Newburgh, 20 April 1781; to Isaac Tuckerman, ADQM, Camp near Dobbs ferry, 20 July 1781; to Colonel Hughes, DQM, Camp, 8 August 1781 (note: Pickering had written William Smith, DQMG, on 6 September 1780, to help Hoey's family move,

but apparently it took almost a year to do so); to Tuckerman, Camp near Dobbs ferry, 8 August 1781; all in Numbered Record Books, M853, roll 25, vols. 125, 126, and roll 26, vol. 127.

87. Gershem Mott to Knox, Mordham near Morristown, 13 July 1781 in The Henry Knox Papers, VI, 109. GLC 2437, The Gilder Lehrman Collection on deposit at The Pierpont Morgan Library (microfilm, David Library).

88. See letters between Lucy and Henry Knox (with ones to William Knox for further insight) written in July 1776; the comment on the Greenes found in 11 July letter. For following year's battle, see their letters from April to August 1777. In Henry Knox Papers.

89. Samuel Adams to Sally (Preston) Adams, Artillery Park at Fredericksburgh, 31 October 1778, and Pluckemin, 6 May 1779, Sol Feinstone Collection (microfilm).

90. John F. Stegeman and Janet A. Stegeman, *Caty: A Biography of Catharine Littlefield Greene* (1977; reprint, Athens: University of Georgia Press, 1985), p. 53.

91. Ibid., pp. 46–47; Nathanael Greene to Catharine Greene, Morristown, 20 May 1777, and N. Greene to Jacob Greene, Pompton Plains, New Jersey, 13 July 1777, in Robert E. McCarthy, ed., *The Papers of General Nathanael Greene*, Part I: 1766–July 1780 (Scholarly Resources, Inc, microfilm).

92. Washington to Greene, Headquarters, 22 January 1780, Sol Feinstone Collection (microfilm).

93. Lucy to Henry Knox, 19 June 1777, IV, 8, sending chocolate and coffee along with spirits, sugar, tea, pepper, etc., in Henry Knox Papers. When she got a chance to visit, the Knoxes borrowed some things from the Baumans, including candlesticks, bed curtains, pillows, a feather bed, etc., as noted in Bauman to Knox, Morristown, 8 December 1778, and Major Shaw to Bauman, 6 and 18 January 1779, in Sebastian Bauman Papers, Vol. 1, 1775–1779, The New-York Historical Society.

94. References to births and children included in Henry to William Knox, New Jersey, 3 April 1779, IV, 161, Major Shaw to William Knox on amusing "prattle," Camp in Bergen, 13 November 1780, V, 101, in Henry Knox Papers. For Catharine Greene and children, see Stegeman, *Caty*, pp. 68, 74.

95. Thacher, Highlands, 27 and 28 July 1778, James Thacher, *Military Journal of the American Revolution* (1862; reprint, New York: Arno Press, 1969), p. 140.

96. Examples of young ladies in camp include a reference to "a very pretty Girl nam'd Betsy a daughter to Capt. Lawrance" on 28 August 1780, [Dobb's Ferry], in Diary by U/I Author, 21 April–25 September 1780, Virginia Historical Society. Henry Knox to brother William, in late 1779, about Lucy being left at Plukemin with Miss Eliza and Sally Winslow, V, 22, in Henry Knox Papers. Alexander Hamilton's courtship of Elizabeth Schuyler is illustrated by his letters to her and about her, also that they planned to return to headquarters soon after the wedding seen in Washington-Hamilton correspondence of 19 and 27 December 1780, in Harold C. Syrett, ed., *The Papers of Alexander Hamilton* (New York: Columbia University Press, 1961), 2:524–26.

97. Blumenthal, *Women Camp Followers*, p. 88; Closen, New Windsor, 1 March 1781, *Revolutionary Journal*, p. 61; Martha Washington's dinners described in introduction by Alan C. Aimone in Edward C. Boynton, ed., *General Orders of George Washington Commander-in-Chief of the Army of the Revolution issued at Newburgh on the Hudson, 1782–1783* (Harrison, N.Y.: Harbor Hill Books, 1973), III.

98. Memorandum, Newburgh, 29 May 1782, Boynton, *General Orders... at Newburgh,* p. 22. The celebration was actually postponed to the 31st. Other examples attending or being invited to celebrations are: Orders, Newburgh, 29 January 1783, Ibid., pp. 66–67; Thacher, April 1778 entry, *Military Journal,* p. 127.
99. Blumenthal mentions the women gathering in Martha Washington's sitting-room to mend uniforms, sew shirts, etc., in *Women Camp Followers,* p. 86; Boynton notes that Mrs. Washington received female callers every morning in her parlor at Hasbrouck House, *General Orders ... at Newburgh,* p. 9. To compare the separation of spheres in the military community to that of the wider society, see Kulikoff, *Tobacco and Slaves,* p. 229, and Nancy F. Cott, *The Bonds of Womanhood: "Women's Sphere" in New England, 1780–1835* (New Haven: Yale University Press, 1977), pp. 168, 172–73.
100. Anna M. Parker to Col. John Brooks, ca. 1779; and Samuel Adams to Sally Adams, West Point, 17 August 1780. Adams told of "Terrible times with the women on the point, their husband's all gone & left them. Mrs. Jackson[,] Mrs. Brooks &c &c left to keep house alone." Sol Feinstone Collection (microfilm).

5

Retainers to the Camp
The Extended Family

> I had various duties assigned me such as the care of the baggage and the property of the mess.
>
> Israel Trask, servant/soldier
Pension application, 1845

Trask was a lad of ten when he volunteered his services in 1775. But was he accepted as servant or soldier? Years later he claimed that he was enlisted as a soldier by his father, Lieutenant Trask, who subsequently handled all matters related to rations, wages, and discharge papers if there were any. But the old man's recollections of his boyhood adventures show him used not as a soldier but as a waiter (a common term for military servants) to officers.[1] Trask's case was not unusual. A number of boys enlisted or tried to enlist in the service and then, whether formally enrolled or not, found themselves utilized by the army as servants. The boys worked alongside adult male servants (most of whom were soldiers), women, and slaves. Whether officially in the army or simply with it, all of these servants performed similar duties and ranked low in both the army's official and social hierarchies.

In comparison, there were the men who, like the boys, volunteered their services out of a sense of adventure and patriotism but who also hoped to enter the army's upper ranks. These men did not want to enlist; they wanted commissions as officers. Of the middling and upper orders of their home societies—some were foreign—they wanted a military rank that would reflect or even better their civilian social rank. They wanted to determine the nature of their service, not have others determine it for them; and yet many, especially in the later years of the war, had to act as supplicants. As such, and to prove their willingness and worth, they fought and labored alongside the men they wished to call brothers-in-arms.

The people in both of these groups—servants and volunteers—entered or remained with the Continental Community as members of extended domestic or military families. They were essentially dependents: dependent on the good graces, care, and commands of those in the army. They were retainers to the camp because they accompanied the army in order to serve themselves or their families and masters. Personal matters had priority; the army's desires or requirements came second. Servants and slaves saw to their masters' needs; if they did their jobs well, their masters could concentrate on military instead of domestic matters. Even the volunteers, most of whom were ardent patriots, concentrated first on finding agreeable positions before turning their attention to the fight. The army, through Article 23, Section XIII, and various other regulations and orders, tried to minimize any negative impact the personal concerns of these attendants and adherents might have had on military matters and maximize all positive contributions.

Private servants and slaves accompanying military personnel belonged to the army only insofar as they owed service to their masters. Their masters or employers established their duties and supervised the work they did within the personal or domestic realm. The army usually remained a secondary supervisor, only adding extra external rules to the ones already imposed on them by their individual masters; but sometimes the army's or public's needs outweighed private ones, and the army appropriated their persons and labor for its own use. At such times the army also generally ordered that soldiers serving as servants return to the ranks and resume combat duty.

As a secondary supervisor, the army tried not to undermine a master's authority; it usually recognized the primacy of the master-servant relationship. The exception to this practice occurred when the army occasionally impressed slaves to serve the army's needs. Even then, the army generally did not commandeer slaves serving military personnel; it tended to impress slaves belonging to civilians just as it did provisions and transport animals. This happened to John Turberville of Westmoreland County in Virginia. In March 1778 the army impressed a wagon, team, and black driver belonging to him in Alexandria to transport soldiers from Virginia to the Continental Army in Pennsylvania. As it happened, the army then detained his property for further public service. When it had still not returned the driver, team, and wagon years later, nor paid for their use, Turberville presented a petition in 1781 to Virginia's House of Delegates for restitution. Although he presented affidavits to support his claim, his case was weakened by the fact that he had not been present at the impressment and had received no certificate recording the seizure. The house rejected his petition.[2] If Turberville was not lying about the impressment, and the driver had indeed disappeared, then it was possible that the driver took impressment as an opportunity to gain his freedom, either driving away from the army after he completed his task or, after declaring himself a freeman, continuing in the military's service either as a soldier or as a wagoner in one of the civil departments. Then, too, the driver may also have died while with the army.

There is no evidence that the army as an organization ever owned slaves itself, but it readily accepted the labor of slaves on loan (whether willingly or unwillingly furnished) and then tenaciously held on to them for as long as possible. General William Smallwood once wrote the president of the Maryland Council to request that the sale of two black women provided for his unit be suspended. He said they provided a valuable service: they released soldiers from kitchen duty.[3] The quartermaster department also benefited from slave labor. When manufacturing armaments in Philadelphia in 1780–1781, it paid owners for the use of their black servants.[4]

In theory, if not always in practice, the American army acknowledged the right of masters to their human property. Military policy forbade the enlistment of indentured servants or slaves. Recruiters and other officers sometimes ignored the stricture when trying to fill their quotas, but it was always at the risk of being discovered and punished. The army looked equally askance at its people usurping the bodies or services of other people's servants for their own (as opposed to military) purposes. A general court-martial held on 8 April 1778 tried Lieutenant William Orr of the 10th Pennsylvania "for ungentlemanlike behaviour [in] conniving with Serj. Heine, in secreting stolen food. 2dly for countenancing him in carrying off & offering for sale a Mulatto Slave belonging to Major Shaw." It found him guilty of the first charge (the record does not mention the results on the second) and sentenced him to be discharged from the service.[5]

The army had to work on a larger scale to determine the status, and thus availability for service, of African Americans when it was inundated with black refugees at Yorktown in 1781. Whereas slaves could be made to follow the army, they were not at liberty to make that choice themselves, especially if they were hoping that following would lead to freedom. Nor could officers and soldiers employ the refugees if doing so was depriving the rightful owner of his or her property. On 9 October, after being informed that some officers had in their possession "Negroes, who have come out of N[ew] York," Washington ordered that reports of all such newcomers be made to the adjutant general. He guaranteed that militia and Continental officers found keeping such persons unreported and in their service would be called to "severest account."[6]

That was not the end of the matter; with the capitulation of the British, the problem of runaway slaves in camp escalated rapidly. Washington noted on 25 October that "many Negroes & Mulattoes the Property of Citizens of these states have concealed themselves on Board the ships in the Harbour, that some still continue to attach themselves to British Officers & that others have attempted to impose themselves upon the Officers of the french & american Armies as Freemen & to make their Escape in that Manner." To close that avenue of escape Washington directed "all Officers of the allied Army & other Persons of every Denomination concerned . . . not to suffer any such Negroes or Mulattoes to be retained in their service but on the contrary to cause them to be delivered to the Guards which will be established for their Reception at one of the Redoubts in York & another in Gloucester." He appointed a Mr. David Ross to superintend the internees and to issue those determined to be slaves passes that would enable them to return to their masters. African Americans who could prove they were free would be allowed to determine their own fate. Washington also mentioned that he wanted the officers who had reported, in response to the order on the 9th, all "Negroes in their Possession" to deliver them to Ross that day or the next.[7]

Washington's concern may have been due to the rumor that the British had sent a large number of blacks sick with smallpox out of Yorktown just before the battle in the hopes of infecting their besiegers.[8] A more probable explanation for Washington's close supervision in the matter was his profound belief that one of the army's duties was to safeguard the property of American citizens—he deplored plundering of any kind. Although he had begun to question the morality and the economic feasibility of slavery before the war, it was not his right or duty as commander in chief to deny owners their possessions, even when those possessions were human beings.

The American military's sensitivity over accepting slaves not only as soldiers but as followers was also a response to British practices and public outrage. John Murray, earl of Dunmore and royal governor of Virginia, issued a proclamation in November of 1775 that sparked outrage and controversy throughout the colonies but especially so in the southern ones. He promised freedom to all black slaves and white bondsmen (with rebel masters) who joined the British army. Thousands of slaves responded to that call during the course of the war. The British army made soldiers of some of them but utilized most as laborers.[9] Americans reacted with fear and anger, threats and closer supervision. They took measures to prevent slaves from reaching British lines and published warnings in their newspapers to be passed on to slaves and those who would help them. Papers included articles describing British mistreatment, including reenslavement, of blacks as well as promises of punishment for those found guilty of insurrection.[10] The 13 December issue of the *Pennsylvania Gazette* carried a 29 November report from Williamsburg, Virginia, that stated that blacks were already deserting Dunmore due to his cruelty. The article warned slaves and masters alike: it told the former that Dunmore intended to place them to the front of the battle lines to prevent them from fleeing, while telling the latter that some blacks had been sent to pillage the neighborhood. The paper concluded its account on the Dunmore/slave issue by reporting the fate of some African Americans who had attempted to attach themselves to the British army instead of remaining with their American masters: "Nine Negroes (two of them women) who have been endeavoring to get to Norfolk [to join Dunmore's forces there] in an open boat, and put ashore on Point Comfort, were fired upon by some persons in pursuit, taken, and brought here on Thursday; two of the fellows are wounded, and it is expected the rest will soon be made examples of."[11]

There were few if any comparably desperate flights on the part of blacks to follow the Continental Army, but then again that army's commanders were not making the same kinds of promises the British ones were. Of interest here, though, would be the fact that Sir Henry Clinton, in response to the American "practice of enrolling Negroes among their Troops," issued a proclamation on 30 June 1779 warning that African Americans taken prisoner while performing any military duty would be sold off but promising all those who deserted the right to practice their occupations within the British lines.[12]

The exodus of slaves continued. In February 1779 David Crane advertised a reward for the return of his mulatto, James, who supposedly sought refuge aboard an English ship in 1777 but had since left that army to lurk around Philadelphia. That July Persifor Frazer also published his loss: "Ran away about 14 months ago, & went into Philadelphia whilst the British troops were there, a young Negroe Wench, named PEG, about 20 years old, very lusty of her age . . . there is great reason to believe she is in, or at no great distance from, Philadelphia, possibly in the Jerseys, as she was seen last winter in the market. Whoever takes up and secures said Wench, so that I may have her again, shall have One Hundred Dollars Reward."[13] On 4 April 1780 Captain John Peebles of the British army in Charleston, South Carolina, reported that five blacks "came in to us having made their escape over the works."[14] A letter from Hampton, Virginia, published in the *Pennsylvania Gazette* on 22 August 1781 mentioned that African Americans were flocking to the British at Yorktown and Gloucester, where they "ease the soldiery of the labourer's work." The paper reported on the issue in a different vein that November: "It must inspire every feeling bosom with horror and resentment, when they are told, that out of upwards of 2000 slaves, who joined Lord Cornwallis's army, upwards of 1500 have perished from disease and famine. . . . provisions were only given to those men who were able to work, whilst the women, children, and men debilitated by sickness, were left to linger out a miserable existence. . . . Many were turned out in such a situation, that they expired before they could reach our army."[15]

The British also stole slaves (there was a fine distinction between American impressment and British stealing—the interpretation rested on who did the taking, who was the victim, and who reported the situation). Joseph Holmes Jr. charged in the *Pennsylvania Gazette* in May 1777 that "on or about the 10th day of December last, Anthony Woodward, junior, of Upper-Freehold, county of Monmouth, in the eastern part of the state of New-Jersey, came to my house, in said township, with others, seised on my Negroe man, two horses and waggon, and sent them into service of the British army." Years later, in August 1781, one of the paper's correspondents in Virginia informed the public that the British, in passing through a plantation about twenty miles from Richmond, stole fifty slaves, thirty horses, and all the cattle, sheep, and hogs and then burned the barns. The author was particularly aggrieved because the slaves, who had been placed on board a British vessel that was shortly thereafter captured by American privateers, had been awarded to the privateers as prizes. He thought there should be a policy change on salvage rights.[16]

Others believed that a policy or legislative change on a broader scale was required; they thought the United States should not worry about compensating owners for human property lost in the war but instead should take the opportunity to abolish slavery altogether. Some Americans agreed with the sentiments expressed by the author of an article in the 7 August 1782 *Pennsylvania Gazette*. They saw a contradiction between the nation's ideology and its practices: it fought for independence under a banner that declared all men equal and deserving of life, liberty, and the pursuit of happiness and yet kept some of its people enslaved.[17] African Americans were aware of the irony. Most had to continue to live with the contradiction because the majority of men with the power to free them either did not see or did not accept the contradiction. A few blacks, however, did use opportunities presented by the War for American Independence to escape bondage. Some African Americans gained their freedom and personal independence by aiding the British rather than the Americans; it was another of the war's ironies.

The evidence strongly indicates that there were more black soldiers and camp followers, as refugees and laborers (including servants), with the British army than with the American forces. This happened even though the British did not free or fairly treat all slaves. Dunmore's proclamation, for instance, did not apply to the slaves of those loyal to the crown. The exodus continued because British policy, flawed as it was, failed to convince Americans to change their own even more flawed practices, even after one state effectively raised a black battalion and individuals such as Alexander Hamilton and John Laurens advocated using slaves as soldiers. Rhode Island, which had had trouble filling its regiments with white recruits, had begun enlisting slaves by 1777 through the use of bounties to the owners and freedom to the slaves. Then in 1778 it mustered its black battalion.[18] Hamilton, obviously looking at the Rhode Island experiment, the successful integration of blacks in other northern units, and British policy, argued "that if we do not make use of them in this way, the enemy probably will; and that the best way to counteract the temptations they will hold out will be to offer them ourselves. An essential part of the plan is to give them their freedom with their muskets."[19] The American army could have become an instrument for social change. Unfortunately for Hamilton, his friend John Laurens, and others who thought like them, and certainly for African Americans, the angrier Americans—especially southern Americans who owned most of the slaves—became over that British policy the less likely they were to imitate it.

On the other hand, American and allied officers, like their British counterparts, continued to employ a number of African Americans as their personal servants. There was no threat to the social or political order in that. Washington's mulatto servant, Bill (or Billy), was a familiar sight around headquarters. Bill sometimes rode behind the commander at parades and accompanied him when he dined outside his own quarters.[20] Baron von Closen, with the French army at Newport in June 1781, mentioned how everyone, especially at the beginning of a campaign, tried to provide for himself when an army left garrison. He himself set out with two servants and four horses. One of his servants, Peter, was an African American who had been born in Connecticut of free parents. Closen described Peter at various times as good, faithful, and honest. While it appears that Peter was a free black, General Rochambeau wrote Governor Harrison of Virginia in June of 1782 that several French army officers, including himself, employed African Americans, some of whom were free and some not.[21]

American officers employed both free and enslaved blacks but seldom differentiated their servants' status when writing about them. Servants were servants, and they all "belonged to" a master, whether that master actually owned them or not. The military position that camp followers belonged to the army echoed this attitude. Officers generally saw their servants as members of their families as well as employees and ordered them about accordingly. They tended to keep a close watch on their conduct, but they also included them in certain pastimes and worried about them when they were ill. When General Hand found a wounded black soldier by the name of Robert, who was suspected of having British sympathies, repeatedly visiting his quarters and his black servant woman, he became disturbed. He had reason to be alarmed; after overhearing a conversation between Robert and the woman, Hand concluded that Robert intended to desert to the enemy and was attempting to seduce the servant to go with him. Hand confined him and then sent him on to Dr. Charles McKnight to be kept under close supervision until he healed and the matter of his loyalties was resolved.[22]

Colonel John Lamb of the 2nd Continental Artillery occasionally had servant troubles as well. In October 1777 an uncle, via another kinsman, sent him Jack, a black servant.[23] Jack was a prisoner of the British by the end of 1779 and then, upon his escape that December, became a slacker as he settled in with his wife at Andrew Breasted's place in Essex County. Breasted wrote Lamb in September 1780 that he had so little work to give Jack that the man did not "half earn his Bread" but that Jack wanted to remain there until his wife gave birth. He continued that he could not bring himself, "as they are both faithful Servants," to send Jack on his way without Lamb's direct orders. Breasted did say that he had repeatedly told Jack that he did not want him to remain "without his Master's Consent & Order'd him to acquaint You of his being here, but having not hear'd from you, and thinking the Letters he wrote you might have miscarried," Breasted decided to write the colonel himself, "as I would not have you think I mean to detain your Servant." What did Lamb want him to do?[24]

While Jack pursued his own ends, Lamb was left with Ichabod and at least one servant boy. Ichabod was industrious enough, but the boy was another matter. When Captain John Harrison wrote Lamb on 14 July 1780, he asked Lamb if he had received the information about his horse that Harrison had sent him in answer to an earlier request. If he had not, the boy who carried the messages "*est un Coquin.*" Apparently Harrison had had a strange conversation with the lad upon his delivering the initial letter. As the boy had been a stranger to Harrison, the captain had asked him if he belonged to Lamb. When the youth answered in the affirmative, he asked what had happened to Ichabod. The boy said he had "gone off." Harrison was astonished, "What! [W]ith Colo. Lambs Baggage[?]" The boy replied, "Yes." Harrison was left to think this "a Devil of an affair" until Ichabod showed up "and set all to Rights."[25]

Dr. Jonathan Potts, as he transferred from his post in the northern department and assumed his duties in the middle department, received word of the death of one servant and the movements of another. On 15 January 1778 Dr. Robert Johnston at Albany wrote Potts that his servant, Mike (apparently left behind because of illness), had died: "When taking Medicines to remove the Eruption he frequently went out, got Drunk & exposed himself to the Cold, which I apprehend were the Occasional Causes of an Inflammation in his Liver, the predisposing Cause of a total Stagnation in the Nervous & Vascular System; which was the Proximate Cause of his Death." On 16 March John B. Cutting at Carlisle wrote to Potts at Reading about transportation problems due to high waters and medical supply problems due to lack of money. He also reported that he had ordered Pott's female black servant to accompany supply wagons to Manheim. The wagons set out ten days ago, "but they were detained so long at the River that Madam grew tired and returned here again." On the 25th Cutting again wrote Potts, this time from Manheim, "I expect a fine Parcel [of volatile salts] manufactur'd at Carlisle, tomorrow, by a Waggon in which, Your Negro Wench was order'd to come hither." The servant woman was apparently being moved around so that she could clean Potts's house(s) and perform other chores in Manheim and Carlisle.[26]

Servants and slaves belonging to military personnel figured not only in personal correspondence but in newspapers, court-martial proceedings, and legislative petitions as well. For example, Andrew Caldwell advertised a reward for the return of "a Mullattoe fellow, named JACK" in the 23 May 1781 issue of the *Pennsylvania Gazette*. After describing Jack's appearance and character, Caldwell mentioned that Jack was "well acquainted with the country, having been two or three times at Boston, and was servant to Doctor Hutchinson when the army were at Valley Forge."[27] Black servants also appeared as either defendants, witnesses, or, when referred to as property, evidence in courts-martial. A brigade court-martial acquitted Anthony, "a Negro belonging to Capt Carter," of the charge of theft in December 1778. When the commanding general upheld the opinion, Anthony was released from confinement. In September 1780 another brigade court-martial tried a wagon conductor, Patrick Quilley, "Chargd with fraud in Exchanging a publick horse for a private one and selling the latter for a Negro Wench which he has as his own property." The court found him not guilty.[28] Although it appears to have been unusual for someone not of the officer ranks to carry a slave with him in the service, Quilley's case proves it was not unheard of.

Not only service in the army but service with a member of the military could occasionally lead a slave to freedom. When the armies faced off or maneuvered around each other, a slave on the American side could escape to freedom within British lines. Thomas Hughes's servant did that. Hughes, probably the Lieutenant Hughes who served with the 2nd and then 7th Virginia Regiments, petitioned Virginia's government in June 1776 for compensation for a slave he had purchased (at twenty pounds) to work for him as a servant. His slave, trained as a soldier, served with spirit in many skirmishes but then deserted to Lord Dunmore's forces on 19 January. The convention rejected the request for compensation. Another slave's service led to legal emancipation. Thomas Walker Jr. petitioned for the emancipation of William Beck, a mulatto slave, first owned by Major Thomas Meriwether and then purchased by Walker from Meriwether's heirs. Walker requested that Beck be declared free because during his servitude he "behaved in a most exemplary manner, while with him, under Colo. Charles Lewis in several Campaigns to the northward" and because Beck had also paid Walker his initial purchase price. Virginia's house and senate agreed to the request.[29]

The slaves who followed the American army were African Americans, but not all African Americans with the army were slaves or worked as enslaved servants. Officers also employed free blacks as servants and used black soldiers as waiters, and the army's staff departments hired black laborers and wagoners. Jehu Grant was most of the above. Grant ran away from his loyalist master in 1777 and enlisted in the service in Danbury, Connecticut. He was put to work as a wagoner, drawing provisions and other supplies for the army until winter arrived and John Skidmore, called wagon master general there (though probably a civilian serving with the army), took him as his waiter. By spring, when at his master's application he was returned to slavery, he was Skidmore's wagoner, having charge of his baggage.[30]

Black servants, whether free, slave, or soldier, worked alongside white ones and generally performed the same duties. There were, however, occasional differences in the duties to which they were assigned, especially when more than one servant attended the higher ranking officers. There may have been a racial dimension to these decisions, but they could also have been due to the training and experience of the servants so assigned. Major General von Steuben provided an example of this mixing of servants as well as a servant hierarchy in a 1779 letter in which he related his 1777 welcome to the United States: "My reception at Boston was just as flattering for me as that at *Portsmouth*. . . . Mr. *Hancock* took upon himself the provision therefor [for Steuben and his suite]. Wagons, sleighs, and pack-horses were procured for me; five negroes were given me as grooms and drivers, and a commissary to provide quarters and forage on the way. Since I had brought along from Paris only one valet and one cook, I engaged two Englishmen in Boston as servants, and made up my field equipage for myself and my officers."[31]

Both soldiers and civilians engaged in domestic or personal chores for the officers. Unfortunately, however, officers seldom indicated which type they were using when they mentioned servants in their letters (often carried by the very servants, acting as couriers, to whom they referred). For example, Major Sebastian Bauman wrote his commander, Lamb, in January 1783, "Please to let me know whether Capt. Hubble has been at Newburgh . . . and if, whether he has left my Subsistance notes with you, if he has, please send them to me by the Bearer my servant."[32] In another situation a few years earlier, Pickering wrote to a Major Willet, one of his assistant deputy quartermasters, to facilitate a servant's errand: "The bearer a servant of captain Rochefontaine waits on you with this request, that you will endeavour to obtain of David Spafford of Sharon (or whomever the horse shall be found with) Capt Rochfontaines horse, which the bearer is to bring to Camp. I have given him two hundred dollars new emission . . . to pay for the keeping of the horse & defray his expences to & from Camp."[33]

Such servants, whether carrying out courier or waiter duties, were often soldiers who had been assigned to the detail in lieu of their primary military occupation; thus they were not and could not be considered camp followers. Washington, however, did not like to see his military manpower diminished in such a manner. He probably preferred that his officers use civilian servants as he himself did. Washington was attended not only by Bill but by a household staff that over the course of the war included a number of civilians. For instance, Ebenezer Austin served as steward of Washington's military household between July 1775 and April 1776. His job included obtaining the provisions and supervising the cooking, cleaning, and laundering, among other domestic duties. When he decided not to follow Washington to New York, supervision of the household staff and accounts fell upon Caleb Gibbs, the commander of Washington's guard. But after Gibbs left headquarters for another assignment in 1780, Washington began a search for a civilian steward again. It was a futile search until he wrote to the Board of War and it appointed John Loveday to the position.[34]

These men directed the women housekeepers who had immediate charge of other domestic staff and tasks. During the transition from Austin's to Gibbs's stewardship, Gibbs simply gave Mary Smith large amounts of money with which to settle household bills. It was only when Elizabeth Thompson took over as housekeeper in June 1776 that Gibbs took over the payment of household accounts. This should not suggest that Thompson was less trustworthy than Smith. Mrs. Thompson, "a very worthy Irish woman," was apparently still seeing to the general's comfort at his New Jersey headquarters in the winter of 1779–1780. When Washington's table was reduced to rations and he did not have a farthing for extra fare, Mrs. Thompson asked him to have an aide attain extra bushels of salt for her. She then bartered the salt among some local people to obtain extra provisions for Washington's dining pleasure.[35] Benedict Arnold followed Washington's example by employing Catherine Martin, the wife of a sergeant major in the 3rd Pennsylvania, as a housekeeper at West Point.[36] But loyal black body servants and female housekeepers were probably the exception, not the rule.

Other senior officers made do with more temporary help and had more servant problems. Lucy and Henry Knox certainly had their share. In July 1776 Lucy asked her husband about the "boy that was mustered out of the regiment." If he was available, she wanted him sent to her, for the "negro is two heavy for the Horse [and] the boy I have is a soldier is anxious to go back to the army." She also mentioned another possible candidate for the servant's position. Henry answered by sending along a servant boy, with indenture and new clothes, by the name of Thomas Eliot. A few days later he assured his wife that the Dutch girl she left with him was behaving well, if the fact that his clothes were kept clean and in pretty good order was any indication. Over a year later Lieutenant Samuel Shaw, apparently acting as Knox's steward (he later became Knox's official aide-de-camp), paid Mary Lary for two months service in the family and for doing extra laundry for the general's brother William and for Captain Treat. Then in May of 1780 Shaw engaged a man to "serve in the family of Genl Knox one year from the date hereof at the aforesaid rate of 200 dollars per month." But by January 1781 Knox had to write his brother that the man, "who for some time past has been as an hired servant to Mrs Knox has gone from us—he was too knowing to be kept long. I wish therefore that you would be so kind as to engage a servant black or white of the following description—rather small in stature, understands how to take care of horses and can ride [postilion]—a good Cook—honest and willing to do any thing he may be let about."[37] Servants were supposed to relieve officers of domestic cares, but it did not always work out that way.

Many officers did not use—indeed, most could not afford to hire—outside help. The economic problem was a natural consequence of the necessity to build an officer corps which included men from outside the gentry. In addition to that, many officers believed they were entitled to military attendants as one of the perquisites of their rank: the use of waiters or batmen in European armies served as precedent. Having servants was not simply a status issue, however. Neat, sober, and honest individuals were needed to cook for them, tend them when they were ill, take care of their horses, and run errands.[38]

Washington understood both the need and desire: when a man was commissioned as an officer, he was also declared a gentleman, and a gentleman had to live in a certain manner. So when the commander in chief found he could not unilaterally prohibit the practice (there were a few attempts),[39] he tried to control it instead. Washington and other commanders wanted, as Artemas Ward put it in 1776, no "superfluous Cooks nor Waiters"[40] and so ordered strict accountability of the usage of their troops. In April 1778 commanding officers of regiments received orders "to be exceeding exact, to mention those offrs. in any Department, who detain any of their Soldiers as waiters or for any other purpose, and every particular circumstance relative to their absence, as his [Washington's] fix'd determination is, that he will know the true state of his army."[41] The 2nd Continental Artillery, as did other units, was still complying with that order in 1783: in its last return, in April, before it was partially disbanded and then reorganized as the New York Corps of Artillery, its muster roll of the field and staff officers and noncommissioned officers not attached to any company included not only the sergeant major, quartermaster sergeant, drum major, and fife major but Privates John Cumbo, James Brown, and Benjamin Chatsey, who were the servants to, respectively, Colonel Lamb, Lieutenant Colonel Stevens, and Doctor Tunison.[42]

Washington and others tried to retard the degradation of the ranks by limiting the number of soldier-servants allowed and by insisting that some of these men continue to bear arms and perform some of their military duties. Robert McCready noted on 26 October 1778 that the western department's commanding general, Lachlan McIntosh, had determined that, according to that week's returns, "above one 20th part of our little Army are employed as officers servants." McIntosh thought that excessive, especially as the having of servants was "Rather an Indulgance than allowd. and the men have hard Ducty between guards and fatigue." The general wanted his gentlemen to restrain themselves to a moderate number of servants, and to make sure that those soldier-servants gathered on the parade once a day to show that their arms and accoutrements were in order.[43] The same problem of juggling soldier versus servant responsibilities occurred in other units and other departments. In November 1779, because of the scarcity of men available for duty, Lamb asked his officers to "detain as few waiters as possible and order some that they have for that purpose to do duty in their compys."[44] Benedict Arnold, West Point's commander, ordered in September 1780 (before he fled to the British later that month) that "Officers on Guard, and fatigue are to take their Waiters with them, who are to be considered as part of the details." He thought it "shamefull and injurious to withhold their services from the Public."[45] A general, probably Benjamin Lincoln, commanding the Yorktown division of which the 1st Virginia Battalion was a part on 16 October 1781, reminded his corps commanders to abide by the general orders issued in 1780 that established the number and disposition of the attendants allowed officers. The orders, or regulations, permitted field officers to have two servants "not Carrying Arms," allowed captains to have one armed and one not, and granted subalterns (lieutenants) one servant who had to bear arms. Servants who carried arms had to turn out with their companies on every occasion but did not have to perform guard duty.[46] On occasion Washington too thought it important to remind his officers that their attendants were part of the army, not personal employees: "He perswades himself that it is totally unnecessary to signify that no retireing officer is at liberty to take with him his waiter be [he?] a soldier, or inlisted at the publick expence, but least through inadvertency such a thing should be attempted, it is hereby strictly forbidden."[47]

Orders issued at the Philadelphia headquarters on 18 and 19 January 1782 more fully established the army's policies on soldier-servants. It tried to limit their use to officers of the line. On the 18th the general ordered that in the future "no Person belonging to the Civil Staff, be permitted to take a Soldier as a servant: and that those Gentlemen in that Department, who now have such, return them to their respective Regts. or Corps, on or before the first day of April next, by which time he hopes they will be able to provide themselves otherwise, without Inconvenience." Washington then asked his corps commanders to attend to that order and, furthermore, recall all men who were absent without proper authority, "especially those with Officers who have retired from the service." The next day's orders informed corps and regimental commanders that they were not to provide servants or wagoners in the future unless expressly ordered to by the commander in chief or the commanding officer of the army to which they were attached. The orders then spelled out the new, limited, allowances for "Officers actually belonging to Regts. or Corps and serving with them." Colonels in the infantry, artillery, and all corps serving on foot could have two servants without arms from their respective corps. Lieutenant colonels and majors were also allowed two servants each, but one had to bear arms. Captains, subalterns, and surgeons and their mates were each permitted to employ one servant who also bore arms. Field officers in the cavalry were allowed two servants each; their servants did not have to bear arms, but they did not receive public horses either. Captains, subalterns, surgeons, and mates received one each, without arms or public horses. Each of the field officers could take one servant with them on furlough, but no one else could take one from his regiment for any reason. Nor could any officer or doctor use a convalescent from the hospitals as a servant.[48]

Then, to take care of the officers who were not in the regiments, the new regulations allowed the general and military staff and "Officers not belonging to Corps" to have servants in the following proportions: major and brigadier generals could each have four and colonels two; lieutenant colonels down to captains, aides-de-camp, and brigade majors could employ one each. When they could not obtain these servants by any other means, they could take them from the army and have them counted as servants "without arms."[49]

Servants carrying arms were exempt from sentry duty and other camp chores but had to appear under arms when their regiment paraded. They also had to mount guard with the officer whom they served. In contrast, servants without arms were "never to appear in Rank or File except at the Inspection." Quite possibly, the individuals so detailed were younger males and black males, those considered less skilled or desirable as soldiers. Enlisted men detailed as servants without arms essentially became servants first, soldiers second. Finally, the regulations stated that when a regiment marched out but left its camp standing, one servant to each company was permitted to remain behind. When a camp disbanded, and the baggage was loaded, all servants were required to join their regiments.[50]

Some officers obeyed the various regulations over the course of the war; others worked around them. Lieutenant Isaac Guion, who had just assumed the additional duties of paymaster for the 2nd Continental Artillery, wrote Lamb about pay and clothing allowances in September 1779. He then asked to be allowed to remain with the artillery park at New Windsor instead of being shipped off elsewhere. He explained that as his quarters were there, a move would create many difficulties for him: "first the want of a Waiter, as I shall have to leave the one I now have, & in my Absence from Camp There'l be no one to take care of my tent & Clothes—likewise forage for my horse"; but he assured Lamb, "I shall be ever ready to my duty from this place." Lieutenant Colonel Richard Varick, an aide-de-camp to Arnold at West Point, wrote to Lamb, who was also at the post in August 1780, that he was "much in want of a Boy" but did not have it in his power to procure a suitable servant. He thought he had the solution, though he presented it rather confusingly, when he wrote, "The Bearer or his Companion a Negro Boy of Tom Ludlow is disposed to inlist in the service for the war. I shall be very happy if You will inlist him & permit me to have as a Servant. The only present Objection thereto is his not being furnished with under Clothes. I hope that Deficiency can be remedied."[51] Varick could have been asking for either the bearer or his companion, but the likelihood is that both men wished to enlist, and Varick wanted Lamb to accept the black recruit as well as the white one and then send him back to Varick.

Timothy Pickering was quite sensitive to the issue of staff officers using soldiers as servants. When Colonel Hughes sent on a boy he had procured from General McDougall to serve Pickering's wife, the quartermaster general thanked him for his thoughtfulness and then explained why he could not accept the gift: "I cannot consent that a servant for my *private family* [as opposed to his military family] be taken from the army. *Groundless* reproaches (and they do not seem to be wanting) I can bear almost without complaining: but I should be mortified with a charge of *public abuse* were I conscious of giving any colour for it."[52] Pickering wanted the servant either returned to West Point or sent to the hospital, wherever he could serve best. It was sometimes difficult enough to justify the use of soldiers as servants to military personnel, but to justify the use of one by a camp follower (as Mrs. Pickering then was) was almost impossible.

Servants, their numbers and use, were an issue throughout the war because they were a public expense. If they were soldiers, they received pay, provisions, and clothing; if they were civilian servants, the army still allocated provisions and clothing, or in 1783 a subsistence allowance, for their upkeep. Pickering tried to explain this to the contractor firm of Comfort Sands and Company in January 1782:

> By your issueing only part of the provisions ordered on Colo. Lutterloh's last return, I supposed you thought no allowance was to be made for servants. But surely Officers who procure their own servants, & pay & clothe them at their own expence, may much more reasonably demand an allowance of provisions for them, than those who take soldiers from the line: yet the latter as *soldiers* cannot be denied. However to remove all doubts I have proposed to the secretary at war that provisions should be allowed to servants enumerated in the inclosed list, and the conditions therin mentioned, to which you will observe, he [h]as agreed.[53]

General Greene in South Carolina that September showed that officers did not necessarily even have to clothe their personal servants. To establish his army's clothing needs, Greene ordered the regimental clothiers to obtain certificates from the proper authorities detailing the number of men mustered, those who had since died and those who had since joined, and "the number of Servants, belonging to Officers, who are not mustered as Soldiers, and are entitled to Clothing." After those numbers were tallied, appropriate deductions were to be made for personnel in the wagon department, Captain Wilmot's detachment, and for all who had left on furlough "either as Bat Men or Servants to Officers."[54]

When the army regulated the number of servants "not carrying arms," it determined not only how many soldiers could be so detailed but how many personal servants could legally be provided for by the army. Officers put such attendants on provision and clothing rolls or, under the new regulations effective in January 1783, provided for them themselves with the subsistence allowance given them for that purpose.[55] So when regulations allowed an officer one or more unarmed servants, and that officer utilized civilians instead of soldiers in that role, he could in all propriety request (for most of the war) that the army provision his private servants as it would have provisioned "government-issue" ones. Indeed, the numerous orders suggest that many officers went beyond propriety and requested (and received) provisions for unauthorized servants as well.

Authorized or unauthorized, thousands of people appear to have served in or with the army as servants. Although many, if not most, of the servants were actually in the military, a great many others qualify as civilian retainers to the camp. Some, like James Anderson (alias Asher Crocket), followed the army as officers' servants until they were old enough or big enough to enlist. Anderson was about sixteen years of age when he ran away from his master in Hampshire County, Virginia, and fell in with the Continental Army. He followed the army into Pennsylvania and New Jersey and stayed with it for two years while serving in the capacity of camp boy and waiter. When, upon his return to Hampshire County, his master attempted to reclaim him, Anderson turned to the army once again. He first tried to substitute for a draftee but was rejected because of his size. He was, however, then allowed to enlist on his own account.[56] Numbering perhaps more than the juvenile males, African Americans comprised the other major servant group. Black slaves and servants either followed their masters to war or were provided by other individuals and organizations to serve the men who served the country. A few women, black and white, and a few adult white males followed the army in the capacity of servants as well. These civilian servants with the military were often people deemed ineligible or undesirable for service in the army but acceptable for service with it.

***

Some individuals who were certainly eligible for military service followed the army in pursuit of preferment because they deemed themselves to be desirable acquisitions and wanted to be recognized and treated as such. Others, less focused on glory and money, like "Mr. Wendell who was of a very genteel family in Boston," became volunteers out of principle[57] or because they wished to retain some measure of independence while serving country and cause. These civilians, for varying lengths of time, lived, worked, and fought alongside their commissioned brethren. As volunteers, the gentlemen accompanying the army without a commission or appointment qualified as retainers. Whether in search of a commission or just proffering aid in a particular situation, they occupied a category somewhat similar to that filled by the family followers of most officers: they were typically of the same class, were not by oath or pay bound to the army, but had to obey regulations pertaining to camp conduct and security. They, like other retainers, followed the army in order to fulfill personal needs or responsibilities; but, unlike the visitors who sometimes swarmed into camps and the many retainers who stayed on the sidelines, they entered camp "not as Spectators, but with a View of Joining the Army & being Active during the Campaign."[58] Retainer-volunteers pursued adventure, honor, and, usually, rank. They accompanied the army in battle, on the march, and into camp, unlike neighborhood volunteers who turned out to defend local territory and then went home. Retainer-volunteers also should not be confused with the men who volunteered to be soldiers and were also occasionally referred to as volunteers. Men who entered the camps so as to enlist seldom experienced much of a delay between their offer and the army's acceptance. Thus they did not have to, nor did they generally offer to, work or fight gratis while waiting for an acceptable appointment (though they often complained, with reason, that they were working for nothing after enlisting).

Gentlemen who wanted a commission had to find a vacancy in one of the army's regiments or departments first. The army did not automatically commission all suitable candidates and then try to find them positions. State control and department politics precluded such an arrangement. States wanted to see their own citizens commanding state regiments. Since they helped pay for these regiments, either in money or provisions, they could insist on it. Civil department chiefs also guarded their right to screen and appoint candidates within their areas. As a result, both American and foreign applicants descended on various regimental, departmental, and higher headquarters, with letters of recommendation in hand, to scout out the situation and present their qualifications. While they waited for a response, many stayed in camp in order to make contacts, perhaps attach themselves to a particular commander or military family, demonstrate their potential, and participate in upcoming military actions. Both Matthias Ogden and Aaron Burr, after being recommended to Washington by John Hancock in July 1775, served as volunteers during Arnold's Quebec campaign in the fall and winter of 1775. They proved themselves to be capable young men. Ogden received a lieutenant colonel's commission in the 1st New Jersey in March 1776. Burr served on Washington's staff for a while that spring and then became an aide to General Israel Putnam. In January 1777 Burr left staff duty to accept a lieutenant colonelcy in Malcolm's Additional Continental Regiment.[59]

Most petitioner-volunteers were young men in search of entry-level positions. Many first approached the units they wished to join. Isaac Bangs was one such applicant. He had served for about two months as a lieutenant in Captain Benjamin Godfrey's company in Colonel Cary's militia regiment. Then, when that militia's time had expired but his desire to serve had not, he cast about for a lieutenant's vacancy. He found both it and officers who supported his candidacy in Colonel John Bailey's 23rd Infantry. On 1 April 1776 Bangs traveled with Lieutenant Colonel John Jacobs from Roxbury to Cambridge to get the general's approval. Needless to say, they "found the Genl. very busie in wrighting dispatches, &c., that he could not attend to Buisness of such small Consequences; but upon Agt. Genl. Gates Promise of my having a Commission if I would follow the Army, I concluded to do it if I had the advice of Coln. Baily." Bailey assured him that he "should be as well used as if Time had permitted the Genl. to have given me a Commission." Bangs spent the evening writing his friends of his decision and then the next morning set out to join the regiment. He caught up with the company with which he was to do service and traveled down with it to New York City, where, on the 20th, he received his commission.[60] Bangs's jaunt as a volunteer was short; others found the route to a commission both longer and more difficult.

If no position was available, sympathetic commanders often referred them to neighboring or higher headquarters for information on vacancies in other units. Washington received a great many of these referrals, especially at the beginning of the war. Inundated as he was with strategy sessions and paperwork, he begged his subordinates to stop the flood of applicants before it reached his door. He was willing to advance the careers of a select few, but he did not want to deal with those unknown to him or to trusted colleagues. In December 1775 he wrote Lieutenant Colonel Joseph Reed, his military secretary at the time, "At the sametime that I thank you for stopping visitors in search of preferment, it will give me pleasure to shew Civilities to others of your recommendation—Indeed no Gentleman that is not well known, ought to come here with out Letters of Introduction, as it puts me in an aukward Situation with respect to my Conduct towards them."[61]

By that time Washington was weary of dealing with all the petitioners: he had been responding to their pleas and those of the men who had recommended them since July. Among the many he helped were John Grizzage Frazer, a fellow Virginian who owed him money and had come recommended by Patrick Henry, and George Lewis, who had accompanied Martha Washington on her journey to Cambridge that November. He had tried to help Anthony Walton White, an applicant recommended by George Clinton in Congress, but when he could not give White (who had lingered in Cambridge for months) a coveted aide-de-camp position, he advised him to go to New Jersey and seek an appointment in one of the two battalions being raised there. Washington's recommendation proved a good one: White became lieutenant colonel of the 3rd New Jersey in February 1776. Washington also forwarded to the Continental Congress his own preferences for candidates to fill senior positions. Impressed by volunteer Henry Knox's help in building area fortifications, Washington wrote Congress on 28 November 1775, "I have now to inform you that Henery Knox Esqr. is gone to New york, with orders to forward to this place, what Cannon & Ordnance Stores, Can be there procured, from thence, he will proceed to General Schuyler, on the Same business.... [I]t would givie Me Much Satisfaction, that this Gentleman, or any other whom you may think qualifyed, was appointed to the Command of the Artillery Regiment." Congress anticipated Washington's request. Knox had actually ceased being a volunteer on 17 November when Congress appointed him colonel of the artillery regiment. A little over a year later he was a brigadier.[62] The early volunteers generally did well; the later ones had to struggle a bit more to make rank.

Although it decreased over the course of the war, there was always a contingent of petitioners and volunteers with the army. Washington continued to deal with a number of them, but departmental and regimental chiefs handled most of the petitioners and supervised those who volunteered their services as well as their presence. In June 1778 Henry Williams, after thanking Lamb for earlier recommending his nephew, Henry Abraham Williams, to Knox when Lamb did not have a lieutenancy to offer, renewed his nephew's appeal. He said the young man had waited in vain for an appointment or commission, but "Being now inform'd, that there is orders for an augmentation to your Regiment, I have taken the liberty to direct my Nephew, to waite personally on you, to renew our former application, hoping and not doubting, but it within your line of duty, you will grant our suit, as He hath given some evidence of his resolution of a Soldier on the day of action at Fort Montgomery as Captn Moody and other Gentn of the core can well inform you." Young Williams evidently fought as a volunteer at the battle of Fort Montgomery in 1777 with Captain Andrew Moodie's company. Lamb, however, could not fulfill his wish for a lieutenancy until September 1780. John Smith, on the other hand, did not have to wait that long for his commission in Lamb's regiment. Lieutenant Colonel William S. Smith asked Lamb in February 1781 to give his brother, John, an appointment. He believed that his brother deserved preferment over any other candidates because of his previous service. John had been an ensign in Colonel Lee's regiment in 1778–1779 but had left the army to join the marine service. Taken prisoner at Charleston and then exchanged, this man of action was eager to resume the fight. Lieutenant Colonel Smith gave further proof of his brother's enthusiasm in his conclusion: "As Lt. Colo. Stephens [Stevens, Lamb's second-in-command] is to command the artillery in the present detachment I shall take him with me & if oppertunity offers he will act with the Corps as a Voluntier." John Smith had to act as a volunteer for just a few months; in June he made second lieutenant. Another petitioner, in June 1782, did not receive preferment in Lamb's artillery despite James M. Hughes's and Colonel Hugh Hughes's recommendations. A former dragoon, who after being wounded had left the service to practice law, Ephraim Kirby had decided to discontinue his practice and once again lead a military life—but this time as an officer. He eventually found a position as an ensign in Olney's Rhode Island Battalion.[63]

Regiments and departments, including Lamb's 2nd Continental Artillery, fostered many volunteers, but they could promote only some of them into the competitive line positions. Captain-Lieutenant Daniel Gano recommended a volunteer to Colonel Lamb in June 1777. The volunteer, Samuel Young, had served as an officer with a Captain Wiley in the summer of 1776 and at the time of Gano's letter had been a volunteer in Moodie's company (of which Gano was a member) for six weeks. In this particular case the volunteer did not get the position he wanted; he had to look elsewhere. In March 1779 a list of gentlemen "under Nomination for appointments in the Corps of Sappers & Miners" included the volunteers Mr. Richard Mount with the 2nd North Carolina or 2nd New York and Mr. Welch with General Huntington's brigade. John Welch made the grade; he became a lieutenant in that corps in August.[64]

There were volunteers outside of the line units as well. Dr. Amos Windship was one of the first of many physicians who volunteered to help in the Continental hospitals. Windship escaped from Boston during the British occupation in 1775 and served without a commission until he received an appointment as surgeon's mate in 1776. Some physicians, mirroring the tactics of other volunteers, provided services with the specific aim of receiving preferment. Patrick Galt gave medical assistance in the early months of 1776 to companies that became part of the 9th Virginia Regiment in the expectation of receiving the regimental surgeon position. When he did not receive the appointment, first he, and then his executor after he died, petitioned the state of Virginia for recompense.[65] Other physicians just offered assistance when the army was stationed in their area.

Quite a few volunteers were to be found working as generals' aides. In that position they were associated with the line but somewhat out of it. The men at headquarters gained more responsibilities and prestige than other volunteers, and by making the right connections they could move into coveted line positions. On a more negative note, membership in a general's military family meant hard and long labor under the eyes of officers who could break as well as make a man's reputation. The volunteer aides worked and learned alongside aides who had military rank. Such volunteers included William S. Smith, who acted as aide-de-camp to General Sullivan during the absence of Major Samuel in 1776; John White, who was appointed volunteer aide-de-camp to Sullivan in September 1777; and James Loyd of Maryland, who served as General Greene's volunteer aide in the fall of 1777. Loyd, in particular, was apparently a fine young gentleman. Greene wrote a female correspondent that November that he was looking forward to a visit to Morristown and was bringing Loyd with him, so she could "tell all the young ladies of the neighbourhood that stand candidates for matrimony to hold themselves in readiness."[66]

Most of the retainer-volunteers had never been in the American army and were seeking their first appointments, but a few were men who had been soldiers, like Ephraim Kirby, or who had served in the militia and now wanted to join the Continental Army, such as Isaac Bangs, or who had resigned or otherwise lost their commissions. Among the latter were those who wished to rejoin, including John Smith, and those who had no desire to reenter the service but wanted to help out for a time. Joseph Reed resigned from the army in January 1777 but served as a volunteer aide to Washington during the ensuing campaign. When Congress offered him an appointment as brigadier that May, Reed declined the honor.[67]

A number of Europeans who sailed across the Atlantic to find positions in the Continental Army would not have declined. Some came with recommendations or guarantees of commissions from American commissioners, such as Benjamin Franklin and Silas Deane, posted abroad. Applicants in the "Rankmad Tribe," as some Americans put it, included men of distinct merit, such as

Colonel, later General, Louis le Begue de Presle Duportail, and Captain, later Major, Francois Louis Teissedre de Fleury. Duportail and de Fleury volunteered for service but never had to serve as volunteers, for they were readily commissioned due to their strong recommendations and military training.[68]

Some foreign applicants had rather dubious antecedents: not all were well qualified or behaviorally suited to the positions they sought. They also created dissension when they demanded, or in some cases were promised, positions in which they would outrank American veterans. Silas Deane recruited Philip Tronson du Coudray for the artillery by promising a generous contract and general's rank. When du Coudray arrived in the spring of 1777, Knox threatened to resign, and other officers vehemently voiced their displeasure as well. Du Coudray was given another position and then conveniently died in the fall. The du Coudray controversy, along with the poor performances of some of the early foreign volunteers, made Congress and the army wary. The result was that some later applicants had to act as volunteers while Congress and the army's general officers debated their qualifications and decided whether or not to offer them commissions. Baron Frederick von Steuben attached himself to the army shortly after his arrival in America and vigorously pursued his duties as a volunteer inspector-general for months before receiving the commissioned rank of major general.[69]

For applicants with weaker military backgrounds, less prestigious recommendations, and imperfect or nonexistent English language skills, even volunteering did not guarantee them the ranks and positions they coveted. When William Clajon recommended a Captain Parison to Lamb in October 1777, he detailed Parison's intentions because the captain could not explain them in English. Clajon wrote:

> He offers his immediate Service as a Volunteer, not to lose the present Opportunity of manifesting his Zeal in our Cause, and desired to be so stationed, as to receive his Orders from you; otherwise, his Usefulness would be lost, he being unable to understand an English Officer, who cannot speak the French Language. Captain Parison is a very respectable Man; and every Body must believe it, when they know he is the first Sergeant in the French Artillery who ever was made an Officer in that Corps. . . .
> When the Enemy are driven off, Capt. Parison inten[ds] to wait on Congress, or General Washington, to solicit the Preferment he expected, when he sailed from France, and not to obtain from you, and General Putnam, the Certificate and Recommendation his Conduct shall entitle him to.[70]

Apparently there was a problem with either Parison or his story. He did not receive a commission in Lamb's artillery unit, nor did he serve as a commissioned officer elsewhere in the American or allied French armies.⁷¹ He either continued to serve as a volunteer or left. Quite a few foreign candidates took the latter action when their applications met with no better results.

American volunteers also left when there was no timely, positive response to their applications and actions. Others may have left due to disillusionment with military life, ill health, or "consumption" of the purse. John Howard, who does not appear to have received the artillery post he so desired, suffered from the latter affliction. In May of 1776 he wrote a letter to Knox that was an apologetic request for monetary assistance, a masterly work of self-promotion, and a fine example of what drove volunteers. He opened the epistle duly noting the obligations and obedience he owed Knox for giving him the honor and hope of serving in the regiment. He then went on to establish himself as an eager patriot and responsible gentleman—in other words, prime officer material.

> I came from home . . . expecting to return in a few days, and therefore was noways prepared for such a journey; much less for a Campaign. I had only 40 Dollars in my Jacket, and but little Cloathing. Our March from Providence (where I overtook Capt. Burbeck) to this City, was slow, fatiguing, and very expensive. Many of the Soldiers were destitute of money; and while I have it myself, it grieves me to se others suffer for Drink. But now my Cash is all gone; I am here among Strangers, and at a great Distance from Home; am still forced to be at considerable Expence, but in a very poor Way to pay it. I am neither an Officer nor a Soldier. This, Sir, is my unhappy Case! I leave it to the Colonel to paint out to himself the Mortification a Person of Spirit must feal in circumstances like these. Were I strip'd by the Misfortune of War, in which I had bravely acted my Part, my Poverty would be to my Honour but here, 'tis low—'tis mean— who can bear it? An Officer should not only be exemplary in his whole Deportment, but also in his Dress: A Candidate should be the same. . . .
>
> I would only intreat the Colonel . . . to put me in some Way to extricate myself from the Difficulties under which I labour; and I hope in return, my conduct may be such as will reflect Honour upon my Colonel, merit it for myself, and do Good to my Country's Cause.
>
> I assure you, Sir, I have no Disposition to be made (to use the Soldier's Phrase) one of the Continent's bad Bargains; I fear there are toomany such already. . . . But it was not the gay Livery of an Officer—it was not a Prospect of Meriment and Selfgratification that led me here: no, Sir, I [ ]ited from other Motives. A Thirst for Honor; The Defence of my own Property & the common Rights of Mankind have, for a long Time, with united Force, invited me to join the Martial Band: . . . Please to do for me as your Wisdom may direct: and as it will be my Honour, Interest, and Duty; so it shall ever be my greatest pleasure and constant Concern to qualify myself for, and faithfully to fulfill the various Duties incumbent uponme.⁷²

Volunteers, including Howard, did not expect to be paid as volunteers; they merely hoped that the time between volunteering and commissioning—and thus between no pay and pay—would be short. The longer they had to wait, the more they had to confront that part of the eighteenth century's definition of gentleman that demanded self-sufficiency.

Although the army did not pay these men, it did provide bed and board. In return, it expected them not only to behave as gentlemen but to obey regulations and the officers of the units to which they were attached. In comparison to the civilian auxiliaries or "Volunteers not under the orders of any officers" who fought and plundered alongside but not always with the army, these volunteers generally did follow orders so as to make a good impression and become Continental officers. Discipline problems appear to have been few or minor and dealt with at a local or personal level: volunteers did not figure in court-martial proceedings nor were they drummed out of camp. If a volunteer's behavior was unacceptable, the officers of the unit to which he was attached could first counsel him and then, if there was no improvement, deny him any chance at a commission and ask him to leave. The army preferred to handle these "informal" officers in informal or unofficial ways.[73]

Volunteers belonged to the army only so long as they wished to belong to it, or as long as the army would have them. They were not under contract as sutlers were, most (those looking for positions in the line, some generals' aides being exceptions) did not receive wages as persons serving with the army did, nor were most tied to family members in the service as the other retainers were. John Parke Custis would be one of the exceptions. He served his stepfather as a volunteer aide at Yorktown—and while there contracted a camp fever and died. Many did not follow the army for economic reasons; they followed because they wanted to be in the army or because they felt they belonged with the army. Tench Tilghman was certainly one of those. Formerly a captain of the Flying Camp in 1776, he became a volunteer at Washington's headquarters that August. In May 1781 Washington sang his praises to General Sullivan, while the latter was in Congress, in urging the award of a commission to Tilghman with a date of rank of 1 April 1777: "He has been a zealous Servant and slave to the public, and a faithful assistant to me for near five years, great part of which time he refused to receive pay." Tilghman was promoted to lieutenant colonel, ranking him with Washington's other commissioned aides.[74] He persevered; other volunteers did not. If camp life did not meet their expectations or if the army did not give them what they wanted, they left. As a group they were perhaps the most temporary of all the camp followers. They could come and go as they pleased while awaiting word on their petitions, and then, upon receiving an answer, they either became officers or departed to seek their destiny somewhere else. Obviously, once they became officers or left the camp with no intention to return, they ceased to be camp followers.

These retainers to the camp, whether high or low in its social structure, were not simply members of extended military families; they were servants to the public. They were dependents, attendants, and adherents. While volunteers retained a measure of independence unknown or disallowed to slaves, some family members, and enlisted men, they too became dependents when they followed the army, entered its camps, slept in its tents, and ate with a mess in their quest to defend the "common Rights of Mankind" and their desire for position, pay, and honor. As attendants to personnel or adherents to the army, servants and volunteers were all subject to orders and all had duties assigned them, whether it be to cook, clean and care for baggage, or correspond, keep accounts, and learn to aim a cannon. In doing their duties they helped the army fight for and survive until national recognition by Britain. Indeed, in simply being with the army, they helped it accomplish that mission (though in the case of African Americans it may have hurt their own cause). While the exodus of slaves into both armies (whether to work as soldiers or servants) and the resulting disruption in work and profits hardened some Americans' attitudes, especially in the South, against black emancipation, it also stiffened resistance against the British government (considered the root of the conflict) and the British army, its instrument.[75] So African Americans by their service in and with the army provided both positive and negative examples (depending on the perspective of the observer) of the costs and possibilities of independence. Volunteers, in turn, by their serving with the army, and especially when they wanted a commission in it, reinforced the idea that the fight was a worthy one and that rank in the Continental Army and American society was something valuable.

Notes

1. John C. Dann, ed. *The Revolution Remembered: Eyewitness Accounts of the War for Independence* (Chicago: University of Chicago Press, 1980), pp. 406–11.
2. Randolph W. Church, comp., *Virginia Legislative Petitions: Bibliography, Calendar, and Abstracts from Original Sources, 6 May 1776–21 June 1782* (Richmond: Virginia State Library, 1984), Petition 1493-P on page 449. John Turberville letter to the Virginia House of Delegates, in Legislative Petitions, General Assembly, Legislative Department, Archives, The Library of Virginia, Richmond.
3. Sally Smith Booth, *The Women of '76* ((New York: Hastings House, 1973), p. 186.
4. Mrs. Elizabeth Lawrence received money in payment for "work done by her Negro man . . . for the Use of the United States in Col. Benjan Flower QMstres Departmt" on 2 October 1780 and 8 February 1781 in Philadelphia. Vouchers in Letters, Orders for Pay, Accounts, Receipts, and Other Supply Records Concerning Weapons and Military Stores, 1776–1801, M927, National Archives (microfilm, David Library of the American Revolution, Washington Crossing, Pennsylvania).
5. Headquarters Valley Forge, 16 April 1778, Major General Heath's Headquarters Orderly Book, From Boston to Providence, 23 May 1777–20 October 1778, War Department Collection of Revolutionary War Records, Record Group 93 (overall

collection referred to hereafter as RG 93), Revolutionary War Miscellaneous Manuscript Collection, National Archives, Washington, D.C. (hereafter cited as Heath's HQ Book).

6. General Orders, before Yorktown, 9 October 1781, Orderly Book, Col. John Lamb's 2nd Regiment, Continental Artillery, 20 June–21 October 1781, The New-York Historical Society's Collection of Early American Orderly Books (microfilm, David Library). Lamb's orderly books (under the same title) in The New-York Historical Society's Collection will hereafter be referred to as Lamb's 2CA Orderly Book and differentiated by date.

7. After Orders, Headquarters near York[town], 25 October 1781, Lamb's 2CA Orderly Book, 7–30 October 1781.

8. Thacher, Yorktown, 3 and 4 October 1781, James Thacher, *Military Journal of the American Revolution* (1862; reprint, New York: Arno Press, 1969), p. 281.

9. Philip S. Foner, *Blacks in the American Revolution* (Westport, Conn.: Greenwood Press, 1976), pp. 44–45, 65.

10. Benjamin Quarles, "Lord Dunmore as Liberator," in James Kirby Martin and Karen R. Stubaus, eds., *The American Revolution: Whose Revolution?* (Huntington, N.Y.: Robert E. Krieger, 1977), pp. 80–81.

11. *Pennsylvania Gazette,* 13 December 1775, p. 2, col. 2.

12. *Rivington's New-York Gazetteer* (renamed *The Royal Gazette* in December 1777), 3 July 1779, p. 3, col. 1.

13. *Pennsylvania Gazette,* 24 February 1779, p. 3, col. 3, and 7 July 1779, p. 3, col. 3.

14. Charleston, 4 April 1780, in John S. Salmon, "A British View of the Siege of Charleston: From the Diary of Captain John Peebles, February 11–June 2, 1780," Master's thesis, College of William and Mary, 1975, p. 54.

15. *Pennsylvania Gazette,* 22 August 1781, p. 3, col. 1, and 14 November 1781, p. 1, col. 3.

16. Ibid., 21 May 1777, p. 1, col. 1, and 29 August 1781, p. 3, col. 1–2.

17. Ibid., 7 August 1782, p. 1, col. 1.

18. Hamilton to Lt. Col. John Laurens, [Middlebrook, New Jersey, April 1779], and [West Point, 11 September 1779], about recruiting African Americans as soldiers and the prejudice against it, in Harold C. Syrett, ed., *The Papers of Alexander Hamilton* (New York: Columbia University Press, 1961), 2:34–38, 165–69. British officer Mackenzie noted while in Rhode Island on 30 June 1777, "that they find it so difficult to raise men for the Continental Army, that they inlist Negroes, for whom their owners receive a bounty of 180 Dollars, and half their pay; and the Negro gets the other half, and a promise of freedom at the end of three years." In *Diary of Frederick Mackenzie: Giving a Daily Narrative of his Military Service . . . during the Years 1775–1781 in Massachusetts, Rhode Island and New York,* 2 vols. (Cambridge, Mass.: Harvard University Press, 1930; reprint, New York: Arno Press, n.d.), p. 145. For more on Rhode Island's Black Battalion see Foner, *Blacks in the American Revolution,* pp. 56–58.

19. Hamilton to John Jay, [Middlebrook, New Jersey, 14 March 1779], in Syrett, ed., *Papers of Hamilton,* 2:18. A good source on black participation and exploitation during the Revolution is Sylvia Frey's *Water from the Rock: Black Resistance in a Revolutionary Age* (Princeton, N.J.: Princeton University Press, 1991).

20. Thacher recounts that in New Jersey on 14 May 1779, Washington, followed by his mulatto servant Billy, reviewed his brigade with a number of Indian chiefs, in *Military Journal,* p. 163; Charles Carroll Mason to James Murray Mason, information to be given to Judge Mason about Thomson Mason (d. 1784), includes a Revolutionary War story about Washington breakfasting at the Mason home accompanied only by his servant Billy, Washington [D.C.], 19 September 1859, in Hugh Blair Grigsby papers, Section 122, Virginia Historical Society, Richmond. British and loyalist propagandists used Billy's name in vain when they published forged letters from Washington in 1777–1778. They said Billy had been taken prisoner in 1776 while these letters were in his possession. *The Royal Gazette,* 14 February 1778, p. 2, cols. 1–2. Washington later refuted the authenticity of the letters, stating that it was a fact "that no part of my baggage, or any of my attendants, were captured during the whole course of the war." In John C. Fitzpatrick, ed., *The Writings of George Washington* (Washington, D.C.: U.S. Government Printing Office, 1931–1944), 35:414–15.
21. Closen, Newport, 10 June 1781, and Virginia, 17 and 26 February 1782, in Evelyn M. Acomb, trans. and ed., *The Revolutionary Journal of Baron Ludwig Von Closen, 1780–1783* (Chapel Hill: University of North Carolina Press, 1958), pp. 82–83, 178–80, 187.
22. Hand to McKnight, New Windsor, 16 May 1781, Numbered Record Books Concerning Military Operations and Service, Pay and Settlement of Accounts, and Supplies in the War Department Collection of Revolutionary War Records (hereafter referred to as Numbered Record Books), M853, roll 17, vol. 162, National Archives (microfilm, David Library).
23. A. Griffiths to Lamb (?), Beverwyck in Morris County, 4 October 1777, in John Lamb Papers, The New-York Historical Society (microfilm), reel 1.
24. Andrew Breasted to Lamb, Essex County, Gothem, 1 September 1780, Ibid., reel 3.
25. Harrison to Lamb, Fishkill, 7 June and 14 July 1780, Ibid., reel 2.
26. Johnston to Potts, Albany, 15 January 1778; Cutting to Potts, Carlisle, 16 March 1778, and Manheim, 25 March 1778, Dr. Jonathan Potts Papers, 1766–1780, Historical Society of Pennsylvania, Philadelphia.
27. *Pennsylvania Gazette,* 23 May 1781, p. 3, col. 3.
28. Brigade Orders, probably Pluckemin, New Jersey, 12 December [recorder put '76 instead of proper '78]. As this said "belonging to Capt Carter" instead of belonging to Capt. Carter's company, I interpreted Anthony's status as that of servant. Brigade Orders, Steenrapie, 15 September 1780. In Lamb's 2CA Orderly Books, 30 November 1778–4 February 1779 (and 11 January–18 February 1780), and 7 September–2 November 1780.
29. Hughes and Beck petitions in Church, *Virginia Legislative Petitions*, Petition 110-P, p. 32, and 1066-P, p. 319. Beck case also in petition from Albemarle C[oun]ty, 23 October 1779, Legislative Petitions, General Assembly, Legislature Department, Archives, The Library of Virginia, Richmond.
30. Dann, ed., *The Revolution Remembered,* pp. 26–28.
31. Steuben to Privy Councillor, Camp near New Windsor on North River, 4 July 1779, in Ray W. Pettengill, trans., *Letters From America 1776–1779: Being Letters of Brunswick, Hessian, and Waldeck Officers with the British Armies During the Revo-*

lution (Port Washington, N.Y.: Kennikat Press, 1924; reprint, 1964), p. 242 in Appendix III.

32. Bauman to Lamb, 22 January 1783, John Lamb Papers (microfilm), reel 2.
33. Pickering to Willet, probably in camp near Dobb's Ferry, 7 August 1781, Numbered Record Books, M853, roll 26, vol. 127.
34. Washington to Artemus Ward, Providence, 6 April 1776, W. W. Abbot, ed., *The Papers of George Washington*, Revolutionary War Series (Charlottesville: University of Virginia Press, 1985), 4:46, 222, footnotes. Washington to the Board of War, Headquarters near Dobbs's Ferry, 16 July 1781, Fitzpatrick, *Writings of Washington*, 22:388.
35. Abbot, ed. *Papers of Washington*, 222 footnote 2. Thacher, New Jersey, 1 January 1780, *Military Journal*, p. 184.
36. Carl Van Doren, *Secret History of the American Revolution* (New York: Viking Press, 1941), p. 294.
37. Lucy to Henry Knox, Stamford, 18 July 1776, II, 162; Henry to Lucy, New York, 28 July 1776, II, 170; Henry to Lucy, New York, 1 August 1776, III, 9; Accounts, 29 September–18 October 1777, IV, 64, V, 84; Receipt, Boston, 16 May 1780, V, 75; Henry to William Knox, New Windsor, 3 January 1781, V, 116, in The Henry Knox Papers, GLC 2437, The Gilder Lehrman Collection, on deposit at The Pierpont Morgan Library (microfilm, David Library).
38. For examples see: Headquarters, 23 August 1776, in Peter Kinnan, *Order Book Kept By Peter Kinnan July 7–September 4, 1776*, intro. by M. E. Kinnan (Privately printed, Princeton, N.J.: Princeton University Press, 1931), p. 80. Regimental Orders, Camp at Trenton, 20 August 1777, Sixth Battalion of North Carolina, Continental Army, Orderly Book, 1777–1778, from the Collection of The Filson Club Historical Society, Louisville, Kentucky. Major Shaw to Captain Bauman, Morristown, 22 March 1777, in Sebastian Bauman Papers, Vol. 1, 1775–1779, The New-York Historical Society. Valley Forge, May 1778, in Joseph Plumb Martin, *Private Yankee Doodle: Being a Narrative of Some of the Adventures, Dangers and Sufferings of a Revolutionary Soldier*, ed. George F. Scheer (1830; New York: Little, Brown, 1962; Popular Library ed., 1963), p. 110. Fort Plank, 12 February 1779, in Almon W. Lauber, ed., *Orderly Books of the Fourth New York Regiment, 1778–1780 [&] the Second New York Regiment, 1780–1783* . . . (Albany: University of the State of New York, 1932), p. 60.
39. Headquarters Morristown, 8 December 1779, Lamb's 2CA Orderly Book, 7 December 1779–27 March 1780. This order repeats an earlier order that had tried to halt the use of soldiers as servants: "The order of the Sixteenth of May 1778 prohibiting the taking of Soldiers from the Army as Servants is to be strictly observed."
40. Artemas Ward to Washington, Boston, 4 May 1776, in Abbot, ed., *Papers of Washington*, 4:203.
41. Valley Forge, 7 April 1778, in *Valley Forge Orderly Book of General George Weedon of the Continental Army under Command of Genl. George Washington, in the Campaign of 1777–8* (1902; reprint, New York: Arno Press, 1971), pp. 281–82.
42. "Muster Roll of the Field and Staff Officer, of the 2nd or New York Regt. Artillery with such Noncommissioned Officers as are not attached to any Company," West Point, (April 1788) 26 May 1788, RG 93, Revolutionary War Rolls, M246, roll 117, National Archives (microfilm, David Library).

43. Fort McIntosh, 26 October 1778, Robert McCready Journal, 4 November–2 December 1778, Manuscript Division, Library of Congress.
44. Warwick, 19 November 1779, Lamb's 2CA Orderly Book, 24 August 1779–20 February 1780.
45. Garrison Orders, West Point, 7 September 1780, in Garrison Orders, West Point, New York, 14 August–29 September 1780. The New-York Historical Society's Collection of Early American Orderly Books (microfilm, David Library).
46. Division Orders, before Yorktown, 16 October 1781, Orderly Book of the 1st Virginia Battalion of 1781, Historical Society of Pennsylvania.
47. Headquarters New Windsor, 31 December 1780, Lamb's 2CA Orderly Book, 17 December 1780–20 February 1781.
48. Orders issued from headquarters at Philadelphia, 18 and 19 January 1782, Lamb's 2CA Orderly Book, 7 February–7 August 1782.
49. Ibid.
50. 19 January orders only, Ibid.
51. Guion to Lamb, New Windsor, 15 September 1779; Varick to Lamb, R[obinson's] House at West Point, 15 August 1780, John Lamb Papers (microfilm), reels 1 and 2.
52. Pickering to Hughes, Camp near Dobb's Ferry, 24 July and 7 August 1781, Numbered Record Books, M853, roll 26, vols. 82 and 127, National Archives. The emphasis on certain phrases is Pickering's.
53. Pickering to Messrs. Comfort Sands & Company, Contractors, [New Windsor]; as this is sandwiched in between two 31 January 1782 entries one may assume this letter was of the same date, Ibid., roll 26, vol. 83.
54. Headquarters Ashley Hill, South Carolina, 16 September 1782, Maj. Gen. Nathaniel Greene's Orders, Southern Army, 1 July–5 November 1782, The New-York Historical Society's Collection of Early American Orderly Books (microfilm, David Library).
55. General Orders, Headquarters Newburgh, 28 December 1782, Fitzpatrick, *Writings of Washington,* 25:480.
56. Pension application for James Anderson [or Asher Crocket] (Sarah). W. 2533; BLWt. 31439-160-55, in *Virginia Revolutionary Pension Applications, Abstracted,* compiled by John Frederick Dorman, 3 vols. (Washington, D.C., 1958–1959), 2:26–28.
57. 16 July 1780, in Continental Army, Military Life, Diary by U/I Author, 21 April–25 September 1780, Virginia Historical Society, Richmond.
58. John Hancock to Washington, Philadelphia, 19 July 1775; the note from Hancock is not transcribed in toto, but the part recommending Ogden and Burr including this comment is given in Abbot, *Papers of Washington,* 1:132.
59. Ibid., p. 132 and footnote 1 on 1:133.
60. Isaac Bangs, *Journal of Lieutenant Isaac Bangs, April 1 to July 29, 1776,* ed. Edward Bangs (1890; reprint, New York: Arno Press, 1968), pp. 5, 7, 20–21.
61. Washington to Joseph Reed, Cambridge, 25 December 1775, in Abbot, *Papers of Washington,* 2:607.
62. Patrick Henry to Washington, Philadelphia, 31 July 1775, and footnote 1; Fielding Lewis to Washington, 14 November 1775, and footnote 1; George Clinton to Washington, 4 July 1775, and footnote 1; Washington to George Clinton, Cambridge, 25 August 1775; Washington to Anthony White, Cambridge, 25 August and 28 October 1775; about Knox in Washington to Jonathan Trumbull, Sr., Cambridge, 2 No-

vember 1775, and footnote 2; Washington to Hancock, Cambridge, 28 November 1775, and footnote 2, in Abbot, *Papers of Washington,* 1:201; 2:371, 373; 1:58–59; 1:361; 1:365; 2:249; and 2:289–90; 2:444–45.

63. Henry Williams to Lamb, Poughkeepsie, 16 June 1778; William S. Smith to Lamb, Headquarters, 17 February 1781; and James M. Hughes to Lamb, Litchfield, 10 June 1782, John Lamb Papers (microfilm), reels 1 and 2.

64. Gano to Lamb, Stratford, 20 June 1777, Ibid., reel 1; Orders, Artillery Park at Pluckemin, New Jersey, 13 March 1779, Lamb's 2CA Orderly Book, 5 February–30 May 1779; Heitman's *Historical Register* has John Welch as a lieutenant in the Sappers and Miners as of 2 August 1779.

65. Washington to Hancock, Cambridge, 21 July 1775, and footnote 2, in Abbot, *Papers of Washington,* 1:144; Smith (executor for Galt), Accomack C[oun]ty, 19 November 1777, Legislative Petitions, Virginia State Archives; Church, *Virginia Legislative Petitions,* 241-P and 472-P, on pages 72 and 145.

66. Washington wrote John Hancock about giving rank and pay to aides-de-camp, as well as described their duties, in letter from New York, 23 April 1776, Abbot, *Papers of Washington,* 4:112–13. Naming aides: Headquarters, 15 August 1776, in *Order Book Kept By Peter Kinnan,* p. 66; General Orders, 25 September, and Headquarters, 29 September 1777, in Sixth Battalion of North Carolina Orderly Book; Greene to Susanna Livingston (?), Camp near Philadelphia, 11 November 1777, in Robert E. McCarthy, ed., *The Papers of General Nathanael Greene,* microfilm edition (of typescripts furnished by Rhode Island Historical Society) published by Scholarly Resources, Inc.

67. Information about Joseph Reed in footnote 3, Abbot, *Papers of Washington,* 1:57. See Heitman, *Historical Register,* p. 461, for brigadier offer; Richard L. Blanco, ed., *The American Revolution, 1775–1783: An Encyclopedia,* 2 vols. (New York: Garland, 1993), 2:1376–77, for a short essay on Reed.

68. James Lovell to Knox, Philadelphia, 26 July 1777, IV, 33, in Henry Knox Papers. Lovell said that he supposed Knox, along with others, had dubbed him "Patron of the whole Rank-mad Tribe" since he had been appointed chairman of the Committee on Foreign Applications, and then went on to recommend Duportail. Major Shaw to Bauman, 30 May 1777, about finding employment for Captain Fleury in the artillery corps, in Sebastian Bauman Papers, Vol. 1, The New-York Historical Society. Also see Robert K. Wright, Jr., *The Continental Army* (Washington, D.C.: U.S. Government Printing Office, 1983), pp. 128–42, for information on foreign volunteers.

69. Knox to Hancock, Camp Middlebrook, 1 July 1777, IV, 24, in Henry Knox Papers. Also, Wright, *The Continental Army,* pp. 128–30, 140–45. Heitman, *Historical Register,* p. 518.

70. William Clajon to Lamb, Fishkill, 6 October 1777, John Lamb Papers (microfilm), reel 1.

71. Parison was not in the list I compiled of 2nd Continental Artillery officers, nor is he listed in Heitman's *Historical Register* as either an American or French officer.

72. Howard to Knox, New York, 14 May 1776 (II-91), in Henry Knox Papers.

73. "Instructions from the Continental Congress" to Washington, Philadelphia, 22 June 1775, Abbot, *Papers of Washington,* 1:21–22. These include: "You are to victual at

the continental expence all such volunteers as have joined, or shall join the united army.... In addition to yr Instructions it is Resolved by Congress, That the troops including the volunteers be furnished with camp Equipage and blankets if necessary at the continental expence." General Orders against plundering by followers and volunteers not under orders, Headquarters near Dobbs Ferry, 1 August 1781, in Fitzpatrick, *Writings of Washington,* 22:443–44. Charles Royster in *A Revolutionary People at War: The Continental Army and American Character, 1775–1783* (New York: W. W. Norton, 1979), pp. 50–51, discussed volunteer irregulars. About discipline: research in various orderly books and other records did not turn up volunteer offenders brought before courts-martial. The few letters that referred to volunteers indicate that the army tended to be both careful and casual (which sounds like a contradiction but was not) in its treatment of volunteers. There was a court-martial at which William Hutton, provost marshall, justified his not following orders, in this case performing an execution, by claiming he had been a volunteer at the time. The court accepted that, but Washington overturned their decision arguing that while "it is true Mr. Hutton had not been appointed in orders as principle in the office till the time he mentions, but he had for some time past been considered as a Deputy, . . . performed the duties & *drawn pay* [italics mine]." Washington dismissed him from office. General Orders, 22 April 1781, in Lamb 2CA Orderly Book, 21 February–28 March [May] 1781.

74. Washington to President of Congress, at Colonel Bassetts near Ruffen's ferry, 6 November 1781, announcing he will be delayed arriving in Philadelphia due to a distressing event (as footnote explained, the death of Custis); Washington to John Sullivan, New Windsor, 11 May 1781, and General Orders, Headquarters New Windsor, 5 June 1781, in Fitzpatrick, *Writings of Washington,* 23:338; 22:70–71, 163–65.

75. The irony and tragedy of black service: while it proved their equality to some, it only served to threaten others. Again, for more information on African American resistance and service, see Frey, *Water from the Rock.*

6

All Persons Serving with the Army

> In an Army properly organized, there are sundry Officers of an Inferiour kind, such as Waggon Master, Master Carpenter, &c.
>
> Washington to Hancock
> Cambridge, 21 July 1775

When Washington referred to those "Officers of an Inferiour kind,"[1] he was not speaking derogatorily; he merely meant that they were not commissioned line officers. They were the appointed staff or public officers who managed or supervised essential support services. As such they belonged within the last category of camp followers mentioned in Article 23, Section XIII, of the 1776 Articles of War: persons serving *with*, but not *in*, the army. True, some officers and soldiers were assigned to the staff departments, and other people—although not part of the military line—were members of the military, but many others were civilians who followed the army or lived within the Continental Community so that they could work in these admittedly somewhat schizoid civil-military departments. These civilians, from managers to laborers, were appointed or employed, as opposed to commissioned or enlisted, in the public service. Many became camp followers because of these professional obligations. As part of the Continental Community, and because they were supposed to contribute to the public good by their labor and conduct within it, they, like their military counterparts, were subject to army regulation.

The administration of the staff departments and their employees was, however, made difficult by the constant reorganization (echoing that seen in the regiments) and personnel shifts from soldiers to civilians and back again. The orders and regulations issued underscored both the civil and military lines' constant attempts to make these departments more effective.[2] Both lines wanted these departments to operate more efficiently and economically. It was necessary that they do so, because the staff departments, speaking here of the quartermaster and commissary ones in particular, performed vital administrative and logistics—what the twentieth-century American army would call "service support"—functions. They moved, supplied, and quartered the troops, performing the duties that could make or break an army.

Although there was agreement on their importance and on what in general these departments were supposed to do, there were numerous conflicts over the nature of their affiliation with the army. Maintaining civilian control of these departments would be a way of maintaining civilian supervision and control of the entire army. There was certainly historical precedent in the British practice of having the civil arm control military transport. But when such control hampered military operations to the point of endangering independence, then the way was open to militarize these departments through both their administration and the people employed in them. Necessity dictated the placement of line officers into staff positions, the use of soldiers as artisans, and the transfer of operational control over some essential civilian labor from the state to the military. The result, over the course of the war, was not only closer affiliation of staff departments, or at least parts of them—when they were divided into civilian and military components—with the army, but also evaluation of and experimentation with the roles and uses of soldiers and civilians performing service-support functions. Armies over the ages had utilized civilians—those recruited from outside and followers assigned from inside the camps—in such positions; however, in the early modern era armies began more fully to incorporate service-support functions, and thus the positions and the people, within the military establishment.[3] The Continental Army was an example of this ongoing evolution in military organizational design: the militarization of the staff departments. Besides putting military members into these roles, there were attempts to shift the remaining civilian workers' focus and affiliation from state to army, for by serving the army one served the state; it did not always seem to work the other way around. This shift presaged the later development of a new corps of followers who would work with and under military command.

Although the demands of the war fostered this militarization of the staff departments, that does not mean the change proceeded easily or evenly. Some people may have feared that such a shift would make the army too independent, and that was not the kind of independence these revolutionaries wanted to foster. There is the possibility then that as frustrating and inefficient as it may have been at times, there was some method to the creation of public and line components within the departments. Members of the Continental Congress not only wanted to retain some control over the staff departments, they may also have wanted to maintain some civilian control within them. It seemed to make sense, for instance, to have the procurement of supplies done by the civil or public side of the quartermaster department, while disbursement could be handled by a military component within it.

Washington, that champion of civilian supervision of the military, preferred to have "inferiour" or public service officers and men in the staff departments. But in this case he also had other motivation: he did not want to see his officers and soldiers pulled from the line. He recognized, however, and then exploited the necessity of assigning his people to these positions and jobs. Enlisted or commissioned into the army, they worked in and for the army even when assigned noncombat jobs. Ideally that meant there was no question of divided loyalties. In contrast, there was some confusion about the affiliation of staff officers and civil department employees: did they work in, with, or for the military? Washington, acknowledging them as fellow public servants, established the premise that they were part of the military establishment—they belonged to the army—and cemented the relationship by subjecting them to military regulation. That was his way of balancing their "checks" on the army. The Continental Congress apparently accepted that and, indeed, went a step further, for in providing pay, pensions, provisions, and, initially, ranks comparable to those given line officers, Congress essentially declared most staff officers to be military officers, but officers answerable to Congress first, as the governing civil body, and then to the army. In theory then, there was a civil-military system of checks and balances. But as more line officers were assigned to the staff departments, the balance tilted to military control.

As for the actual staffing of the civil departments, Congress usually followed the recommendations of the department heads and the commander in chief. When Washington and other line and staff commanders concurred that military regularity would be best served by enlisting rather than employing staff personnel, Congress gave them the go-ahead. Companies of artificers were the most visible result; however, the shortage in manpower eventually forced the advocates of the new system to retreat from a full militarization of the staff departments and hire civilians. The result of all of this experimentation was civil-miliary conflict and confusion. Enlisted men and employees mixed together, each demanding the privileges accorded the other, and each claiming that different rules applied to their individual groups. Commanders and staff managers, sometimes perplexed as to who was actually in the army and who was serving with it, tried to surmount these difficulties by providing comparable provisions to service members and employees alike, and by insisting that all of them, civilians included, obey army regulations and the orders of their officers.

The problem of status—that is, whether these people had civilian or military standing—and rank, which determined their authority and privileges, began at the top of the staff department hierarchy. The first staff position, one already fully incorporated within the military establishment, was that of adjutant general, and Brigadier General Horatio Gates received the appointment. His successors were also officers with line commissions, as were most of their subordinates; however, there were a few civilians, generally clerks, operating within the department. The adjutant general's department managed personnel by keeping track of enlistments, commissions, and the army's actual as opposed to paper strength, among other things.

In comparison to that very militarized staff department, there were the ordnance and clothing departments. The former, created early in the war, and the latter, which developed over time until organized by congressional command in 1779, focused on acquiring, making, and fixing their designated stores: respectively, ammunition, weapons, clothing, and the materials necessary to produce them. The ordnance department had both military and civil branches; the first was run by a commissary of military stores who served with the troops in the field, while the second, as odd as it sounds, had a commissary general of military stores who, defined by military rank as well as job title, headed the laboratories. The clothing department reflected that of ordnance in that it had military and civil arms. The clothier general was expected to accompany the army, as were some of his personnel, but there were also deputies or agents assigned to the states to facilitate purchasing. None of the clothier generals nor their deputies held a line rank.[4]

Neither Joseph Trumbull, the commissary general of stores and provisions and later, after the commissariat was reorganized into two branches (purchases and issues), the commissary general of purchases, nor his successors or deputies held line commissions, although they were sometimes addressed by military rank. These support officers concentrated on provisioning the Continental Army, while their colleagues in the quartermaster general's department focused on the acquisition, transportation, and utilization of other supplies. The quartermaster department eventually consisted of two branches, civil and military, for acquisition and issue, and supervised two subordinate divisions: the wagon and forage departments. Considered the most vital of all the staff departments, it was also, despite its civil branch, one of the most military in personnel and function; indeed, it was occasionally referred to as the quartermaster's line instead of department. The quartermaster general, such as Thomas Mifflin, usually held a commission (Stephen Moylan, the quartermaster general for a few months in 1776 who first received his military or line rank with that office, was the exception) and was expected to be well versed in military strategy. He acted as an adviser to the commander in chief, and his deputies, military and civilian, acted in the same capacity on regional and regimental levels.[5]

The last important staff division was the hospital department, and it was the department that maintained the clearest distinctions between military and civilian labor. This department dealt with the care and repair of people and, on paper, was initially the best organized of all the staff departments. In practice there were some serious problems. Regimental surgeons and their mates owed their appointments to their regimental commanders and so gave their allegiance to their individual line units instead of to the hospital department. The result was a continuing power and supply struggle between surgeons of the line and their commanders, and the director-general and his deputies in the hospital department. Yet whether or not they identified with a line unit or the staff department, surgeons and surgeon's mates were officers. The army did not assign them line ranks such as colonel or lieutenant; it continued to address them by job title, but the army formally established their relationship when it formulated their pay, benefits, and pensions. Assisting these medical officers in the hospital department were apothecaries and their mates, clerks, storekeepers, orderlies, nurses, and laborers. A few of these had enlisted in the army's line and then been detailed to the department; others had enlisted specifically for such duties; but most of the men, and all the women, were civilians. They did not hold military rank, nor did they generally receive military pensions.[6]

The relatively clear distinction between military and civilian personnel seen in the hospital department was seldom mirrored in the other staff departments. In the early years of the war, line officers complained about Congress's tendency to give military, or more precisely line, rank to staff appointees and, when Congress was not the culprit, the tendency of staff officers to assume such ranks. The "warriors" did not want to be outranked by, made answerable to, or even be required to share privileges with some of those other public servants. To use a modern colloquialism, military officers did not want rank accorded to those who merely "talked the talk" instead of "walked the walk." Washington could not revoke titles given by Congress, but he could try to end the latter practice of staff personnel assuming titles of rank. In August 1777 Washington declared, "As the Congress never have & the Genl. is persuaded never do Intend to give Rank to any of the Waggon Masrs. in this Army, except the Waggon Masr. Genl., They are order'd not to Assume the title of Majors Captains &c. but to be Distinguish'd by the names of Division or Brigade Waggon Masrs. . . . Waggon Masrs. are useful in every Army & will be supported in all their Just Priviledges, but the way for them to obtain respect is by a diligent & faithful discharge of their respective Duties. . . . This Order is to extend to Persons in every other Department who have not rank given to them by their Commissions or appointments by Congress."[7] Most line officers considered staff officers, the quartermaster and adjutant generals excepted, to be civilians with supporting, as opposed to military or, more precisely, combat, duties. While Congress seemed to substantiate this position by its desire to have the civil departments acting as checks on military units, it appeared to act contrary to that when it gave these officers ranks associated with the line. That method of equating staff officers with line officers may, however, have simply been another way to reward and empower these public servants. Most staff officers saw their employment as military service: they were serving country, commander in chief, and army. In May 1778, however, Congress did make a concession to the line officers; it ruled that no one appointed to the civil staff after that time would be entitled to any rank in the army solely because of such a staff appointment. That did not totally rid the army of excess colonels and captains, however, for staff personnel continued to use complimentary ranks.[8]

Also, to confuse the issue further, if a line officer took such an appointment as an additional duty, he could keep his rank. So, were staff officers in the army or with it; in other words, were they or were they not professional camp followers? If one accepts the evaluation of most line officers, staff officers were not in the army. If one prefers to accept the judgment of some members of Congress as well as the opinion of staff officers, then the answer is yes, they were.

The problem of status and rank existed at lower management as well as labor levels in the support departments. The civil departments, in trying to maintain sufficient personnel levels, resorted to numerous expedients: employing civilians for prescribed lengths of time or hiring them to do piecework; enlisting civilians into special companies of artificers or wagoners; and drawing officers and soldiers from the line. At any time and in any place a department could be staffed by one or more of the preceding methods. For example, by 1780 the wagon department's top staff included the wagon master general and eleven deputy wagon masters general. The middle-management spots were held by 108 enlisted wagon masters (those who had enlisted directly into the department), three wagon masters taken from line units, and two hired or civilian wagon masters. Filling up the ranks were 256 enlisted wagoners, 104 wagoners diverted from the line, and 272 civilian wagoners. The department also hired some packhorse masters and men.[9]

In 1776 Commissary General Trumbull submitted to Congress a list of persons employed in his department: they were all hired civilians or departmental enlistees, and they were all anxious to be paid. They included four storekeepers, twenty-three clerks, two bookkeepers, a commissary for Colonel Arnold's detachment, twenty-two laborers, six coopers, two cooks, and one man "employ'd constantly in Riding, to one Place & another to get in Stores, pro[visions,] Teams &c."[10] That early return showed a very civilian department. The adjutant general's department made a distinct contrast. It had always been a militarized organization, but the congressional resolution of 1 August 1782 showed just how military its staff was. Congress resolved that it would appoint the adjutant general from the general officers, colonels, or lieutenant colonels in the army. It authorized the adjutant general to appoint two assistants and one clerk, insisting only that the appointments be approved by the commander in chief. The assistants were to be majors or captains, but the clerk could be a subaltern or volunteer. Deputy adjutant generals attached to each of the separate armies had to be field officers. They could each have one assistant, who was to be either a major or a captain.[11]

The quartermaster department showed more of a personnel mix than either of the previous two, perhaps reflecting the strongly dualistic nature of its role: its military and civil branches handled both administration and logistics. Quartermasters played an important role in the administration of the army and individual units as well as managed logistic operations. In comparison, commissaries were purely logistic personnel, while adjutants operated solely as administrators. The army readily accepted civilians in the former supply role but preferred its own people in the latter. The adjutant general's department was also more elitist: it was a management organization that did not require a contingent of manual laborers. The quartermaster department had both managers and laborers; civilian appointees and military officers filled the first group, while civilian employees and enlisted men made up the second. A 1780 return shows deputy quartermasters for the states both with rank and without. It included Major Richard Claiborne of Virginia (line rank) and Colonel Hugh Hughes of New York (rank attained when Congress gave them to staff officers in 1777), as well as Donaldson Yates, Esq., taking care of Maryland and Delaware, and Ralph Pomeroy, Esq., of Connecticut. The return also divulges that some brigades employed lieutenants and captains as quartermasters while others looked outside the line; a few sergeants were forage masters as were some civilians; and some deputy wagon masters held line ranks while others did not. The return does not mention rank for the many clerks, hostlers, and express riders.[12]

Quartermaster General Timothy Pickering proposed to militarize the military side of his department even more thoroughly in 1782. That March, perhaps using the adjutant general's department as a guide, Pickering recommended that all, if possible, of the department's higher staff personnel be taken from the line. His recommendation served two purposes: not only would it help him staff his department with proper military personnel, but it would also offer an alternative to supernumerary officers who were losing their places in the shrinking army. He did add, however, in April, after hearing about a congressional committee's deliberations on a new plan for his department, that additional pay would have to be offered in order to entice line officers, who enjoyed light duties and high honors, to take on the drudgery of staff work. Later, although still promoting the use of line officers in his department, Pickering altered his position a bit when he indicated that the initial plan was impractical and unjust because it would compel the dismissal of some experienced and worthy staff officers in favor of the supernumeraries.[13]

The congressional committee and then Congress listened to Pickering's opinions. When Congress resolved later that year to reorganize the department, to be effective 1 January 1783, it implemented a number of his suggestions. Congress authorized the quartermaster general to appoint, with the approbation of the commander in chief, the following officers for the armies of the United States: one deputy quartermaster, one wagon master, one commissary of forage, one director and one subdirector of a company of artificers, "and as many Assistants as the service may require in the Main and Southern Army, to perform the Duties of Quarter Masters of Brigades, Storekeepers, Clerks, and such other Duties in the Quarter Masters Departments as the service may require, and also as many Waggon Conductors." It then went on to state that the wages listed in the resolution included their pay in the line. Having dealt with the military branch, Congress turned to the civil side and resolved that the quartermaster general could appoint, with the approbation of the secretary at war (as opposed to the commander in chief), "so many Assistants to reside in the several States as the publick service may require." It then resolved that all of these officers, "of whatever denomination," had to take "the Oath of Allegience and the Oath of Office precribed by Congress."[14] Obtaining high office in the public service, mirroring the acquisition of rank in the military service, required a demonstration of commitment.

The dual nature of the quartermaster department, and of most of the other staff departments for that matter, meant that debates ensued over the issue of control: who controlled the staff departments, and, in turn, who and what did the staff departments control? Officially, Congress created the staff departments, appointed their senior officers, and had a final say over their affairs; however, it often formally delegated its power of appointment to military commanders and informally relinquished its supervisory powers to them as well. In July 1775, writing to Washington that the Continental Congress had made Trumbull the commissary general of stores and provisions agreeable to Washington's recommendation, President John Hancock said that the appointments of quartermaster general, commissary of musters, and commissary of artillery were left to Washington's discretion because "Congress not being sufficiently acquainted with persons properly qualified for these offices" did not want to make the decisions.[15] Two years later, being somewhat disorganized at the time, Congress authorized Major General Israel Putnam, the commander at Peekskill, to appoint deputy commissary generals for that area if the deputies chosen by it declined the posts. A month later Congress told the governor of Connecticut he could choose the officers if Putnam did not.[16] Congress's willingness to abide by military recommendations and to delegate the power of appointment led some officers to assume powers of control over staff functions. Washington, as commander in chief, exercised a great deal of control over the civil departments. The heads of those departments accepted his authority, and at times his interference, because he was their secondary commander under Congress. But the staff chiefs deeply resented attempts by other military commanders to control their departments. They did not want interference from the line in the management of their personnel and functions, especially when they saw such interference occurring in the civil branches of their departments.

Attempts by military commanders to control staff department affairs could and did lead to feuds which disrupted supply functions and forced the parties to redefine their operational boundaries. When a military commander acted upon the assumption that the civil departments worked for the line instead of with it, invariably he encountered opposition from the staff officers who supposed otherwise. One such feud over support services, and the autonomy of the staff department personnel that provided them, erupted in the winter of 1780–1781 when Pickering engaged in a vigorous, and at times venomous, dispute with General William Heath and Colonel Moses Hazen over the control of his department's people and activities at Fishkill. The staff-line battle began when Pickering forbade his officers to obey any of Hazen's orders that would have infringed on department business. Then Heath issued orders at West Point that were designed to regulate public issues at Fishkill but, according to Pickering, would only "unhinge all public business there & go near to disolve my departmt in the State." Pickering asked Washington to intervene, for he believed Heath issued the orders "at the instigation of Colo. Hazen, whose overbearing disposition aimed at the absolute control of every transaction at that post." The quartermaster general had not wanted to bother the commander in chief about this matter but had to do so because Heath entertained "a mistaken principle in the case." Heath had censured Hazen's initial orders because he believed that Hazen "had no right to interfere with the *great branches* of the staff departments," but when he added that Hazen had the right to control the subordinate officers and the issuing of public supplies, he cleared the way for further incursions. Pickering felt Heath's mistake came "from his confounding a civil with a military post. Were Fishkill a mere place of arms, and a Garrison posted there for its defence, the commanding officer ought undoubtedly to regulate & controul the distribution of every species of stores: for he would be answerable for its safety.... In like manner when an issuing officer is appointed merely to serve a military corps, he must be subject to the controul of its commanding officer." But Fishkill was a magazine for a wide variety of public stores and served not only troops but various persons in the public (as opposed to military) service as well. "Colo. Hazens Regt. is accidental. It is not necessary for the security of the place. A captains guard could perform all the *military* duties of the post." Pickering bolstered his argument by stating that he did not think the situation would have escalated as it had if Colonel Hughes had not been engaged in important business at Albany. "Had he been present Genl. Heath would hardly have thought of requiring the deputy quartermaster of the state to carry his provision return to be countersigned by Colo. Hazen or perhaps one of his captains." Pickering warned that if the orders were not revoked Hughes was sure to resign as were his assistant and other subordinate officers and "his large collection of excellent artificers."[17]

After asking Washington for his help in the matter, Pickering wrote Major (apparently another one of those courtesy titles) John Keese, the assistant deputy quartermaster at Fishkill (the assistant ready to resign), "I shall not cease my attention to the case till the rights of the department are acknowledged and guarded against future incroachments." He wanted everyone to await Washington's decision. Pickering also stated that he believed Heath would not have issued the offensive orders "had he adverted to the resolves of Congress, which his orders, if executed, would in effect repeal. By the plan for the Commissary's department established June 10 1777 'the quarter master general & any of his Deputies or Assistants' are authorized to give Orders for the issues of Provisions. The right thus given to you no General Orders can take away: for it will not be denied that an Order of Congress is of superior authority." So he ordered Keese to demand, as usual, the rations due the department and to continue, as usual, making issues within the department. "There is a variety of business to be done at the post which has no connection with the military. The deputy of the State is answerable that that business be executed. But for this purpos[e] he must employ a variety of Persons & he must furnish them with the means of doing that business. These means are principally (as money is wanting) fuel and provisions. . . . Your right & power to order the issues of these Articles is delegated to you by Congress, with which no person . . . delegated by inferiour authority to Colo. Hazen can come in competition."[18]

The problem was that Pickering saw the personnel at Fishkill as part of the civil branch of the staff department at an essentially civil post, while the army commanders there looked upon the resident quartermaster personnel as supporting a military unit at a military post. The combatants worked through the problem but never fully resolved it, partly because the line between the two branches was often negligible or indistinct. Indeed, that August, Pickering himself further confused the issue (if not for those originally involved then at least for historians trying to untangle civilian from military personnel). At that time Pickering chose Hughes to be deputy quartermaster to the army under Heath's command. He said, "The probable situation of this army will admit of his [Hughes] attending to the business in the state as well as if he resided at Fishkill." Pickering guaranteed that Heath or anyone who might succeed him could depend on Hughes "for every kind of supply, & the means of transportation by land & water. Nine tenths of the business will be of a civil nature, which nobody could manage better than Colonel Hughes; and his intimate acquaintance with every part of this state & its resources will I trust be singularly useful. In the military branch of his new office he will not be embarrassed: if more military knowledge & experience than his line of duty has led him to acquire be needful, he is sure of every necessary aid." After declaring Hughes and his people essentially separate from the army's command structure, Pickering now attached them to it. He appointed Keese deputy commissary of forage, Captain Hasfield White deputy wagon master, and Joseph King storekeeper for Heath's army.[19] They now straddled the military and civil branches of the quartermaster department.

A lot of people straddled the civil-military staff department fence. They included those essentially civilian, such as Keese and King, and those who never let anyone forget that they were first and foremost military, including Nathanael Greene when he was quartermaster general and Lieutenant Francis

Brooke when he assumed a staff position. When Greene, happily finished with his staff appointment, appointed Brooke quartermaster of the park of artillery for the southern army in 1781, Brooke only accepted "on the express condition that I should not lose my rank in the line; as I did not come into the army to go into the staff." Brooke added that "having two duties to perform, I was very attentive to that in the line."[20] Brooke's sentiments were echoed by many of the other officers detailed to staff duties.

Line officers generally had a poor opinion of staff department or public officers. This developed in some cases out of resentment, envy, and a suspicion that public service was rewarding those servants more than its military ones. It was also partly due to the inability, perceived or real, of some staff officers to perform their duties. What line officers failed to recognize was that staff officers had an immense amount of work to do, and had to do it while coping with congressional meddling as well as the states' hostility and lack of cooperation at times.[21] This meant that some staff officers established priorities that were unpopular with military officers who wanted their needs met immediately. There were, however, also some inept staff officers. Colonel Walter Stewart, who was actually acting in a staff capacity himself at the time, blamed his problems on the latter when he irritatedly wrote Lamb in July 1782, "I find nothing but disappointment takes place when we depend upon the Publick Officers to execute Business." Lamb's muster rolls had lain at the quartermaster general's office in Philadelphia for days, holding up Stewart's work as inspector for the main army. After waiting for the office to send the rolls out, Stewart went by to speed things up only to find they finally had sent them out. But the delay meant that now he had to ask that Lamb's officers prepare the rolls as quickly as possible so that they (along with their troops) would be ready for his review later that morning.[22] Stewart knew he would find a sympathetic audience in Lamb. Just a few years earlier Lamb, after inspecting the laboratory at Springfield, had written the Board of War about the deficiencies of a public officer there: "I find on the strictest enquiry, that Mr. Eayres, Superintendant of Artificers an Ignorant overbearing Man/ has been the origin of all the disputes and uneasiness, that has happened between the Officers and has constantly kept in a state of anxiety ever since he has been considered as a Major in Flower's Regiment." He also discovered that Eayres kept an office and employed his son, "a Lad about 15 years of Age," as a clerk, both at the public's expense. Lamb believed, "Both the Office, and Clerk . . . may be dispensed with. . . ."[23]

Accustomed as they were to looking down on staff officers and cursing them for malfeasance or incompetence, most line officers found it disconcerting and degrading when they were appointed to staff positions. Actually, the staff's poor reputation may have been a result of just such appointments: some line officers were ill-equipped, by disposition, education, or intellect, to handle staff duties. Nonetheless, some line officers did find themselves with staff duties when there was no one else to perform them. The 2nd Continental Artillery needed both an adjutant and quartermaster in June of 1777. Lieutenant Daniel Gano did recommend to his colonel a candidate for the latter position, but apparently the candidate was either not acceptable or the regiment was not efficient in procuring him, for a week later Lieutenant Colonel Oswald wrote Lamb, "We are in great want of an Adjutant & Quarter Master, as I am oblig'd to do their Duty as well as my own—Our Officers here [Subalterns?] seem to think it a degradation to act in either Capacity, however I have appointed Lt. Ashton to do Adjutant Duty. I have been obliged to go myself to Fish Kill, for Cloathing. . . ." At one time or another the problem and the solution (with the commander making the appointment or the officers voting on who received the appointment) were echoed by the army's other regiments and by the staff departments.[24]

Washington and his subordinate commanders did not perceive the appointment of line officers to staff positions within regiments as a terrible hardship; actually it was common practice, for the officers remained with their units and could continue to perform combat duty as well as staff duty. What they did not like was the appropriation of line officers by the staff departments. In July 1779 Washington, after being "informed that some commissioned officers hold appointments in the commissary and forage departments," ordered the practice to be discontinued: "The demands upon the line for the Staff officers authorized by congress are so numerous that it would be injurious to the service, to permit any other than they have pointed out."[25] Circumstances conspired to prevent wholesale adherence to that order. As the staff departments continued to suffer from a shortage of manpower, the army continued to loan them officers and soldiers from the line. For example, in August 1782 Greene's orders noted that Lieutenant North of the Pennsylvania line was appointed deputy wagon master to the southern army and that Sergeant Samuel Filson received an appointment as wagon conductor to the Maryland line.[26] Then, of course, there were those congressional resolutions in late 1782 that promoted the use of line officers in the staff departments.

Although there were many line officers doing duty in the staff departments, most staff officers were originally civilians who received direct appointments. For a good number of them such appointments served as stepping-stones to line commissions. In contrast to the volunteers with the regiments, they were able to support themselves with such paid positions as they made their connections. Washington made John Parke an assistant to the quartermaster general in August of 1775; within a year Parke crossed over to the line and became an ensign in the 2nd Pennsylvania Battalion. John Grizzage Frazer, appointed to be another assistant to the quartermaster general in September 1775, left his staff post to assume the duties of major in the 6th Continental Infantry the following January. In March 1778 Congress appointed Matthew Clarkson and Major (he went the other way, moving from a military into a civil role) John Clark auditors to settle and audit the army's accounts. Within months Clarkson had resigned from that post to become a major and aide-de-camp to General Arnold. And Theophilus Brower wrote to Colonel Lamb in May 1780 recommending a commission for his brother William, who had served for the past twelve months as a conductor of military stores and now wished to join the 2nd Continental Artillery, noting that Colonel Stevens had assured William that he would, pending Lamb's approval, receive the first open appointment in the regiment.[27]

Other appointees preferred to stay (to the amazement of some line officers) within the staff departments, serving with the army if not in it. Jeremiah Wadsworth, who had been a deputy commissary general of purchases in 1777, became the commissary general of purchases in April 1778 and remained in that post until 1780. Deputy Quartermaster Hugh Hughes of New York gave years of service and both appointed and supervised numerous assistant deputy quartermasters within his district. In 1782 alone these assistants included John Campbell, Daniel Carthy, John Keese, Edward Kiers, Uriah Mitchell, Nicholas Quackenbush, and Charles Tillinghast.[28] Stationed at different posts, such as Fishkill, West Point, and Newburgh, these public servants supervised lesser officers and employees in the acquisition, storage, and issuance of quartermaster supplies. Their staffs included forage masters, storekeepers, paymasters, and clerks. Such personnel acted as the middlemen between the purchasing agents or deputies in the civil side of their departments and the military units who were the ultimate recipients of their goods and services.

As Congress neglected to provide the staff departments with an adequate number of workers, sometimes actually undermining recruiting efforts by establishing limits on the number of staff employees allowed and caps on the wages allowed them, some staff chiefs went out and hired departmental assistants, clerks, and other personnel on their own. They found some of the people they needed already in the camps, such as volunteers for clerks, men and boys for laborers, and women for nurses, but had to go outside the Continental Community for others. They then put their people on the public payroll and presented Congress with a fait accompli. Both Mifflin and Trumbull staffed their departments this way. Other officials, especially in the hospital department, preferred to complain and make Congress take action.[29] The staff officers and Congress also turned to the army for help in ameliorating civil department personnel shortages. These three methods—personal initiative, congressional resolution, and army intervention—defined staffing procedures throughout the war.

Staff officers often worked on their own initiative, instead of acting upon specific congressional or state recommendations, in hiring certain departmental personnel such as storekeepers, paymasters, and barrack masters and office personnel such as clerks or assistants. Six months after Congress appointed him the commissary general of stores and provisions, Trumbull had established four major magazines or stores (Cambridge, Roxbury, Prospect Hill, and Medford), each under the supervision of a storekeeper, at least three of whom had previous commissary experience. He also either provided each with staffs of clerks and laborers or approved the storekeepers' own choices of subordinates before he submitted the staff list to Congress so that the employees could begin to receive their pay.[30]

Clerks were hired to handle business and sometimes personal correspondence, take care of certain monetary transactions, keep department accounts, and maintain office operations when their superiors were away. Although a few clerks were enlisted men, such as Thomas Jones of the artillery artificer unit (he enlisted in June 1777), most, like those employed in the public service by Deputy Quartermaster Hughes, were civilians stationed at various posts that housed substantial staff department contingents. Some of the clerks on Hughes's payroll in 1782 were Jacob Boerum, clerk to the issuer of forage at Fishkill; Theunis Bogert at the Continental Village; Anthony Byvanck, clerk to the assistant deputy quartermaster at Fishkill; George Denniston at West Point; John Gilbert at Kings Ferry; and Dirick Hunn at Albany. They were paid between twenty and thirty-five New York dollars per month for their services.[31]

Decent and regular pay was vital to the retention of these important employees, and an issue of continuing concern to their employers. Pickering wrote Hughes in October 1780: "The pay of Storekeepers, Clerks, artificers [&]c whom you shall find necessary for the service, you will fix at your discretion, according to their merit & services respectively: but if engaged for more than two months the plan directs that the condition be approved by the Quarter Master Genl. . . . However if I rightly recollect, Col[o]. Miles expected to engage all his storekeepers and Clerks at from thirty to forty or forty five dollars at most P month, they finding [for; meaning provisioning] themselves." A little over a year later Pickering told Major Richard Claiborne, a line officer and deputy quartermaster, that "the pay of clerks you must fix on the best terms in your power; they are essential in business."[32]

Myriad other workers, including supervisors, tradesmen, and laborers, were also essential to staff department business. Indeed, because the departments could not function without them, staff officers resorted to various measures in their efforts first to obtain and then to keep these people. Staff officers began by hiring (and then continued to employ) civilian workers, but when too many of them proved transient and insubordinate, the officers (with Congress's approval) tried enlisting men directly into their departments. The results were not decisively positive: the departments did get some people in this manner, but not enough to fill their ranks. Tradesmen, knowing their worth on the open market, often did not want to enlist and thereby decrease their mobility and earning power. If they did enlist, it was generally for limited periods instead of a soldier's enlistment of three years or the war's duration. The tradesmen also insisted upon, and received, better pay and more rations than the average soldier; even so, the departments continued to have personnel shortages and had to resort to drafts on the line.

Soldiers labored for the staff departments from the war's beginning to its end. On 1 October 1775 Washington ordered that "the Colonels and commanding Officers of Corps, are upon application from the Qr Mr General, immediately to employ under his direction, all the Carpenters in their several regiments, to erect barracks for the Regiments and Corps they respectively belong to."[33] The next fall Washington first commanded the brigades of Putnam's division to furnish men for the hospital and then ordered that no officer (in any brigade) was "to take off any Soldier who is employed either as Waggoner, Butcher, Tallow Chandler or other Business under the Q. Master Gen or Comm. Gen without first applying to the Head of the Department."[34] Staff officers late in the war followed their predecessors' examples. In May 1781, when Pickering felt that boat building and repairs were proceeding too slowly at some Hudson River posts, he asked Hughes, "Will it not be adviseable to get a draught from the line of a number of ship carpenters or boat builders, to make all the repairs at West point, under the direction of one good man of yours? . . . Will it not even be adviseable to apply for a dozen of ship carpenters & boat builders to be taken from the line, to be employed at Wappens creek, untill the army takes the field?"[35] Unit commanders and post commandants usually tried to comply with the continuous demands on their troops. The commandant at Burlington Barracks in March of 1782 directed that the "Mechanecks in the Artillery" who were willing to assist the artificers be lent to Mr. Thorp. As there was little time remaining before the opening of the year's campaign and still much to be done, the commandant asked that the men who worked last year do so again. He assured them that they would be paid for their work. The commandant at West Point in June 1783 also guaranteed "proper encouragement" (extra pay or rations or both) to the masons, brick makers, carpenters, and blacksmiths in the corps who helped to construct the magazines at that post.[36]

Soldiers knew that civilian or enlisted artificers in the staff departments received more provisions and higher pay than they did and wanted to reap the same benefits if they performed the same labor, especially if it was done in addition to their military duties. As department chiefs and line commanders preferred to have motivated volunteers rather than disgruntled draftees perform the work, they often did provide inducements. They promised extra money to the pay-deprived privates; furthermore, there may have been a greater chance of actually getting the money if it was to come out of departmental rather than regimental pay chests. The soldiers simply had to make sure they submitted proof of their extra service. The commandant at Burlington Barracks ordered the soldiers who worked with the artificers the previous year, in 1781, to get "certificates from the Commanding officer of that Corps, of time they respectively Served & give them to Lt Allen on Monday morning that he may make

Out an Abstract of the whole & procurr the money."[37] The headquarters at Newburgh issued a similar order in June 1783: "All Noncommissiond officers and soldiers who have money due them for Services in the Qr. Master Generals Department will lodge the Certificates thereof with orders for payment thereon in the hands of their pay masters, who will Settle for the same."[38]

As obliging, however, as most commanders were about providing extra manpower to the staff departments, they had no intention of relinquishing all control over the services of their men. They reminded staff officers that the soldiers were loans, not gifts, and insisted that their men be free to take up arms upon demand. Administrative changes implemented at Morristown in January 1780 required that returns include an additional column, titled extra service, under which wagoners, artificers, and "all others who are so Imployd" were to be counted and considered "as Part of the Effective force of the Army." A later addendum required that "those that cannot appear under Arms in time of Action" also be recorded.[39] A few months later, on 5 April, headquarters requested that general and staff officers not of the line "inform the Adjutant General what guards, fatigue parties, artificers or assistants they have, or may want, from the army" so that they may be given them on or before the 8th, as all other troops belonging to the line however employed would be recalled after that date.[40] Commanders were also less likely to release noncommissioned officers than enlisted men for such special details. Garrison orders at Fort Schuyler on 9 January 1778 illustrated that reluctance: "No Sergt. or Corpl. to be Employ'de as Artificers unless a especial Order from the Commanding Officer."[41]

The Continental Army and its accompanying community created a vast and diverse labor pool. That was one of the advantages of having a volunteer force that was composed of men from all walks of life and various professions or trades. Staff officers took full advantage of what was available, but, given all the strictures and complaints they heard about their demands on the line, it was no wonder most preferred to create their own departmental labor force. They not only employed civilians in their departments; they also enlisted people into what they called the public service. The quartermaster general and commissary general of military stores in particular enlisted men into companies of wagoners or artificers.

The commissary and commissary general of military stores engaged a number of wagoners and conductors (who supervised armorers as well), but it was the quartermaster general, usually under the aegis of his subordinate agency, the wagon department, who controlled most of the rest of the wagons, wagoners, conductors, and other transport personnel and equipment. From 1777 to 1780 the wagon department hierarchy included the wagon master general, deputy wagon masters general, wagon masters, and wagoners. Staff officers without line rank filled the first two positions; civilians, men drawn from the line, and others enlisted into the staff department filled the latter two. After the 1780 reorganization wagon masters were the senior officers, deputy wagon masters next, then conductors (those who had formerly been called wagon masters), and finally wagoners. Furthermore, the quartermaster general, with the approval of Washington or the commanders of the separate armies, could draw officers from the line to fill the higher positions.[42]

Pickering did look to the line when choosing candidates for some of the prime posts. Washington would even at times push candidates Pickering's way: "As the direction of the Waggon Department is a charge of great importance (in foreign Armies generally intrusted to a Field officer of the line) and as it is thought the service will be benefitted by a similar practice in our Army Major [Thomas] Cogswell of the first Massachusett's regiment is appointed Waggon Master to the Main Army and is to be obeyd as such."[43] Some deputies were also drawn from the line in this example of militarization, but others, such as Alexander Lamb at Fishkill, were appointees in the public service. Wagon conductors, too, could be either appointees, like Kamp Ayres (another member of the Fishkill contingent), or line personnel.[44]

Recognizing their integration into and their importance to the military, the army in the last years of the war thought wagon masters should be compared to field officers and treated their deputies and conductors similarly to (and sometimes better than) company-grade officers. When Washington restricted officers of the line to one ration each in the winter of 1780–1781, Quartermaster General Pickering attempted to insure his staff's exemption so that men who had drawn two rations earlier would continue to do so. He also arranged for an equitable rum allowance: conductors receiving the same amount as subalterns, and deputy wagon masters that of captains.[45]

In a role similar to that of company-grade line officers, conductors (or, before 1779–1780, wagon masters) supervised small units of men, in this case wagoners, and generally conducted small-scale operations, though these were actions involving supply, not combat. They could act as supervisors in brigades of wagoners, as James Login did in 1779, or perform as adjunct officers in line units. In 1781 Pickering wrote Lieutenant Colonel John Popkin of the 3rd Continental Artillery, "I told Mr[.] Fisher Conductor at the park that he must go with the Detachment Being an officer of the Brigade he is subject to your orders as Commanding Officer—It is most proper he should go, as he is acquainted with the particular mode of geering the Artillery Horses & management of what pertains to the artillery."[46] When serving with the line, especially during an active campaign, conductors, as Pickering reminded Mr. Fisher, received their day-to-day instructions from line commanders. When Lamb wanted to move some artillery pieces and ammunition out of Fishkill in June 1778, he ordered Mr. Mavins, his conductor of stores, to carry out the assignment. Lamb also told Mavins how many horses belonging to the regiment were available for the operation before writing Lieutenant Colonel Udney Hay, an assistant deputy quartermaster general, to apprize him of the situation and warn him that he had told Mavins to apply to him for extra horses.⁴⁷ Conductors also operated under the direct orders of their staff department supervisors. In early December 1780 Pickering sent out a flurry of letters to wagon conductors and associated personnel ordering them to proceed to various places where the horses could be wintered.⁴⁸

The reliance of the army upon the transportation system translated into the dissemination of numerous orders to minimize disruptions or mishaps and maximize utility. Both line and staff officers expected wagon masters or conductors to supervise their wagoners properly, see to it that the horses and oxen were cared for, and insure that the wagons were always ready to roll. Washington clearly stated the priorities in September 1777 when he ordered "that every night the Waggon horses be put to the Waggons & there kept—& if it be necessary at any time for them to go to grass, that it be in the day time only, and then the Waggoners must be with them constantly, that they may be ready to tackle at the shortest notice—The Waggon Masters are requir'd to see this order carefully executed."⁴⁹ Commanders also expected wagoners to keep their four-legged charges from disrupting camp, trampling neighboring fields, or disappearing altogether. Carelessness was unacceptable. As a brigade order stated in September 1778, "When ever a Horse Strays away the Waggon Master is to Report the Waggoner in whose care said Horses was to the Officer Commanding the Regt. who is Directed to have the Matter Immediately enquired into and the Delinquent Punished."⁵⁰

Line and staff commanders also promised punishment if the wagoner was so delinquent as to allow himself to stray. If a man enlisted as a wagoner for a proscribed period in the public service and left before fulfilling his obligation, the army considered him a deserter. Alexander Turner, a deputy wagon master general, made that clear in June 1780 when he advertised in the *Pennsylvania Gazette* for apprehension of the wagoners James Parker, Irish-born, "a taylor by trade, about 48 years of age . . . [and] much addicted to liquor," and Michael Sellsar, a Pennsylvanian of Dutch (probably German) extraction who could only speak broken English.⁵¹ And when the military was not busy rounding up its human strays, it was usually engaged in combating the malfeasance of those who remained. Wagoners, or drivers as they were also sometimes called, had a reputation for untrustworthiness and unreliability. They not only embezzled supplies but destroyed them as well. In trying to lighten a heavy load, they sometimes drained the brine preserving the salt pork from the casks and thereby spoiled the meat. If they could not drain away the load, they sometimes simply dumped it on the roadside.⁵² Officers tried stricter supervision and punishment, but they could not halt the practices nor could they circumvent them by doing without wagoners—the army had too much need of them.

The army had a lot of trouble with wagoners, but the matter of disciplining the ones it had paled in comparison to the problem of obtaining enough of them. One problem was money, another was the nature of the job, and yet another was the treatment of the wagoners themselves. When Congress tried to control costs by limiting wages, which it did for a good part of the war, but especially in the early years, civilian wagoners preferred to work in the more lucrative private sector than in the public service. Then when the quartermaster department tried to enlist wagoners, it found that people did not want to take on such laborious duties. Even when the army raised the wages it was willing to pay, it drove wagoners away by not always delivering what it promised in recompense or security. It sometimes lacked the cash to pay the wagoners or the forage to feed their teams. Furthermore, wagoners found that while they did not rate high for convenient quarters, their gear rated high among thieves.[53]

Nonetheless, the quartermaster generals continued to try to furnish the army with enough wagoners for its needs throughout the war. Mifflin employed civilian wagoners in 1775, and then in the fall of 1776 he suggested that when enough could not be hired, soldiers be used. Washington did not like the solution. Before the 1777 campaign began, the commanding general ordered the quartermaster general to look to the neighboring inhabitants and not his soldiers. To make such service appear more attractive, Washington covered both public virtue and private interest in his ruling that people so engaged would be considered in the service over the period of their contract and thus would be excused from militia duty. It was not a strong enough inducement: Mifflin still had to divert soldiers from the line. Washington again tried to end the practice in January 1778 and again had to swallow his objections during the succeeding campaign.[54]

Colonel Lamb's and his conductor Mr. Mavins's difficulties in getting artillery pieces and other equipment moved that summer of 1778 were not unusual. On 1 June, the same day he had written Hay for horses, Lamb informed General Gates that he could not move the artillery from Farmington as soon as he would like "for want of Horses, and Drivers." On the 2nd he wrote Nehemiah Hubbard, an assistant quartermaster general at Hartford, to ask how many horses and drivers he had obtained and to urge him to procure a full complement "as speedily as possible," for getting the artillery to headquarters was extremely important. Hubbard answered that he had enough horses, "but am afraid we shall meet with Difficulty in Raising Drivers—Mr[.] Bingham Return'd without any, have sent him out to hire Men to go to Head Quarters with the artilery & there be Discharg'd—he'll Return next Monday—will then inform you of his success." Bingham was apparently unsuccessful, for on 4 July Lamb asked Hay to engage some drivers and forward them to Farmington because Hubbard was still having difficulty procuring (he crossed out "inlisting") enough drivers.[55] If Hay was not able to oblige, Lamb would have been forced to detail some of his artillerymen to do the work.

In April 1779 Congress eliminated its earlier wage restrictions by authorizing the quartermaster general to employ wagoners at the best terms he could obtain, as long as Washington approved them.[56] If the quartermaster officers thought that would solve all their problems, they soon discovered they had been overly optimistic. They still could not hire or enlist enough wagoners; as a result, they continued to request drafts from the line for the rest of the war. Money continued to be a major factor in the procurement problem. Pickering used the lack thereof as his reason in June 1781 for asking the adjutant general for soldiers. To make his request more palatable he noted his willingness to take those least combat ready, especially as he wanted them for the entire campaign. "Perhaps," he suggested, "there are some men too old as well as too young for military duty, and some newly recruited negroes, who may without any material deduction from the effective Strength of the army be furnished to the waggon department."[57]

Pickering was following an already established precedent in his request. When taking waiters and wagoners from the line, officers tended to choose those soldiers deemed least effective. For example, a year earlier down south a runaway servant boy of limited intelligence and education by the name of William Burnett enlisted in the army. One day he recognized his former master's wagon and team, which had been pressed into service. He mentioned to his captain that he had formerly driven that team, and next thing he knew, he was taken from the ranks, placed under the supervision of a wagon master, and put to work driving that team.[58]

When the quartermaster department could not hire enough teams it sometimes resorted to impressment, and although impressment officially applied only to livestock and equipment, it sometimes resulted in the acquisition of a driver as well. A master might send a slave along to keep an eye on his property or he might drive his team and wagon himself. William Anderson of Rockbridge County in Virginia did the latter in the summer of 1781. As a result, the rather unwilling camp follower was "in hearing of the cannon when Cornwallis surrendered."[59] Impressment, however, remained an undesirable and unreliable method for obtaining manpower, resorted to only when civilian recruitment and drafts from the line proved insufficient for the military's needs. The quartermaster department always preferred to use its own enlisted or employed wagoners, such as Peter Archer, William Hunn (an African American), and Jacob Barbazet, or hire team owners like Major Adams and Jacob Hanch to fill its brigades of wagons.[60]

The quartermaster department employed a number of other public servants to transport supplies. As the new nation lacked a good road system, and bad weather adversely affected the condition of the roads that did exist, the department tried to use boats and boatmen whenever and wherever possible. British naval patrols limited the use of transport boats and ships along the coast, but the army did employ ferries and other boats on many inland waterways. In July 1775, before the quartermaster department was organized, Washington contacted Joshua Davis, a Boston ship captain, about building and manning a hundred boats for the army. Davis answered with a plan calling for 601 men exclusive of officers. He included a master boat builder at captain's pay, twenty-five boat builders at sergeant's pay, a boat master for each boat at sergeant's pay, and six men to crew for each boat. The plan was never implemented in its entirety because the army did not require or, more specifically, could not afford so many nautical employees or followers; however, from 1778 to 1780 the quartermaster department did include a boat department with a "superintendent of naval business," ferry operators, shipwrights, and their supervisors. When Pickering became quartermaster general, he closed out the subordinate department by reducing personnel, but he did not discontinue its functions; instead he incorporated them back within the larger department. Also, throughout the war quartermaster officers contracted with the owners or captains of privately owned vessels to transport army supplies and hired artisans and boatmen to care for and crew the boats the department itself owned.[61]

Other quartermaster department employees had the task of delivering information rather than supplies. Express or post riders were couriers: civilian employees appointed by the quartermaster general to convey dispatches and to obey or carry out any other related orders or duties (such as delivering a horse or two to another officer or post) given them by certain designated officers, such as the commander in chief, the quartermaster general, or his deputies. They were generally furnished with a Continental horse (though some may have used their own), which they could exchange in camp or on the road when necessary, so as to carry out their duties.[62]

As expresses were expensive, the army at times tried to cut costs by eliminating certain routes and reducing the number of men so employed; but invariably it had to reestablish chains of expresses to keep the information exchange open along key routes or in strategic areas. Furthermore, the cost could be justified not only by the dispatches delivered but as proper care and compensation for the information gathered and the risks taken by the expresses. Elijah Bennet was a favored post rider between the generals in New York in 1776 because he could be trusted to deliver oral as well as written dispatches and relay news he picked up along his route.[63] Bennet and other expresses did court danger in the course of their duties, for they were prime targets of enemy operatives in search of information. Lieutenant John Moody of the 4th Battalion of the New Jersey Volunteers made quite a few guineas by intercepting the rebel mail around New York City in 1781. As *The Royal Gazette* crowed after one exploit: "The Capture of this Mail is extremely consequential, and gives the Commander in chief the most perfect knowledge of the designs of the enemy."[64]

Although the expresses were vital links between the various commands and departments of the Continental Community, it does not appear that the army or the staff departments ever tried to enlist express riders. One reason may have been that many were boys or slight young men who would not strain the horses. The nature of the work and the fact that only a few needed to be stationed at any one place may also have hindered militarization here. The army did, however, occasionally use dragoons for the task. An account tallied up at Newburgh on 1 January 1782 showed that twelve dragoons carried dispatches between the army on the Hudson and Hartford and that thirteen hired expresses carried the dispatches between Hartford and Boston.[65]

Associated personnel included directors or superintendents of expresses, who, like Robert Dunn at Tappan in October 1780, were directed to examine daily and see to it that the expresses "are provided with suitable horses and other things requisite to enable them properly to perform their duty; to send every rider in his proper tour, so that each may do his proper share of duty in the most equal manner; to keep a register of the times when the riders go out and return & to examine their horses when they come in; and if any do not return in due season; of if their horses appear to have been ill used, you are to report the same to me [Pickering]."[66] And if need be, they could be ordered to ride express as well. There were also stable keepers like Vincent Carter, who also, on occasion, acted as a measurer of grain and express rider, and hostlers like George Hutton in the public service.[67]

The army needed not only post riders but producers. Pickering may have been correct for one brief moment when he told one of his deputies, Hughes, in November 1780 that the artificers with the army were either enlisted or "draughted from the Line,"[68] but such a simple declaration was not possible before that time or after. The Continental Army, from the day it was formed to the day it was formally disbanded, needed workers to manufacture and repair buildings and boats, tents and wagons, clothing and equipment, and weapons and ammunition. In order to wage war effectively, it needed not only soldiers but multitudes of artisans and mechanics. Those were the kinds of followers the army wanted, and so it went out and recruited them. It obtained the services of civilians in and out of the Continental Community by hiring them by the day or the piece, by enlisting them in the line and then transferring them to an artificer company, by enlisting them directly into staff department artificer units, or by detailing soldiers to do the work for specified periods.

During the first year of the war there was no established policy on the employment and regulation of artificers. Army commanders and the quartermaster general simply tried to negotiate the best terms possible when employing the necessary civilian artisans. Although negotiations did not substantially lower wages, the army continued to use civilians, but it began to arrange them into companies so as better to supervise their labor.[69] Then in June 1776 Washington ordered the formation of a provisional artificer regiment: "As many useful men belonging to the army have been drafted and others have been hired for the different works of the camp and as their assistance may be wanted to repel the enemy such carpenters, armourers, Smiths and other artificers as are now under the direction of Capns Post, Pollard, Bruin[,] Ford and Bacon are forthwith to be formed into a distinct Corps under the Command of Col. Jonn. Brewer and Mr. Parke Asstn QM Genl. who are to act pro-temporary as their Col. and Lt. Col." Washington wanted the regiment operational and flexible, its personnel continuing their normal duties but prepared for combat during the "present exigency" and then disbanded at campaign's end, which turned out to be that November.[70] By 1777 the army was unifying the employment and direction of artificers under specific departments.

Most artificers belonged to the quartermaster general or the commissary general of military stores, but some belonged to the artillery. In accordance with Washington's orders of January 1777, Lieutenant Colonel Benjamin Flower, the commissary general of military stores, raised three companies of artillery artificers, including one deployed with the artillery in the field, and one company of artillerymen laborers to work at his laboratories in Carlisle and Philadelphia. In 1778 the collective companies became the Regiment of Artillery Artificers. Over that same period General Knox enlisted a company of carpenters, one of blacksmiths, another of wheelwrights, one of armorers, and a company of harness makers under the artillery's direct command at Springfield. Then in February 1778 Congress placed all artillery artificers except those in the field under Flower's command.[71] Artificers following the army into the field belonged to the line unit to which they were attached. As Knox put it when he wrote Lamb about Captain Anthony Post of the artificers at Fredericksburg in August 1777, "I have given him Instructions to consider himself as belonging to the Artillery, and to take his particular orders from you." Years later, in 1780, Knox still kept some artificers under the artillery's direct command. He told Lamb, "Whatever terms the Q.M. General engages his artificers upon may be given for those wanted for the artillery." He wanted more blacksmiths, carpenters, and wheelwrights engaged for the war or three years, and if enough could not be enlisted, Lamb was to ask his garrison commander to draft some of the troops to fill the jobs. Lamb was also to detail some of his own artillerymen to serve as artificers for a year.[72]

As Knox knew, the quartermaster generals engaged artificers upon varying terms according to the year or month they were hired and the place they were to work. Throughout the war the quartermaster department preferred to hire civilian artificers for short terms so as to minimize the expense of their wages. At various times it would also contract with civilians for piecework. But when the army's needs for artificer goods and labor indicated that longer periods of service would be necessary, the department preferred to enlist workers into companies of artificers. From 1775 to 1778 a few army commanders, such as General Schuyler of the northern department when he needed boats in 1776, and the quartermaster general contracted with master artisans to raise companies of civilian artificers. These companies were designed as temporary "shops," established to perform a certain task or fill a specific order and then be discharged. Then in 1778 the quartermaster department decided to create permanent companies of artificers and began to enlist (for three years or the war's duration) men possessing the appropriate skills, such as carpenters and wheelwrights. The department promised enlistees good pay, a bounty, a suit of clothes, fatigue rations (usually larger than a soldier's ration by half), and such other compensation as was granted by Congress to soldiers in the line. In return it got a more stable workforce that was without question subject to the army's rules and regulations. In July 1778 Quartermaster General Greene appointed Colonel Jeduthan Baldwin commander of the quartermaster artificers. Baldwin remained in command of the Regiment of Quartermaster Artificers (commonly called Baldwin's regiment or Baldwin's artificers) until early 1781, when Congress dissolved it. The quartermaster department had supplemented the ranks with civilian artificers during that time, but now its new director, Pickering, decided once again to rely on a civilian workforce (which made an interesting contrast to his advocacy of military officers in the management positions) while reducing the number of enlisted artificers.[73]

Pickering decided on this reversal within months of assuming office. When he became quartermaster general in August of 1780, he first focused on reforms within the regiment. He felt that the companies were not only necessary in army manufactures but could also form a useful corps in action as the men were equipped with arms and occasionally instructed in how to use them. But as he examined the companies in response to Congress's decision to reduce the regiment, and as he tried to economize, Pickering came to believe that the regiment was too expensive and enlisted artificers too slothful. On 31 January he wrote Hughes, "I have been long disgusted with the manner of doing Continental work. Artificers in general who have fallen under my observation did not do half a days work in a day. This occasions prodigious loss to the public, the Indolent will eat as much as the industrious, and in the present mode we are obliged to employ double the number which would be other wise requisite. My wish is therefore to employ none but good workmen, to allow them just and even generous Pay, and then to compell them to work with diligence." A day later he informed Baldwin, "For my own part, I am very far from thinking a Regimental Establishment of Artificers the most eligible. I am certain that at this Period of the war it is not the best way to procure artificers remarkable either for their Skill or Industry."[74]

When he wrote to Richard Peters, a member of the Board of War, on 2 February seeking further clarification of Congress's intentions relative to the reduction of artificer companies, Pickering offered another solution to the organizational as well as economic problem:

> This I am certain of from my own observation, that one hundred skillful & industrious artificers, would do more & infinitely better service, than the whole new regt. if composed of such men as Col. Baldwin's. The expence of that regt. has been prodigious. There is all the parade about it of a regiment of soldiers; The officers assume as much state, and so as little work, as the officers of other regiments, and are allowed the pay of artillery officers. I declare again, that I am sicke of the establishment, & wish it were done away. Yet I would not in dissolving the corps discharge the men: there are about 90 inlisted for the war. I have suggested to Genl. Knox that these might be annexed to his company of artillery artificers. ... He was much pleased with the idea. But some artificers will be necessary with my department: and if I might take my own method in getting them, I would hire one director of the whole and two or three master workmen, who with fifty journeymen . . . ; would perform all the services requisite in my department.

The Board of War and Congress decided to implement Pickering's ideas. On 29 March 1781 Congress resolved to disband Baldwin's regiment and have the remaining enlistees reassigned by order of the commander in chief (he transferred most to the artillery artificers and others to garrison laboratories).[75]

Within two months Pickering authorized the raising of a new company of artificers. Although he had spoken against the regiment of artificers and had advocated the employment of civilian workmen, he retreated from his earlier stand when he realized, first, that he did not have enough civilian artificers immediately available and, second, that he needed workmen to serve with the main army during the campaign just then getting under way. He appointed Stephen Clapp, a carpenter, captain of the new company and directed him to appoint one lieutenant, who was also to be a carpenter, as his deputy and enlist four foremen, fifty privates, and six cooks. The distribution of the foremen and privates was to be in the following manner: twenty-five carpenters, fifteen smiths, six wheelwrights, four boat builders, two saddlers, and two harness makers. Pickering wanted the company raised in the western areas of Massachusetts and Connecticut and the men marched from there to join the army. The big difference between this company and the earlier ones was the term of enlistment. In a change that seemed to hark back to the limited terms of expeditionary forces in the colonial wars, instead of enlisting for three years or the duration of the war, these artificers were only to be engaged to serve until the last day of December, unless sooner discharged. Pickering did, however, state that if any of the men were "disposed to inlist for a longer period, it may be done; provided the engagements extend to an intire Campaign, or to the last of December in each year." He said he actually preferred such long enlistments.[76]

After arranging for this new company of artificers in the military arm of his department, Pickering shifted his focus to the civil side as he tried to supplement the artificer shops in various garrisons. He authorized Mr. Cheeseman, his director of masons, "to inlist six masons to be imployed at West point or elsewhere as the public service shall require. . . . to serve until the first day of January next, unless sooner discharged." In this case Pickering equated the verb *enlist* with *hire* or *contract*. He did not give Cheeseman a rank as he did Clapp, nor did he make the masons privates. He also specifically said, "You are to keep correct accounts of the number of days that all the artificers under you shall be employed distinguishing those that are hired from those drawn from the line."[77] Again, this difference in definition can be explained by the fact that Cheesemen and his masons worked in garrisons and were seen as public servants in the civil branch of the department: they were district artificers as opposed to field artificers.

When some artificers in Hughes's New York district accused Pickering of partiality and injustice because he managed to get two months pay for the company of artificers with the army but none for them, Pickering defended himself by pointing out the hazards of following the army in order to serve with it: "Let it now be noticed that these artificers have been exposed to all the hardships of service in the field—that they marched 500 miles with the army to Virginia—that such fatigue & change of climate endangered their hea[l]ths & lives—that two of the company have in fact died during the expedition, & that several others at this day if alive remain sick at the hospital at Williamsburgh. After hearing this detail of facts, who can with reason blame me for paying these field Artificers in preference to others?"[78] But the district artificers' complaints did affect Pickering's enlistment and organization of artificers for the next year's campaign.

During the winter of 1781–1782 Pickering resolved to discharge all artificers in the public service and instead procure quartermaster stores by the piece. He wanted to apply the contract system to artificers. He also decided to engage some of the former district artificers as field artificers for the new campaign. Pickering began the switch in December when he informed Colonel Jabez Hatch to start discharging artificers at public or army posts. As he explained to Hatch, Major Richard Claiborne (another deputy quartermaster), General McDougall, and just about everyone else with whom he corresponded, public artificers were indolent and expensive. Henceforward, artificers (no question about their being civilian now) were to be paid by the piece instead of by the day or month. By 19 February Pickering was able to inform Secretary of Finance Morris that "this change took place in New York the beginning of January. I have since permitted two or three artificers to be continued at Albany till farther orders, as they would have employment, and the prices of work done by the piece were extravagantly high there. There were some kinds of work immediately necessary for the army in the Highlands, for which I have contracted to pay by the piece." He added, for the sake of comparison, that the contracted prices were lower than those charged by the artificers in Philadelphia. One of Pickering's contracts was with

Mr. Jacob Reeder (who, in turn, employed five workers) at Newburgh, who was to do the smith's work required by the main army.[79]

After taking care of that business, Pickering focused on the continuing need for field artificers. He wrote to Captain Clapp that he would again have need of a company of artificers for the coming campaign but that he could not appoint him to the new command because "motives of humanity & the public interest . . . require the company should be formed of the artificers lately employed by Colo. Hughes, all of whom where discharged the beginning of January." Pickering explained that the artificers could not easily move from the state to find employment and had families which were suffering. Also, "as the city of New York will be the object of our operations the ensuing campaign, the engaging artificers that were originally citizens thereof, promises much advantage. The public interest will also be promoted in this way—that the New york artificers are on the Spot, and there will be no wages or expences paid for the time lost in travelling to camp & home again." He then contacted Mr. John Parsell, who had been the superintendent of wheelwrights at Fishkill, and authorized him to enlist carpenters, smiths, wheelwrights, a collier, woodcutters, boat builders, saddlers, and cooks to serve with the army during the coming campaign. Interestingly, Pickering made no mention of rank other than the job titles of director, subdirector, and foreman.[80]

That artificers, whether enlisted or employed, were necessary there was no doubt. They performed a multitude of tasks at all the army's camps and garrisons. Most served as colliers, bellows makers, smiths, coopers, rope and tent makers, masons, and carpenters, but a few occupied rarer positions, as did, for example, Mr. Morgan, the cutler sent to Morristown in December 1780. Carpenters, if not outnumbered by smiths, made up the largest contingent among the artificers. They acted as both district and field artificers in the quartermaster department, enlisted as artillery artificers, and worked for the commissary general of military stores. As quartermaster and artillery artificers, they built the army's barracks and huts, erected the necessaries or outhouses, measured cannons so as to hew gun mounts, and occasionally acted as wheelwrights, making axles and wheels.[81] In the civil branch the commissary general of military stores, Benjamin Flower, utilized their talents, along with other specialists, laborers, and women doing piecework in his laboratories from Philadelphia to Springfield. They worked at various jobs from cobbling shoes to making cartridges.[82]

Many persons served with the army as unskilled laborers. Deputy Quartermaster General Hughes employed William Adams as an overseer of the fatigue men with the engineers (those who planned and built roads and fortifications). Adams, other public service overseers, and line officers supervised crews of laborers who dug ditches, leveled and repaired roads, built bridges, and raised redoubts and revetments. Many of these fatigue men were African Americans, for the army hired black followers and detailed black soldiers to do much of the hard labor associated with military operations.[83] This division of labor was quite evident in the southern army in 1782. In July Greene ordered the quartermaster to "collect all the Negroes and have the roads repaired this evening, between this and Mr. Cattle's plantation on the Ashley River." Then, after a summer of such special assignments, Greene commanded that "all the Negro's that have been employed on different kinds of service with the army, and upon extra duty, are to be sent into the quarter Master General's, who will appoint a Captain of pioneers [engineers] to superintend them, as the service may require."[84] He thereby culled a good many of the blacks out of the ranks of soldiers and followers and established them as laborers under the quartermaster department in an engineering or pioneer unit.

Other departments also utilized hired and enlisted fatigue men to handle some of their more laborious duties. The hospital department, in particular, used quite a number of them at all its associated facilities—from the field and regimental hospitals to the general hospitals more remote from camp and combat. These laborers figured rather prominently in Boston-area hospital accounts from 1775 to 1776. They worked in the army's general hospitals there, both in the main one and the smaller "sick houses," as well as the smallpox house (a building set aside for those recovering from inoculation as well as the "natural" illness). Many of the workers were white, but a few were black, the latter including slaves hired out to the hospitals. For instance, the hospital department paid David Wart for the services "of his Negro Man Sam as Waiter & his Negro Woman as Washer for 4 Months."[85] As this indicates, hospital laborers not only toted the bales or dug the ditches (in this case probably for necessaries) as engineer laborers did; they also took on service tasks similar to those engaged in by followers who acted as servants and domestics with the line units. This was further illustrated by an advertisement for female nurses in the 4 March 1776 issue of the *Boston Gazette and Country Journal* which also asked for male laborers who would act as assistants to the nurses; it mentioned that men from the distressed seaport towns would be given preference.[86]

As the war progressed and the department established more hospitals in other military districts and near other garrisons, it not only hired civilians to do such chores but requested and received details of soldiers as well. In June 1776, while on Long Island, Greene ordered the camp colormen out of three regiments to attend not only to the camp but also to work at the hospital. Patient and personnel returns for the hospital at Albany in 1778 included fatigue men, numbering anywhere from five to over a dozen, detailed from neighboring regiments.[87]

At the same time some soldiers were being detailed to the hospitals to perform maintenance, others were ordered there to nurse. Greene had wanted not only the colormen; he wanted colonels in command to send nurses to tend their sick in the hospital. Those Albany personnel returns of 1778 included tallies of soldiers taken from the line to do nursing duty and female nurses hired for the job. The hospital there had an even distribution of twelve to thirteen male and eleven to twelve female nurses over the early months of 1778. As this begins to indicate, although the hospital department hired many general laborers, it also employed a great many other workers for more specific duties.

The congressional resolution of 27 July 1775 established the medical department's initial hierarchy by authorizing one director general and chief physician, four subordinate surgeons or physicians, an apothecary, and twenty surgeon's mates, as well as assistants in the form of a clerk, two storekeepers, a nurse to every ten patients, and occasional laborers as needed. By 1780 the establishment had expanded to include the director, chief hospital physicians, chief physicians and surgeons of the army, physicians and surgeons, purveyors, apothecaries, assistant purveyors, and assistant apothecaries. They were to be appointed and commissioned by Congress and receive all the benefits enjoyed by officers of the line. Assisting these gentlemen of the hospital, and sharing in their status if not their benefits, were a few civilian adjunct and volunteer surgeons, but the majority of hospital employees occupied lower status and lower-paying positions. From the start Congress authorized the director and chief hospital physicians (and after 1781, in the absence of the aforementioned personages, other physicians and surgeons of the hospital) to employ as many persons as needed "for the good of the Service," or as later stated, "for the regular management of the hospitals." These people included clerks, storekeepers, stewards, ward masters or managers, apothecary laborers, matrons, and nurses.[88]

Civilians serving with the army in the medical department worked either in hospital administration or medical service. Clerks, storekeepers, stewards, ward masters, and matrons were administrators or managers. They accounted for supplies, distributed provisions, maintained the physical plant, and supervised their subordinates. Hospital mates, apothecary laborers, nurses, and fatigue men (when acting as orderlies) assisted the surgeons and other medical personnel and attended to the patients. Hospital mates occupied a position similar to that of surgeon's mate but one with additional duties. As Dr. John Morgan wrote his colleague Jonathan Potts, "Let me give You a piece of Advice or Hint that may be useful to You, which is to make it a part of the Duty of the Mates to assist the Apothecary in making up & dispensing Medicines. I call all Mine Hospital Mates, not merely Surgeons Mates, because I will not suffer Names to mislead, or allow any of them to refuse that Duty under a Notion that they are Surgeons Mates, & that it is not part of their Duty to assist the Apothecary. . . ." Actually, few if any of these mates served as civilians (or volunteers) for a substantial length of time, for most quickly obtained an officer's appointment within the department. The method of appointment, however, could and often did differ. Whereas regimental surgeon's mates received direct commissions from Congress, hospital mates (who, despite Morgan's practice, were also called surgeon's mates in hospitals) were appointed, and certified by warrant, by the director of the hospital department. They were, in effect, warrant officers with the duties and privileges of commissioned officers. Nurses, on the other hand, never received commissions or warrants, or, indeed, ever enlisted as nurses in the service. Some nurses were enlisted men, but they were soldiers taken from the line for temporary duty. The other nurses, whether male or female, were always hired to serve with the army, never in it, and their employment was contingent upon demand. When Dr. Dirk Van Ingen set up a small hospital in two rooms of the barracks at Schenectady in August 1777, he immediately hired "a Couple of Women and a Couple of men to attend on the Sick," and when his patients multiplied (on the 16th he had forty-three of them), he looked around for more.[89]

The hospital department hired matrons and nurses from civilian communities and the Continental Community. When the General Hospital in Massachusetts wanted nurses for its houses at Cambridge and Roxbury in the spring of 1776, its advertisement noted that preference would be given to Boston and Charlestown women. A few months later the Continental Hospital at Williamsburg, Virginia, published its need of nurses in the *Virginia Gazette* and promised that anyone with good recommendations would "have good encouragement."[90] General officers and regimental commanders also encouraged, sometimes quite strongly, female retainers (the "women of the army") to take nursing positions. In July 1776 Greene declared, "The sick Being Numerous in the Hospital And But few Women Nurses to be Had, the Regimental Surgeon must Report the Number Necessary for the sick of the Regt and the Colonels are Requested to supply accordingly. A Daily Report to Be made to the Commanding Officers of Corps by the Surgeons of the Watchers wanting in the Hospital Which are to be supply'd Accordingly."[91] The colonels could supply male or female nurses, but females were preferred because every male detailed from the line meant one fewer soldier available to fight. Therefore commanders sometimes drafted women followers as nurses, first, by promising full rations and an allowance for volunteers and, second, by threatening to withhold all rations from those reluctant to take on the duty.

A few commanders also apparently thought of hospital duty as a way to test a woman's loyalty and used the institution as a sort of low-security reformatory or prison. Although this attitude was probably rare, General Israel Putnam demonstrated it in April 1777 when dealing with a woman named Elisabeth Brewer. Brewer was apprehended coming out of British-occupied New Brunswick, New Jersey, and questioned on the reasons for her movements. During the interrogation she gave information against a number of men, two of whom Putnam secured and another who, after discounting her testimony, he released on the condition that the man inform the Americans of British movements. Putnam informed Governor William Livingston that Brewer "has an Inclination of entering the Hospital as a Nurse; in which employment she has been before employ'd at this place, and the Surgeon giving her a good Character, I have that purpose to detain her here for that purpose—If you have any Objections and will let me know, I will send her Immediately to you." There must have been objections, for in June a general court-martial found Brewer guilty of espionage and recommended incarceration.[92]

Actually, hospital work might have proved a harsher and more fitting punishment for Brewer and other such criminals if it were not for the fact that the patients would have had to suffer from their ministrations. Most Continental hospitals were overcrowded, unsanitary, and poorly ventilated. When Dr. Lewis Beebe described the hospital serving Mount Independence and Ticonderoga, he described most of the army's other medical facilities as well: he said the sick were "crowded into a dirty, Lousy, stinking Hospital, enough to kill well men."[93] Decades after the war a veteran of the battle of Germantown recalled entering a hospital "where the necessary surgical operations were performing and there beheld a most horrid sight. The floor was covered with human blood; amputated arms and legs lay in different places in appalling array. . . ."[94] The hospitals were as much a health hazard to the people who worked there as they were to the people treated there. And for the nurses illness posed a threat to their livelihoods if not their lives. After asking Doctor Potts whether nurses were allowed any liquor, Dr. Joseph Young asked if nurses who took sick were "entitled to nurses wages during their Illness."[95] It can be hoped that Potts answered in the affirmative. Of course, some hospitals were better than others. In April 1778 the Reverend James Sproat, hospital chaplain of the middle department, commented that the hospital at Yellow Springs was "very neat, and the sick comfortably provided for," and that the French Creek Church hospital was "very neat and clean, and the sick seem well attended." That June he again commended the facilities at those locations, specifically mentioning their airiness.[96]

In good conditions and bad, matrons and nurses labored to assist the surgeons and aid the sick. Although her activities included drinking tea with the doctors and providing hospitality to visiting officials, a matron was usually busy supervising the nurses and directing housekeeping activities. The steward would issue supplies, such as wine, brandy, rum, sugar, raisins, and other items prescribed by the surgeons, to the matron, and she, in turn, would see that they were distributed according to orders. She also toured the hospital two to three times each day so as to check that the patients had their food properly prepared, that the nurses were doing their duty, and that the wards and their inhabitants were clean and neat. Nurses attended to the immediate needs of the sick and performed housekeeping duties. They dealt more with hygiene than medicine: only when the hospital or surgeon's mates were not available did they administer medicines and dress wounds. Nurses generally concentrated on obeying the matron and keeping wards and patients clean. Their duties included keeping themselves clean and sober; emptying the chamber pots as soon as possible after use into necessaries or vaults dug for that purpose; washing newly admitted patients and then returning to wash their hands and face and comb their hair every morning; changing patients' linen as directed by the surgeons; sweeping out the wards every day if necessary and sprinkling them with vinegar three or four times a day; and delivering the effects of dead patients to the ward master. They were never to be absent without leave from the physicians, surgeons, or matron, and they were never to steal from their patients or colleagues. Offenders would be punished.[97]

The work was hard and the pay poor—conditions that adversely affected both the recruitment and retention of matrons and nurses. In 1775 Congress authorized a salary of four dollars a day for the director general and chief physician of the department but only four dollars a month for the matron and two dollars a month for the nurses. In comparison, soldiers received six and two-thirds dollars a month. But as the need for nurses grew, Congress periodically increased their wages (though inflation may have been at work here as well). In 1776 nurses' salaries doubled, and then in 1777 their wages were set at eight dollars a month. There was no specific legislation on nurses' pay after that time, but hospital directors and chief physicians exercised discretion in the matter when attempting to maintain their nursing staffs. But poor as the pay was, it was better than nothing. That pay plus the supplementary rations and, in the case of camp retainers, command inducements attracted women to hospital duty. The Albany hospital in July 1777 counted nine women—Eunis McNabe, Elisabeth Simson, Catrinea Sullvan, Nancy Smith, Loies Hart, Ellaner Staries, Mrs. Obrain, Mary Weston, and Sealley Tonstor—among the nurses on wards N1 to N10; only N6 had two male nurses instead of one of each sex, and N10 may have been bereft of a partner for Tonstor. The same hospital in March 1780 rationed its female personnel and their children as well as female and child patients. The matron, Sarah Ray, received two rations for herself and her son. Nurses Rachel Clement (who had two children) and Mary DeCamp (with one) also each received two rations. But their colleagues, Mrs. Perkins (with three children) and Sarah Lancaster (with her one child), only received one ration apiece. The other nurses, Grace Gilbert, Susannah Low, Mary Antrim, Sarah Demont, and Mrs. McMurry, were listed without children and received the standard one ration each. For comparison's sake, the hospital provided its carpenter, Edmd. Kingsland, and his wife and three children with three and one-half rations a day and divided twelve rations among the nine women and ten children patients.[98]

Both the army's and Congress's struggles to recruit and retain staff department personnel through pay and provision incentives indicate that these people were deemed necessary to the army's survival and success. As Lieutenant Colonel Henry Beekman Livingston put it in 1776 when he asked Washington about a barrack master and conductor of stores, "they are Persons we Can Scarcely do without."[99] That was true of persons both high and low in the departmental hierarchies. The staff officers, who considered themselves to be, and sometimes were, skilled businessmen, not only managed department operations and personnel but they often acted as liaisons between the civil governments and the military command. Their employees, whether unskilled laborers or master artisans, performed the thousands of supporting tasks "belonging to," meaning inherent to, an active army.[100]

Despite the acknowledged need for the services of staff department personnel, the extent and difficulty of their work was not always recognized, much less appreciated. When there was any disruption in army operations, they were often blamed, even when the problem was in the line not logistics. For that very reason, Major General Philip Schuyler felt obliged to defend staff department personnel on at least two occasions in 1776. Artisans, wagoners, and bateau men had been working hard to get the troops moving by land and water. But the troops did not make the task easy: their most "Amazing Quantity of Baggage" overloaded or bogged down the transports, and they abused both the persons and property of the wagoners and bateau men. The situation so deteriorated that some employees left and others threatened to, even if it meant forfeiting their wages. Furthermore, while it was true that some wagoners undoubtedly tapped the pork barrels to make transporting them easier, Schuyler, contrary to Brigadier General John Sullivan's allegations, did not think the wagoners at fault for all the bad pork. Some of it arrived in Albany without having been properly pickled in the first place.[101] So some officers and soldiers did denigrate the very people they had to depend upon. Sometimes there was reason to do so; but the army attempted to keep the reasons to a minimum.

The army expected all persons serving with it to obey regulations and follow orders. Some civilians supervised other civilian employees within the staff departments, but ultimately the military directed the actions of all of them. Sometimes the direction was quite general, as when the commander in chief established an area of operations and informed the hospital, quartermaster, commissary, and other staff departments to set up the appropriate administrative and logistics agencies, networks, and personnel to support the army's actions. At other times the direction was specific and personal, as when military officers directly supervised civilian operatives. Peter Gansevoort, colonel-commandant of Fort Schuyler, paid strict attention to the artificers working at his post. In January 1778 he reminded the carpenters that they could not under any "pretence whatsoever quit work until Ordered." Then in March he appointed a line officer, Lieutenant William Tapp, superintendent of the "Engineers-Business" and ordered the artificers and "others" to obey Tapp as such. Gansevoort also took the opportunity to state, "All the Artificers who work under Cover are to begin to work in the Morning when the Drum beats the Troop for Roll Calling [sunrise]." But in April the commander still expressed himself dissatisfied with artificer productivity. He wanted every subsequent officer of the day to walk around the works and observe if all the working parties and artificers were diligently employed; the officer was to note deficiencies on the back of the guards' morning reports. The reports apparently revealed patterns of abuse, for a month later Gansevoort ordered the superintendent of the engineers department to make sure the artificers kept the proper hours at mealtimes and to dock them one quarter of a day for every quarter of an hour they were late at the works.[102]

When artificers and other persons serving with the army disobeyed orders or abused privileges, military commanders both promised and delivered punishment. After hearing that soldiers had been seen reeling out of the carpenter's shop "very much disguised in Liquor," Gansevoort made his displeasure known in garrison orders published on 8 April: "The Commanding Officer takes this Method of acquinting the Carpenters; that if any of them are found out in disposing of any Spiritous Liquors to the Soldiers, Their allowance of Rum shall be Withheld from the said Carpenters and the person found to Offend by Transgressing of this Order shall be Tried by a Court Martial, And punish'd for Disobedience of Orders." The commander soon got the chance to deliver on his promise. "John Duncan a Carpenter employed about the Works at this place having been found Guilty of transgressing the Order of the Eight of this Month, in not only selling Rum Contrary to the said-Order but Receiving a Soldiers Blankett for pay for the said Rum. . . . The Commissary is to Issue no more of the allowance of Rum, which may hereafter be due to the said John Duncan, nor is Mr Gardner the Master Carpenter to include him in his Rum Return for the Time to come."[103] For comparison, in the earlier case concerning the wagoners and tapped pork barrels, Sullivan would not have been content with such a "civil" punishment, he was out for blood. He figured that the wagoners had "Learnt this piece of Skill in the Last War, for which Some of them were we[ll flogged,] and I hope Some of them may Share the Same fate—again."[104]

Staff officers, even when in public as opposed to military service, were no more immune to military prosecution and punishment than their subordinate civilian employees. A court-martial found Mr. Edward Miles, a deputy assistant in the commissary department who was attached to the light troops of the southern army, guilty in August 1782 "of a breach of the first article, twelfth Section of the articles of War" and sentenced him to be dismissed from the department and to forfeit all pay due for his services.[105]

Officers and employees in the staff departments found out soon after taking their positions that they belonged not only to the public (i.e., Congress) and their respective departments but to the army as well. The degree of such belonging was a matter of much debate between those in the military and civil lines, especially as officers in the former wanted to master those in the latter.

The exigencies of war and the demands of commanders battered the sensibilities of staff officers and workers and at times disrupted civil-military cooperation within the Continental Community. When that happened the army attempted more coercive methods of ensuring services and supplies: by more fully integrating, that is, enlisting, support personnel into the military.

Actually, service with the army was already much like service in it, mainly in that both public service and military personnel lived with regulation, regimentation, and deprivation. Differences could be distinguished, however, in terms of work performed, personal freedom, public recognition, and pay. Public service personnel provided support services for the military. Their work in administration or logistics allowed line personnel to concentrate on tactics and strategy. Because they were not combat personnel, most appointees and employees were free to resign or quit their positions at any time. Only those who enlisted or signed a contract for a term of service relinquished that freedom; but their enlistments still often differed from those of soldiers in the line by being of much shorter duration. Many, but not all, public service employees also obtained better pay than that given soldiers. The grumbling of the military men certainly attested to that. On the other hand, laborers and nurses did not do as well. Nor did most of these public servants do as well in terms of public recognition for their contributions to the cause.

The very nature of their employment often precluded civilian staff personnel, both those who remained in garrison and those who followed the army in combat, from receiving the accolades accorded officers and soldiers of the line. Senior staff officers received some recognition, but as public instead of military servants, as artisans and laborers instead of soldiers, most of the others serving with the army were ranked not with the "virtuous warriors" but with the camp followers. They provided essential services and supplies to the Continental Army, but because they were often perceived as feeding from instead of contributing to the public trough, and because they were workers instead of warriors, they found little glory—though plenty of regulation—in public service.

Notes

1. Washington to John Hancock, Cambridge, 21 July 1775, in W. W. Abbot, ed., *The Papers of George Washington,* Revolutionary War Series (Charlottesville: University Press of Virginia, 1985–), 1:139–40.
2. Washington to James McHenry, Philadelphia, 11 December 1781, in John C. Fitzpatrick, ed., *The Writings of George Washington* (Washington, D.C.: U.S. Government Printing Office, 1931–1944), 23:380–81. Washington mentioned McHenry's "transition from the Military to the Civil Line" in connection with his election to the Maryland Senate instead of a transfer to a staff department.
3. Rupert C. Jarvis, "Army Transport and the English Constitution: With Special Reference to the Jacobite Risings," in *The Journal of Transport History* 2 (1955–1956):

101. (Courtesy of Adam Lynde.) Frederick Bernays Wiener, *Civilians Under Military Justice: The British Practice since 1689 Especially in North America* (Chicago: University of Chicago Press, 1967), pp. 87–88. Wiener noted that in time many of the thousands of civilians in the staff departments of the British army would become militarized. A comparison of both armies during the Revolution indicated that the American army may have proceeded a bit more quickly on this course.

4. Erna Risch, *Supplying Washington's Army* (Washington, D.C.: Government Printing Office, 1981), pp. 265, 275, 310–15. Risch did a good job of unraveling the mechanisms by which the staff departments operated. Of particular note here are the ordnance and clothing departments. Another excellent source on staff department operations: Wayne E. Carp's *To Starve the Army at Pleasure: Continental Army Administration and American Political Culture, 1775–1783* (Chapel Hill: University of North Carolina Press, 1984).

5. Risch, *Supplying Washington's Army,* pp. 160–71 on the commissariat, and 29–30 on the quartermaster department. As for mention of a Quartermaster Line instead of department, see Knox's letter to Lamb, Valley Forge, 11 May 1778, in the John Lamb Papers, The New-York Historical Society (microfilm), reel 1. In that note Knox began to refer to it as a department, but then crossed it out and inserted line. He may have done so as a concession to Greene, who had just taken over the department and was carrying the letter to Lamb. James A. Huston, in *Logistics of Liberty: American Services of Supply in the Revolutionary War and After* (Newark: University of Delaware Press, 1991), p. 17, noted that the quartermaster general was "the principal staff officer of a British field army in the eighteenth century."

6. Carp, *To Starve the Army,* pp. 25–26. Congressional resolutions acknowledged that medical officers were also officers in the army. Examples include: Congressional Resolution of 11 June 1781, stating, "that the officers of the Hospital and Medical Department, now in service be allowed the Depreciation upon their pay, in same manner as officers of the Line of the Army," published in General Orders, 21 June 1781, Orderly Book, Colonel John Lamb's 2nd Regiment of Continental Artillery, 20 June–21 October 1781, The New-York Historical Society Collection of Early American Orderly Books (microfilm, David Library of the American Revolution, Washington Crossing, Pennsylvania). Lamb's orderly books (under the same title) in The New-York Historical Society's Collection will hereafter be referred to as Lamb's 2CA Orderly Book and differentiated by date. Congressional Resolution of 16 May 1783 dealing with pensions, published at Headquarters Newburgh, 27 May 1783, Lamb's 2CA Orderly Book, 28 March–25 June 1783.

7. General Orders, Headquarters, 22 August 1777, *Valley Forge Orderly Book of General George Weedon of the Continental Army under Command of Genl. George Washington, in the Campaign of 1777–8* (1902; reprint, New York: Arno Press, 1971), pp. 14–15. Risch, *Supplying Washington's Army,* p. 71.

8. Footnote 5 to Benjamin Harrison's letter notifying Washington that he could appoint some officers to the staff, 21 (–24) July 1775, Abbot, *Papers of Washington,* 1:145, 149, mentioned that John Adams was not pleased about allowing Washington to appoint staff officers. Adams felt such officers should act as checks upon Washington and he, in turn, should serve as a check on them; such a close connec-

tion could hinder that. Risch, *Supplying Washington's Army,* pp. 46–47. In discussing the issue of rank, Risch did not mention the adjutant general because she focused on the personnel and operations of the logistics branches; the adjutant general department was a purely administrative one. Carp, *To Starve the Army,* p. 157, on the ways by which staff officers described their roles expressed their patriotism.

9. Risch, *Supplying Washington's Army,* pp. 74–75.
10. Trumbull, "Lists of Persons employ'd in the Comissary General's Department in the Continental Army," Cambridge, 20 January 1776, Sol Feinstone Collection (microfilm), David Library of the American Revolution, Washington Crossing, Pennsylvania.
11. 1 August 1782 Congressional Resolution, published in General Orders, at Headquarters Newburgh, 26 December 1782, Lamb's 2CA Orderly Book, 27 November 1782–5 January 1783.
12. Quartermaster department personnel list, n.d but c. 1780, in Numbered Record Books Concerning Military Operations and Service, Pay and Settlement of Accounts, and Supplies in the War Department Collection of Revolutionary War Records (hereafter referred to as Numbered Record Books), M853, roll 25, vol. 126 (microfilm, David Library).
13. Pickering to Lincoln, Philadelphia, 23 March 1782, and to Scott, Cornel, & Dickinson (committee for arranging the officers in the staff departments), Philadelphia, 27 April 1782, Ibid., roll 26, vol. 83.
14. Congressional Resolution reorganizing the Quartermaster Department, 23 October 1782, published in General Orders, Headquarters Newburgh, 28 December 1782, Lamb's 2CA Orderly Book, 27 November 1782–5 January 1783.
15. Hancock to Washington, Philadelphia, 24 July 1775, Abbot, *Papers of Washington,* 1:165.
16. Risch, *Supplying Washington's Army,* p. 175.
17. Pickering to Washington, Newburgh, 14 January 1781, Numbered Record Books, M853, roll 25, vol. 123.
18. Pickering to Keese, Newburgh, 15 January 1781, Ibid., roll 25, vol. 123.
19. Pickering to Heath, Kings Ferry, 26 August 1781, Ibid., roll 26, vol. 127.
20. Francis J. Brooke, *A Family Narrative of a Revolutionary Officer* (1849; 1921; reprint, New York: Arno Press, 1971), p. 95.
21. Thomas M. Doerflinger, *A Vigorous Spirit of Enterprise: Merchants and Economic Development in Revolutionary Philadelphia* (Chapel Hill: University of North Carolina Press, 1986), pp. 231–32.
22. Stewart to Lamb, Bristol, 8 o'clock, 3 July 1782, John Lamb Papers (microfilm), reel 2.
23. Lamb to Board of War, Springfield, 21 February 1780, John Lamb Papers (Letterbooks) 1778–1782, The New-York Historical Society (microfilm).
24. Gano to Lamb, New Haven, 19 June 1777; Oswald to Lamb, Peekskill, 25 June 1777; and Washington to Lamb, West Point, 13 August 1780, John Lamb Papers (microfilm), reels 1 and 2. Washington wrote that a resolution of Congress stated that paymasters were to be chosen by majority vote of all the officers in a regiment while quartermasters and adjutants were to be chosen by the field officers. He did

not indicate whether appointees had to already be in the military; however, according to orders from headquarters at New York on 16 August 1776, a commissioned officer could not be appointed paymaster unless he resigned his former commission, in Peter Kinnan, *Order Book Kept by Peter Kinnan July 7–September 4, 1776,* intro. by M. E. Kinnan (Privately printed, Princeton, N.J.: Princeton University Press, 1931), pp. 67–68.

25. Orders, Camp near Chester, New York, 1 July 1779, Lamb's 2CA Orderly Book, 8 June, 14 June–19 August 1779.
26. Orders, Ashley Hill, 9 and 16 August 1782, Orderly Book: Maj. Gen. Nathaniel Greene's Orders, Southern Army, South Carolina, 1 July–5 November 1782, The New-York Historical Society's Collection of Early American Orderly Books (microfilm, David Library).
27. General Orders, Headquarters Cambridge, 16 August and 22 September 1775, Abbot, *Papers of Washington,* 1:312; 2:35. Parke recorded in Heitman's *Historical Register,* on page 424, and John Grizzage Frazer (or Fraizer) is entered as John Gizzard Frazer on page 236. Orders, Valley Forge, 25 March 1778, *Valley Forge Orderly Book,* p. 269. Brower to Lamb, Pompton, 18 May 1780, John Lamb Papers, (microfilm) reel 2.
28. James Giles to Lamb, Pluckamin, 15 May 1779, sounded rather amazed or perturbed that Mr. Richards declined a commission, "and does Duty again [emphasis his] in the Ordnance Store Department." In John Lamb Papers, (microfilm) reel 1. Risch, *Supplying Washington's Army,* p. 180; Wadsworth noted in Heitman, *Historical Register,* p. 562. The assistants and their times and places of service are recorded in the War Department Collection of Revolutionary War Records (called Record Group 93 and hereafter referred to as RG 93) in Compiled Service Records of American Naval Personnel and Members of the Departments of the Quartermaster General and the Commissary General of Military Stores Who Served During the Revolutionary War, M880 (hereafter referred to as Compiled Service Records, M880), National Archives, Washington, D.C. (microfilm, David Library), roll 1.
29. Carp, *To Starve the Army,* pp. 28–29.
30. Risch, *Supplying Washington's Army,* p. 161; Trumbull, "Lists of Persons employ'd in the Comissary General's Department in the Continental Army," Cambridge, 20 January 1776, Sol Feinstone Collection (microfilm).
31. Clerks listed in Compiled Service Records, M880, rolls 1 and 2.
32. Pickering to Hughes, Camp at Tappan, 1 October 1780, and to Claiborne, no place mentioned, November 1781, in Numbered Record Books, M853, roll 25, vol 126, and roll 26, 127.
33. General Orders, Headquarters Cambridge, 1 October 1775, Abbot, *Papers of Washington,* 2:76.
34. Headquarters New York, 2 September and 3 October 1776, George Washington's Headquarters Orderly Book, New York, 31 (misprint in records says 21) August–4 October 1776, in RG 93, Revolutionary War Miscellaneous Manuscript Collections, National Archives.
35. Pickering to Hughes, Newburgh, 18 May 1781, Numbered Record Books, M853, roll 26, vol. 127.

36. Garrison Orders, Burlington Barracks, 26 March 1782, and Garrison Orders, West Point, 24 June 1783, Lamb's 2CA Orderly Book, 7 February–7 August 1782, and 28 March–25 June 1783.
37. Garrison Orders, Burlington Barracks, 16 March 1782, Lamb's 2CA Orderly Book, 7 February–7 August 1782.
38. General Orders, Headquarters Newburgh, 5 June 1783, Fitzpatrick, *Writings of Washington,* 26:469–70.
39. General Orders, Morristown, 23 January and 5 February 1780, and General Orders, New Windsor (?), 27 May 1781, Lamb's 2CA Orderly Books, 7 December 1779–27 March 1780, and 21 February–28 March (actually goes to 28 May) 1781. In the latter Washington basically reiterates the earlier command, "only such men as are not expected to do duty with arms Viz- Genl. Field & Staff Officers Servents, Waggoners, Butchers, Bakers, Commy. QM & Forage Mastr. Assistants, and one Armourer for each Regt. in each Brigade to which a Travelling Forge is attach'd be returned on Extra service. That all others on duty in Camp or Garrison, whether with Arms, on fatigue or occasionally employed as Artificers (except Guards placed for the security of Magazines of Ammunition, Clothing or Provisions not in Garrison) be returned present on Duty, and comprised in the Number fit for action."
40. General Orders, Headquarters Morristown, 5 April 1780, Fitzpatrick, *Writings of Washington,* 18:221.
41. Garrison Orders, Fort Schuyler, 9 January 1778, Mss. Orderly Book kept at the Headquarters of LTC Marinus Willett of the 3rd New York Regiment, 17 February 1777–21 May 1778, The New-York Historical Society (microfilm).
42. Risch, *Supplying Washington's Army,* p. 89.
43. General Orders, Headquarters Orangetown, 30 September 1780, Fitzpatrick, *Writings of Washington,* 20:101–2. Heitman's *Historical Register* recorded that Cogswell became a lieutenant colonel in the 15th Massachusetts on 26 November 1779.
44. Lamb and Ayres listed in Compiled Service Records, M880, roll 1.
45. Pickering to Cogswell, Camp Phillipsburgh, 9 July 1781, and to Stewart, Camp Near Dobb's Ferry, 2 August 1781, Numbered Record Books, M853, roll 26, vol 82. Apparently there were still some problems over the double rations that summer, even though Pickering thought he had cleared it all up earlier.
46. Login recorded in Compiled Service Records, M880, roll 1; Pickering to Popkin, Newburgh, 24 January 1781, Numbered Record Books, M853, roll 25, vol. 124.
47. Lamb to Hay, Farmington, 1 June 1778, John Lamb Papers, (microfilm) reel 1.
48. Numerous letters from Pickering to wagon conductors about winter quarters for horses are in Numbered Record Books, M853, roll 25, vol. 123.
49. General After Orders, Headquarters Wilmington, 6 September 1777, *Valley Forge Orderly Book,* p. 38.
50. Brigade Orders, probably the Artillery Park near Fredericksburg, 26 September 1778, Lamb's 2CA Orderly Book, 26 September–27 November 1778.
51. *Pennsylvania Gazette,* 7 June 1780, p. 3, col. 3.
52. Carp, *To Starve the Army,* p. 62.
53. Ibid., 44, 61. James A. Huston, *Logistics of Liberty: American Services of Supply in the Revolutionary War and After* (Newark: University of Delaware Press, 1991), p.

196. Many wagoners quit at Morristown because of lack of pay, forage, convenient housing, and theft of horses and gear.
54. Risch, *Supplying Washington's Army,* p. 75.
55. Lamb to Gates, Farmington, 1 June 1778; to Hubbard, Farmington, 2 June 1778; Hubbard to Lamb, Hartford, 5 June 1778; Lamb to Hay, Farmington, 4 July 1778; all in John Lamb Papers, (microfilm) reel 1.
56. Risch, *Supplying Washington's Army,* pp. 79–80.
57. Pickering to Hand, Newburgh, 21 June 1781, Numbered Record Books, M853, roll 26, vol. 127.
58. John C. Dann, ed., *The Revolution Remembered: Eyewitness Accounts of the War for Independence* (Chicago: University of Chicago Press, 1980), pp. 371–74.
59. Anderson, William (Nancy), R. 197, pension application, in John Frederick Dorman, comp., *Virginia's Revolutionary Pension Applications, Abstracted,* 3 vols. (Washington, D.C., 1958–1959), 2:47.
60. Archer was an enlisted wagoner in wagon conductor James Login's brigade of wagoners in 1779. Adams was in John Springer's brigade in the state of Delaware for a few weeks in 1779, while Hanch was on David Boggs's payroll for a number of days, again in Delaware, in 1780. Hunn and Barbazet were stationed at Albany while wagoners in the public service under Hughes in 1782. All recorded in Compiled Service Records, M880, roll 1.
61. Davis to Washington, Cambridge, 22 July 1775, Abbot, *Papers of Washington,* 1:156. Risch, *Supplying Washington's Army,* pp. 80, 129, 132–33.
62. Pickering to William Dunn, appointment as express rider, "The like form given to the other expresses named," 5 October 1780, and Pickering to the Duke de Lauzun, Newburgh, informing him that "The bearer Mr. Lyons, one of my expresses, waits on you with a horse for your journey eastward," 4 June 1781, Numbered Record Books, M853, roll 25, vol. 126, and roll 26, vol. 127.
63. During 1780–1781 there were a number of letters referring to express operations. They included: Washington to Greene, Headquarters Morristown, regarding dismissal of expresses except those with the main army and at certain posts, 27 January 1780, in Sol Feinstone Collection; and Pickering to John Neilson, Newboro (Newburgh), on establishing a permanent express at Trenton, 2 December 1780; Pickering to Abraham Appleton, Newburgh, "Expresses are too expensive to be employed on any but extraordinary services that do not admit of delay," 15 December 1780; Pickering to Hughes, Newburgh, "chain of Expresses to be reestablished from Head Quarters to Rhode Island," 2 February 1781; last three examples in Numbered Record Books, M853, roll 25, vol. 124. Bennet was mentioned in: Schuyler to Washington, 12, 27 April and 21 May 1776; Varick to Washington, 23 May 1776; Washington to Hancock, and to Schuyler, both on 13 June 1776, in Abbot, *Papers of Washington,* 4:54, 147, 363, 375, 512, 515.
64. Frederick Mackenzie, *Diary of Frederick Mackenzie: Giving a Daily Narrative of his Military Service as an Officer of the Regiment of Royal Welch Fusiliers during the Years 1775–1781 . . . ,* 2 vols. (Cambridge: Harvard University Press, 1930; reprint, New York: Arno Press, n.d.), pp. 497–98, 536, 698–99. Mackenzie noted Moody's exploits on 31 March, 5 June (with note on the consequential nature of the

captured mail), and 20 November 1781. Interestingly, Washington wrote Rochambeau on 3 June, from New Windsor, to tell him that one of their messengers had been taken, and that among the dispatches he had was the one Rochambeau had addressed to the ministers of France. He added hopefully that "the enemy can gain no material information from my letters, and shall be happy to hear that they will be disappointed in yours." In Fitzpatrick, *Writings of Washington,* 22:155.

65. John Burrows, "The Revolutionary War Reminiscences of John Burrows," written in 1830, edited by John G. Barrett in 1975. Typescript copy of a handwritten copy that was owned by Mrs. Henry Maclin in 1975, in Virginia Historical Society, Richmond. Burrows noted that his father always kept light boys for riders to carry the mail, and then went on to recall his service as an express during the fourteen months he was a member of Washington's household (pp. 2, 8–9). "Estimate of Money due for Expresses Sta[ ] on the Road leading from Hudson River to Boston, Newburgh, 1 January 1782, in Letters, Returns, Accounts, and Estimates of the Quartermaster General's Department, 1776–1783, In the War Department Collection of Revolutionary War Records, M926, National Archives (microfilm, David Library), 1 roll.
66. Pickering to Dunn, Camp at Tappan, 5 October 1780, Numbered Record Books, M853, roll 25, vol. 126.
67. Carter and Hutton listed in Compiled Service Records, M880, roll 1.
68. Pickering to Hughes, Camp Totowa, 8 November 1780, Numbered Record Books, M853, roll 25, vol. 123.
69. Among the "Questions for the [Congressional] Committee," Cambridge, c. 18 October 1775, was one asking if it was acceptable to continue employing artificers at the high rates they demanded, in Abbot, *Papers of Washington,* 2:188; Risch, *Supplying Washington's Army,* pp. 152–53.
70. Evening Orders, Headquarters, 29 June 1776, Orderly Book of the Pennsylvania Rifle Regiment, vol. 1, Historical Society of Pennsylvania; Robert K. Wright in *The Continental Army* (Washington, D.C.: U.S. Army Center of Military History, 1983) discussed the artificer regiment on page 89.
71. Risch, *Supplying Washington's Army,* pp. 327–28.
72. Knox to Lamb, Derbey (prob. Darby), Pennsylvania, 25 August 1777, and Camp at Pracaness (Preakness?), 13 October 1780, John Lamb Papers, (microfilm) reels 1 and 2.
73. Risch, *Supplying Washington's Army,* pp. 152–57.
74. Pickering to Governor Trumbull, Camp at Totowa, 22 October 1780; to Washington, Camp [Totowa], 10 November 1780; to Hughes, Newburgh, 31 January 1781; and to Baldwin, Newburgh, 1 February 1781, Numbered Record Books, M853, roll 25, vols. (in order for letters) 126, 123, 124, 125.
75. Pickering to Peters, Newburgh, 2 February 1781; and to "To whom it may concern," Newburgh, 13 April 1781; after mentioning what arrangements had been previously made for the officers of the artificers' regiments, he mentions that Baldwin's regiment had been dissolved, Ibid., roll 25, vol. 125.
76. Pickering to Clapp, Newburgh, 19 May 1781, Ibid., roll 26, vol. 127.
77. Pickering to Cheeseman, Newburgh, 26 May 1781, Ibid., roll 26, vol. 127.
78. Pickering to Hughes, New Windsor, 4 January 1782, Ibid., roll 26, vol. 83.

79. Pickering to Hatch, New Windsor, 18 December 1781; to Claiborne, New Windsor, 16 January 1782; to McDougall, New Windsor, 14 January 1782; to Morris, Philadelphia, 19 February 1782; to Joseph Bowne (storekeeper), New Windsor, 1 February 1782; to Comfort Sands, Esq. & Co., New Windsor, 1 February 1782; to Washington, Philadelphia, 8 February 1782; Ibid., roll 26, vols. 82, 83.
80. Pickering to Clapp & Parsell, both letters from Philadelphia, 26 February 1782, Ibid., roll 26, vol. 83.
81. See Compiled Service Records, M880, roll 1, for listing of names and occupations of artificers employed in the Quartermaster General's Department. Mr. Morgan, the cutler, named in letter from Pickering to Aaron Forman (assistant deputy quartermaster at Morristown), Newburgh, 20 December 1780, Numbered Record Books, roll 25, vol. 124. Garrison Orders about building "a good Necessary," Fort Schuyler, 17 March 1778, Mss. Orderly Book kept at the Headquarters of LTC Marinus Willett of the 3rd New York Regt., The New-York Historical Society (microfilm). Mott to Lamb, about carpenter measuring cannon, Fort Constitution, 2 September 1777, and about carpenters working on axletree and wheel of six-pound artillery piece, Farmington, 27 July 1778, in John Lamb Papers (microfilm), roll 1.
82. Flower's leather accoutrements factory muster in Philadelphia in the fall of 1778 included whitesmiths, shoemakers, burers, and laborers. In the munitions industry there, people like John Beaks and his wife Deborah, Sarah Cribbs, Catherine Faries, Ann Eyres, and Elizabeth Young, among others, made cartridges from the fall of 1780 to spring 1781. Another woman, Rebecca Young, made thousands of brushes and wires. Names, some of their trades, and dates hired and quit, of personnel in Commissary General of Military Stores Department found in Compiled Service Records, M880, rolls 1 and 2. Voucher Record and Letter Book from Commissary General of Military Stores Department, Philadelphia, 2 October 1780–2 June 1781, in Letters, Orders for Pay, Accounts, Receipts, and Other Supply Records Concerning Weapons and Military Stores, 1776–1801, M927, National Archives (microfilm, David Library). Entries on John Beaks are numbers 655, 689, 729, 772, 816, and 872 (the last two mention cartridges made by his wife. Entries on Deborah Beaks include 642 and 697. Cribs is mentioned in 643, 698, 733, 791, and 894; Faries in 895, Eyres in 897, Elizabeth Young in 901, and Rebecca Young in 862.
83. Compiled Service Records, M880, include William Adams as overseer of fatigue men, and William Boerum as a fatigue man, among others in the Quartermaster Department, roll 1. Philip S. Foner in *Blacks in the American Revolution* (Westport, Conn.: Greenwood Press, 1976), p. 68.
84. Orders, Headquarters near Bacon's Bridge, 6 July 1782, and Headquarters Ashley Hill, 4 September 1782, in Orderly Book: Greene's Orders, Southern Army, South Carolina, 1 July–5 November 1782.
85. Wart payment, 15 April 1776, Financial Account from American Continental Hospital to Dr. John Morgan, 8–28 December 1775 and 31 March–3 May 1776, in RG 93, Revolutionary War Rolls, 1775–1783, M246, National Archives (microfilm), roll 135. For definition/description of hospitals, see Richard L. Blanco, "American Army Hospitals in Pennsylvania during the Revolutionary War," *Pennsylvania History* 48 (October 1981): 355.

86. Ad mentioned in "Army Nurse Corps History," unpublished work out of Washington, D.C.: Center of Military History, n.d. Copy at U.S. Army Military History Institute, Carlisle Barracks, Pennsylvania.
87. Orders about colormen duties, [Long Island], 13 June 1776, in Robert E. McCarthy, ed., *The Papers of General Nathanael Greene,* Part I: 1766–July 1780 (Scholarly Resources, Inc., microfilm). A Return of the present state of the Generl. Hospitals N. Departmt at Albany & Schenectady, January 1778; A General Return of the sick & Wounded in the General Hospital Northern Departmt. Albany, 16 February 1778; and A General Return of the sick Wounded &c in the General Hospital at Northern Department, Albany, 16 March 1778, all in Dr. Jonathan Potts Papers, Historical Society of Pennsylvania.
88. 1775 resolution and hospital hierarchy in "Army Nurse Corps History," p. 4; "Plan for Conducting the Hospital Department," 30 September 1780, in Jonathan Potts Papers; Congressional Resolution of 17 January 1781 recorded on 10 February in Lamb's 2CA Orderly Book, 17 December 1780–20 February 1781; examples of hospital personnel listed in Morgan to Potts, Copy of Congressional Resolves of 17 June 1776, sent 26 July 1776, and Dr. Samuel Stringer to Potts, Albany, 30 December 1776, Jonathan Potts Papers.
89. Morgan to Potts, New York, 28 July 1776; "Plan for Conducting the Hospital Department," 30 September 1780; Van Ingen to Potts, Sch[e]nectady, 16 August 1777, Jonathan Potts Papers.
90. Ads from *Boston Gazette and Country Journal,* 4 March 1776, and *Virginia Gazette,* 26 July and 2 August 1776, mentioned in "Army Nurse Corps History," p. 8.
91. Orders, [Long Island, New York], 11 July 1776, McCarthy, *Papers of Nathanael Greene* (from Mitchell Orderly Book).
92. Putnam to Livingston, Princeton, 25 April 1777, Sol Feinstone Collection (microfilm). Headquarters Princeton, 11 June 1777, Capt. Robert Kirkwood's Delaware Regiment Orderly Book, 1 March–21 December 1777, Force Manuscripts, 7E, Recl. 16, Entry 67, Manuscript Division, Library of Congress.
93. Risch, *Supplying Washington's Army,* p. 374; Journal Entry, Mt. Independence/Ticonderoga, 16 September 1776, Frederick R. Kirkland, ed., *Journal of Lewis Beebe: A Physician on the Campaign Against Canada, 1776* (Philadelphia: Historical Society of Pennsylvania, 1935), p. 23.
94. Dann, *The Revolution Remembered,* pp. 150-51. The veteran was William Hutchinson.
95. Young to Potts, no date, Jonathan Potts Papers.
96. Journal Entries, 25–27 April and 10–12 June 1778, John W. Jordan, ed., "Extracts from the Journals of Rev. James Sproat, Hospital Chaplain of the Middle Department, 1778," *Pennsylvania Magazine of History and Biography* 27 (October 1903): 442–44. Blanco in "American Army Hospitals in Pennsylvania," pp. 358–65, described hospital conditions.
97. On 12 and 13 June 1778 Sproat mentioned drinking tea with the doctors and matron and being "Genteely treated by Dr. Otto and the matron, Mrs. Adams," in "Extracts from the Journals of Rev. James Sproat," pp. 443–44; "Army Nurse Corps History," listed the matron's duties as described in "Rules and Directions for the better regulation of the Military Hospital of the United States," and nurses duties, pp. 13–14.

98. Pay issues, Ibid., pp. 4–5, 9. "Names of the nurses in the following wards," Albany, 27 July 1777, in Jonathan Potts Papers; A Return of the Officers &c. belonging to the Gen. Hospital, Northn. Department, Albany, 20 March 1780, Revolutionary War Rolls, M246, roll 135.
99. Livingston to Washington, Fort Constitution, 11 [–14] June 1776, in Abbot, *Papers of Washington,* 4:501.
100. Doerflinger, *Vigorous Spirit,* p. 224; Knox to" Committee of the honorable Congress now in Camp," Headquarters Harlem Heights, 27 September 1776 (III-58), in Henry Knox Papers, III, 58. GLC243, The Gilder Lehrman Collection, on deposit at the Pierpont Morgan Library, New York (microfilm, David Library). In making his suggestions for the improvement of the artillery, Knox wrote, "Exclusive of the Artificers at the said Laboratories there must be an hundred of different branches attachd to the Artillery—to repair Carriages when broken, make platforms and a thousand other matters belonging to the Artillery."
101. Schuyler to Washington, Albany, 10 May and 15 June 1776, in Abbot, *Papers of Washington,* 4:264, 533–34. Although officers often scorned the lower orders, one noted a time when he had to revise his opinion. "An Instance that even the lowest class of men are not entirely divested of tender Sensations, happen'd this morning—A waggoner who had a good and faithful dog that took sick and for some days and Nights kept a continual howling which made it necessary out of mercy to the dog & ourselves to rid him of a Life that could be only troublesome—the Waggoner was sent for and the orders given for killing the dog—the poor fellow with tears in his Eyes replied 'Gentlemn yon poor dog has been as faithful a dog to take care of my waggon as ever was;—I know it would be an act of Mercy . . . but I canot find it in my heart to do it my self'—the Simplicity and Gratitude of the man really affected me[.] How often do we observe persons in higher Stations of Life do not possess half the humanity of this poor waggoner." 8 July 1780 entry, in Continental Army, Military Life Diary by U/I Author, 21 April—25 September 1780, Virginia Historical Society, Richmond.
102. Garrison Orders, Fort Schuyler, 31 January, 10 March, 17 April, and 19 May 1778, Mss. Orderly Book kept at the HQ of LTC Marinus Willett of the 3rd New York.
103. Garrison Orders, Fort Schuyler, 8 and 26 April 1778, Ibid.
104. Sullivan to Washington, Albany, 18 May 1776, in Abbot, *Papers of Washington,* 4:336.
105. Greene's Orders, Headquarters Ashley Hill, South Carolina, 17 August 1782, Orderly Book: Greene's Orders, Southern Army, South Carolina, 1 July–5 November 1782.

7

Subject to Orders and the Discipline of War

> All suttlers and retainers to a camp, and all persons whatsoever serving with the armies of the United States in the field, though no inlisted soldier, are to be subject to orders, according to the rules and discipline of war.
>
> *Article 23, Section XIII,*
> *American Articles of War,*
> *20 September 1776[1]*

To visitors and residents alike, the Continental Community sometimes appeared to be a chaotic rather than an ordered community. It may also at times have appeared to be the antithesis rather than the champion of the new American republic and all for which it stood. The image of stalwart male citizens shouldering their arms, kissing their families good-bye, and resolutely forming up into orderly lines to march off to win the war for independence was shattered by the reality of not just combat but life with the army. Children shrieked and ran around the tents and clambered aboard wagons. Women looked up from their chores to shout at their offspring or make rude remarks to sergeants and officers passing by. Drunken soldiers engaged in riotous behavior, and independent-minded ones, when they did not desert, sometimes spat at their commanders' feet and questioned orders, while their enraged officers occasionally responded with blows. Even among the higher echelons of the military hierarchy peace and order were seldom maintained; officers dueled among themselves, both verbally and physically. And under cover of this apparent confusion, thieves and spies sneaked through the lines to pilfer supplies or gather information.[2]

The army not only had the enemy to defeat, it also had itself to control and, as it turned out, to mold. It had to control the individualism that at times threatened to run rampant in response to cries of rights and paeans of liberty, while it molded individuals into a respectable army of soldiers and adjunct personnel with responsibilities that equaled if not exceeded their rights. Maintaining order, a sense of purpose, and the individual's role in that purpose presented a constant challenge to military commanders throughout the war. Furthermore, they had to impose discipline and instill that sense of professional purpose and pride within not only the military context but the republican one as well. Discipline meant not only subordination within the ranks and community but subordination to the wishes of the public as expressed by the people's governments; only then would there be success in both war and revolution.

As the Congress and military command grappled with the question of why such discipline had to be imposed, they also wrestled with the problem of how it was to be applied. From the beginning, starting with General Washington's encampment at Cambridge, a reliance on the virtues supposed inherent in American revolutionaries as well as on the civilian courts and procedures proved both inadequate and inconvenient for maintaining the discipline necessary in an effective military force. As a result, Congress and the army collaborated to create a military justice system by which officers, soldiers, and associated personnel were controlled not only by the local laws governing all people but by additional and more stringent rules of war. The Continental Congress, demonstrating its control over and within the military, erected the constitutional framework for military law by passing the 1775 and subsequent 1776 Articles of War, the ordinances governing the army. Military commanders then had a legislative as well as a strategic or tactical basis for issuing the orders—written and verbal commands, whether general orders or regulations issued by a general officer to control an army or specific orders given by a company commander to a subordinate—that further restrained or initiated actions conducive to military success or community welfare. Finally, and also importantly, military and associated personnel were bound by the custom of war, the established or customary principles and practices peculiar to army life, that at times acted as the military's version of the common law. These three tiers of authority—laws, orders, and custom—not only regulated but also helped to create a military community that was something more than an assembly of officers, soldiers, and followers.

A focus on laws, orders, and military custom was necessary to ensure order in this new community, especially since the already weakening deferential behaviors that supported discipline in civilian communities were further disrupted by the move into the Continental Community. But laws, orders, and custom were not only mechanisms for discipline; they also served to define and then reflect the developing institutional culture of this new American community.[3] As the army, with Congress's approval, created and implemented military and martial law, it strove not only to impose its will upon its people but to substitute its own social (that is, sociomilitary) structure and norms for the ones the newcomers brought with them and to build within them, if they did not have them already, such republican virtues as subordination and self-sacrifice (putting cause and community first above individual interests), as well as courage and discipline. Furthermore, acceptance of and obedience to the precepts and practices of this legal system helped foster a creedal as well as operational conformity and solidarity—a professional ethos—among the people of the Continental

Community that would help them meet the demands and survive the rigors of the war.

Revolutionaries declared independence and worked on establishing a republic while claiming that the former would be won and the latter successful because Americans were a good and noble people—people who would pledge their lives, fortunes, and honor to the cause. While some people were inherently good and others determined to do good, many did not fit the virtuous mold. Washington dealt with that reality by the imposition of discipline. Essentially, Washington seemed to work on the premise that if we declare we are a good people then we must attempt to appear to be so, and in learning to appear so, we can become such. The general had begun the process when he took command but redoubled his efforts with the commencement, on 1 January 1776, of the new army, "which, in every point of View is entirely Continental." After reminding the army of the importance of the cause, he acknowledged that "our men are brave and good; Men who with pleasure it is observed, are addicted to fewer Vices than are commonly found in Armies"; but, he went on, "it is subordination & discipline (the Life and Soul of an Army) which next under providence, is to make us formidable to our enemies, honorable in ourselves, and respected in the world."[4]

Washington knew that instilling such an ethos would not be an easy task. "To bring Men well acquainted with the Duties of a Soldier, requires time—to bring them under proper discipline & Subordination, not only requires time, but is a Work of great difficulty; and in this Army, where there is so little distinction between the Officers and Soldiers, requires an uncommon degree of attention." But he knew it was an essential task if his people were successfully to fend off the foe. Commanders could not depend on the natural bravery or hope of reward that could be found in both recruit and veteran to carry the day. Instead there also had to be an instilled fear of punishment—that coercive element of discipline—to prompt men to discharge their duties in combat.[5] Unfortunately, as the general pointed out, short enlistments and egalitarian practices interfered with the acceptance of such discipline.

An insistence on and exercise of equality compromised authority, and when authority was compromised there was little discipline. Therefore, the first things Washington had to do were establish the righteousness and authority of the army itself, settle the hierarchy or chain of command within it, and insist upon recognition of both. To make the first point, he approved the courts-martial and convictions of those who spoke disrespectfully of the American government or army.[6] To facilitate the second point, he had promotions published and established insignias of rank. Since many officers did not have a distinctive uniform that would set them apart from the rank and file, Washington had them wear cockades and ribbons of different colors. Once soldiers could recognize an officer, even outside of their own companies, they were supposed to act accordingly. Ignorance was no longer a viable plea, and disrespect was punished via fines and a variety of corporal punishments.[7]

Along with insisting that soldiers show respect, Washington insisted that officers earn it. He certainly would not have wanted to hear stories about troops "*pretending* to exercise and maneuver" and being "haw'd about by a set of Ignoramus's and made the sport and ridicule of spectators."[8] Instead he wanted his officers to study the various manuals and treatises on the military sciences and discipline and then apply what they learned. He also wanted the officers out on the parade ground, in the field, and in camp so that they could properly supervise their troops and thus ensure discipline. One person who tried to do exactly that was Benjamin Gilbert. As an enlisted man and then as a junior officer Gilbert was not exactly a prime example of deference himself, but over the course of his military service he did acquire a little self-discipline, and he did put in some time disciplining his own troops. The latter was a frustrating experience because of a constant need to train new recruits. As he wrote in October 1780, "Ever since I came to camp I have been up at day-brake a dissiplining the levies and every afternoon when off duty on the same or Business. As soon as they are learned their times are out and we must take new ones that makes us perpettual slaves." He then echoed the lament of other officers in saying that such troops were a disadvantage to the officers over them, for not only was it tiring and troublesome to be constantly training them, but you could not trust them to do their duty, whether as sentry or soldier in battle. He bemoaned the fact that "the Bravest officer may lose his honour by having such soldiers."[9]

Gilbert was protesting against the practice that Washington had for years pointed out as detrimental to military discipline—that of short enlistments. New recruits were always needed and thus welcomed, but the army also needed a core of veterans that could train the newcomers by example and stabilize them in battle. Veteran officers and soldiers were the disciplined elements of the army. Lieutenant Gilbert showed himself to be one when he commented on how disagreeable it was to be "obliged to conform to the strick regulations and implicit obedience of a Military government" after having visited home for a while, but he then went on to admit that "this being become habitual and familiar I am tolerably reconciled to my present situation."[10] The veteran Joseph Plumb Martin, years later, reminded people why troops so habituated were needed, and how they got that way.

> [Militia troops] would not have endured the sufferings the army did; they would have considered themselves (as in reality they were and are) free citizens, not bound by any cords that were not of their own manufacturing, and when the hardships of fatigue, starvation, cold and nakedness . . . begun to seize upon them . . . they would have instantly quitted the service. . . . That the militia did good and great service . . . I well know . . . but I still

insist that they would not have answered the end so well as regular soldiers.... The regulars were there and there obliged to be; we could not go away when we pleased without exposing ourselves to military punishment, and we had trouble enough to undergo without that.[11]

Some of the regulars did, of course, expose themselves to military punishment when they proved themselves to be "Deaf to the Cause of Justice and reason"[12] by deserting, mutinously protesting, or trying to alleviate, in illegal ways, the hardships of which Martin wrote. That was when the military's system of law and discipline really showed itself.

The establishment of this legal system occurred concurrently with the creation of country and army. It thus reflects not only British precedents (as did so much else in colonial culture) but revolutionary principles and experimentation. At the same time the colonists were fighting for their independence from Britain, they continued to borrow heavily from it. As the colonists had no tradition of a standing army themselves (militias and expeditionary forces were different organisms), they adopted British military law and custom to create their national army and to promote the necessary discipline within it. Rather unconsciously, by the way, they were also adopting the precepts and practices of an army developed not only to defend national interests but promote imperial ones. Furthermore, this was a military legal system proposed and implemented by elites (congressional and military officers) that did not want to have a social revolution, hence the emphasis on a discipline that would not only help inculcate the deference essential to battlefield operations but that would create an orderly community. They did, however, modify some of the principles and penalties inherent to British military law to bring them into closer conformity with revolutionary beliefs. Deference in the American camp would supposedly be fostered by the virtue of subordination and the respect earned by leaders, instead of being given simply due to social and military rank or because it was beaten into the soldiers. British military discipline, especially via the whip, could be Draconian, so the revolutionaries, idealistically believing in republican virtue but realistically recognizing recruiting and retention problems, moderated the prescribed punishments.

When the fighting commenced at Lexington Green, the Massachusetts militia was already operating under articles of war passed by the Provisional Congress of Massachusetts Bay on 5 April 1775. The Massachusetts assembly resolved that the "Articles, Rules and Regulations for the Army, that may be raised for the defence and security of our lives, liberties, and estates, be, and are hereby earnestly recommended to be, strictly adhered to, by all Officers, Soldiers, and others concerned, as they regard their own honour and the publick good."[13] The legislators copied most of their articles almost verbatim from those then in force in the British army, and both sets of rules in turn were models for the American Articles of War that followed.

The Continental Congress enacted the first American Articles of War on 30 June 1775. These articles became effective on 10 August. Following the Massachusetts example, this code of law made punishment less severe than that required by British law. Again, this was, as stated above, due to a practical evaluation of available manpower, and because most of the lawmakers thought that the patriotism and dedication of the American soldier would make harsher punishment unnecessary. Many Americans believed that native courage reinforced by the love of freedom was enough to make a revolutionary into a good soldier, but within months, if not within days, the new army's general officers decided that courage could not replace discipline. Although they continued to recruit by appealing to patriotism, and continued to vaunt their soldiers' determination to preserve liberty, the generals often saw their subordinates' dedication to personal freedom as a military drawback and tried to temper it with military ritual and law.[14] This proved a difficult task.

Washington's first attempt at uniform regulation met with rejection. After the 1775 Articles of War were passed, he tried to get all the officers and soldiers to subscribe to them. Many refused because they feared it would lengthen their service obligation; in essence they were afraid that they would be signing a new contract or entering into a new compact. Washington decided not to press them on the issue, for he "did not experience any such Inconvenience from their Adherence to their former Rules [Massachusetts articles], as would warrant the Risque of entering into a Contest upon it: More especially as the Restraints necessary for the Establishment of essential Discipline & Subordination, indisposed their Minds to every Change, & made it both Duty & Policy to introduce as little Novelty as possible." He believed the difficulty would cease with the establishment of the new army in 1776.[15] In the meantime, the courts-martial decided cases using either the Massachusetts or 1775 Continental articles depending on the status of the defendants. For example, on 15 November 1775 a general court-martial found Lieutenant Soaper (possibly Amasa Soper) and Ensign (Avery) Parker guilty "of a breach of the 46th Article [conduct unbecoming an officer and gentleman] of the Rules and Regulations for the Massachusetts Army." Their abuse of two other lieutenants led to their dismissal from the army.[16]

While the commander in chief struggled to establish the legal code and system upon which military discipline would depend, Congress made further provisions. It amended the original code on 7 November 1775, only to repeal it within a year and replace it with the American Articles of War of 1776, passed on 20 September. The new articles echoed the British law more closely and remained in force throughout the war. This military law extended over officers, enlisted men, and "civilians who served with or accompanied the army in the field." The qualifier "in the field" was meant to indicate that this legal system's jurisdiction was restricted to times of war. Even so, many of these civilians, along with other Americans, objected to a legal system "in which indictment by grand jury and other fundamental rights were unknown"; but military necessity—an argument made all the more potent by the fact that without military success everyone could be facing another legal system backed by an angry government—was considered justification for military (rules regulating military personnel) or, more specifically, martial (regulation over all people within a militarily controlled area) law.[17] Although it made note of the objections, Congress, during the war and later, accepted the necessity of this system of law just as it had accepted the necessity of an army. Congress reiterated its approval of the rules and articles in force during the Revolution by adopting them (with the 1786 revision of Section XIV) under the Constitution on 29 September 1789. They continued in force until replaced by the Articles of War of 1806.[18]

Military commanders issued orders and regulations within the limitations imposed by civilian legal codes, articles of war, and the chain of command. Such orders took on the force of law; violation or disobedience could result in a court-martial. Officers at all levels issued orders, but the regulations ordered by a general took precedence over all others. General orders affected entire armies; division, brigade, and regimental orders applied to those specific units; while further down the organizational ladder, even more restricted in scope, were company-level commands. Finally, all officers could give direct orders to anyone under their command.

There were standing orders and situational orders. The first kind covered activities no matter what the time, locale, or circumstance. A standing order could be a prosaic outline of administrative functions or provide a fine example of revolutionary principles operating in the military sphere. Washington issued one such standing order against plundering in September 1776: "The General does not admit of any Pretence for plundering—whether it is Tory Property—taken beyond the Lines or not it is equally a Breach of Orders & to be punished in the Officer who gives Orders or the Soldier who goes without."[19] This was in line with Articles 16 and 21, Section XIII of the 1776 Articles of War. Article 16 declared that the malicious destruction of "any property whatsoever belonging to the good people of the United States, unless by order of the then commander in chief . . . to annoy rebels or other enemies in arms . . ." would result in a punishment determined by the nature of the offense, and by the judgment of either a regimental or a general court-martial. Article 21 stipulated that an officer or soldier convicted of leaving his post in search of plunder could be sentenced to death by a general court-martial.[20] Congress and Washington allowed no one to forget that this fight was about personal and political liberty, not the "liberation" of property.

Situational orders rarely held a political subtheme though they could include a succinct lesson on virtue. Generally, they were job-specific. Some were as arbitrary and deadly as the order before Germantown on 15 September 1777 that commanded officers in the rear to execute immediately "any man who is not wounded whether he has Arms or not, turns his back on the Enemy & attempts to run away or retreat before orders are given for it. . . . The Man does not deserve to live, who basely flies, breaks his solemn engagements & betrays his Country."[21] In this case the commander in chief wanted to make sure he did not lose a battle because of cowardice and the panic caused by soldiers fleeing to the rear. That was clear enough; however, he then went on to explain why the punishment would be so severe: essentially, the virtuous soldier should see cowardice as a mortal sin. Most other situational orders reflected a milder temper, especially when they dealt with a common irritant: on 1 September 1777, when the line of march for Wilmington was published, officers were "desired to prevent the Waggons being loaded with men & weomen, none to ride but those soldiers who are unable to march."[22] While that order was directed at the officers supervising the baggage train, it essentially further empowered them to command camp followers. And while only officers had the right to give orders, the duty to obey was not confined to the military ranks.

On the march or in garrison, officers regularly posted orders for the regulation of civilians in the proximity of the troops. As mentioned in an earlier chapter, army officers, high and low, regulated sutlers closely. Captain Joseph Bloomfield certainly did. On 1 September 1776 at German-Flatts, he noted that some of his soldiers crossed the river, got drunk, and did not make it back to garrison at night. To correct such misconduct, he ordered out a guard to round up the miscreant soldiers and forbade the selling of liquor by any sutler except Lieutenant Colonel Belinger, who already had permission to sell near the garrison.[23] A year later sutlers with General Weedon's brigade at Wilmington were ordered to move away from the front of the encampment. Then, on 1 November general orders directed the commissaries to buy, at a reasonable price, all the liquor held by sutlers. If the two parties could not agree on a common price, the sutlers were to cart their stock away, for "no Sutler shall be allowed to continue in the army after the 5 Inst." That proved to be a temporary situation. Sutlers and other sellers were almost always around; and the army was always ready to order their affairs. This was evident at Valley Forge, where the army supervised a number of camp markets. The adjutant general had the market regulations printed on handbills and then delivered to the brigades so that they could be read to each regiment; but the officers and soldiers were not the only ones made familiar with market procedures and prices; the civilians who manned the market also received the handbills.[24]

The army was as equally determined to control its female followers. Commanders constantly reminded women when they could accompany the forces, how they could travel with the troops, and what they could or could not do in camp. Orders regulated the most intimate parts of their lives. On 1 July 1777, at Lincoln Mountain while on the march from Princeton, the commander of the Delaware Regiment ordered "That the Weomen belonging to the Regt. be paraded tomorrow morning & to undergo an examination [for venereal disease] from the Surgeon of the Regiment at his tent except those that are married, & the husbands of those to undergo said examination in their stead. All those that do not attend to be immediately drumed out of the Regiment."[25]

Regardless of their sex, all civilians with the army or just passing through its lines had to deal with intrusive army tactics. Officers had orders to check out "all strange faces & suspicious Characters which may be discover'd in Camp, & if upon examination, no good account can be given why they are there, they are then to carry them to the Majr. Genl. of the day for further examination." This was to be done in as inoffensive a manner as possible.[26] It was a necessary order only in that it told the officers what to do with suspicious characters; otherwise, it served only to remind them of a customary and prudent duty: checks were necessary for the proper management of the troops and the security of the camp.

Custom, as much as military law and orders, also regulated life in and with the army. The custom of war, or what was in effect the common law of the army, was not a formal written code. It was, instead, "collected from the general regulations of the army, and from the habits, practices, and rules which prevail[ed] in the military body."[27] This military common law served as a supplementary reference and guide in the administration of army justice. Congress formally recognized custom as a component of military regulation and judicial proceedings in Article 3, Section XIV, of the 1776 Articles of War. Article 3 required that each member of a court-martial swear to "duly administer justice according to the rules and articles for the better government of the forces of the United States of America, without partiality, favor, or affection; and if any doubt shall arise, which is not explained by said articles, according to your conscience, the best of your understanding, and the custom of war in the like cases."[28] The custom of war supplemented the Articles of War; it did not supersede them, nor could it be used to oppose them. It extended military authority and jurisdiction by filling in any gaps left by the written laws.

The decision to hang Major John André for his espionage and role in Benedict Arnold's treason, for example, was based on the custom of war. André had asked to be shot, but "it was thought this indulgence being incompatible with the customs of war could not be granted."[29] Hanging was considered to be an ignominious way to die and thus appropriate for those, like André, taken as spies in civilian clothing. Although André had garnered a great deal of sympathy among American officers who considered him to be essentially honorable, though tarred by Arnold's treason, they felt themselves bound by the custom of war as both a determinant of law and behavior. Perhaps the Americans clung to the custom as closely as they did because such action demonstrated and legitimized their positions as army officers, not just rebels: they were acting in accordance with established military procedure. The British, as upset as they were over the sentence and nature of execution, had to understand the decision because they too operated under this custom of war. This is not to say that the custom of war was rigid or static. The Americans adopted much of what they knew of the British custom of war, but they also adapted it, as they did statute law, as needed. It did evolve over the course of the war, especially in deciding punishments, but nonetheless generally acted as a conservative cultural and legal device.

All three forms of regulation—the articles, orders, and custom—were essential to the survival of the Continental Army as well as the welfare of its community. They were the muscles attached to the administrative skeleton. Policing of this community was necessarily rigorous and enforcement swift, for dissent within such a self-contained organization undermined discipline and impaired the ability of the army to wage war effectively.[30] As mentioned before, enlistment or the acceptance of a commission entailed the subordination of individual interests to those of the army. Soldiers temporarily surrendered some of the very rights and liberties they swore to defend. Commitment to American independence supposedly compensated for any feeling of sacrifice. Unfortunately, as Lieutenant Colonel Edward Hand of Thompson's Pennsylvania Rifle Battalion found out, convincing soldiers that army life and successful campaigns required the subordination of their individual interests proved difficult. As early in the war as September 1775, the officers of that unit had to put down a small revolt triggered by the disciplining of a sergeant.[31]

Mutinies flared up periodically, desertions were frequent, and insubordination was commonplace. In September 1775 a general court-martial found Moses Pickett, a soldier in Captain Merrit's (probably Lieutenant John Merritt) company of Colonel John Glover's regiment, guilty of "disobedience of orders, and damning his Officers." It sentenced him to receive thirty lashes and then to be drummed out of the regiment.[32] The problem continued throughout the war, but as the army could not afford to dismiss men just for insubordination, punishments remained painful but less extreme (especially when the culprit refused to obey a noncommissioned, as opposed to commissioned, officer's orders). At what was probably a regimental court-martial, Anthony Parras of the 2nd Continental Artillery was found guilty of "disobedience of Orders, and Insolence towards Sergt Cochran" in 1782. The court sentenced him to "wear the Log," attend all parades and perform fatigue duty for one week, and ask the sergeant's pardon at parade.[33]

Officers, who were supposed to be good examples to their men, were often as guilty of insubordination and disobedience when they questioned orders or sidestepped their duties. The commander in chief tried to squelch such maneuvers by reminding officers of their obligations:

> It is not for every Officer to Know the principles upon which orders are issued, and to Judge how they may, or may not be dispens'd with or Suspended: but their duty to carry them into execution with the greatest punc-

tuality and exactness—They are to consider that military movements are like the working of a Clock, and will go equally regular and easy if every Officer does his duty: but without it, be as easily disorder'd; because neglect in any one part, like the stop[p]ing of a Wheel disorders the whole.[34]

The officers and troops of the Continental Army did learn to accept discipline and to act with it. Indeed, they displayed such discipline and tenacity (some opponents thought it sheer perversity) in the face of hardship that foreign observers came to admire them.

Civilians entering the army's camps had a choice: to obey or begone. In other words, camp followers also had to accept military discipline, for they were admitted into the military community and allowed to remain only so long as they did not disrupt it. As merchants licensed to sell in camp, sutlers were obligated to conform to camp policies, obey orders, and adhere to the stipulations of their contract. This meant that they agreed to having their products, premises, and practices regulated and inspected. Moreover, they knew that if they were accused of illegal actions, essentially disobeying orders, they could be tried by court-martial and upon conviction forced to forfeit stock, pay a fine, or lose their suttling license and thus have to leave the area.[35]

Compared to the sutlers, women in camp were in a more precarious situation, for their tenure depended more on sufferance than on contracts. The army never established a formal policy to regulate camp women beyond their accountability to the articles of war, so subordinate commanders, generally according to custom, established their own ways to discipline them. If the women did not live by the rules, they could, and often were, summarily punished. Such was the case on 16 July 1777, when Captain Robert Kirkwood of the Delaware Regiment recorded that a woman belonging to the division was ducked for stealing and insolence.[36] The meticulous Kirkwood made no mention of a trial preceding the punishment.

The army demanded that all civilians, not just sutlers and women, serving with the military accept the regulations imposed on those serving in "uniform." The government of the United States backed the army on this point, making specific reference to civil department officers. Congress on 10 June 1777 resolved

> That the Commissy. Genl. of purchaces and Issues and their respective deputies for neglect of Duty or other offences in their respective Offices shall be subject to Military Arrests and trial by order of the Commander in Chief or any Genl. Commanding a Division in the Army, Post or Department, where such neglect of duty or Offences may happen and their respective Assistants of the D[eputy] C[ommissary] Genl. of purchases and Issues shall for the same causes be liable to Military Arrests as

Commissd. Officers in the Army by any Genl. Officer or any Officer Commandg. at a Detach'd Post to which Such Assistant may be Assigned.[37]

In practice the rule extended to quartermasters, wagon masters, surgeons, nurses, clerks, and artificers as well. Some of these people held dual appointments: although commissioned or enlisted in the military line, they also filled staff positions. In such cases there was no problem about military jurisdiction. For those people in the staff departments, however, who held no military rank, this ruling clarified their position under military law.

Camp-follower compliance with military regulations and orders did not depend on the discretion of the followers themselves. To have depended solely upon their acquiescence would have been asking too much of virtue on both sides. Commanders governed camp civilians, or imposed discipline upon them, by invoking custom, common sense, and courts-martial. They used both social custom and military custom to control women and servants. Men, as husbands and masters, were expected to be able to influence their wives' and servants' actions. Men, as officers and soldiers, were within a chain of command and as such responsible for the care and regulation of their dependents. When custom and habit provided no guidelines in a particular situation, commanders relied on their own judgment in dealing with followers. The use of custom and common sense was neither unusual nor illegal in eighteenth-century local government and jurisprudence, but should any camp follower have protested that such a practice was not a legal basis for the military's disciplining of civilians, he or she would have found that loop-hole closed when American military jurisdiction over camp civilians became a matter of law.

In 1775 the Massachusetts Articles of War included a statute for the control of all sellers to a camp and persons serving with (not in) the Massachusetts army in the field. The Continental Congress took Article 31 of the Massachusetts articles and with the appropriate modifications included it as Article 32 in the 1775 American Articles of War passed that June. Military legal jurisdiction over camp civilians was confirmed by Article 23, Section XIII, of the 1776 Articles of War. These statutes, reflecting earlier British ones and repeated in later revisions of military law, have historically allowed wartime commanders to control all persons within their areas of operation. In peacetime the army handed such civilians over to local civilian courts for disciplining, but most legislators agreed with military men that war required swift and decisive action. Thus all sutlers, retainers to the camp, and persons serving with the armies of the United States in the field were subject to orders according to the rules and discipline of war, and whether connected with the army accidentally, temporarily, or permanently, they were liable, "by order of the commander, to trial by court-martial for any breach of good order, whether as affecting the discipline of the army, or the private rights of individuals."[38]

The justification for Article 23 and all other regulations concerning the army's civilians was always the necessity to maintain good order. These dependents and adjunct personnel enjoyed certain privileges, including rations and tent space, in return for the services and conveniences they offered to the soldiers. Coming with that exchange though, when they voluntarily entered the army community with all its additional and distinctive laws, they indicated their willingness to conform to those laws or suffer the penalty when they broke them.[39] For even as the commander was responsible for his people, all his people, so too were these people obliged to obey him.

Ignorance did not justify disobedience; echoing his orders of July 1775, Washington again put a halt to such pleas in September 1777 when, upon learning that many regiments had only one orderly book, he ordered all regimental commanders "to see that the Officers & Men are clearly Inform'd of every order which relates to them respectively, by reading or causing the same to be read to them" until each company had an orderly book.[40] Additional steps were taken to make sure followers got the message. From his headquarters at Verplanck's Point on 8 September 1782 Washington decreed: "As there are many orders for checking irregularities with which the women, as followers of the army, ought to be acquainted, the ser[g]eants of the companies to which the women belong, are to communicate all orders of that nature to them, and are to be responsible for neglecting so to do."[41] Washington was only formalizing what was already standard operating procedure for many units.

In a wartime situation a commander had to be able to control accompanying dependents and civilians just as he controlled his soldiers. These people became "to all intents and purposes, so far as crime may be committed, members of the army." They could not be considered separate from it, for their crimes might disgrace the service and could lead to its disorganization. There was also the possibility that if they were not punished by a military tribunal, they would escape justice and serve as bad examples to soldiers as well as other civilians.[42]

The security of both government and army, as well as the morale and discipline of the troops, required that these civilians be governed in like manner as the people with whom they associated.[43] Furthermore, the full weight of the military legal system fell not only upon legitimate camp followers but upon unauthorized ones as well. As a closed camp was an impossibility, despite the pickets and patrols assigned to guard against espionage, security ultimately rested upon the discretion and patriotism of all the people who passed through the checkpoints. Soldiers had a responsibility to prevent disclosure of military information to the enemy, but not all followers accepted that responsibility. Some people did not pledge their allegiance to the United States, and others put personal gain ahead of any nation. That being the case, spies regularly observed and infiltrated the camps. And some got caught.

There was some confusion and argument over the status of spies and thus over the appropriate jurisdiction for their trials. But generally spies were considered, by most interpretations of the law and as supported by the custom of war, to be associated with military forces even if they were not in them. Article 19, Section XIII, of the 1776 Articles of War declared that "Whosoever shall be convicted of holding correspondence with, or giving intelligence to the enemy, either directly or indirectly, shall suffer death, or such other punishment as by a court-martial shall be inflicted." The legislators purposefully did not add the caveat to restrict this to uniformed personnel that was present in the 1775 articles, nor did they mean to restrict culpability by sex; they considered women quite capable of committing espionage and treason. The Continental Congress made that point earlier in the conflict when it declared that all residents of the United Colonies, "and deriving protection from the laws of the same," owed their allegiance to those laws.[44]

In time of war a person, whether soldier or civilian, charged with spying and abetting the enemy was usually tried by military tribunal. Occasionally the tribunal was not a regular court-martial, as in the case of Thomas Shanks. Shanks, formerly an ensign in the 10th Pennsylvania, had been cashiered for stealing shoes in October 1777. He then decided to act as a spy for the British. Unfortunately for him, a British deserter betrayed him. Washington thought it best "to avoid the formality of a regular trial," especially as Shanks had made some sort of a confession, and asked the Board of General Officers on 2 June 1778 to examine the prisoner. He said that "if his guilt is clear, his punishment will be very summary." Shanks was hanged on 4 June.[45] Most tribunals, however, were courts-martial. One in Philadelphia that August pronounced George Spangler a spy. He was executed on the common near the city. Another such military court at the American headquarters at Providence, on 1 October 1778, tried four civilians at once: Job Tibbots, James Austin, Joseph Hunt, and Nathanael Noyes, accused of being spies for the enemy, pleaded not guilty and were released for lack of evidence. Seth Meed and Abraham Knap were either not so guiltless or lucky: a general court-martial in the Highlands of New York in June 1780 sentenced them to be "hung by the Nect" for their crimes.[46]

The legality of trial by courts-martial for unassociated civilians was a bit more problematic for other treasonable offences (crimes against the state as opposed to crimes against the army). Yet in the early months of 1778 numerous civilians were tried by military courts for attempting to supply the enemy. Many were convicted and suffered the lash, fines, and imprisonment. Washington was careful to note that inhabitants so charged were not triable under the Articles of War (even though Article 18, Section XIII—"Whosoever shall relieve the enemy with money, victuals, or ammunition . . . shall suffer death, or such other punishment as by a court-martial shall be inflicted."—allowed a more general application) but were being tried by courts-martial according to the special resolution Congress passed on 8 October 1777 and then extended that December.[47] Indeed, in October 1779, with the British long gone, it was a civilian court (at a session of oyer and terminer) in Philadelphia that tried and acquitted three men charged with treason. The stability of an area, as well as legal concerns, certainly played a role in all of these cases. In the former instances, including the aforementioned espionage cases, the suspects had been brought up on charges in areas that had recently seen military action and remained under the control of the army; in the last case the military presence was slight and local courts were fully functional. Military trials for civilians were not popular, but when a city or state was beset by internal and external enemies, it could authorize the army to try civilians charged with treason and other high crimes against the state. Both New York and Pennsylvania gave such authority to the Continental Army in 1777, but Washington, who preferred civil trials, sometimes handed over the offenders to civilian authorities anyway.[48]

Camp followers as civilians themselves, although subject to various military laws at specified times, were not subject to military law per se. Military law was, and is, intended for service members and employed to maintain military discipline. It is applied in conjunction with the common and civil law, for the soldier retains his responsibilities as a citizen and is answerable to the civil courts for his actions in that capacity.[49] When accused of military crimes or offenses within the military arena, however, the soldier can be arraigned before a court-martial.

The military judicial system embraces private citizens through martial law. An army or government uses martial law to administer and control all people in a military situation in a time of war or national crisis. It "is the application of military government—the government of force—to persons and property within the scope of it, according to the laws and usages of war, to the exclusion of the municipal government, in all respects where the latter would impair the efficiency of military law or military action."[50] Martial law is invoked when the exigencies of war demand it. Camp followers with the army on campaign or in occupied areas, which include encampments, are almost always subject to this law. The custom of war and Article 23, Section XIII, which specifically made them "subject to orders, according to the rules and discipline of war," ensured that subordination during the Revolutionary War.

Even in wartime, however, followers were not always, or indiscriminately, punished by military courts. If a civil court was available, and the alleged crimes were punishable under civil statutes or common law, then followers were supposed to be, and sometimes were, handed over to a local magistrate. This did not constitute special treatment for followers; Article 1 of Section X of the 1776 Articles of War guaranteed the same procedure for service members:

> Whenever any officer or soldier shall be accused of a capital crime, or of having used violence, or committed any offence against the persons or property of the good people of any of the United American States, such as is punishable by the known laws of the land, the commanding officer and

officers of every regiment, troop or party, to which the person or persons so accused shall belong, are hereby required, upon application duly made by or in behalf of the party or parties injured, to use his utmost endeavours to deliver over such accused person or persons to the civil magistrate. . . .[51]

The pertinent phrase was "upon application." Civilian authorities had to ask that the accused be delivered to them. The "Commissioners for detecting &c Conpiracies" in Poughkeepsie did this in September 1780. They asked Colonel Lamb, then in command at West Point, to send the prisoner Frederick Cookingham, who was in confinement there, to them "to be dealt with as his crime deserves." Cookingham may not have been a soldier, but if his alleged treasonable activities included espionage (or other actions against the army), as was suggested by his confinement at that post, he could be confined and tried by the military unless a civilian court claimed precedence. In return, civilian courts and magistrates delivered fugitives accused of military crimes over to the army. Joseph Chandler, a justice of the peace, sent a man he judged to be a deserter up to Lamb under militia guard in October 1780.[52] Occasionally there was a struggle over jurisdiction, as at the Head of Elk in December 1781 when a soldier killed a civilian, but Washington generally supported the supremacy of civilian jurisdiction, as he did in that case.[53]

If no application for justice by civilian authorities was made, or no court action ensued, army authorities could act as they saw fit and choose either civilian or military tribunals for soldiers and others accused of crime within the military arena. Commanders employed the application rule with followers as well, though apparently in at least one instance Washington tried to get around it or at least delay it. This was the case concerning the forage master Mr. Coldebrugh. Washington wrote that he was unhappy "that any differences should arise between Citizens and Persons belonging to the Army. It is not my wish that any who have been guilty of Crimes properly cognizable by the Laws of the Land should be exculpated, or schreened from justice. At this stage of the Campaign, however, it would be very inexpedient to direct a Person to be taken from the execution of his duty, whose services could not possibly be so essential at any other period as at the present."[54]

The application rule did not come into play when a follower committed a military offense. Maintaining discipline in the ranks meant that all offenders, whether in uniform or out, had to be punished. The army refused to countenance civilian neglect or disobedience of orders; nor did it tolerate insolence to the commander or to any commissioned officer. As such offenses were only punishable by military tribunals, the army had to provide justification (beyond the necessity created by war) before hauling civilians in for judgment. Article 23 again provided the answer: it gave commanders the legal authority or jurisdiction to try the perpetrators of such offenses in a military court. The most serious offenses were tried by general courts-martial; others could be tried either by the general or the regimental courts, depending on the persons involved. For minor breaches of order or law, officers often utilized their authority to judge and punish miscreants summarily. Thus people within the military community were never outside of the law; rather they were regulated by a tight network of both municipal (civil and criminal) and martial (which included army regulations and custom) law.

When a crime was committed, the army responded in a variety of ways. If the perpetrator was seen and recognized, apprehension was generally swift. If the crime was committed by an unknown person, notices were sent out and searches undertaken. The army's orderly books held numerous advertisements for the return of lost or stolen goods. Many victims offered a reward for the return of their property and promised to ask no questions. One advertisement guaranteed no questions and twenty dollars to whoever returned a pair of brass mounted pistols stolen off of General Peter Muhlenberg's horse at the Skippack headquarters on 6 October 1777. Exactly one month later, at the White Marsh headquarters, someone made off with a chest of surgical instruments (as well as some clothing of no great value). In that case the amount of the reward was not specified, but again there was the promise of no questions. If the crime was great or the victim willing to wait upon more formal police action, officers initiated searches. When John Grant was robbed as the Jersey troops marched through White Marsh around 1 December 1777, headquarters responded by ordering the officers of those units to inspect the packs of their men.[55]

The pursuit of justice was not confined within the military community. Advertisements describing military criminals or stolen goods appeared in public newspapers as well. The *Pennsylvania Gazette,* on 20 August 1777, ran a notice about the stolen goods found in the possession of one Catherine Wilson, the wife of James Wilson, an enlisted man in Captain Alexander Patterson's company. The advertiser, Samuel Rea, stated that the items were thought to be stolen from the army (and its people) and listed them as a small roan horse, a Hessian cutlass, a regimental blue coat, one blue and one white vest, two white hunting shirts, eight linen and tow shirts, two pairs of cloth breeches, one pair leather breeches, seventeen pairs of stockings, leggings, and six Indian blankets. People could claim their property by proving it was theirs and paying applicable charges to the subscriber. J. Hiltzheimer's *Gazette* advertisement, on 5 January 1779, promised a hundred-dollar reward for the return of two Continental Army horses and the apprehension of the thief, who was identified as John Anny, a wagoner in the service of the United States.[56]

Once an accused person was apprehended, a decision had to be made, especially if the person was a civilian, on how to handle his or her case. An order dated 6 November 1777 and meant to cover civilians both in camp and out addressed this: "All prisoners not being Continental Soldiers and suspected

Persons are to be carried to the Major Genl. of the day to be examined and dealt with as he shall see fit."[57] It was up to the general to determine if a camp follower accused of criminal activity should go before a general court-martial. At least one of the generals so involved appeared especially vigilant in the apprehension and examination of sutlers. Long before the headquarters in Pennsylvania issued the order detailing the arrest procedure for civilians, Major General Schuyler was following it in the Simpson case. On 19 August 1776, at German-Flatts, Captain Bloomfield received a letter from Schuyler ordering him to arrest the sutler Simpson for stealing things from Johnson Hall. Bloomfield spent the next day questioning Simpson and then sent him under guard to the general in Albany.[58] If a camp follower stood accused of a lesser offense, however, his or her arrest and confinement often remained the concern of the immediate commanding officer. That reflected the accepted practice for dealing with soldiers accused of petty crimes. An order issued out of the Princeton headquarters in May 1777 stated that in the future all soldiers so charged were to be "confined in Qr. Guards and tried by a Regimental Court Martial."[59]

Generally, the apprehension of camp civilians closely followed the procedures used in detaining noncommissioned officers and enlisted men. Soldiers, unlike officers, were imprisoned upon being charged (officers under arrest were honor-bound to remain in camp or garrison) and remained in custody until tried by court-martial or discharged by a proper authority. According to an April 1776 order, prisoners were to be held by the provost marshal if they were to be tried by a general court-martial, or confined in the barrack guard of the regiment to which they belonged if they were to be tried by a regimental court. The Articles of War specified that pretrial custody be short, preferably not longer than eight days. They also required the arresting officer to provide the provost marshal with a written statement specifying the charges when delivering the accused to him. The provost marshal, in turn, was to deliver a statement of charges to the regimental commander (when the offense related only to that corps) or the commander in chief. That was how it worked in ideal situations. Unfortunately, justice often lacked a swift sword; the result was crowded jails and case backlogs. That was the situation at Valley Forge on 30 December 1777. It was cold outside the prison, and freezing inside. As a great number of prisoners were suffering, the order went out to set up brigade general courts-martial, which were to sit every day until every man awaiting trial in the respective brigades had his day in court.[60]

The only military court legally qualified to try "every description of persons known to the rules and articles of war, and for every offence declared by them" was the general court-martial. It also served as the military's appellate court.[61] A general court-martial consisted of at least thirteen commissioned officers, with the president of the court holding the rank of field officer or above. It was the only court allowed to pass a sentence of death, but it could do so only when two-thirds of the officers there concurred. After that, the sentences of the court could not be executed until a report of the proceedings had been presented to Congress or to the commander in chief of the forces of the United States and approval obtained.[62]

Regimental courts-martial could mediate disputes and judge criminal actions not specifically reserved to the higher courts. They generally judged soldiers (camp civilians were usually referred to the higher court) accused of drunkenness, being absent without leave, selling or wasting military stores, or harassing people bringing supplies into camp. The court consisted of five officers appointed by the regiment's commander, except when it was impossible conveniently to assemble that many, in which case three was sufficient. Judgment was by majority opinion. The judges could recommend corporal punishment for small offences, but no sentence could be carried out until the commanding officer (if not a member of the court) or the commandant of the garrison confirmed it.[63]

There were similarities in the operation of both courts. Both adjudicated cases within specific military units or between them. A general court-martial could be convened within one brigade (or division), the judges drawn out of that body's officers, to try cases falling within the jurisdiction of that unit. A general court-martial could also have more sweeping jurisdiction with the presiding officers chosen from the entire army and the accused a member of either the army or the civilian community. The nature of the crime, who committed it, and where it took place would determine whether the court-martial was to be handled at the brigade or army level. Regimental courts-martial could be called to deal with matters within one regiment or between regiments. In all of these situations the judge advocate general, or a person appointed by him, presented the prosecution in the name of the United States of America. Both the prosecution and the defendant (who faced court and prosecutor without counsel) could call on people to give evidence. Witnesses testified under oath and if they refused to testify could themselves be court-martialed.[64]

While the pretrial wait was sometimes prolonged, the trials themselves, especially those of junior officers, enlisted men, camp followers, and civilians, were both simple and speedy. Prosecutor and defendant argued their cases, presented their evidence, and heard judgment passed, often all in one day or less. It was quite common for the court to hear numerous cases in a single day. This was possible because of the way in which the courts-martial operated. "In a certain sense the court-martial of the Revolution was not really a court at all but merely a hearing conducted by a board of officers who examined the evidence and rendered a verdict which was reviewed by the commanding officer. There was no judge or jury nor was the prisoner entitled to defense counsel."[65]

Although the court determined the verdict, execution of the sentence awaited the concurrence of the commanding officer. If the commander believed due process (proper procedure) had not been observed or the sentence was improper, he could reject it and order a new trial. Washington did exactly that for the former reason in February 1778 when inhabitants were tried by a general court-martial that had been improperly appointed and conducted according to the Articles of War instead of the proper congressional resolution. He did it again in March, but for the second reason, when he reviewed the sentences of deserters Thomas Coshall and Samuel Burress of Colonel Lamb's regiment. After both prisoners pleaded guilty, the brigade court-martial sentenced them to five hundred lashes each. Washington denounced the sentences as illegal (five hundred lashes were over the legal limit of one hundred) and ordered a new trial by general court-martial.[66] If, on the other hand, the commander believed the verdict and sentence appropriate, he gave his formal approval and the sentence went into effect.

It was only after the general approved a not-guilty verdict that a prisoner was released from custody. Hanna Taylor and Barbara Boure, charged with trying to persuade soldiers to desert, faced separate general courts-martial in May 1777. Upon their being found not guilty, the general ordered their release. At Valley Forge, Thomas Scott, a wagon master charged with taking forage contrary to the general orders of 31 December, was acquitted at a general court-martial on 22 January 1778. The general approved the verdict and ordered his release on 28 January. A day earlier a division (general) court-martial acquitted William McIntosh of the 2nd Virginia Regiment, John Keyton of the 10th Virginia, and Ann McIntosh (probably for incitement) of the charges mutiny and desertion. The general approved the court's findings and ordered them released from confinement eight days later on 29 January. On 31 March 1778 a general court-martial acquitted Lieutenant (probably Abner) Dunn of Colonel John Patton's regiment, General Charles Scott's brigade (the 4th Virginia), of charges of striking and behaving ungentlemanly toward Lieutenant Street (possibly Benjamin Street of Hartley's Continental Regiment); but he was not discharged from his arrest until the commander in chief confirmed the verdict on 6 April. Washington, always concerned about the military's treatment of private citizens, tried to be especially quick in his review of cases involving civilians. Samuel Harvey, an inhabitant of Pennsylvania, was tried at a general court-martial at Valley Forge on 15 April 1778 for attempting to supply the enemy with provisions. When Harvey was proven innocent of the charge, the discharge order came through three days later on 18 April.[67]

When a commander approved a guilty verdict, punishment commenced. It generally was performed publicly so as to be a lesson on authority and discipline not only to the criminal but to the observers. Article 51 of the 1775 Articles of War listed what punishments besides death the courts-martial could mete out. They included "degrading, cashiering, drumming out of the army, whipping not exceeding thirty-nine lashes, fine[s] not exceeding two months pay of the offender, imprisonment not exceeding one month." The 1776 articles were more severe. Offenders could be sentenced to one hundred lashes, have stoppages put on pay until the loss or damage was recovered or repaired (officers, store-keepers or commissaries convicted of embezzlement, etc., could be made to pay for the loss or damage out of their own pockets, forfeit all pay, and be dismissed from service), or suffer "such other punishment as by a court-martial shall be inflicted."[68] The Articles of 1776 declared that offenders could be sentenced to death for "mutiny, sedition, striking an officer, desertion, sleeping at or abandoning a post when on duty, giving a false claim, misbehavior or cowardice in action, discarding arms and ammunition, making known the watchword, aiding the enemy and plundering."[69] Within those limits, the military courts had a great deal of freedom in which to determine appropriate punishment. Determination generally was based upon custom and the status of the individuals convicted.

The varied nature of legal discipline, both in style and severity, could be seen in the treatment meted out to those brought before a court for blatantly transgressing the professional ethos of deference and subordination. A number of officers were involved in some heated displays of insubordination and unbecoming conduct in the summer of 1777 at Trenton. When Colonel Thomas Polke got into an argument with Colonel Alexander Martin, Martin charged him with disobedience of orders and contemptuous and disrespectful language. A court of inquiry decided that Polke's disobedience was justifiable and his language the result of provocation; therefore Polke was discharged from arrest and the charges dropped. The same court determined that Lieutenant Thomas Blunt did make "an attempt on Captn [Richard] Cook with a draw Sword agreeable to the charge, but as Captn. Cook had so repeatedly provoked him they think a Court Martial on the Occasion unnecessarry." Blunt then turned around and filed charges against Cook for "behavior unbecoming Officer & Gent. Profane curseing & swearing & striking the 'complainent.'" But Cook was found not guilty at a general court-martial. At that same court-martial, however, Captain Pugh Williams was found guilty of a "breach of good Order & Milletarry Discipline" for spitting in Captain Jorlow's face, hitting him, and treating him to "much abusive language." The court sentenced Williams to a reprimand from the general, but the general hoped that reflection on the part of both gentlemen would prevent the need for a reprimand.[70] As General Knox pointed out to Major Bauman a few years later when reflecting on another nasty situation, cases arising out of malice were an abuse of the system. Knox felt that such malefactors should be punished, for they were "as great a nuisance to an Army as a pettifogger is to Civil Society."[71] But besides showing that officers used the courts as dueling grounds, these cases illustrate the fact that rank could at times mitigate punishment for behavior that would never have been deemed acceptable in enlisted personnel.

Throughout the war soldiers suffered corporal punishment, often the maximum allowed, for disobedience of orders, insulting or provoking language, and striking officers (the latter, according to Article 7 in the 1775 and Article 5, Section II, in the 1776 Articles of War, could result in a death sentence, but courts seldom went that far unless the blows had been struck in conjunction with some other abominable crime). In May 1776 Frederick Roach, a matross in the artillery, was tried for insulting and hitting Captain William Hull as well as insulting some inhabitants of Long Island, while John Lewis of the 3rd New York was tried for insulting and striking Lieutenant (Marcus) Cole. Both were found guilty and sentenced to thirty-nine lashes, which was the limit then allowed. In comparison, near West Point in June of 1779 John Tings of the light infantry was whipped only thirty times for disobedience of orders and insulting language, but then he did not hit anyone. At the same roll call Moses Whitford was whipped fifteen times for insulting and abusing a noncommissioned officer when on duty. Thomas Stevens of the 3rd Massachusetts got the maximum in February 1783 when he was found guilty of insulting and striking Lieutenant Josiah Smith: he was sentenced to have his honorary badge removed and to receive one hundred lashes. The only thing that saved Smith from a very sore back was that he benefited from the general pardon given in honor of the anniversary of the French alliance.[72]

Camp followers, under Article 23, Section XIII, could be charged with most of the offenses listed in the 1776 Articles of War and sentenced accordingly, but again there were variations due to one's social or professional status. Although the army insisted that sutlers were subject to the same military discipline as all other camp inhabitants, military courts generally did not handle sutlers and other contracted vendors in the same manner they dealt with officers, enlisted men, and most other followers. The distinct nature of their relationship was illustrated by the crimes they were most often charged with and the punishments that followed conviction. Sutlers and other vendors brought before a court-martial were generally accused of abusing their privileges as sellers and suppliers. In turn, their punishment was usually the severing of the association and revocation of privileges. Punishment could also involve the confiscation of property. A December 1782 general court-martial at West Point tried Samuel and Sarah Warren, sutlers, for "recieving a Sign Board, from a Soldier in Colonel Cranes Regiment of Artillery.—contrary to the rules of the Garrison, for the Government of Sutlers. Secondly—encouraging Soldiers to bring Hogs, from Constitution Island the property of William Dean, and James Forsyth. Thirdly.—For Stealing four Barrells of Flour the property of Gamelial Babesch." It was determined that they were guilty of the first charge, that the second was unsupported, "and that the 3rd Charge is entirely of a private and civil nature, and cannot come under the Cogni[z]ance of the Court." The court sentenced the Warrens to leave West Point on or before the 14th of the month.[73]

Retainers, specifically women of the army and servants, commonly suffered the punishments allotted to enlisted men. The same court-martial that acquitted Ann and William McIntosh, and John Keyton, pronounced others guilty of similar charges. Edward Driver of the 2nd Virginia was sentenced merely to be reprimanded before all the troops by the division's commanding officer. Jeremiah Bride of the same regiment received a sentence of one hundred lashes on his bare back. The court reserved its harshest punishment for a woman. It sentenced Mary Johnson, charged with plotting (her own as well as some soldiers'?) desertion to the enemy, to receive one hundred lashes and then be drummed out of the army (camp) by all the drums and fifes in the division.[74] While retainers in the ranks appeared before the courts, there was virtually no evidence that any of the army's ladies or its gentlemen volunteers were ever brought before a court-martial.

Quartermasters, commissaries, and other staff department appointees serving with the army had the standing of officers, and the courts-martial treated them as such. If found guilty of a crime, they could be reprimanded, fined, dismissed (cashiering, the severest form of this, was usually reserved for officers found guilty of cowardice or multiple offences), or drummed out of camp, but they could not be sentenced to corporal punishment.[75] In January 1778 a general court-martial heard the evidence against Dunham Ford, a commissary in General Greene's division, charged with theft. The court found him guilty and sentenced him to pay Mr. Spencer and Mr. Hotawell two hundred dollars. After procuring a certificate from Greene that he had delivered the appropriate payment, Ford was to "be brought from the Provost Guard mounted on a horse back foremost without a Saddle, his Coat turn'd wrong side out his hands tied behind him & be drum'd out of the Army (Never more to return) by all the Drums in the Division to which he belongs and that the above sentence be published in the News papers." Washington approved the sentence.[76] That March a brigade court-martial tried, "with his own consent," Mr. Robertson, the adjutant of the 13th Virginia Regiment, on charges of encouraging a soldier's wife to sell liquor in Muhlenberg's brigade without permission, for taking the liquor after it was seized by order of the brigade's commander, for refuting the order, and "for Repeatedly getting Drunk and behaving in an Ungentlemanlike manner." The court found Robertson guilty of "detaining & using seized liquors & saying it shouldnt be taken away" and sentenced him to be reprimanded in brigade orders. He was acquitted of the other charges.[77] In 1782, while the southern army (which acted under the same law and custom as the main army) was in South Carolina, a general court-martial found William McKenzie, apothecary's mate to the general hospital, guilty of *"refusing to do his duty."* General Greene approved the court's sentence of dismissal from the service, remarking as he did so "that it is difficult for him to conceive how an Officer in the Medical department, knowing the critical Stages of disorders, could urge a slight indisposition to excuse himself from making up a prescription, on which the life of his brother officer might depend."[78] Officers and civilian adjuncts of comparable status, if convicted of disorderly conduct or crime, could expect punishments that struck at a man's honor, face (standing in army and civilian communities), and pocketbook.

Military courts tried and punished low-ranking staff department employees much in the same manner as they handled enlisted personnel. The only differentiation in the sentencing was perhaps a tendency to be more sparing in the use of the whip and a greater willingness to get rid of troublemakers by simply dismissing them from employment. A general court-martial at West Point in 1778, after determining that Elishee Printer of the artificers was guilty of leaving the post without permission and neglecting his duty, sentenced him to be dismissed from the service. Two years later a general court-martial found Gabriel Gill, a wagon conductor, guilty "of carting private property whilst in public service" and sentenced him to refund the money he received or was to receive for carrying the private iron instead of public flour. General Arnold thought the sentence too lenient to serve as a proper deterrent against future offenses of a similar nature and recommended that the court reconsider. It obliged by adding corporal punishment. A general court-martial at Steenrapie in September 1780 tried the express rider Reubin George "for Delaying 300000 Dollars on the road which he had in charge to Deliver to Moore Furman Esqr. D.Q.M.G. [deputy quartermaster general] for the express purpose of forwarding provisions to the army which delay if not early discovered would have been attended with the most fatal consiquences to the army. 2dly for expending part of the mony and making preparation to desert to Virginia with the Residue." The court decided that George did delay the delivery of the money but did not realize the serious consequences that would have resulted if the problem had not been discovered in time. It also determined that he did spend some of the money, but that it did not appear that he intended to desert to Virginia with the rest. George's sentence included repayment of the money spent, one hundred lashes on his bare back, and dismissal from employment. When Washington approved the sentence, he added that George was to remain under provost guard until released by General Greene. The same court found Joseph Smallwood, a wagoner in Continental service, guilty of "insulting & knocking Lt. Barret off his horse on the publick Road on the 23d last" and sentenced him to suffer one hundred lashes on his bare back.[79]

Civilians found guilty of spying or otherwise aiding the enemy, if not sentenced to death, faced imprisonment (which could include hard labor) or punishments similar to those given service members and followers. Courts-martial seldom sentenced soldiers to imprisonment, for such a sentence deprived the army of valuable manpower.[80] Confining disaffected civilians, however, deprived the enemy of supporters and suppliers, even as it increased the security of the American army. A general court-martial at Princeton in 1777 tried Mary Quin (also spelled Quan) and Elisabeth Brewer on charges of being enemies to their country. The court released Quin for lack of evidence but found Brewer guilty of spying. It sentenced her to imprisonment. The general approved the sentence and ordered her to be sent to Philadelphia and confined there "in Such place as the Commanding Officer shall direct during the War."[81]

The commander in chief could not only approve, reject, or mitigate sentences, he could also pardon offenders. Regimental commanders had the same power when reviewing the actions of regimental courts-martial.[82] This addition to the military system of law, along with the more restrained use of the whip when compared to the British military, again appears to be a reflection of the revolutionaries' belief in virtue: not just that of mercy but that inherent in true patriots. There was the hope that when such people demonstrated a lapse in discipline, they did not always need to be punished; they needed merely to be chastised and reminded of their duty to do it. All too often that put too much faith in human nature, as the revolutionaries acknowledged when they were forced to implement stronger punishments. Washington, however, remained quite liberal with his pardons; he lived always in the hope that his clemency would engender gratitude and future better behavior in the offenders and remind observers that the system was just.

The commander in chief pardoned offenders of all ranks and set aside sentences of varying severity. Lieutenant Armours (probably Thomas Armor) of the 1st Pennsylvania was guilty of conduct unbefitting an officer and sentenced to be discharged in March 1778. The court recommended a pardon, however, in consideration of the excellent character references given on his behalf and the fact that the prosecution appeared to have been malicious. The general agreed with the court and delivered the pardon. That same year, after word of the French alliance reached the United States, Washington was in a magnanimous mood. He wanted to reclaim rather than punish offenders; so, as part of the 6 May 1778 celebration of the alliance, Washington was merciful toward two men guilty of having been misled by traitors. He pardoned William McMath, of the artillery, and John Marrel, of Colonel Henry Jackson's Additional Continental Regiment, both of whom had been awaiting death.[83] Camp followers benefited from such consideration by Washington and other generals as well. The sutlers Samuel and Sarah Warren, who had been ordered to leave West Point by 14 December 1782 after being found guilty of disobeying General McDougall's orders for the regulation of sutlers at the garrison, were given a reprieve on the 13th after garrison orders published that day noted that "Many Officers of high Rank, and respectable Characters" had requested the sentence be remitted because of the former good behavior of the sutlers. The general (either Washington or Knox, who was then commanding West Point) complied but hoped that "the most punctual attention to all orders, respecting Sutlers will be the consequence of this Lenity."[84]

Death, imprisonment, and substantial corporal disciplining were all judicial punishments. They could be imposed only by a court-martial in response to major offenses that threatened military authority and operations. Individual commanders, however, could order nonjudicial or immediate punishment for minor offenses that disturbed the order, welfare, and security of the community. One of the most common offenses was the disorderly firing of weapons. Commanders constantly harangued their men about shooting their muskets in camp: it was a waste of ammunition, it could harm innocent bystanders, and it could frighten camp residents into thinking there was an attack (if that happened the offender could be condemned to death by court-martial). So as to prevent such dire results, the commanders promised immediate retribution to all offenders. An order of 22 December 1777 stated, "Every soldier found discharging his Musket without Leave and in an irregular manner is to receive 20 Lashes immediately upon the Spot." Four months later the stakes were raised; a soldier or noncommissioned officer caught in the act was to be brought before a commissioned officer who "shall order him to be tied up immediately, and receive 39 lashes on his bare back."[85]

As cleanliness in the camps was also a vital concern, appropriate punishment for the hygienically negligent was important. New vaults or necessaries were built, old ones were filled in, and the men were ordered to use them. Disobedience in this matter was, at first, a court-martial offense, but over time commanders came to rely on summary punishment. In October 1777 a man caught not using the necessary was supposed to be dragged before a regimental court-martial. A few months later, in March of 1778, one caught not using the proper facilities could have the scare of his life, for General Weedon had commanded that sentinels be posted with orders to fire on any man found in a compromising position; but that order was soon mitigated. In April the sentinels were ordered just to take such person prisoner and deliver him to his regimental commander, who was immediately to order five lashes.[86] Women could be summarily punished for any similar, or greater, disregard of the camp's welfare. For instance, in July 1777 Captain Kirkwood reported that "there was a Woman Duct & Drummed out of our Encampment." Her crime? She passed on "the Venerieal Disorder."[87] The men, who could and did give such diseases to women, might be fined, but they were usually just given medical treatment and then sent back to the lines.

Nonjudicial punishment was to be used with caution and never excessively; to have done the latter would have antagonized community members, diminished the effectiveness of it as a corrective, and possibly led to a questioning of its propriety if not its legality. This field-expedient method of justice (which could be considered a component or derivative of the custom of war) offered commanders a way in which to deal quickly with minor problems before they could become major ones; unfortunately commanders did not always record offenders and offenses dealt with in this manner and thus left incomplete records on how they managed refractory, though not criminally disruptive, troops and followers. In contrast, commanders did usually name defendants appearing before courts-martial and record the results of judicial actions. Judicial punishment was the preferred method for dealing with army personnel and followers charged with crimes (rather than the misdeeds that followers were likely to be accused of), for, and this was important to the revolutionaries, it had the sanction of law and followed only upon the conclusion of the military legal process.

The American army during the Revolution built a legal system based upon custom, orders, and law. The custom of war was a repository for the common culture of the military. It could be found in the stories, lessons, and directives passed on orally, as well as discerned in the various military manuals read by those eager to study the profession of arms. As a body of communal wisdom, it acted as the army's common law. Officers, soldiers, and even followers used the custom of war to check their decisions and actions against the unwritten code of habit and historical precedent that formed this institutional memory. They often referred to this body of unwritten law, as adopted from long-established European military practices and adapted to fit American sensibilities, when governing camp followers. Custom alone, however, could not control an army and its community, so commanders issued orders as well. Orders regulated both the minutiae and overall plans of both camp and battle. They were often the most current and concrete of all the rules governing the army and its followers. These directives offered a form of immediate, specific, and external discipline. Finally, blanketing the entire Continental Community, and some civilians outside of it as well, were the American Articles of War. These laws took precedence over all other military regulations and furnished the framework for the military judicial system. They defined military crime, established military legal jurisdiction, instituted courts-martial, and provided guidance on appropriate punishments. These articles in combination with orders and custom provided the discipline and direction the army and most of its people needed to survive a long war and successfully challenge an extremely capable, professional army.

In the process of creating, instituting, and applying this threefold legal system, the army not only disciplined itself but defined itself. It defined itself as a professional organization certainly, but an organization, and a community, supposedly built upon virtue and order. It was to embody the values the revolutionaries believed inherent in Americans. To a certain extent it did so; but the interpretation and application of law and discipline within the system also demonstrated the ephemeral nature of virtue and the limits of equality within the community. In doing so, it reflected not only American dreams but American realities.

Notes

1. William Winthrop, *Military Law and Precedents*, 2d ed. (1920; reprint, New York: Arno Press, 1979), p. 967. Winthrop's appendix contains military legislation from the Ordinance of Richard I in 1190 to extracts from the new Army Regulations of 1895. Of significance here are the Articles of War of Gustavus Adolphus (1621), The First British Mutiny Act (1689), the British Articles of War in force at the beginning of the War for Independence, the Massachusetts Articles of War, the American Articles of War of 1775, and the American Articles of War of 1776.
2. James C. Neagles, *Summer Soldiers: A Survey & Index of Revolutionary War Courts-Martial* (Salt Lake City, Utah: Ancestry Inc., 1986). This offers many examples of people brought to trial for disorderly and criminal conduct, including insubordination and striking an officer. Captain Havelman's trial (on wounding a soldier in response to insolence) in General Orders, Headquarters at the Gulph, 18 December 1777, John C. Fitzpatrick, ed., *The Writings of George Washington* (Washington, D.C.: U.S. Government Printing Office, 1931), 10:169.
3. Lawrence M. Friedman in *Crime and Punishment in American History* (New York: Basic Books, 1993), pp. 6–10, noted the interrelationship between social structure, social norms, and the legal system of a society.
4. General Orders, Headquarters Cambridge, 1 January 1776, in W. W. Abbot, ed., *The Papers of George Washington,* Revolutionary War Series (Charlottesville: University of Virginia Press, 1985), 3:1.
5. Washington to John Hancock, Cambridge, 9 February 1776, Ibid., 3:275–76.
6. Examples are in General Orders, Headquarters Cambridge, 16 September 1775, and General Orders, Headquarters New York, 10 May 1776, Ibid., 2:1 and 4:250–51.
7. Louis Clinton Hatch, *The Administration of the American Revolutionary Army* (1904; reprint, New York: Burt Franklin, 1971), pp. 14–15.
8. E. Marvin to U/I, Norwich, 26 February 1776, #884, in Sol Feinstone Collection, David Library of the American Revolution, Washington Crossing, Pennsylvania, on deposit at the American Philosophical Society (microfilm at David Library).
9. Gilbert's lack of deferential behavior (and other behaviors) described in the introductions of both books: Rebecca D. Symmes, ed., *A Citizen-Soldier in The American Revolution: The Diary of Benjamin Gilbert in Massachusetts and New York* (Cooperstown: New York State Historical Association, 1980), and John Shy, ed., *Winding Down: The Revolutionary War Letters of Lieutenant Benjamin Gilbert of Massachusetts, 1780–1783* (Ann Arbor: University of Michigan Press, 1989). Gilbert's comments on troop discipline, written while he was at Totoway, New Jersey, 15 October 1780, found in the latter, pages 25–26.
10. Totoway, 13 October 1780, Ibid., p. 23.
11. Joseph Plumb Martin, *Private Yankee Doodle: Being a Narrative of Some of the Adventures, Dangers and Sufferings of a Revolutionary Soldier,* ed. George F. Scheer (1830; New York: Popular Library ed., 1963), p. 239.
12. Headquarters Princeton, [4–5] June 1777, [Sergeant Long's Orderly Book], Capt. John Belfield's Troop, First Regiment of Light Dragoons, 30 January–22 August

1777, in Military Records Collection, Accession 21334, Archives, The Library of Virginia, Richmond. Richard Burriss, convicted of desertion, was to be shot on the public parade. Soldiers caught attempting to desert from the scouting parties, out pickets, or deserting to the enemy were to be immediately hanged or shot.

13. Massachusetts Articles of War, in Winthrop, *Military Law,* p. 947.
14. Maurer Maurer, "Military Justice Under General Washington," in *Military Analysis of the Revolutionary War,* ed. *Military Affairs* (Millwood, N.Y.: KTO Press, 1977), p. 58; Charles Royster in *A Revolutionary People at War: The Continental Army and American Character, 1775–1783* (1979; reprint, New York: W. W. Norton, 1981), pp. 28–29, 41, 70, discussed idealism and dedication versus discipline.
15. Washington to Hancock, Cambridge, 21 September 1775, in Abbot, *Papers of Washington,* 2:24–30.
16. Washington's General Orders, Headquarters Cambridge, 15 November 1775, Ibid., 2:377.
17. Maurer, "Military Justice," p. 58.
18. William C. DeHart, *Observations on Military Law, and the Constitution and Practice of Courts Martial* (New York: Wiley & Putnam, 1846), pp. 3–4.
19. Headquarters, 24 September 1776, in George Washington's Headquarters Orderly Book, New York, 31 August 1776–4 October 1776, War Department Collection of Revolutionary War Records, Record Group 93 (hereafter referred to as RG 93), Revolutionary War Miscellaneous Manuscript Collections, National Archives, Washington, D.C.
20. American Articles of War of 1776, Winthrop, *Military Law,* p. 967.
21. Headquarters (Germantown?), General Orders, 15 September 1777, *Valley Forge Orderly Book of General George Weedon of the Continental Army under Command of Genl. George Washington, in the Campaign of 1777–8* (1902; reprint, New York: Arno Press, 1971), p. 52.
22. Pennsylvania State Headquarters Chester, 1 September 1777, in Capt. Robert Kirkwood's Delaware Regiment Orderly Book, 1 March 1777–21 December 1777, Force Manuscripts, 7E, Recl. 16, Entry 67, Library of Congress (hereafter cited as Kirkwood's Delaware Regiment Orderly Book).
23. German-Flatts, 1 September 1776, Mark E. Lender and James Kirby Martin, eds., *Citizen Soldier: The Revolutionary War Journal of Joseph Bloomfield* (Newark: New Jersey Historical Society, 1982), p. 103.
24. Brigade Orders, Headquarters Wilmington, 6 September 1777; Headquarters, 1 November 1777; Headquarters Valley Forge, 8 February 1778, *Valley Forge Orderly Book,* pp. 38, 112, 228–29.
25. Regimental Orders, Lincoln Mountain, 1 July 1777, Kirkwood's Delaware Regiment Orderly Book.
26. General Orders, Headquarters Wilmington, 6 September 1777, *Valley Forge Orderly Book,* pp. 36–37.
27. John O'Brien, *A Treatise on American Military Laws, and the Practice of Courts Martial; with Suggestions for Their Improvement* (Philadelphia: Lea & Blanchard, 1846), p. 223. While records of the laws, orders, and courts-martial were available, little was available on the interpretation of military law in the Revolutionary period; thus my use of later works that build upon the Revolution's precedents. O'Brien, in his preface, mentioned that army officers had long needed a treatise on military

law. They needed to know "not merely what principles are applicable, but also what decisions have heretofore been made in similar cases, and also the reasons and arguments on which these decisions are founded."
28. S. V. Benét, *A Treatise on Military Law and the Practice of Courts-Martial* (New York: D. Van Nostrand, 1862), pp. 9–10; DeHart, *Observations on Military Law*, pp. 20–21; American Articles of War of 1776, Winthrop, *Military Law*, pp. 967–68.
29. Hamilton to Lt. Col. John Laurens, [Preakness, New Jersey, 11 October 1780], in *The Papers of Alexander Hamilton*, ed. Harold C. Syrett (New York: Columbia University Press, 1961), 2:468.
30. Robert Harry Berlin, "The Administration of Military Justice in the Continental Army During the American Revolution, 1775-1783," Ph.D. dissertation, University of California, Santa Barbara, 1976, pp. 119–20.
31. Richard Reuben Forry, "Edward Hand: His Role in the American Revolution," Ph.D. dissertation, Duke University, 1976, p. 62; Washington's orders recorded the problems in Thompson's battalion, Headquarters Cambridge, 11 and 13 September 1775, in Abbot, *Papers of Washington*, 1:449, 454–55.
32. Washington's General Orders, Headquarters Cambridge, 15 September 1775, Abbot, *Papers of George Washington*, 1:465.
33. Garrison Orders, Burlington Barracks (or possibly West Point), 30 April 1782, Orderly Book, Col. John Lamb's Second Regiment of Continental Artillery, New Jersey, 7 February–7 August 1782, The New-York Historical Society's Collection of Early American Orderly Books (microfilm, David Library of the American Revolution). Lamb's regimental orderly books (listed under the same title) in The New-York Historical Society's Collection will hereafter be referred to as Lamb's 2CA Orderly Book and differentiated by date. When a soldier was sentenced to "wear the log," he had a heavy log or board attached to his back; he was also usually ordered to perform fatigue duties while so encumbered.
34. General Orders, Headquarters, 10 October 1777, *Valley Forge Orderly Book*, p. 78.
35. O'Brien, *Treatise on American Military Laws*, p. 112; Headquarters Valley Forge, 26 January 1778, *Valley Forge Orderly Book*, pp. 209–10.
36. Afternote to Headquarters New-borough entry of 16 July 1777, Kirkwood's Delaware Regiment Orderly Book.
37. Copy of congressional resolution of 10 June 1777, Headquarters Valley Forge, 1 February 1778, *Valley Forge Orderly Book*, p. 219.
38. Benét, *Treatise on Military Law*, p. 29.
39. Ibid., p. 30.
40. General Orders, Headquarters (Germantown?), 26 September 1777, *Valley Forge Orderly Book*, p. 59.
41. Walter Hart Blumenthal, *Women Camp Followers of the American Revolution* (Philadelphia: George MacManus, 1952), p. 78, quoting Washington out of Fitzpatrick, *Writings of Washington*, 25:139.
42. O'Brien, *Treatise on American Military Laws*, p. 151.
43. Winthrop, *Military Law*, p. 98.
44. American Articles of War of 1776, Winthrop, *Military Law*, pp. 102–3, 967; Linda K. Kerber, *Women of the Republic: Intellect and Ideology in Revolutionary America* (Chapel Hill: University of North Carolina Press, 1980), p. 121. Showing the problem of jurisdiction: there is an example of Washington ordering a prisoner accused

of spying to be handed over to the civilian authorities, in letter to Col. Oliver Spencer, Headquarters Middle Brook, 9 April 1779. There were also numerous examples of spies being tried in the military courts, including the cases of David Farnworth and John Blair reported in General Orders, Headquarters Fredericksburgh, 23 October 1778, and the cases of Joseph Betts and Stephen Smith, reported in General Orders, Headquarters New Windsor, 4 July 1779, in Fitzpatrick, *Writings of Washington,* 14:357–58; 13:139–40; 15:364.

45. Washington to the Board of General Officers, Headquarters Valley Forge, 2 June 1778, Ibid., 12:11. Execution reported in *The Royal Gazette,* 17 June 1778, p. 2, col. 3.
46. Spangler's execution in *The Royal Gazette,* 26 August 1778, p. 2, col. 3. Other trials recorded in: Headquarters Providence, 1 October 1778, Major General Heath's Headquarters Orderly Book, from Boston to Providence, 23 May 1777–20 October 1778, RG 93, Revolutionary War Miscellaneous Manuscript Collection, National Archives. General Orders, Headquarters Highlands, 22 June 1780, *Orderly Books of the Fourth New York Regiment, 1778–1780 [&] the Second New York Regiment, 1780–1783 . . . ,* ed. Almon W. Lauber (Albany: University of the State of New York, 1932), p. 376.
47. Articles of War of 1776, Winthrop, *Military Law,* p. 967. Washington to Lt. Col. Adam Hubley, Headquarters, 14 February 1778, Fitzpatrick, *Writings of Washington,* 10:458.
48. *Pennsylvania Gazette,* 6 October 1779, p. 3, col. 2. At a session of Oyer and Terminer on 20 September, John Holden, Robert Strettel Jones, and Edward C[]tbuth were tried for treason and acquitted. Bills for high-treason were found against Peter Miller, Richard Mason, William Cassedy, and Joseph Wirt. Don Higginbotham, *The War of American Independence: Military Attitudes, Policies, and Practice, 1763–1789* (1971; reprint, Boston: Northeastern University Press, 1983), p. 279.
49. DeHart, *Observations on Military Law,* p. 16.
50. Benét, *Treatise on Military Law,* p. 14.
51. Articles of War of 1776, Winthrop, *Military Law,* p. 964.
52. Commissioners for detecting &c Conpiracies to Lamb, Poughkeepsie, 13 September 1780; Joseph Chandler to Lamb, Bethlehem, 7 October 1780, John Lamb Papers, The New-York Historical Society (microfilm), reel 2.
53. Washington to the Continental Officer Commanding at the Head of Elk, Philadelphia, 30 December 1781, telling him to deliver the soldier accused of killing an inhabitant to the civil authority, in Fitzpatrick, *Writings of Washington,* 23:414.
54. Washington to John Cleves Symmes, Headquarters near Dobbs Ferry, 14 August 1781, Ibid., 22:498.
55. Headquarters Skippack, 6 October 1777, *Valley Forge Orderly Book,* p. 69. Headquarters White Marsh, 6 November and [1–2 December] 1777, Copy of Orderly Book, 1777–1778, Virginia State Infantry, 1st Regiment, Mss12:1777 Nov. 2:1, Virginia Historical Society, Richmond.
56. *Pennsylvania Gazette,* 20 August 1777, p. 4, col. 1, and 5 January 1779, p. 1, col. 2. Hiltzheimer promised eighty dollars for the apprehension of Anny, and ten dollars for each horse recovered.
57. Headquarters (?), 6 November 1777, *Valley Forge Orderly Book,* p. 119.

58. German-Flatts, 19 August 1776, Lender and Martin, eds., *Citizen Soldier*, p. 101.
59. Headquarters Princeton, 28 May 1777, Kirkwood's Delaware Regiment Orderly Book. Reflects earlier Cambridge, 10 July 1775 order, in Abbot, *Papers of Washington*, 1:82.
60. General Orders, Headquarters New York, 22 April 1776, Abbot, *Papers of Washington*, 4:103; Winthrop, *Military Law*, p. 969. Articles 15 through 19 in Section XIV of 1776 articles outline arrest and confinement procedures. Headquarters Valley Forge, 30 December 1777, *Valley Forge Orderly Book*, p. 173.
61. Benét, *Treatise on Military Law*, p. 38. Benét discussed the military courts under the American Articles of War of 1806 (appeals allowed under Article 35), but his observation applies to the Revolution's courts as well (appeals under Article 2, Section XI, Articles of War of 1776).
62. Winthrop, *Military Law*, pp. 967–68. See 1, 5, and 8, Section XIV, of 1776 Articles of War.
63. Footnote 2 to Washington's General Orders of 10 July 1775, in Abbot, *Papers of George Washington*, 1:83; Winthrop, *Military Law*, p. 968, specifically 1776 articles 10 and 11.
64. Ibid., pp. 967–68, articles 2, 3, 5, 6, and 9. More evidence on jurisdiction over civilians seen in the Valley Forge headquarters entry for 15 March 1778, *Valley Forge Orderly Book*, pp. 258–59; for the next day's general court-martial: "all Evidences & persons concern'd are desired to attend at the time & place mentioned, more Especially against the Inhabitants of this State now confined in the Provo, as their Tryal will come on tomorrow[.]"
65. Berlin, "Administration of Military Justice," pp. 82–83, 124.
66. Washington to Lt. Col. Adam Hubley, Headquarters, 14 February 1778, Fitzpatrick, *Writings of Washington*, 10:458; Headquarters Valley Forge, 10 March 1778, *Valley Forge Orderly Book*, p. 253. The brigade court-martial was held on 8 March. Article 3, Section XVIII, of the Articles of War of 1776 limits the number of lashes allowed. These were exceeded at times as military courts tried to punish offenders for crimes "worth" more than 100 lashes but less than the death penalty. There was debate too over corporal punishment versus incarceration.
67. Headquarters Princeton, 21 and 23 May 1777, Kirkwood's Delaware Regiment Orderly Book. Headquarters Valley Forge, 28 January 1778; Regimental Orders, Valley Forge, 29 January 1778; on 6 April 1778, Washington approved the acquittal, but took the occasion to declare that too many proceedings seemed to originate out of personal prejudice and private animosities. He wanted officers to consider themselves a band of brothers. All in *Valley Forge Orderly Book*, pp. 213, 215–16, 280–81. Headquarters Valley Forge, 18 April 1778, Heath's Headquarters Orderly Book.
68. Articles of War of 1775, Article 51; Articles of War of 1776, Article 3, Section XVIII; Articles 1, 3, and 4, Section XII; the quote was the final proviso in a number of the articles, in Winthrop, *Military Law*, pp. 957, 970, 965–67.
69. Berlin, "Administration of Military Justice," pp. 70–71.
70. Camp at Trenton, 19, 21, and 24 July 1777; Camp near Chester, 1 August 1777, in Sixth Battalion of North Carolina, Continental Army, Orderly Book, 1777–1778, in collection of The Filson Club, Louisville, Kentucky.
71. Knox to Bauman, New Windsor, 25 September 1779, Sebastian Bauman Papers,

vol. 1, 1775–1779, The New-York Historical Society.
72. General Orders, Headquarters New York, 3 May 1776, Abbot, *Papers of Washington,* 4:189–90; 19 May 1776, Orderly Book of Col. Alexander McDougall's 1st New York Regiment, New York, 25 March 1776–15 June 1776, The New-York Historical Society's Collection of Early American Orderly Books (microfilm, David Library). Tings and Whitford's punishments noted by Gilbert, [Constitution Island near West Point], 29 June 1779, Symmes, ed., *Citizen-Soldier,* p. 54. General Orders, Headquarters Newburgh, 8 February 1783, Fitzpatrick, *Writings of Washington,* 26:109–10.
73. General or Garrison Orders, West Point, 3 December 1782, Lamb's 2CA Orderly Book, 27 November 1782–5 January 1783.
74. Regimental Orders, Valley Forge, 29 January 1778, *Valley Forge Orderly Book,* p. 215.
75. Berlin, "Administration of Military Justice," p. 203; Doctors also liable to courts-martial as officers, p. 207.
76. Headquarters Valley Forge, 5 January 1778, *Valley Forge Orderly Book,* p. 180.
77. Headquarters Valley Forge, 10 March 1778, Ibid., pp. 252–53.
78. General Orders, Headquarters Ashley Hill, 17 September 1782, Maj. Gen. Nathaniel Greene's Orders, Southern Army, South Carolina, 1 July–5 November 1782, The New-York Historical Society's Collection of Early American Orderly Books (microfilm, David Library).
79. General or Garrison Orders, area of Fredericksburg, New York, 13 October 1778; General Orders, Headquarters Robinson's House, New York, 14 August 1780; Headquarters Stee[napie], 10 September 1780, Lamb's 2CA Orderly Books, 26 September–27 November 1778, 14 August–29 September 1780, 7 September–2 November 1780.
80. Berlin, "Administration of Military Justice," p. 139.
81. Headquarters Princeton, 22 and 29 May, 11 June 1777, Kirkwood's Delaware Regiment Orderly Book. Kirkwood wrote on 22 May that Mary Quin was confined on suspicion of being an enemy. Then on the 29th recorded that a court of inquiry checking on Mary Quin and Elisabeth Brewer was in session. The court-martial's decisions were published on 11 June. Brewer was to be sent to Philadelphia in the company of James Cox, who had been convicted of desertion and sentenced to a hundred lashes and confinement. He was not specifically referred to as a soldier, but he probably was, and as such was one of the few service members so imprisoned.
82. 1776 Articles of War, Article 2, Section XVIII, Winthrop, *Military Law,* p. 970. Berlin, "The Administration of Military Justice," pp. 26–27.
83. General Orders, Headquarters Valley Forge, 16 March, and Orderly Office Valley Forge, 6 May 1778, *Valley Forge Orderly Book,* pp. 262, 309–10.
84. "After" Garrison Orders, West Point, 13 December 1782, Lamb's 2CA Orderly Book, 27 November 1782–5 January 1783.
85. Headquarters Valley Forge, 22 December 1777; 11 April 1778, *Valley Forge Orderly Book,* pp. 165, 286.
86. General Additional Orders, Headquarters Skippack, 1 October 1777; Brigade Orders, Headquarters Valley Forge, 13 March 1778; Valley Forge, 14 April 1778;

Ibid., pp. 255, 288–89. As noted in chapter 2, nn. 155 and 157, in 1779 at least one brigade resorted to the use of fines for this offense, and in 1781 another commander was threatening court-martial.
87. Camp at [Ramapaugh?] Clove, 12 July 1777, Kirkwood's Delaware Regiment Orderly Book. Kirkwood, usually quite thorough in his entries, made no mention of a trial or sentence, just the punishment and the reason for it. As he mentioned other women's trials, my assumption is that this was summary punishment.

8

Contributors to a Glorious Work

> [That person] will be the best Soldier, and the best Patriot, who contributes most to this glorious work, whatever his [or her] station, or from whatever part of the Continent he [or she] may come.
>
> *George Washington*
> *New York, 1 August 1776*[1]

There were thousands of men and women with the Continental Army who did as much to win the war for independence as those who served in it. They all belonged to the army, but when those "citizen-soldiers" marched off into history, somehow most of the followers got left behind. These civilians, whether they accompanied the American army so as to exploit military personnel, remain with loved ones, or find employment, also served, and in legitimate, sometimes even heroic ways. To dismiss camp followers because this title has often been thought synonymous with that of whores is not only to demean them but to miss their vital contributions to the army's survival and thus the Revolution's success.

Yes, some prostitutes did follow the Continental Army. They were, however, a minority; it has only been the public's (as well as the soldiers') interest in their activities that has magnified their presence in the army's train. In actual numbers, there were probably more gentleman volunteers than prostitutes with the troops, but few people remember that they, too, were civilians following the army. Actually, sutlers and other vendors, servants and slaves, family members, and civilian or public service employees made up the majority of the army's followers.

After the Continental Congress recognized the inevitability of civilians with the army, it defined followers and their status in camp in the 1775 and 1776 American Articles of War. Article 23, Section XIII, of the 1776 Articles categorized followers as sutlers, retainers to camp, and all persons whatsoever serving with the armies of the United States. The military, by applying that legislation in orders, regulations, and courts-martial, then enlarged the definition. For example, it determined that rules pertaining to sutlers could be applied to other sellers, extending the name itself to cover a wide variety of merchants who were not technically sutlers, meaning licensed vendors to the troops in camp. Wives, children, servants, and slaves fell under the designation of retainers to the camp and were the people most commonly thought of when that term was used (indeed, when the term *follower* was used). But another group of followers, volunteers, also came under this heading, because they, like the other retainers, accompanied the army, without a contract to bind them or guaranteed pay and positions to hold them, to fulfill personal as opposed to military needs. Although different from the other retainers in terms of position, power, and dependency, volunteers legally ranked as retainers. Although not all people in the public service worked with or for the army, persons serving with the army were officers or employees in the public service. They worked for the staff or civil departments that provided administrative or logistics support to the army. Generally, the army tended to see sutlers, contractors, and other sellers as adjuncts, namely as business people who added to or complemented the military supply system; retainers as domestic attendants or regimental adherents, bound by personal affection or interests; and persons serving with the army as auxiliaries who transported, supplied, and quartered the troops and thus were more intrinsically part of the military organization than any of the other camp followers.

Although some of these followers did hinder army operations, most did not, and their contributions, much like those of many civilians elsewhere, have to be seen as patriotic service for they certainly resulted in little personal or group gain and recognition. Most sutlers and contractors did not get rich; most slaves with the army for American independence did not gain their freedom; the majority of the women with the army were not liberated by the experience; and many of the army's civilian employees did a lot of work for little money and even less glory.

Each person's service, whether disbursing cartridges or doing laundry, had value, but the power of that assistance only truly became manifest when it was harnessed and used in tandem with the service of others. The army saw to that. Washington and the other commanders did not like being burdened with followers, but they discovered that they needed their help. They therefore gave directions to make it so. Followers did not necessarily like the orders, but they, in turn, often desired the army's aid and protection. This symbiotic, civilian-military relationship became the basis of a new community: a community whose people performed the myriad tasks necessary to keeping an army in the field for eight long years. If basic survival of the army—not just winning battles, or profound leadership, or foreign aid and French troops—was one key to independence, then the camp followers performed work as glorious as that of other patriots.

Officers, soldiers, and followers all belonged to the army, but in varying degrees. Men who accepted a commission or signed an enlistment essentially delivered themselves into the army's possession; they surrendered their personal freedom so as to serve the public good.[2] Belonging was not merely a matter of association in their case; it was a matter of ownership: the army owned their services for the duration of their contracts—in an officer's case until resignation, dismissal, or discharge, and in the soldier's, until discharge or expiration of enlistment. The army also possessed its civilian followers, but possession, more specifically control, was more tenuous: it rested upon mutual interests such as patriotism, defense, and survival; upon sacrifice, the army forgoing a measure of security and mobility, and the followers, comfort and security; and on formal and informal agreements that (despite the sacrifices) association and subordination would benefit both army and followers. When sutlers, contractors, and staff department employees accepted appointments or made formal arrangements to provide goods and services, they entered into a contract with the army. The army assured them of access to the camps, guaranteed their markets or wages, and provided military protection for as long as they were needed and heeded its regulations. In the case of retainers, the military evidently believed that if it fed them, it owned them. But "belonging to" was not defined merely by the army's claim of ownership or control; it also described the feeling of connection with the military that some followers had. Although many followers never looked beyond their own business or personal concerns, many others strongly identified with the army and its mission: while they may have acknowledged they were not in the army, they felt themselves to be a part of a broader military organization.

This broader military organization or society was the Continental Community. The core of this society was the army: it supplied a reason for the community's existence, provided employment, created a market, and established a form of government. It was a mechanical (as opposed to an organic or naturally developing) society in that it maintained itself primarily by focusing on an outside threat, through administrative and legal constraints, and by a controlled and systematic distribution of labor.[3] Civilian followers not only helped to create this community by establishing a symbiotic relationship with the army and its uniformed personnel but legitimized the army's command structure as the government of the community by accepting its rules. In doing so, the Continental Army and its followers established the precedents upon which the modern American military community would be built. By accepting, rejecting, and modifying both earlier and contemporary models of this civil-military relationship, the revolutionaries established the rules by which later civilian residents of the American military community would be governed. These appeared, echoing the earlier practices, in an 1846 interpretation of the legality of military authority over camp followers:

> *camp followers* entering into a new society, having peculiar laws of its own, by their own voluntary act, must conform to those laws, as such is an understood condition of their admission: they are therefore liable to

receive the orders of their military superiors, and are to act in conformity thereto, though rather in a civil than in a military capacity. These persons cannot be called upon to perform military duty; but in all that relates to the maintenance of the peace and order of the camp the observance of rights, public or private, the arrangement of their goods, horses and carriages, and in matters pertaining to the police, safety or convenience of the camp, they are as liable to military command, and punishment for the non-observance of the same, as the enlisted soldier; . . . they should . . . make themselves acquainted with the orders and regulations by which they are governed; . . . ignorance of the law is no excuse for offences.[4]

The Continental Community did not exist merely because of a mechanical legal and social solidarity. It was also a community built upon shared beliefs—those brought into the community and those engendered or ennobled within it—such as liberty, freedom, and military glory, as well as the virtues (including, as they discovered, the virtue of discipline[5]) needed to realize these beliefs. Army service attracted people intent on American independence and willing to achieve that end by military means. Although such sentiments, which waxed and waned throughout the war,[6] were generally strongest in the officers and soldiers, some civilians decided to follow and serve the army as their contribution to the cause.

The army also fostered a creedal solidarity in its personnel and followers. It promoted this through patriotic lectures and displays, religious sermons, fireside debates, and even the courts-martial. All served to reinforce appropriate existing beliefs and indoctrinate soldiers and followers alike in revolutionary political ideology and the need for American unity—a unity that needed to be displayed in the Continental Community so that it could serve as an example to the states. Yet all too often that unity was not evident in the Continental Community (thus a dependence on external controls such as regulations and courts-martial). Americans, especially the Americans in and with the army, had much in common, but they had a great deal of difficulty in learning how to work together. Continental Army or Community life tested the ability of revolutionary Americans "to live continentally as well as to think and talk continentally." Some could not do it; they could not operate in this unfamiliar, new, and temporary community that had a national as opposed to local orientation. A few responded by causing trouble in the community; others simply left or deserted. But others were profoundly "Continentalized" or nationalized by the experience of living and fighting alongside men and women from the different states.[7]

The war itself—the battles, constant movement, and deprivations—also fostered that sense of community—of belonging to the army—in the army's officers, soldiers, and followers and encouraged in them a belief that the army or nation owed them something for their services in that community. Officers and soldiers did receive recognition and eventually some recompense, but the great majority of followers did not, even though they not only endured the same hardships and encountered the same hazards as the officers and soldiers but sometimes suffered additional misfortune due to their jobs with or services to the military. Sutlers lost their stores, while contracted laborers and other employees lost their property and the tools of their trade. They, along with other followers, could find themselves prisoners if they did not remain in a secure position on march or in battle. If not laid low as Martha Washington once was by the diseases that ravaged the camps, they could be killed, as a volunteer was at the contested occupation of Plowed Hill in or near Cambridge on 26 August 1775, or wounded by musket balls and artillery fire.[8]

African Americans, whether as slaves, free servants, or free laborers following the army, were among those who suffered. Some slaves ran away to one or the other of the opposing armies in attempts to gain freedom only to be captured after a military engagement and returned to their owners. Both slaves and black freemen—some with an army, some not—were also captured, commandeered, or killed by both armies at various times. Lucretia Pritchett and William Churchill, executors for the estate of Joseph Pritchett, asked for and received compensation from the Virginia legislature for the loss of the male slave, Minny, who was killed in action against a British tender in the Rappahannock River while serving as a volunteer. Anne Cocke, James Taylor, and Anne Burwell also all received compensation from Virginia for slaves lost to them. Cocke's slave had first been impressed by the American army to help ferry the 2nd Virginia Regiment from Jamestown to Edward's Landing below Cobham and then was captured by the British in November 1775. Taylor lost two slaves who had been moved to Great Bridge (sometime in 1776 or early 1777) to help prepare fortifications and then died there, and Burwell's slave was accidentally drowned while transporting ammunition for the Virginia troops in December 1776.[9] In these cases compensation was awarded to persons who had not followed the army themselves but had assigned others to do so: the payment was for persons who had fallen while following or serving the army as part of their duties. The black soldiers, servants, and laborers who lived, worked, and had comrades die in the Continental Community were integral parts of that society but, reflecting what was common in the rest of American society, seldom saw their services recognized and rewarded outside of a few slaves receiving their freedom and a few others quietly honored for their efforts.

There was little or no reconsideration for the status of women on account of their fortitude and actions with the army. As they had with African Americans, many white male Americans found it difficult to work with women followers (as opposed to just ordering them to do something) and did not always think to accord them recognition for hardships endured and jobs done well. Women and children lost husbands and fathers (Captain Richard Shortridge's two young sons saw their father buried at Crown Point on 8 July 1776) and were injured or killed themselves by accidents in camp, as a woman was when a musket carelessly snapped by a soldier fired, or during engagements with the enemy, as Margaret Corbin was at Fort Washington. The British and American armies also sometimes captured their enemy's retainers.[10] Recognition though, usually through the awarding of pensions, was given in only a few extraordinary cases, such as those involving Mary Ludwig Hays, Margaret Corbin, and Anna Maria Lane, where the women had performed above and beyond the call for women's duties. Women belonged to the army, but they belonged to it in the same way they belonged to anything else—as domestic attachments. Even the nurses, women and men, in the hospital department worked primarily within the domestic, not medical, sphere and because of that received little financial or public reward for their labor.

Civil or staff department officers and employees sometimes felt that they were not receiving proper recognition and recompense, but Congress did award some of them official titles or ranks, especially those working within the military branches of their departments, and promised pensions and land grants to those appointed as officers or those who enlisted in the public service. On the other hand, the public seldom acknowledged or praised these public servants the way it did officers and soldiers of the line. There was little glory in staff work. In fact the public tended to see some of them, especially the public agents or purveyors and contract employees, as opportunists feeding off the army and often blamed them (sometimes with reason) for the administrative and logistics problems that plagued the military throughout the war.

After the war, as it created a mythology of the Revolution, the new nation ignored the roles played by most camp followers. Americans preferred to concentrate on tales that ennobled the ragtag fighters who surmounted all odds to win the war. In contrast, although they celebrated the exploits of a few individuals, they generally saw nothing noble about ragtag women or men who wielded account books or artisans' tools instead of swords and muskets.

Such neglect was aided both by the advent of peace and by a continuation of the militarization of civilian support services to the army. In June 1783 Washington furloughed most of his noncommissioned officers and soldiers, and in October Congress declared that the Continental Army would be officially disbanded as of 3 November (thus belying predictions that once America was free of Great Britain it would continue under a military government[11]). When the men dispersed and returned to their homes, they took their retainers with them. As the military market shrank (the new American army was tiny), sutlers and other sellers also left. As there was no need for large-scale administrative and logistical support, civil department personnel were dismissed. Therefore, when historians and mythmakers (they are not necessarily the same thing), even those writing immediately after the war, looked to a current army as a model, they did not see a prominent contingent of civilian followers affecting army operations and so did not think to include them in their analysis of the earlier army. And when they talked with veterans and their descendants and then wrote about the war, they focused on battles, not camp life. The myopia increased over time, especially as armies began to enlist people or train soldiers to do the tasks once done by followers.

The Continental Army, although it experimented with tactical and organizational techniques that would be fully implemented in the armies of the nineteenth century, was ultimately an army for and of its time: an eighteenth-century army that still relied heavily on nonmilitary support services and personnel. Its reliance on such people placed it historically with the European armies it took as examples; even the methods whereby it controlled its camp followers were copied from the British model. But the army's eagerness to control these people more tightly, evidenced by its willingness to court-martial them and its attempts to incorporate them within the army (as in the case of enlisted artificers), foreshadowed the increasingly professional armies of the next century. Armies became, more than ever, communities of uniformed men.[12] The need for camp-follower support declined as the army incorporated service functions within the organization, and as the need declined, people forgot that such support was ever necessary and that a great number and variety of civilians once not only followed the American army but were part of its creation and essential to its success.

Notes

1. General Orders, Headquarters New York, 1 August 1776, in John C. Fitzpatrick, ed., *The Writings of George Washington* (Washington, D.C.: U.S. Government Printing Office, 1931), 5:361–62.
2. Charles Royster, *A Revolutionary People at War: The Continental Army and American Character, 1775–1783* (1979; reprint, New York: W. W. Norton, 1981), pp. 67–68.
3. This is Emile Durkheim's distinction (though perhaps not his precise definition) of mechanical vs. organic social solidarity. Durkheim's methodology is discussed in Robert A. Nisbet's *The Sociological Tradition* (New York: Basic Books, 1966), pp. 82–97.
4. William C. DeHart, *Observations on Military Law, and the Constitution and Practice of Courts Martial* (New York: Wiley & Putnam, 1846), pp. 26–27.
5. Headquarters New York, 27 April 1776, W. W. Abbot, ed., *The Papers of George Washington,* Revolutionary War Series (Charlottesville: University Press of Virginia, 1985), 4:140–41. Washington said, "It should be the pride of a Soldier, to conduct himself in such a manner, as to obtain the Applause, and not the reproach of a people, he is sent to defend; and it should be the business, as it is the duty of an Officer to inculcate and enforce this doctrine."
6. Circular to the States, 31 January 1782, Fitzpatrick, *Writings of Washington,* 23:479. Washington hoped that "soon might that day arrive, soon might we hope to enjoy all the blessings of peace, if we could see again the same animation in the cause of

our Country inspire every breast, the same passion for freedom and military glory impel our Youths to the field, and the same disinterested patriotism pervade every rank of Men, as was conspicuous at the commencement of this glorious revolution."

7. Robert Middlekauff, *The Glorious Cause: The American Revolution, 1763–1789* (New York: Oxford University Press, 1982), p. 331. Although I agree with Royster, *A Revolutionary People at War,* p. 62, about the army testing the revolutionaries' ability to live continentally, I do not see Americans in camp as being spiritually on their own. Don Higginbotham mentioned how army service fostered a national perspective in many officers in *The War of American Independence: Military Attitudes, Policies, and Practice, 1763–1789* (1971; reprint, Boston: Northeastern University Press, 1983), pp. 438–39. Joseph Plumb Martin is an example of this phenomenon, as revealed in *Private Yankee Doodle: Being a Narrative of Some of the Adventures, Dangers and Sufferings of a Revolutionary Soldier,* ed. George F. Scheer (1830; New York: Popular Library ed., 1963), pp. 122, 167.
8. Washington to Fielding Lewis, Peaks-Kill, 28 June 1781, wrote that Martha Washington had been ill for over a month with a kind of jaundice, in Fitzpatrick, *Writings of Washington,* 22:284. Washington to Hancock, Cambridge, 31 August 1775, Abbot, *Papers of Washington,* 1:391, 393 footnote 6.
9. Petitions 89-P (Pritchett and Churchill, 15 June 1776), 107-P (Cocke, 21 June 1776), 349-P (Taylor, 30 May 1777), and 486-P (Burwell, 22 November 1777), in Randolph W. Church, comp., *Virginia Legislative Petitions: Bibliography, Calendar, and Abstracts from Original Sources, 6 May 1776–21 June 1782* (Richmond: Virginia State Library, 1984), pp. 25–26, 31–32, 103, 148. The Pritchett-Churchill petition states that Minny was killed while voluntarily serving under Hugh Walker. Walker is not mentioned in Heitman's *Historical Register* or Sanchez-Saavedra's *Guide to Virginia Military Organizations in the American Revolution.*
10. Beebe mentioned that Shortridge was buried at Crown Point, 8 July 1776, in Frederick R. Kirkland, ed., *Journal of Lewis Beebe: A Physician on the Campaign Against Canada, 1776* (Philadelphia: Historical Society of Pennsylvania, 1935), p. 17. Woman killed incident is in Betty Sowers Alt and Bonnie Domrose Stone, *Campfollowing: A History of the Military Wife* (Westport, Conn.: Greenwood Press, 1991), p. 15. Story of Margaret Corbin in William Davison Perrine, *Molly Pitcher of Monmouth County, New Jersey and Captain Molly of Fort Washington, New York, 1778–1937* (Princeton Junction, N.J., pamphlet, 1937). *Pennsylvania Gazette,* 15 November 1775, p. 4, col. 2, reported that American forces took the garrison at St. John's on Lake Champlain with 180 prisoners total, including women and children; and reported on 7 November 1781, p. 2, col. 2, that among the 7,247 prisoners taken at Yorktown were 6039 rank and file and 80 "followers of the army."
11. *The Royal Gazette,* 19 September 1778, p. 3, col. 2. In answer to queries sent from the country, the author gave the opinion that should America be "detached" from Great Britain, she would continue under a military government.
12. Barton Hacker, "Women and Military Institutions in Early Modern Europe: A Reconnaissance," *Signs: Journal of Women in Culture and Society* 6, no. 4 (1981): 645, 664–65; Myna Trustram, *Women of the Regiment: Marriage and the Victorian Army* (Cambridge: Cambridge University Press, 1984), p. 3. Both Hacker and

Trustram mentioned how militarization affects the supporting roles of camp followers. For information on camp followers after the American Revolution, check Edward M. Coffman, *The Old Army: A Portrait of the American Army in Peacetime, 1784–1898* (New York: Oxford University Press, 1986). For discussion on military legal jurisdiction over camp followers, see Maurer Maurer, "The Court-Martialing of Camp Followers, World War I," *American Journal of Legal History* 9 (1965).

Bibliography

I. Manuscript Primary Sources

A. Letters, Papers, and Records Other than Orderly Books

Ambler, Elizabeth Jacquelin. Papers. Library of Congress, Manuscript Division. Photocopy.

Backhouse, Richard. "Receipt and Account Book of Richard Backhouse of the Revolutionary Army 1775." Historical Society of Pennsylvania, Philadelphia.

Blackwell, Robert. Letters & Documents of Rev. Robert Blackwell in Wallace Family Papers. Historical Society of Pennsylvania, Philadelphia.

British Intelligence, New York, 1778. Library of Congress, Manuscript Division.

Browne, [Charlotte]. Journal of Mrs. Browne, Braddock's Expedition, 1754–1757. Copy in The New-York Historical Society. Extracts of diary printed in the *Virginia Magazine of History and Biography* (1932). Printed in full from manuscript in Library of Congress, in Isabel M. Calder, *Colonial Captivities, Marches and Journeys*. New York, 1935.

Burrows, John. "The Revolutionary War Reminiscences of John Burrows," John G. Barrett, ed. Written in 1830; ed. in 1975. Mss5:1B9466:1 is a typescript copy of a handwritten copy on deposit (owned by Mrs. Henry Maclin in 1975) at Virginia Historical Society, Richmond.

Campbell Family Papers, 1744–1859. Personal Papers collection, Accession 14014. Archives, The Library of Virginia, Richmond, Virginia 23219.

Champion, Deborah. Papers. Library of Congress, Manuscript Division. Copy.

Clinton Papers (with special mention for John Andre's Letter Book, 1778–1780, and Intelligence Volume, 1779–1780). William L. Clements Library, University of Michigan, Ann Arbor.

Compiled Military Service Records. National Archives, Washington, D.C. War Department Collection of Revolutionary War Records, Record Group 93: Compiled Service Records of American Naval Personnel and Members of the Departments of the Quartermaster General and the Commissary General of Military Stores Who Served During the Revolutionary War, M880 (microfilm); Compiled Service Records of Soldiers Who Served in the American Army During the Revolutionary War. M881 (microfilm); Revolutionary War Miscellaneous Manuscript Collections Revolutionary War Rolls, 1775–1783. M246 (microfilm).

Compiled Revolutionary War Records. National Archives, Washington, D.C. Additional Revolutionary War Records, Record Groups 39, 53, 92, 93, 94, 107, and 217: Letters, Orders for Pay, Accounts, Receipts, and Other Supply Records Concerning

Weapons and Military Stores, 1776–1801. M927 (microfilm); Letters, Returns, Accounts, and Estimates of the Quartermaster General's Department, 1776–1783. M926 (microfilm); Miscellaneous Numbered Records, 1775–1790s. M859 (microfilm). Numbered Record Books Concerning Military Operations and Service, Pay and Settlement of Accounts, and Supplies. M853 (microfilm).

Continental Army, Military Life Diary by U/I Author, 21 April–25 September 1780. Mss5:1Un3:10 in the Virginia Historical Society, Richmond. Author may have been Elias J. Parker (Mass.).

Continental Hospital Returns, 1777–1778, in Alison Papers. Historical Society of Pennsylvania, Philadelphia.

Feltman, William. Military Journal, 1781–1782. Historical Society of Pennsylvania, Philadelphia. Also published: "The Journal of Lieut. William Feltman, of the First Pennsylvania Regiment, from May 26, 1781, to April 25, 1782, Embracing the Siege of Yorktown and the Southern Campaign." *Collections of the Historical Society of Pennsylvania* 1 (1853): 303–48. Reprint. New York: Arno Press, 1971.

First Virginia Regiment Provision Returns, 1783. Military Records Collection, Accession 24834, Richmond, Virginia 23219.

Greene, Nathanael. Collection. Series IIIA. Library of Congress, Manuscript Division.

Grigsby, Hugh Blair. Papers, 1745–1944. Mss1G8792b in the Virginia Historical Society, Richmond.

Hand, Edward. Papers, 1777–1788. Manuscript Group 66. Pennsylvania State Archives, Harrisburg.

The Henry Knox Papers, GLC 2437. The Gilder Lehrman Collection, on deposit at The Pierpont Morgan Library, New York.

"Itinerary of the Pennsylvania Line, 1781." In Wayne Papers, Historical Society of Pennsylvania, Philadelphia. Also published: "Itinerary of the Pennsylvania Line from Pennsylvania to South Carolina, 1781–1782." *Pennsylvania Magazine of History and Biography* 36 (1912): 273–92.

John Lamb Papers. The New-York Historical Society, New York City. Microfilm.

Legislative Petitions, General Assembly, Legislative Department. Archives, The Library of Virginia, Richmond, Virginia 23219.

Martin, Lt. Charles. May 1797 Provision Return, Ft. LeBoeuf. Military Manuscripts Collection (MG7). Pennsylvania State Archives, Harrisburg.

McCready, Robert. Journal, New York, November–December 1778. Library of Congress, Manuscript Division.

Mercereau, John. Papers. Catalogued under Merserau in Miscl. Manuscripts. The New-York Historical Society, New York City.

"Molly Pitcher" Papers. U.S. Army Military History Institute, Carlisle Barracks, Pennsylvania. Includes copies of a variety of manuscripts and documents such as camp follower Jane Norton's declaration for benefits and Robert Young's statement of service in Revolution.

Pennsylvania Gazette. 1775–1783.

Potts, Jonathan. Papers, 1766–1780. Historical Society of Pennsylvania, Philadelphia.

Revolutionary War Miscellaneous Collection. U.S. Army Military History Institute, Carlisle Barracks, Pennsylvania. Contains copies of such things as Louis DuPortail's letter to the Count de St. Germain, 12 "9ber" 1777, and Lt. Robert Magaw's letter of 13 August 1775.

Rivington's New-York Gazetteer, known as *Rivington's New-York Loyal Gazette* from 18 October 1777 to 8 November 1777, and then *The Royal Gazette* from 13 December 1777 to 8 November 1783.

Schoff Revolutionary War Collection, William L. Clements Library, University of Michigan, Ann Arbor.

Sebastian Bauman Papers. Vol. I, 1775–1779. The New-York Historical Society, New York City. Microfilm.

Shippen Family Papers. Specifically Anne Hume Shippen Livingston Letters. Library of Congress, Manuscript Division.

Sol Feinstone Collection, David Library of the American Revolution, on deposit at the American Philosophical Society. Microfilm at David Library, Washington Crossing, Pennsylvania.

Washington Family Papers. Especially Martha Washington Letters. Library of Congress, Manuscript Division.

B. Orderly Books

The Filson Club Historical Society, Louisville, Kentucky
Sixth Battalion of North Carolina, Continental Army, Orderly Book, 1777–1778.

Historical Society of Pennsylvania, Philadelphia
Orderly Book of Brigadier General Anthony Wayne. Combined Pennsylvania Battalions, 1781. In Wayne Papers.
Orderly Book of the Pennsylvania Rifle Battalion. June–December 1775.
Orderly Book of the Pennsylvania Rifle Regiment. Vol. I, 16 June–3 September 1776. Vol. II, 4 September–4 October 1776. Copies.
Orderly Book of the 1st Pennsylvania Regiment. 26 July 1778–20 December 1778, 24 May–25 August 1779, 13 June–5 August 1780.
Orderly Book of the 4th Pennsylvania Battalion. 10–30 April 1776, 21 June–20 September 1776.
Orderly Book of the 1st Virginia Battalion of 1781.

Library of Congress, Manuscript Division, Washington, D.C.
Kirkwood, Robert. Delaware Regiment Orderly Book. 1 March–21 December 1777. Force Manuscripts, 7E, Recl. 16, Ent. 67.
Myers, Christian. German Regiment of Pennsylvania Orderly Book. 25 June 1779–29 March 1780.

National Archives, Washington, D.C.
George Washington's Headquarters Orderly Book. New York, 31 August–4 October 1776. Record Group 93. Revolutionary War Miscellaneous Manuscript Collections.
Headquarters Valley Forge Orderly Book. 1–31 January 1778. Record Group 93. Revolutionary War Miscellaneous Manuscript Collections.
Major General Heath's Headquarters Orderly Book. From Boston to Providence, 23 May 1777–20 October 1778. Record Group 93. Revolutionary War Miscellaneous Manuscript Collections.

The New-York Historical Society, New York City
Collection of Early American Orderly Books (microfilm at the David Library of the American Revolution, Washington Crossing, Pennsylvania): American Headquarters, Morristown, New Jersey, 21 February–17 May 1780; Brigade of Artillery with Washington's Main Army, New York and New Jersey, 23 July–31 December 1778; Colonel Alexander McDougall's 1st New York Regiment, New York, 25 March–15 June 1776; Garrison Orders, West Point, New York, 14 August–29 September 1780; General George Washington, Headquarters, Massachusetts, 31 August–24 September 1775; Major General Nathaniel Greene's Orders, Southern Army, South Carolina, 1 July–5 November 1782.

John Lamb's Second Regiment of Continental Artillery, 26 September–27 November 1778; 30 November 1778–4 February 1779 and 11 January–18 February 1780; 5 February–30 May 1779; 8 June, 14 June–19 August 1779; 24 August 1779–20 February 1780; 7 December 1779–27 March 1780; 28 March–12 June 1780; 21 June–6 September 1780; 26 June–30 December 1780 and 4 August–13 October 1781; 7 September–2 November 1780; 2 November–16 December 1780; 17 December 1780–20 February 1781; 21 February–28 March (notation error, actually goes to May) 1781; 29 May–22 June 1781; 20 June–21 October 1781; 7–30 October 1781; 7 December 1781–4 February 1782; 7 February–7 August 1782; 9 August–27 November 1782; 27 November 1782–5 January 1783; 6 January–19 February 1783; 20 February–28 March 1783; 28 March–25 June 1783.

Mss. Orderly Book kept at the Headquarters of LTC Marinus Willett of the 3rd New York Regiment, 17 February 1777–21 May 1778 (microfilm).

Pennsylvania State Archives, Harrisburg
O'Neill, Sergeant John. Orderly Book. February–September 1779. Military Manuscripts Collection (MG7).

Virginia Historical Society, Richmond
Virginia State Infantry, 1st Regiment. Order Book. 2 November 1777–4 March 1778. Mss12:1777 Nov.2:1. Copy.

The Library of Virginia, Archives, Richmond, Virginia 23219:
[Sergeant Long's Orderly Book], Captain John Belfield's Troop, First Regiment of Light Dragoons, Order Book, 30 January–22 August 1777. Military Records Collection, Accession 21334.
Unidentified Military Orderly Book, two leaves, 1777. Military Records Collection, Accession 23647.

William L. Clements Library, University of Michigan, Ann Arbor
Sir William Howe Orderly Book, 27 January 1776–1 May 1778.

II. Published Primary Sources

Acts of the General Assembly of the Commonwealth of Pennsylvania Passed . . . on Tuesday the Fourth Day of December, in the Year . . . One Thousand Eight Hundred and Twenty-One. . . . Harrisburg: Gleim, 1822. (Copies of title page and p. 32 in Molly Pitcher Papers, U.S. Army Military History Institute, Carlisle Barracks, Pennsylvania.)

Adjutant and Inspector General's Office. *Military Laws and Rules and Regulations for the Armies of the United States*. Washington: Adjutant and Inspector General's Office, 1 May 1813. Rare Book Room, U.S. Army Military History Institute, Carlisle Barracks, Pennsylvania.

Bangs, Isaac. *Journal of Lieutenant Isaac Bangs, April 1 to July 29, 1776*. Edited by Edward Bangs. Cambridge: John Wilson and Son, 1890. Reprint. New York: Arno Press, 1968.

Beebe, Lewis. *Journal of Lewis Beebe A Physician on the Campaign Against Canada, 1776*. Edited by Frederick R. Kirkland. Philadelphia: Historical Society of Pennsylvania, 1935. Originally published in *Pennsylvania Magazine of History and Biography* 59 (October 1935): 321–61.

Benét, S. V. *A Treatise on Military Law and the Practice of Courts-martial*. New York: D. Van Nostrand, 1862.

Black, Jeannette D., and William Greene Roelker, eds. *A Rhode Island Chaplain in the Revolution: Letters of Ebenezer David to Nicholas Brown, 1775–1778*. Port Washington, N.Y.: Kennikat Press, 1949.

Bloomfield, Joseph. *Citizen Soldier: The Revolutionary War Journal of Joseph Bloomfield*. Edited by Mark E. Lender and James Kirby Martin. Newark: New Jersey Historical Society, 1982.

Boynton, Edward C., ed. *General Orders of George Washington Commander-in-Chief of the Army of the Revolution issued at Newburgh on the Hudson 1782–1783*. Reprint of 1909 edition. Harrison, N.Y.: Harbor Hill Books, 1973.

Brooke, Francis Taliaferro. *A Family Narrative of a Revolutionary Officer*. 1849, 1921. Reprint. New York: Arno Press, 1971.

Carlisle Herald, Carlisle, Pennsylvania. Copy of 26 January 1832 paper in Molly Pitcher Papers, U.S. Military History Institute, Carlisle Barracks, Pennsylvania.

Closen, Ludwig von, Baron. *The Revolutionary Journal of Baron Ludwig Von Closen 1780–1783*. Translated and edited by Evelyn M. Acomb. Chapel Hill: University of North Carolina Press, 1958.

Dann, John C., ed. *The Revolution Remembered: Eyewitness Accounts of the War for Independence*. Chicago: University of Chicago Press, 1980.

Dann, John C., and John Harriman, eds. "The Revolution Remembered—By the Ladies." *American Magazine and Historical Chronicle* 3 (Autumn–Winter 1987–1988): 68–83.

DeHart, William C. *Observations on Military Law, and the Constitution and Practice of Courts Martial. . . .* New York: Wiley & Putnam, 1846.

Fridlington, Robert. "A 'Diversion' in Newark: A Letter from the New Jersey Continental Line, 1778." *New Jersey History* 105 (Spring–Summer 1987): 75–78.

Garden, Alexander. *ANECDOTES of the AMERICAN REVOLUTION . . . ,* 2d Series. Charleston: A. E. Miller, 1828. Rare Book Room, U.S. Army Military History Institute, Carlisle Barracks, Pennsylvania.

Gilbert, Benjamin. *A Citizen-Soldier in the American Revolution: The Diary of Benjamin Gilbert in Massachusetts and New York*. Edited by Rebecca D. Symmes. Cooperstown: New York State Historical Association, 1980.

———. *Winding Down: The Revolutionary War Letters of Lieutenant Benjamin Gilbert of Massachusetts, 1780–1783*. Edited by John Shy. Ann Arbor: University of Michigan Press, 1989.

Greene, Nathanael. "A Letter to His Wife." *Pennsylvania Magazine of History and Biography* 41, no. 2 (1917): 271.

———. *The Papers of General Nathanael Greene*. Edited by Robert E. McCarthy (microfilm) edition (of typescripts furnished by Rhode Island Historical Society) published by Scholarly Resources, Inc. At David Library of American Revolution, Washington Crossing, Pennsylvania.

Hamilton, Alexander. *The Papers of Alexander Hamilton*. Edited by Harold C. Syrett and Jacob E. Cook. 26 vols. New York: Columbia University Press, 1961–1979.

Kinnan, Peter. *Order Book Kept by Peter Kinnan July 7–September 4, 1776*. Intro. by M. E. Kinnan. Privately printed at Princeton University Press, 1931.

Lauber, Almon W., ed. *Orderly Books of the Fourth New York Regiment, 1778–1780, [&] the Second New York Regiment, 1780–1783. By Samuel Tallmadge and Others with Diaries of Samuel Tallmadge, 1780–1782, and John Barr, 1779–1782*. Albany: University of State of New York, 1932.

Mackenzie, Frederick. *Diary of Frederick Mackenzie: Giving a Daily Narrative of his Military Service as an Officer of the Regiment of Royal Welch Fusiliers. . . .* 2 vols. Cambridge: Harvard University Press, 1930; Arno Press reprint.

Mann, Herman. *The Female Review: Life of Deborah Sampson*. 1797, 1866. Reprint of 1866 version. New York: Arno Press, 1972. Originally published as *The Female Review; or Memoirs of an American Young Lady. . . .* Dedham: Nathaniel and Benjamin Heaton, 1797.

Martin, Joseph Plumb. *Private Yankee Doodle: Being a Narrative of Some of the Adventures, Dangers and Sufferings of a Revolutionary Soldier*. 1830. Edited by George F. Scheer. New York: Popular Library, 1963.

Murray, J. A. "Molly McCauley." *American Volunteer* (Carlisle, Pennsylvania), 12 September 1883. Copy in Molly Pitcher Papers, U.S. Army Military History Institute, Carlisle Barracks, Pennsylvania.

Nagle, Jacob. *The Nagle Journal: A Diary of the Life of Jacob Nagle, Sailor, From the Year 1775 to 1841*. Edited by John C. Dann. New York: Weidenfeld & Nicolson, 1988.

O'Brien, John. *A Treatise on American Military Laws, and the Practice of Courts Martial; with Suggestions for their Improvement*. Philadelphia: Lea & Blanchard, 1846.

Parker, Robert. "Journal of Lieutenant Robert Parker of the Second Continental Artillery, 1779." Edited by Thomas R. Bard. *Pennsylvania Magazine of History and Biography* 27 (1903): 404–20; 28 (1904): 12–25. Reprinted in New York (State) Division of Archives and History, *The Sullivan-Clinton Campaign in 1779*, pp. 188–210. Albany, 1929.

Pettengill, Ray W., trans. *Letters from America 1776–1779: Being Letters of Brunswick, Hessian, and Waldeck Officers with the British Armies During the Revolution*. 1924. Reprint. Port Washington, N.Y.: Kennikat Press, 1964.

The REMEMBRANCER; or, Impartial Repository of Public Events. For the Year 1778. Vol. 6. London, 1778. Rare Book Room, U.S. Army Military History Institute, Carlisle Barracks, Pennsylvania.

Sproat, James. "Extracts from the Journals of Rev. James Sproat, Hospital Chaplain of the Middle Department, 1778." Edited by John W. Jordan. *Pennsylvania Magazine of History and Biography* 27 (1903): 441–45.

Thacher, James [Surgeon]. *A Military Journal during the American Revolutionary War, from 1775–1783*. Boston, 1823. Also, *Military Journal of the American Revolution*. 1862. Reprint. New York: Arno Press, 1969.

Valley Forge Orderly Book of General George Weedon of the Continental Army under Command of Genl. George Washington, in the Campaign of 1777–8. 1902. Reprint. New York: Arno Press, 1971.

Washington, George. *The Diaries of George Washington*. 6 vols. Edited by Donald Jackson. Charlottesville: University of Virginia Press, 1976–1979.

———. *The Diaries of George Washington, 1748–1799*. Vol. II. Edited by John C. Fitzpatrick. Boston & New York: Houghton Mifflin, 1925.

———. *The Papers of George Washington*. Revolutionary War Series. Edited by W. W. Abbot et al. Charlottesville: University of Press Virginia, 1985– .

———. *The Writings of George Washington from the Original Manuscript Sources 1745–1799*. 39 vols. Edited by John C. Fitzpatrick. Washington, D.C.: Government Printing Office, 1931–1944.

Winthrop, William. *Military Law and Precedents*. 2d ed. 1920. Reprint. New York: Arno Press, 1979. (Original edition published 1886.)

Wister, Sarah. *The Journal and Occasional Writings of Sarah Wister*. Edited by Kathryn Zabelle Derounian. London & Toronto: Associated University Presses, 1987.

III. Secondary Sources

A. Reference Works

Berg, Fred Anderson. *Encyclopedia of Continental Army Units: Battalions, Regiments and Independent Corps*. Harrisburg, Pa.: Stackpole Books, 1972.

Blanco, Richard L. *The American Revolution, 1775–1783: An Encyclopedia*. 2 vols. New York: Garland, 1993.

Burgess, Louis A., comp. *Virginia Soldiers of 1776: Compiled from Documents on File in the Virginia Land Office Together with Material Found in the Archives Department of the Virginia State Library, and Other Reliable Sources*. 3 vols. Richmond: Richmond Press, 1927–1929. Reprint ed. Spartanburg, S.C.: Reprint Co., 1973.

Church, Randolph W., comp. *Virginia Legislative Petitions: Bibliography, Calendar, and Abstracts from Original Sources, 6 May 1776–21 June 1782*. Richmond: Virginia State Library, 1984.

Colonial National Historical Park Staff. "A Bibliography of the Virginia Campaign and Siege of Yorktown, 1781: Being a Part of the Master Bibliography of Colonial National Historical Park, Yorktown, Virginia, as of September, 1941." Undated mimeograph publication.

Daughters of the American Revolution, National Society. *Daughters of the American Revolution Magazine*. July 1892– . Index, vols. 17–71. Genealogical index for vols. 1–84.

———. *DAR Patriot Index*. Washington, D.C.: DAR, 1966. Supplement. Washington, D.C., 1969.

Deutrich, Mabel E. *Preliminary Inventory of the War Department Collection of Revolutionary War Records (Record Group 93)*. Washington, D.C.: National Archives, 1962.

Dorman, John Frederick, comp. *Virginia's Revolutionary Pension Applications, Abstracted*. 3 vols. Washington, D.C., 1958–1959.

Duncan, Louis C. *Medical Men in the American Revolution, 1775-1783.* Army Medical Bulletin, no. 25. Carlisle Barracks, Pa.: Medical Field Service School, 1931.

Flagg, C. A., and W. O. Waters, "A Bibliography of Muster and Pay Rolls, Regimental Histories, Etc., with Introductory and Explanatory Notes." *Virginia Magazine of History and Biography* 19 (October 1911): 402–14; 20 (January, April, July 1912): 52–68, 181–94, 267–81; 22 (January 1914): 57–67.

Gwathmeny, John Hastings. *Historical Register of Virginians in the Revolution: Soldiers, Sailors, Marines; 1775–1783.* Richmond: Deitz Press, 1938. Reprint ed. Baltimore: Genealogical Publishing Co., 1973.

Hamersly, Thomas H. S., ed. *Complete Regular Army Register of the United States (1778–1879), Together with ... Various Tables.* Washington, D.C., 1880.

Heitman, Francis B. *Historical Register of Officers of the Continental Army during the War of the Revolution, April, 1775 to December, 1783.* 2d. rev. ed. Washington, D.C.: Rare Book Shop Publishing Co., 1914. Reprint. Baltimore: Genealogical Publishing Co., 1982.

Holst, Donald W. "Eighteenth Century Military and Naval Terms." *Military Collector and Historian* 31 (Spring 1979): 4–7.

Kail, Jerry, and others, eds. *Who Was Who During the American Revolution.* Indianapolis: Bobbs-Merrill, 1976.

Linn, John Blair, and William H. Egle, eds. *Pennsylvania in the War of the Revolution, Battalions and Line, 1775–1783.* Pennsylvania Archives, 2d ser., vols. 10, 11. Harrisburg, 1880.

Listing of Revolutionary War Personnel for Memorialization Consideration. Circular No. 1–44. Washington, D.C.: Headquarters Department of the Army, 29 April 1975. In Revolutionary War #5 Miscl. Bibliography Folder, Military History Institute, Carlisle Barracks, Pennsylvania.

Matthews, William, and Roy Harvey Pearce. *American Diaries: An Annotated Bibliography of American Diaries Written Prior to the Year 1861.* Boston: J. S. Canner, 1959.

Military Service Records: A Select Catalog of National Archives Microfilm Publications. Washington, D.C.: National Archives & Service Administration, 1985.

National Archives. General Index to Compiled Military Service Records of Revolutionary War Soldiers. Record Group 93 (microfilm) publication M860.

Neagles, James C. *Summer Soldiers: A Survey & Index of Revolutionary War Courts-Martial.* Salt Lake City: Ancestry Inc., 1986.

Nebenzahl, Kenneth. *A Bibliography of Printed Battle Plans of the American Revolution 1775–1795.* Chicago: University of Chicago Press, 1975.

Newman, Debra L., comp. *List of Black Servicemen Compiled from the War Department Collection of Revolutionary War Records.* National Archives Special List no. 36. Washington, D.C.: National Archives, 1974.

New York (State) Comptroller's Office. *New York in the Revolution as Colony and State.* 2 vols. Albany: J. B. Lyon Co., 1901–1904.

Palmer, William P., ed. *Calendar of Virginia State Papers and Other Manuscripts ... Preserved in the Capitol.* Vols. 1–3. Richmond, 1875–1883.

Peckham, Howard H., ed. *The Toll of Independence: Engagements & Battle Casualties of the American Revolution.* Chicago: University of Chicago Press, 1974.

Peterson, Harold L. *The Book of the Continental Soldier being a compleat account of the uniforms, weapons, and equipment with which he lived and fought.* Harrisburg: Stackpole Co., 1968.
Sanchez-Saavedra, E. M., comp. *A Guide to Virginia Military Organizations in the American Revolution, 1774–1787.* Richmond: Virginia State Library, 1978.
Schulz, Constance B. "Daughters of Liberty: The History of Women in the Revolutionary War Pension Records." *Prologue* 16 (Fall 1984): 139–53.
———. "Revolutionary War Pension Applications: A Neglected Source for Social and Family History." *Prologue* 15 (Summer 1983): 103–14.
Sellers, John R., and others. *Manuscript Sources in the Library of Congress for Research on the American Revolution.* Washington, D.C.: Library of Congress, 1975.
Sons of the American Revolution. *A National Register of the Society Sons of the American Revolution.* 2 vols. New York: A. H. Kellogg, 1902.
Trimble, K. W. "Some Old Yorktown Maps." *Military Engineer* 23 (September–October 1931): 439–43.
Virginia Revolutionary War State Pensions. Richmond: Virginia Genealogical Society, 1980.
Virginia State Library, Department of Archives and History. *List of Revolutionary Soldiers of Virginia.* Compiled by H. J. Eckenrode. Special Report for 1911. Supplement, Special Report for 1912. Richmond: D. Bottom, 1912, 1913.
White, J. Todd, and Charles H. Lesser. *Fighters for Independence: A Guide to the Sources of Biographical Information on Soldiers and Sailors of the American Revolution.* Chicago: University of Chicago Press, 1977.
Wright, Robert K. "The Continental Army: Bibliography." Center of Military History, Washington, D.C. Photocopy.

B. Monographs, Articles, and Dissertations

Alden, John Richard. *The American Revolution, 1775–1783.* The New American Nation Series. New York: Harper & Row, 1954. Harper Torchbook edition, 1962.
Alt, Betty Sowers, and Bonnie Domrose Stone. *Campfollowing: A History of the Military Wife.* Westport, Conn.: Greenwood Press, 1991.
Anderson, Fred. *A People's Army: Massachusetts Soldiers and Society in the Seven Years War.* 1984. Reprint. New York: W. W. Norton, 1985.
Benson, Mary Sumner. *Women in Eighteenth-Century America: A Study of Opinion and Social Usage.* New York: Columbia University Press, 1935.
Berkin, Carol Ruth, and Mary Beth Norton, eds. *Women of America: A History.* Boston: Houghton Mifflin, 1979.
Berlin, Robert Harry. "The Administration of Military Justice in the Continental Army During the American Revolution, 1775–1783." Ph.D. diss., University of California, Santa Barbara, 1976.
Blanco, Richard L. "American Army Hospitals in Pennsylvania during the Revolutionary War." *Pennsylvania History* 48 (October 1981): 347–68.
———. *Physician of the American Revolution: Jonathan Potts.* New York: Garland STPM Press, 1979.
Blanton, Wyndham B. *Medicine in Virginia in the Eighteenth Century.* Richmond: Garrett & Massie, 1931.

Blumenthal, Walter Hart. *Women Camp Followers of the American Revolution.* Philadelphia: George MacManus, 1952.
Booth, Sally Smith. *The Women of '76.* New York: Hastings House, 1973.
Buel, Joy Day, and Richard Buel Jr. *The Way of Duty: A Woman and Her Family in Revolutionary America.* New York: W. W. Norton, 1984.
Bushman, Richard L. *The Refinement of America: Persons, Houses, Cities.* New York: Alfred A. Knopf, 1992.
Carp, E. Wayne. *To Starve the Army at Pleasure: Continental Army Administration and American Political Culture, 1775–1783.* Chapel Hill: University of North Carolina Press, 1984.
Center of Military History. Army Nurse Corps History. Unpublished draft. Center of Military History, Washington, D.C. (Copy at U.S. Army Military History Institute, Carlisle Barracks, Pennsylvania.)
Clinton, Catherine, and Nina Silber. *Divided Houses: Gender and the Civil War.* New York: Oxford University Press, 1992.
Coffman, Edward M. *The Old Army: A Portrait of the American Army in Peacetime, 1784–1898.* New York: Oxford University Press, 1986.
Cohn, Michael. "Evidence of Children at Revolutionary War Sites." *Northeast Historical Archaeology* 12 (1983): 40–42.
Contamine, Philippe. *War in the Middle Ages.* Translated by Michael Jones. Oxford: Basil Blackwell Publishers Ltd., 1984.
Cott, Nancy F. *The Bonds of Womanhood: "Woman's Sphere" in New England, 1780–1835.* New Haven & London: Yale University Press, 1977.
Countryman, Edward. *The American Revolution.* American Century Series. New York: Hill & Wang, 1985.
Deakin, Carol C. "Support Personnel: Women with General Braddock's Forces." In *Proceedings of Northern Virginia Studies Conference, 1983,* edited by James Allen Braden. Alexandria: Northern Virginia Community College, 1984. pp. 85–94.
Demos, John. *Past, Present, and Personal.* New York: Oxford University Press, 1986.
De Pauw, Linda Grant. "Women in Combat: The Revolutionary War Experience." *Armed Forces and Society* 7 (Winter 1981): 209–26.
Doerflinger, Thomas M. *A Vigorous Spirit of Enterprise: Merchants and Economic Development in Revolutionary Philadelphia.* Chapel Hill: University of North Carolina Press, 1986.
Eckenrode, H. J. *The Story of the Campaign and Siege of Yorktown.* Washington, D.C.: Government Printing Office, 1931.
Ellet, Elizabeth F. *The Women of the American Revolution.* 2 vols. New York, 1849.
Evans, Elizabeth. *Weathering the Storm: Women of the American Revolution.* New York: Charles Scribner's Sons, 1975.
Foner, Philip S. *Blacks in the American Revolution.* Contributions in American History, no. 55. Westport, Conn.: Greenwood Press, 1976.
Forry, Richard Reuben. "Edward Hand: His Role in the American Revolution." Ph.D. diss., Duke University, 1976.
Frey, Sylvia. *The British Soldier in America: A Social History of Military Life in the Revolutionary Period.* Austin: University of Texas Press, 1981.
———. *Water from the Rock: Black Resistance in a Revolutionary Age.* Princeton, N.J.: Princeton University Press, 1991.

Friedman, Lawrence M. *Crime and Punishment in American History.* New York: Basic Books, 1993.
Greene, Francis Vinton. *The Revolutionary War and the Military Policy of the United States.* New York: Charles Scribner's Sons, 1911.
Hacker, Barton. "Women and Military Institutions in Early Modern Europe: A Reconnaissance." *Signs: Journal of Women in Culture and Society* 6, no. 4 (1981): 643–71.
Hall, David D., John M. Murrin, and Thad W. Tate, eds. *Saints & Revolutionaries: Essays on Early American History.* New York: W. W. Norton, 1984.
Hall, Edward Hagaman. *Margaret Corbin: Heroine of the Battle of Fort Washington, 16 November 1776.* New York: American Scenic and Historic Preservation Society, 1932.
Hatch, Louis Clinton. *The Administration of the American Revolutionary Army.* 1904. Reprint. New York: Burt Franklin (Lenox Hill Publ. & Dist. Co.), 1971.
Higginbotham, Don. *The War of American Independence: Military Attitudes, Policies, and Practice, 1763–1789.* 1971. Reprint. Boston: Northeastern University Press, 1983.
———. *War and Society in Revolutionary America: The Wider Dimensions of Conflict.* Columbia: University of South Carolina Press, 1988.
Huston, James A. *Logistics of Liberty: American Services of Supply in the Revolutionary War and After.* Newark: University of Delaware Press, 1991.
Isaac, Rhys. *The Transformation of Virginia, 1740–1790.* 1982. Reprint. New York: W. W. Norton, 1988.
Jarvis, Rupert C. "Army Transport and the English Constitution: With Special Reference to the Jacobite Risings." *The Journal of Transport History* 2 (1955–1956): 101–20.
Kaplan, Roger. "The Hidden War: British Intelligence Operations during the American Revolution." *William and Mary Quarterly* 47 (January 1990): 115–38.
Kein, Randolph. "Heroines of the Revolution." *Journal of American History* 16 (January 1922): 31–35.
Kelly, Amy. *Eleanor of Aquitaine and the Four Kings.* Cambridge: Harvard University Press, 1950.
Kerber, Linda K. *Women of the Republic: Intellect and Ideology in Revolutionary America.* Chapel Hill: University of North Carolina Press, 1980.
Kopperman, Paul E. "The British High Command and Soldiers' Wives in America, 1755–1783." *Journal of the Society for Army Historical Research* 60 (1982): 14–34.
———. "Medical Services in the British Army, 1742–1783." *Journal of the History of Medicine and Allied Sciences* 34 (1979): 428–55.
Krueger, John William. "Troop Life at the Champlain Valley Forts During the American Revolution." Ph.D. diss., State University of New York at Albany, 1981.
Kulikoff, Allan. *Tobacco and Slaves: The Development of Southern Cultures in the Chesapeake, 1680–1800.* Chapel Hill: University of North Carolina Press, 1986.
Kurtz, Stephen G., and James H. Hutson, eds. *Essays on the American Revolution.* Chapel Hill: University of North Carolina Press, 1973. Reprint. New York: W. W. Norton, 1973.
Landis, John B. "Investigation into American Tradition of Woman Known as 'Molly Pitcher.'" *Journal of American History* 5 (January 1911): 83–95.
Levin, Phyllis Lee. *Abigail Adams: A Biography.* New York: St. Martin's Press, 1987.
Lewis, Jan. *The Pursuit of Happiness: Family and Values in Jefferson's Virginia.* Cambridge & New York: Cambridge University Press, 1983.

Logan, Mary S. *The Part Taken by Women in American History.* American Women: Images & Realities Series. 1912. Reprint. New York: Arno Press, 1972.

Mackesy, Piers. *Could the British Have Won the War of Independence?* Bland-Lee Lecture, September 1975. Worcester, MA.: Clark University Press, 1976.

Martin, James Kirby, and Mark Edward Lender. *A Respectable Army: The Military Origins of the Republic, 1763–1789.* Arlington Heights, Ill.: Harlan Davidson, 1982.

Martin, James Kirby, and Karen R. Stubaus, eds. *The American Revolution: Whose Revolution?* Huntington, N.Y.: Robert E. Krieger, 1977.

Maurer, Maurer. "The Court-Martialing of Camp Followers, World War I." *The American Journal of Legal History* 9 (1965): 203–15.

Mayers, Lewis. *The American Legal System.* New York: Harper & Brothers, 1955.

McKenny, Janice E. "'Women in Combat': Comment." *Armed Forces and Society* 8 (Summer 1982): 686–92.

Middlekauff, Robert. *The Glorious Cause: The American Revolution, 1763–1789.* New York & Oxford: Oxford University Press, 1982.

Military Affairs editors. *Military Analysis of the Revolutionary War.* Millwood, N.Y.: KTO Press, 1977. Anthology includes articles by Maurer Maurer, Howard Lewis Applegate, and Durand Escheverria & Orville T. Murphy.

Neimeyer, Charles Patrick. "America Goes to War: Race, Class, and Ethnicity in the Continental Army." Draft manuscript for New York University Press, 1995.

Nisbet, Robert A. *The Sociological Tradition.* New York: Basic Books, 1966.

Norton, Mary Beth. *Liberty's Daughters: The Revolutionary Experience of American Women, 1750–1800.* Boston & Toronto: Little, Brown, 1980.

Onuf, Peter S., ed. *Patriots, Redcoats, & Loyalists.* Vol. 2 of *The New American Nation, 1775–1820.* New York: Garland, 1991. Note articles by Stephen Conway, John E. Ferling, Robert Middlekauff, and Charles Royster.

———, ed. *The Revolution in American Thought.* Vol. 1 of *The New American Nation, 1775–1820.* New York: Garland, 1991. Note article by Ruth H. Bloch.

———, ed. *The Revolution in the States.* Vol. 3 of *The New American Nation, 1775–1820.* New York: Garland, 1991. Note article by Joseph S. Tiedemann.

Perrine, William Davison. *Molly Pitcher of Monmouth County, New Jersey, and Captain Molly of Fort Washington, New York, 1778– 1937.* Princeton Junction, N.J., 1937. Pamphlet.

Piemonte, Robert V., and Cindy Gurney. *Highlights in the History of the Army Nurse Corps.* Washington, D.C.: U.S. Army Center of Military History, 1987.

Powell, Barbara MacDonald. "The Most Celebrated Encampment: Valley Forge in American Culture, 1777–1983." Ph.D. diss., Cornell University, 1983.

Quarles, Benjamin. *The Negro in the American Revolution.* 1961. Reprint. New York: W. W. Norton, 1973.

Ranlet, Philip. "The Two John Lambs of the Revolutionary Generation." *American Neptune* 42 (October 1982): 301–5.

Rees, John. "'. . . the multitude of women,' An Examination of the Numbers of Female Camp Followers with the Continental Army." *The Brigade Dispatch.* Part I, 23 (Autumn 1992): 5–17. Part II, 24 (Winter 1993): 6–16. Part III, 24 (Spring 1993): 2–6.

Risch, Erna. *Supplying Washington's Army.* Washington, D.C.: Government Printing Office, 1981.

Robson, Eric. *The American Revolution in Its Political and Military Aspects, 1763–1783*. The Norton Library. New York: W. W. Norton, 1966.

Rotundo, E. Anthony. *American Manhood: Transformations in Masculinity from the Revolution to the Modern Era*. New York: Basic Books, 1993.

Royster, Charles. *A Revolutionary People at War: The Continental Army and American Character, 1775–1783*. 1979. Reprint. New York: W. W. Norton, 1981.

Salmon, John S. "A British View of the Siege of Charleston: From the Diary of Captain John Peebles, February 11–June 2, 1780." Master's thesis, College of William and Mary, 1975.

Selesky, Harold E. *War and Society in Colonial Connecticut*. New Haven: Yale University Press, 1990.

Shimmell, Lewis S. *Border Warfare in Pennsylvania during the Revolution*. Harrisburg, Pa.: R. L. Myers, 1901.

Shy, John. *A People Numerous and Armed: Reflections on the Military Struggle for American Independence*. Rev. ed. Ann Arbor: University of Michigan Press, Ann Arbor Paperbacks, 1990.

Smith, Daniel Blake. "The Study of the Family in Early America: Trends, Problems, and Prospects." *William and Mary Quarterly* 39 (January 1982): 3–28.

Stegeman, John F., and Janet A. Stegeman. *Caty: A Biography of Catharine Littlefield Greene*. 1977. Reprint. Athens: The University of Georgia Press, 1985.

Stone, Lawrence. *The Family, Sex and Marriage in England 1500–1800*. Ab. ed. New York: Harper Colophon Books, 1979.

Stryker-Rodda, Harriet. "Militia Women of 1780: Monmouth County, New Jersey." *Daughters of the American Revolution Magazine* 113 (April 1979): 308–12.

Treadway, Sandra Gioia. "Anna Maria Lane: An Uncommon Soldier of the American Revolution." *Virginia Cavalcade* 37 (Winter 1988): 134–43.

Trussell, John B. B., Jr. *Birthplace of an Army: A Study of the Valley Forge Encampment*. Harrisburg: Pennsylvania Historical and Museum Commission, 1979.

Trustam, Myna. *Women of the Regiment: Marriage and the Victorian Army*. Cambridge: Cambridge University Press, 1984.

Van Doren, Carl. *Mutiny in January: The Story of a Crisis in the Continental Army now for the first time fully told from many hitherto unknown or neglected sources*. New York: Viking Press, 1943.

———. *Secret History of the American Revolution*. New York: Viking Press, 1941.

Watson, G. R. *The Roman Soldier*. Ithaca, N.Y.: Cornell University Press, 1969.

Webster, Graham. *The Roman Imperial Army, of the first & second Centuries A.D.* 2nd ed. New York: Harper & Row, 1979.

Wiener, Frederick Bernays. *Civilians Under Military Justice: The British Practice since 1689 Especially in North America*. Chicago & London: University of Chicago Press, 1967.

Wright, Robert K. *The Continental Army*. Army Lineage Series. Washington, D.C.: Center of Military History, United States Army, 1983.

Index

Aaron, Aaron (Captain), 128
Acland, Christian Henrietta (Lady Harriet), 15
Acland, John (Major, British), 15
Adams, Abigail, 19
Adams, John, 19, 61
Adams, Major (team owner), 211
Adams, Sally (Mrs. Samuel Adams), 148
Adams, Samuel (surgeon), 148
Adams, William (overseer), 218
Adjutant General department, 194, 197, 198, 207. *See also* Staff departments
Administration, Continental Community, 22, 34, 47
African Americans, 16, 57, 185, 274; in courts-martial, 169–70; and enlistment controversies, 44, 73–74n 59, 186n 18; as enlisted soldiers, 167, 170; in exodus to British, 165–66, 167, 170; as laborers, 218–19; as Yorktown refugees, 164. *See also* Servants; Slaves.
Albany, N.Y., 112–13, 134, 205, 217, 219, 223, 224, 253
Alcohol abuse, 109–110, 225, 243, 258
Alexander, William (General). *See* Stirling, Lord
Allen, Jane (supplier), 97
Anderson, James (servant, soldier), 177
Anderson, William (team owner), 211

André, John (Major, British), 244
Animals, 67, 83n 173, 105, 235n 101
Anny, John (wagoner), 252
Anspach, Peter (clerk, paymaster), 139
Anthony (slave), 169
Antrim, Mary (nurse), 223
Archer, Peter (wagoner), 211
Armours, Lieutenant (Thomas Armor?), 260
Arnold, Benedict, 60, 132, 173, 175, 178, 204; and John André, 244; and servants for, 139, 172
Arnold, Benjamin (Ensign), 52
Articles of War, American, 91, 262; 1775 vs. 1776 Articles, 13, 87, 94, 241, 255–56; 1776 Articles: Article 5, Section II, 257; Articles 2 and 3, Section VII, 51; Articles 1–4, Section VIII, 87–88, 94; Article 1, Section X, 250; Articles 16 and 21, Section XIII, 242; Articles 18 and 19, Section XIII, 249; Article 23, Section XIII, 5, 86, 135, 163, 192, 236, 247–48, 250, 257, 270; Article 3, Section XIV, 244; other articles in 267nn 60, 61, 62, 63, 64, 66, 68. *See also* Legal system, military
Articles of War, British, 13, 87, 240–41
Artificers: from artisans in ranks, 62–63, 206; duties, 218, 233n 82, families, 218; organizations, 194, 213, 215–16, 217; pay and

Index

rations, 215, 217; recruitment, 213, 214–15, 216; in Regiment of Artillery Artificers, 214; work locations, 214, 217, 218
Ashton, Joseph (Lieutenant), 203
Austin, Ebenezer (steward), 171
Austin, James (alleged spy), 249
Ayres, Kamp (wagon conductor), 208

Backhouse, Richard (contractor), 97
Bacon, Captain (William?), 214
Bailey, John (Colonel), 178
Baldwin, Jeduthan (Colonel), 215
Baldwin's Regiment of Artificers, 132, 147, 215
Bangs, Isaac (Lieutenant), 55, 111, 178–79, 181
Bans, Solomon (soldier), 59
Barbazet, Jacob (wagoner), 211
Barret, Lieutenant, 259
Barton, William (Lieutenant), 20
Bauman, Sebastian (Major), 62, 76n 91, 171, 256
Beach, John (matross), 44
Beaches, Mary (follower), 134
Beck, William (slave to freeman), 170
Beebe, Lewis (physician), 53, 60
Belinger, Lieutenant Colonel (Ballinger, Fred?), 94, 116n 26, 243
Belonging to the army: definitions, 5, 36, 122, 168, 224, 225; civilian vs. military, 194, 270–72; means regulation, 88, 128; secondary for servants, 163
Bennet, Elijah (express), 212
Bill (Billy, servant-slave), 168, 171, 187n 20
Bingham, Mr. (quartermaster employee), 210
Blaine, Ephraim (commissary general of purchases), 99

Blair, John (spy), 38–39
Blooman, John (civilian), 41
Bloomfield, Joseph (Captain), 141, 243, 253
Blowers, Robert (and wife), 133
Blunt, Thomas (Lieutenant), 256
Board of War, 99, 102, 130, 171, 202, 215–16
Boat department, 211–12
Boerum, Jacob (clerk), 205
Bogert, Theunis (clerk), 205
Bolter, Captain (with artificers), 147
Boure, Barbara (prisoner), 255
Braddock, Edward, 8–9, 24n 17
Breasted, Andrew (correspondent), 168
Brewer, Elisabeth (spy/nurse), 221–22, 260, 268n 81
Brewer, Jonathan (Colonel), 106, 214
Bride, Jeremiah (soldier), 258
British army: description, 18; African Americans, as prisoners, 166; African Americans, use of, 165; women with, 8–10
Brooke, Francis (Lieutenant), 54, 201–202
Brooks, John (Colonel), 150–51
Brooks, Mrs. John, 150–51
Brower, Theophilus (correspondent), 204
Brower, William (conductor), 204
Brown, James (soldier-servant), 173
Brown, Mrs. W., 146–47
Brown, W. (William?, Captain), 146–47
Brown, William (physician), 111
Browne, Charlotte (matron, British), 8
Bruin, Captain (Jeremiah Bruen?), 214
Burgoyne, John (General, British), 15
Burlington Barracks, N.J., 61, 64, 66, 101, 136, 206

294   Index

Burnett, William (soldier, wagoner), 211
Burr, Aaron (volunteer), 178
Burress, Samuel (soldier), 255
Burwell, Anne (slave owner), 274
Byvanck, Anthony (clerk), 205

Caldwell, Andrew (servant/slave master), 169
Cambridge, 15, 30, 34, 36, 44, 57, 63, 86, 88, 179, 221, 237, 274
Campbell, John (assistant deputy quartermaster), 204
Camp color men, 63–64, 219
Camp followers: definition, 1, 5, 23–24n 11, 270; contributions of, 2, 21, 271; effect on movement; 47–50; perceptions of 5, 9; regulation of, 35–36. *See also* specific people, departments, and items, such as Women followers, Numbers of, Quartermaster department, and Rations, etc.
Carlisle, Pa., 41, 169, 214
Carter, Captain (slave owner), 169
Carter, Vincent (stable keeper), 213
Carthy, Daniel (assistant deputy quartermaster), 204
Cary, Mrs. Elihu (cook), 132
Castner, Catharina (follower), 135
Champion, Deborah (courier), 158n 73
Chandler, Joseph (justice of the peace), 251
Charleston, S.C., 57, 166
Chatsey, Benjamin (soldier-servant), 173
Cheeseman, Mr. (director of masons), 217
Children, 126, 129, 132, 133, 138, 149, 223, 274
Churchill, William (estate executor), 274

Civil departments. *See* Staff departments
Claiborne, Richard (Major), 198, 205, 217
Clajon, William (correspondent), 182
Clapp, Stephen (Captain), 216, 217, 218
Clark, John (Major), 203–4
Clarkson, Matthew (auditor), 203–4
Class (rank) issues: African-American service and status, 167–68, 170; command-rank relations, 51; servants and officers' status, 172–73; social mobility, 52– 53, 162; social stratification, 21, 51, 57, 77n 103, 162; status and military legal system, 247, 253, 256–59; status of staff personnel, 194, 196–97, 198, 224; and among women, 15, 122–23, 127, 146, 151
Clement, Rachel (nurse), 223
Clerks, 205. *See also* Staff departments
Clinton, George (in Congress), 179
Clinton, Sir Henry, 166
Closen, Baron Ludwig von, 55, 57, 145, 168
Clothier General, 195
Civil-Military relations, 3, 11, 41–42, 61–62, 135; affected by social interaction, 59; and government regulation, 42; and plundering, 41, 135–36
Cochran, John (physician), 111
Cochran, Sergeant, 245
Cocke, Anne (slave owner), 274
Cockron, Mary (follower), 122
Cockron, William (soldier), 122
Cogswell, Thomas (Major), 208
Coldebrugh, Mr. (forage master), 251

Cole, Marcus (Lieutenant), 257
Colles, Mr. (instructor), 113
Comfort Sands and Company (contractor firm), 99, 100, 105, 176
Commissary department (commissariat), 45, 67, 97–99, 129, 195, 197; personnel, 207; purchasing agents, 97–98; magazine/store locations, 204; and specific supply system, 98–99
Commissary of Military Stores, 195, 214
Conductors, 207, 208. *See also* Staff departments; Wagon department
Continental Army: formation, 2, 17–18; image vs. reality, 3,4, 68–69; reputation, 41, 42; size, 22n 1. *See also* Continental Community
Continental Artillery: 1st Continental Artillery, 54; 2nd Continental Artillery, 44, 56–57, 58, 59, 92–93, 95, 101, 108, 109, 110, 113, 129, 131, 139, 147, 173, 175, 180, 203, 204; 3rd Continental Artillery, 48,148, 208.
Continental Community: definition, 1, 3, 4, 30–31, 271, 272; formation, 12–13, 86, 237, 272–73; organization, 4; providing workers, 204; relationship with army, 2, 49–50, 271; setting precedents, 272, 276; social change, agent for, 274–75. *See also* Image vs. reality; Public perceptions
Continental Congress: and army establishment, 2, 44; and army pay, 43, 73n 55 and 56; and Articles of War, 87, 94, 241; and military legal system, 237, 242, 246–47, 249; and officer applicants, 179, 182; organizing logistics system, 96–99; staff departments control, 193, 196, 197, 198–99, 203, 204, 210–11, 214, 215, 216, 220, 223
Continental Infantry: 6th Continental Regiment, 203
Contractors, 86, 97; checks and balances, 101; difficulties, 99–100; firms, 99–100; initial use of, 97; later procedures, 102–104; suttling on side, 93
Cook, Richard (Captain), 256
Cooking, 63. *See also* Food; Rations; Women's work
Cookingham, Frederick (prisoner), 251
Corbin, John (matross), 144
Corbin, Margaret (follower), 50, 144, 275
Cornell, Ezekiel (inspector), 101, 102
Cornwall, David (soldier), 141
Cornwall, Mrs. David (washerwoman), 141
Cornwallis, Lord Charles, 166, 211
Coshall, Thomas (soldier), 255
Coudray, Philip Tronson du (volunteer), 182
Courts-martial: for noncamp civilians, 38–39, 40–41. *See also* Legal system, military
Crane, David (slave owner), 166
Crane, John (Colonel), 48–49, 51 (possibly the Crane mentioned), 58, 257
Cregier, Mrs. (cook), 140
Crocket, Asher. *See* Anderson, James
Crown Point, N.Y., 53, 91, 93, 274
Cruise, Walter (Captain), 52
Culp, Philip (civilian), 41
Cumbo, John (soldier-servant), 173

Custis, John Parke (volunteer), 184
Custom of war, 244, 261–62. *See also* Legal system, military
Cutting, John B. (correspondent), 169

Davis, Joshua (ship captain), 212
Dean, Moses (artificer), 131–32
Dean, Sergeant, 51
Deane, Silas, 181, 182
DeCamp, Mary (nurse), 223
Delaware, General Assembly of: on servant enlistments, 58; on soldiers' debts, 42
Delaware Regiment, 122, 243–44, 246
Demont, Sarah (nurse), 223
Denniston, George (clerk), 205
Desertion, 58–59, 245; and espionage, 37; and punishment, 80n 127; 263–64n 12; of staff department personnel, 209
Discipline: definition, 237; and authority, 238–39, 245–46; need for, 6, 32, 128, 236–37; for effectiveness, 33–34, 135, 163, 192, 245, 262; for professional ethos, 237; for virtue, 86, 238; and for women, 123
Disorder: civil-military in staff departments, 194, 199–200; culture clashes, 52; personal conflicts, 51. *See also* Mutiny
Dobbs Ferry, N.Y., 108
Draper, George (physician), 111
Driver, Edward (soldier), 258
Duer and Parker (contractor firm), 99
Duncan, John (carpenter), 225
Dunmore, earl of (John Murray), 16, 165, 167, 170
Dunn, Abner (Lieutenant), 255
Dunn, Robert (director of expresses), 213

Duportail, Louis le Begue de Presle, 182

Eayres, Mr. (superintendant of artificers), 202
Eliot, Thomas (servant), 172
Emersly, John (soldier), 134–35
Espionage, 37–39, 212, 231–32n 64, 248–49
Eustis, William (physician), 46
Evans, John (civilian), 41
Express riders, 212–13

Farnsworth, David (spy), 38–39
Fatigue men, 218–19
Feltman, William (Lieutenant), 50
Feminine sphere/domesticity, 123–24, 138, 144, 152n 2 & 3. *See also* Gender issues
Filson, Samuel (Sergeant, wagon conductor), 203
Fishbourne, Mary (patriot), 20
Fisher, Mr. (conductor), 208
Fishkill, N.Y., 11, 34, 60, 132, 140, 147, 200–201, 203, 204, 205, 208, 218
Flagley, John (matross), 110
Fleming, George (Captain), 110, 141
Fleury, Francois Louis Teissedre de, 182
Flower, Benjamin (Lieutenant Colonel), 214, 218
Flower's Artillery Artificer Regiment, 147, 202
Food, 67–68; at markets, 106; sutler stock, 92. *See also* Cooking; Rations
Forage department, 195
Ford, Captain (artificers), 214
Ford, Chilion (Lieutenant), 92
Ford, Dunham (commissary), 258
Foster, John (Ensign), 52

Fort Constitution, 93
Fort George, 142
Fort Montgomery, 180
Fort Schuyler, 35, 39, 51, 64, 104–105, 106, 109, 135, 147, 207, 224
Fort Sullivan, 128, 134, 137
Fort Washington, 144
Franklin, Benjamin, 181
Frazer, John Grizzage (volunteer), 179, 203
Frazer, Persifor (slave owner), 166
Freeman, Mr. (sutler), 108
French army, 37, 49, 55, 108, 164, 168, 183
French and Indian War, 8–10
Furloughs, 56–57, 126
Furman, Moore (deputy quartermaster general), 259

Galt, Patrick (physician), 181
Gano, Daniel (Captain-Lieutenant), 180, 203
Gansevoort, Peter (Colonel), 104–105, 106, 109, 224–25
Gardner, Mr. (master carpenter), 225
Gates, Horatio, 38, 91–92, 178, 194, 210
Gay, Samuel (female soldier), 20–21
Gender issues, 122–24, 127, 159n 76, 247, 274–75. *See also* Feminine sphere; Masculinity
George, Reubin (express), 259
Gérard, Conrad Alexandre (French minister), 54
German-Flatts, N.Y., 94, 243, 253
Germantown, Pa., 47, 48, 64, 144, 222
Gibbs, Caleb (officer and steward), 171–172
Gibson, Hezekiah (artificer), 131–32
Gibson, Mrs. Hezekiah (cook), 132
Gilbert, Benjamin (Ensign), 42, 55, 112, 239

Gilbert, Grace (nurse), 223
Gilbert, John (clerk), 205
Gill, Gabriel (wagon conductor), 259
Glover, John (Colonel), 245
Godfrey, Benjamin (Captain), 178
Government: state vs. continental controls, 2, 88, 178, 199, 251. *See also* Continental Congress; specific states
Grant, Jehu (African American, servant/wagoner), 170
Greene, Catharine, 15, 54, 147–48, 149
Greene, Nathanael, 54, 59–60, 64, 106, 143, 148, 150, 176, 181, 219, 221, 258; as quartermaster general, 98–99, 201–202, 215, 259; with southern army, 203, 219, 258
Guion, Isaac (Lieutenant), 175

Hamilton, Alexander (Lieutenant Colonel): as aide-de-camp, 131–32; on African Americans in war, 167; on wife's/women's roles, 20, 150
Hanch, Jacob (team owner), 211
Hancock, John, 31, 171, 178, 192, 199
Hand, Edward, 245; as adjutant general, 58, 100, 130; servant problem, 168
Harrison, John (Captain), 169
Hart, Loies (nurse), 223
Harvey, Samuel (civilian), 255
Hatch, Jabez (Colonel), 217
Hay, Udney (Lieutenant Colonel, assistant deputy quartermaster general), 208–209, 210
Hays, John Casper (Sergeant), 144
Hays, Mary Ludwig ("Molly Pitcher"), 21, 29n 60, 50, 144, 275

Hazards of following, 14, 217, 222, 274–75
Hazen, Moses (Colonel), 200–201
Head of Elk, Md., 49, 137, 251
Health and hygiene, 63–65, 82n 157 & 158, 222, 261; venereal disease, 134, 244, 261. *See also* Medicine
Heap, John (servant's master), 127–28
Heath, William, 143, 200–201
Hendershot, John (supplier), 97
Henry, Patrick, 179
Herrin, Jane (follower), 134
Hicks, Giles (Captain-Lieutenant), 146
Hicks, Hester (Mrs. Giles Hicks), 146
Hiltzheimer, J. (advertiser), 252
Hinslee, Daniel (supplier), 98
Historical precedents: early, 7; from British army, 8–10, 12, 128, 130, 193, 227nn 3 & 5; for military legal system, 240, 245. *See also* French and Indian War
Hodgdon, Samuel (commissary), 39
Hoey, Benjamin (Lieutenant), 147
Holmes, Joseph Jr. (civilian), 166
Hospital department, 46, 195; department organization, 219, 220; hospital conditions, 222; hospital locations, 65, 134, 142, 219, 221, 222; personnel, 195–96, 219–221; personnel duties, 219, 220, 222; recruitment/rations/pay, 219, 220, 221, 223
Housing, 65–67; for followers, 134, 148–49
Howard, John (volunteer), 183
Howe, Robert, 103
Hubbard, Nehemiah (assistant quartermaster general), 210
Hubbell, William (Lieutenant), 57
Hubble, Captain (Hubbell, Isaac?), 171
Hughes, Hugh (Colonel, deputy quartermaster), 45, 175, 180, 200–201, 204, 205, 206; and artificers, 213, 215, 217, 218; and department rations, 101, 102, 132–33; and rank, 198
Hughes, Thomas (Lieutenant?, slave owner), 170
Hull, William (Captain), 257
Hunn, Dirick (clerk), 205
Hunn, William (African-American wagoner), 211
Hunt, Joseph (alleged spy), 249
Huntington's Brigade, 180
Huntington, Ebenezer (Colonel), 142
Hutchinson, Margaret (spy), 40
Hutton, George (hostler), 213
Hutton, William (volunteer), 191n 73

Ichabod (servant), 168–69
Identity/Ideology: patriotism or nationalism, 18–19, 85; women's patriotism, 19–20, 124–25, 143–45, 153n 5; reasons for service, 18, 27n 50, 31–33, 177; training, 69, 273
Image vs. reality: army of citizen-soldiers, 17–18, 57, 270; Continental Community as symbol, 68–69, 273; independence/slavery, 167; and military legal system, 240–41; virtue, 59–61, 85–86, 110–11, 125, 236, 275
Irvine, Matthew (Captain), 128

Jack (Caldwell servant/slave), 169
Jack (Lamb servant/slave), 168
Jackson, Henry (Colonel), 260
Jacobs, John (Lieutenant Colonel), 178

Index 299

James (slave), 166
Johnson, Mary (follower), 258
Jones, Thomas (enlisted clerk), 205
Jones, Thomas (commissary), 40, 67
Jorlow, Captain, 256

Keese, John (assistant deputy quartermaster), 200–201, 204
Keyton, John (soldier), 255, 258
Kiers, Edward (assistant deputy quartermaster), 204
King, Joseph: as clothier, 45; as storekeeper, 201
Kingsland, Edmd. (carpenter), 223
Kirby, Ephraim (volunteer), 180, 181
Kirkwood, Robert (Captain), 122, 134, 136, 246, 261
Knap, Abraham (spy), 249
Knox, Henry, 48, 50, 58, 182, 256; and artillery artificers, 214, 216; and servants, 139, 172; and sutlers, 94–95; as volunteer, 179; and wife, 147–48; and women's rations, 131
Knox, Lucy, 139, 147–48, 149, 172

Lamb, Alexander (deputy wagonmaster), 208
Lamb, John (Colonel), 46, 56–57, 110, 133, 141, 146, 171, 175, 202, 204, 214, 255; and civil-military issues, 61, 251; and contractors, 104; and family, 145; and logistics, 208, 210; and servant issues, 139, 168–69, 173; and sutler, 108; and volunteers, 180, 182
Lancaster, Sarah (nurse), 223
Lane, Anna Maria (follower), 144–45, 275
Lary, Mary (servant, washerwoman), 172

Laundry, 46, 64, 141–42. *See also* Women's work
Laurens, John (volunteer, Lieutenant Colonel), 167
Lee, Charles, 52
Legal system, military: components of, 237, 245, 262; conjunction with civil law, 250–52; courts, 253–54; establishment, 237, 248; follower accountability and access, 134–35; jurisdiction, 247, 248, 249–52, 265–66n 44; and maintenance of social order, 240; military vs. martial law, 242, 250; and outside civilians, 249–50, 259–60; procedures, 252–255; punishments, 255–262; and staff personnel, 246, 258–59; and sutlers, 243, 246, 253, 257, 260; and women, 243, 246, 247, 248, 255, 258, 260, 261. *See also* Articles of War; Continental Congress; Custom of war; Orders and orderly books
Lewis, Charles (Colonel), 170
Lewis, George (Captain?), 179
Lewis, John (soldier), 257
Linch, Michael (substitute matross), 44
Lincoln, Benjamin, 173; as secretary at war, 102, 130
Livingston, Abraham (purchasing agent), 98
Livingston, Henry Beekman (Lieutenant Colonel), 223
Livingston, William (New Jersey governor), 221
Lloyd, Mrs. (cook), 140
Login, James (conductor), 208
Loveday, John (steward), 171
Low, Susannah (nurse), 223
Loyd, James (volunteer), 181

Mackenzie, Frederick (Captain, British), 15
Malcolm's Additional Continental Regiment, 178
Malcome, Colonel (Malcolm, William?), 149
Marechaussee Corps, 48, 94
Markets, 86, 106; regulation of, 86, 90–93, 107–109, 243
Marrel, John (soldier), 260
Martin, Joseph Plumb (soldier), 126, 239–40
Martin, Alexander (Colonel), 256
Martin, Catherine (follower, housekeeper), 172
Maryland, government of: on apprentice/servant enlistments, 58; on loan of slaves, 164
Masculinity, 52, 76–77n 95, 123; and military brotherhood, 54, 162, 267n 67. *See also* Gender issues
Massachusetts, military units: 1st Brigade, 66; 3rd Brigade, 66; 3rd Regiment, 257; 5th Regiment
Massachusetts, government of, 33, 63, 88; 1775 state articles of war, 240, 247
Mavins, Mr. (conductor), 208–209, 210
McCarty, Mr. and Mrs. (British deserter and wife), 133
McClure, John (sutler), 95
McDougall, Alexander, 34, 110, 111, 175, 217, 260
McGraugh, John (sutler), 96
McIntosh, Ann (follower), 255, 258
McIntosh, Lachlan, 173
McIntosh, William (soldier), 255, 258
McKenzie, Samuel (surgeon), 112
McKenzie, William (apothecary's mate), 258

McKnight, Charles (physician), 168
McMath, William (soldier), 260
McMurry, Mrs. (nurse), 223
McNabe, Eunis (nurse), 223
Medicine: care for female followers, 127, 134; diseases, 65, 134, 165; small pox inoculation, 65, 219. *See also* Health and hygiene
Meed, Seth (spy), 249
Meng, Christopher (storekeeper), 139
Meriwether, Thomas (Major), 170
Merrit, Captain (Lieutenant John Merritt?), 245
Mifflin, Thomas (quartermaster general), 195, 204, 210
Miles, Colonel (deputy quartermaster?), 205
Miles, Edward (deputy assistant, commissariat), 225
Miller, William (carpenter, soldier), 37
Minny (slave), 274
Minor, Asa (market clerk), 106
Miralles, Don Juan de (Spanish agent), 54
Mission, military, 2, 3, 12, 18. *See also* Identity/Ideology
Mitchell, Uriah (assistant quartermaster), 204
Mnthorn, John (Sergeant), 133
Monmouth, N.J., 144
Montgomery, Mary (servant), 127–28
Moodie, Andrew (Captain), 135, 146, 180
Moodie, Mrs. Andrew, 146; and perhaps Mrs. Moody, 135
Moody, John (Lieutenant, Loyalist), 212
Morgan, John (director-general, hospital department), 147, 220

Morgan, Mary (Mrs. John Morgan), 147
Morgan, Ralph (soldier), 126
Morris, Robert, 99, 100, 101, 102, 104, 130, 131, 217
Morristown, N.J., 15, 51, 55, 62, 134, 149, 181, 207, 218
Mott, Gershem (Captain), 147
Mott, Isaac (soldier), 135
Mount, Richard (volunteer), 180
Moylan, Stephen (quartermaster general), 195
Muhlenberg, Peter, 252, 258
Mutiny, 51, 143, 245

Nagle, Jacob (soldier), 140
Native Americans, 39; Iroquois, 39, 128.
Neilson, John (Colonel, deputy quartermaster general), 104
Newburgh, N.Y., 11, 69, 90, 95, 103, 105, 106, 109, 111–12, 142, 150, 171, 204, 207, 213, 218
New Hampshire line, 66
New Jersey, government of, 58
New Jersey, military units: 1st, 133, 178; 2nd, 128; 3rd, 179
Newspapers: about African-American flight, 165–67; about army, 61; on deserters, 58–59, 209; on military punishment, 258; on nurses, 221; on runaways, 58; about servants, 15, 169; about thefts, 252; on women's patriotism, 19–20
New Windsor, N.Y., 105, 133, 147, 150, 175
New York City, 11, 36, 54, 55, 59, 98, 111, 145, 147, 178, 212, 218
New York, government of, 250
New York Highlands, 15, 54, 129, 132, 217, 249

New York, military units, 130–131; 1st, 111, 2nd, 129, 180; 3rd, 34, 104, 128–129, 257; 4th, 129; 5th, 129; with women and children, 128–29
North, Lieutenant (deputy wagonmaster), 203
North Carolina, military units: 2nd, 180
Norton, Jane (follower), 142
Norton, William (Drum Major), 142
Noyes, Nathanael (alleged spy), 249
Numbers of followers: attempts to limit, 129, 136; established via returns, 35–36, 128–130, 133–134; servants, 176; British quota, 10
Nurses. *See* Hospital department; Women's work

Obrain, Mrs. (nurse), 223
Officers: disputes among, 51–52, 76n 91, 256; as examples, 35, 60, 245–46; medical, 220; motivation, 43–44, 183; rations, 67–68, 84n 179, 117–18n 55; resignation, 56; staff positions, 202–203; social status, 52–53, 76n 91; training, 54, 62, 239
Ogden, Matthias (volunteer), 178
O'Neill, John (Sergeant), 141–42
Orders and Orderly Books, 34, 35, 248; orderly book support for policy, 130; general, situational, and standing orders, 242
Ordnance department, 195
Orr, William (Lieutenant), 164
Osborn, Sarah (follower), 137, 140
Oswald, Eleazer (Lieutenant Colonel), 56–57, 203

Painter, Gamaliel (Captain), 147

Parison, Captain (volunteer, French), 182
Parke, John (quartermaster general assistant), 203, 214 (possibly same man)
Parker, Anna M. (follower correspondent), 150
Parker, Avery (Ensign), 241
Parker, James (wagoner), 209
Parras, Anthony (soldier), 245
Parsell, John (artificers superintendent), 218
Parsell, Sarah (cook), 140
Patterson, Alexander (Captain), 252
Patterson, James (soldier), 105
Patton, John (Colonel), 255
Peebles, John (Captain, British), 166
Peekskill, N.Y., 38, 199
Peg (slave), 166
Pennsylvania, government of, 11, 250
Pennsylvania, military units: 1st Brigade, 92; 1st Regiment, 50, 65, 260; 2nd Regiment, 141, 203; 3rd Regiment, 172; 6th Regiment, 52; 10th Regiment, 146, 164; Pennsylvania Rifle Regiment (1st Continental Regiment), 33; Thompson's Rifle Regiment, 97, 245
Pepin, Lieutenant (Peppin, Andrew), 147
Perkins, Mrs. (nurse), 223
Perry, David (Lieutenant), 145
Persons serving with army, 6, 192. *See also* specific staff departments
Peter (servant), 168
Peters, Sergeant (also cook), 143
Philadelphia, Pa., 12, 39–40, 48, 49, 105, 111, 137, 174, 214, 217, 218, 249

Pickering, Timothy (quartermaster general), 45, 67, 85, 99, 205, 206, 208, 211, 212, 213, 215–18; and command of department, 200–201, 208, 209; and contractors, 100, 101, 102, 104; employing women, 139; helping families, 131–133, 147; servants, 171, 175–76
Pickett, Moses (soldier), 245
"Pierce's notes," 105–106, 118n 64
Piercy and Marvin, Messrs. (sutlers), 94–95
Piper, Benjamin, and Pencan (sutlers), 109–110
Pitcher, Molly. *See* Hays, Mary Ludwig
Platt, Richard (deputy quartermaster), 132, 147
Pluckemin, N.J., 95, 113
Polke, Thomas (Colonel), 256
Pollard, Captain (Benjamin?), 214
Pomeroy, Ralph (deputy quartermaster), 100, 198
Popkin, John (Lieutenant Colonel), 208
Post, Captain (Anthony?), 214
Post riders. *See* Express riders
Potts, Jonathan (deputy director-general, hospital department), 112, 220, 222; and servant problems, 169
Printer, Elishee (artificer), 259
Pritchett, Lucretia (executor, slave owner), 274
Prospect Hill, Mass., 109, 112
Prostitution, 5, 86, 110–12
Proud, Chas. (soldier, artificer), 139
Proud, Mrs. Chas. (servant), 139
Provost marshall, 91, 94, 253
Public perceptions: of army, 42, 61; of army and community, 69, 125, 236, 275–76
Putnam, Israel, 178, 182, 199, 206, 221

Quackenbush, Nicholas (assistant quartermaster), 204
Quartermaster: department, 45, 97, 99, 104, 140, 195; general's duties, 66–67, 90, 147; impressment, 211; military vs. civil components, 193, 195, 197–98, 199, 201–202, 216–17; pay and rations, 208; personnel, 164, 197, 198–99, 204, 207, 214, 218, 224. *See also* Boat department; Forage department; Pickering, Timothy; Wagon department
Quilley, Patrick (conductor), 170
Quin, Mary (alleged enemy/spy?), 260, 268n 81

Rand, Abraham (forage master), 104
Rations: for female followers, 68, 103; for officers, 67–68, 117–18n 55; for soldiers, 67; for quartermaster/staff department personnel, 101, 102, 132–33; quotas/regulations, 14, 128–133
Ray, Sarah (matron), 223
Rea, Samuel (advertiser), 252
Reed, Jacob (Captain-Lieutenant), 58
Reed, Joseph (volunteer, Lieutenant Colonel), 131, 179, 181
Reeder, Jacob (smith), 218
Refugees, 11–12, 25n 27, 113, 130, 145, 147
Regulations. *See* Administration; Articles of War; Discipline; Legal system
Religion/morality: and mission, 33; vs. vice, 60–61, 110–11. *See also* Image vs. reality: virtue
Retainers: definition, 5, 122, 185, 271; as attendants/adherents, 6, 271; as servants and volunteers, 162–63, 271; contribution to mission, 185. *See also* Camp followers
Rhode Island, government of: on enlistment issues, 58, 167
Rhode Island, military units: black battalion, 167; Olney's Battalion, 180; 2nd Rhode Island, 52
Riedesel, Baroness Frederika, 15
Roach, Frederick (matross), 257
Robertson, James (adjutant), 258
Robinson, Polly (alleged prostitute), 112
Rochambeau, Jean Baptiste Donatien, comte de, 37, 168
Rochefontaine, Captain, 171
Ross, David (superintendent internees, Yorktown), 164–65

Sackett, Nathaniel (sutler), 95
St. Clair, Arthur, 52, 92
Sampson, Deborah (woman soldier), 20–21; 159n 76
Sappers and Miners, corps of, 101, 105, 180
Schuyler, Elizabeth (Mrs. Alexander Hamilton), 20, 150
Schuyler, Philip, 52, 179, 214, 224, 253
Scott, Thomas (wagonmaster), 255
Security, camp, 36–37, 39–41, 103–104, 143, 244, 248
Seeley, Silvanus (sutler), 95
Sellsar, Michael (wagoner), 209
Servants, 15–16, 162, 168, 179, 176–77; issue of enlistment, 164; private vs. public, 163, 170; in officer households, 170–72. *See also* Soldiers; Waiters; Women's work; and specific officers
Shanks, Thomas (spy), 249
Shaw, Samuel (Lieutenant, steward), 172

Shortridge, Richard (Captain), 274
Shreve, Israel (Colonel), 128
Simpson (sutler), 253
Simson, Elisabeth (nurse), 223
Sinnex, William (soldier, servant?), 139
Skidmore, John (wagonmaster), 170
Slaves: army use of, 163–64; impressment of, 163, 211; hospital service, 219; personal use of, 168; service and freedom, 170. *See also* Servants
Smallwood, Joseph (wagoner), 259
Smallwood, William, 56, 164
Smith, John (volunteer), 180, 181
Smith, Josiah (Lieutenant), 257
Smith, Mary (housekeeper), 171, 172
Smith, Nancy (nurse), 223
Smith, William S. (volunteer, Lieutenant Colonel), 180, 181
Smithes Clove, N.Y., 35, 136
Smith and Lawrence (contractor firm), 102
Snook, Ann (supplier), 97
Soaper, Lieutenant (Soper, Amasa?), 241
Social Life: officers, 53–56; soldiers, 59–60; women, 55–56, 60, 149
Social mobility. *See* Class issues
Soldiers: duties, 62–63; enlistment of boys and servants, 57–58, 79n 122; as entrepreneurs, 105–106; motivation, 43–44; rations, 67; as servants, 171, 172–176; substitutes, 44, 74n 61; working for staff departments, 206–207. *See also* African Americans; Women's work
Southern army, 176, 203, 219, 225, 258
Spangler, George (spy), 249
Spies. *See* Espionage; André, John
Sproat, James (chaplain), 222

Staff departments, 16, 178, 275; civil-military checks and balances, 194, 227n 8; line vs. staff issues, 196, 199, 202; militarization of, 17, 45–46, 138, 192–93, 197, 206, 208, 212–13, 226, 275; pay, 45, 205, 210; rank, 74n 63, 196–97; recruitment, 205–206; staffing procedures, 204–205, 228–29n 24. *See also* specific departments
Staries, Ellaner (nurse), 223
Steuben, Baron Frederick von, 58, 170–71, 182
Stevens, Ebenezer (Lieutenant Colonel), 139, 141, 173, 180, 204
Stevens, Thomas (soldier), 257
Stewart, Walter (Colonel), 141, 202
Stirling, Lady (and daughter Kitty), 148
Stirling, Lord (Alexander, William), 38
Stone, Mrs. (follower, British), 9
Street, Lieutenant (Benjamin?), 255
Styres, Joseph (spy), 38
Sullivan, John, 96, 107, 181, 184, 224, 225
Sullvan, Catrinea (nurse), 223
Sutlers, 86–96; definition, 5, 86; business, 13, 46; courts-martial, 95–96, 253, 257 impressment of stores, 96; payment, 91, 92, 93, 106; rations, 129; regulations, 86, 90–91;

Tapp, William (Lieutenant), 224
Taylor, Hanna (prisoner), 255
Taylor, James (slave owner), 274
Thacher, James (physician), 47, 50, 52, 65–66; motivation for service, 32–33, 43–44; officers' social pursuits, 53–54, 55, 112–13, 149

Index   305

Theft, 17, 39, 210, 252–53
Thomas, Hannah (cook), 140
Thompson, Elizabeth (housekeeper), 171–72
Thorp, Mr. (director of artificers), 206
Tibbots, Job (alleged spy), 249
Ticonderoga, N.Y., 47, 91, 142, 222
Tidrey, Nel (alleged prostitute), 112
Tilghman, Tench (volunteer, Lieutenant Colonel), 184
Tillinghast, Charles (assistant quartermaster), 204
Tings, John (soldier), 257
Tonstor, Sealley (nurse), 223
Trask, Israel (soldier-servant), 162
Trotter, John (dance teacher), 112–13
Trumbull, Joseph (commissary general), 45, 195, 197, 199, 204
Tunison, Garret (surgeon), 101, 173
Turberville, John (slave and team owner), 163
Turner, Alexander (deputy wagon master general), 209

Valley Forge, Pa., 15, 40–41, 52, 56, 62, 65, 66, 67, 89–90, 107, 128, 133, 134, 142, 148, 169, 243, 253, 255
Van Cortlandt, Philip (Colonel), 34
Van Ingen, Dirk (physician), 221
Van Wagenen, Garret H. (Lieutenant), 133
Varick, Richard (Lieutenant Colonel), 139, 175
Varnum, James Mitchell (Colonel), 126
Verplanck's Point, N.Y., 68, 95
Virginia, government of, 163, 168, 170, 274
Virginia, military units: 1st Virginia Battalion, 173; 2nd Virginia Regiment, 255, 258, 274; 4th Virginia Brigade (General Charles Scott's Brigade), 255; 9th Virginia Regiment, 181; 10th Virginia Regiment, 255
Visitors: spectators of war, 75n 81, 177; wives, 145, 147
Volunteers: definition, 177–78, 183; backgrounds of, 181; as generals' aides, 181; as medical personnel, 220; problems, 183–84; process to positions, 178–181, 203, 204; process for foreign applicants, 181–83; provisions, 185, 190–91n 73; regulation/discipline, 184, 191n 73
Von Heer, Bartholomew (Captain), 94

Wadsworth, Jeremiah (commissary general), 204
Wagon department, 195; personnel hierarchy, 197, 207–208; wagoners, 207, 208, 209–211. *See also* Staff departments; Quartermaster
Waiters, 162, 173; batmen precedent, 172.
Walker, Robert (Captain), 145, 146
Walker, Thomas Jr. (slave owner), 170
Ward, Artemas, 111, 173
Warren, Samuel and Sarah (sutlers), 257, 260
Wart, David (slave owner), 219
Washington, George: establishing army and community, 30, 31, 32, 33–34, 238; on alcohol abuse, 109; on camp health, 64–65; and conflict with Greene on housing, 149; on contract system, 100; on desertion, 59; establishing civil-

military relationships, 3, 11, 251; and female followers, 14, 125–7, 129–31, 138; on furloughs, 56, 78n 113, 79n 125; ideological basis of leadership, 3, 69, 238; ideology and impressment, 67; ideology and plundering, 41, 242; ideology and slavery, 164–65; on military legal system, 241, 242, 255, 260 on officer; study/training, 62, 239, 276n 5; on officer conflicts, 51–52; and servant Bill, 168, 171, 187n 20; on servant-soldier practices, 171, 173; and social life, 55, 150; and staff department personnel issues, 192, 193–94, 199, 200, 203, 206, 208, 209, 210, 213–14; on sutlers, 88–93; on volunteers, 179, 184
Washington, Martha, 15, 147, 148, 150, 179, 274
Wayne, Anthony, 51
Wear, Andrew (cook), 140
Weedon, George, 47, 128, 243, 261
Weedon, Nancy (follower), 51
Welch, John (volunteer), 180
Weston, Mary (nurse), 223
West Point, N.Y., 35, 37, 46, 49, 55, 66, 92–93, 105, 107–108, 109, 110, 129, 133, 136, 137, 138, 139, 140, 142, 143, 149, 150, 151, 172, 173, 175, 204, 205, 206, 217, 251, 257, 259, 260
White, Anthony Walton (volunteer), 179
White, Hasfield (Captain), 201
White, John (volunteer), 181
Whitford, Moses (soldier), 257
White Marsh, N.Y., 40, 252
White Plains, N.Y., 35, 38, 94

Willet, Major (deputy quartermaster), 171
Williams, Henry (petitioner), 180
Williams, Henry Abraham (volunteer), 146, 180
Williams, Pugh (Captain), 256
Williamsburg, Va., 49, 55, 165, 217, 221
Wilson, Catherine (Mrs. James Wilson), 252
Wilson, James (soldier), 252
Windship, Amos (volunteer physician), 181
Wister, Sarah (civilian), 40, 56
Women followers, officers' wives: camp life vs. homelife, 145, 149, 150; causing discord, 146, 147–48; housing, 147, 148–149; the "sisterhood," 150–51
Women followers, "Women of the Army": description/perception, 125–27; patriotism, 124–25, 143–44; rations/returns, 128–33, 137–38, 155–56n 37; reasons for following, 123; regulation, 136; traveling with army, 136–38. *See also* Camp followers
Women's work: and military work in general, 7–8, 13–14, 138; as "artificers," 218, 233n 82; as cooks, 132, 140; in domestic service, 139–40; as seamstresses, 139; as washerwomen, 46, 140–42; as matrons, nurses, 17, 142–43, 219, 220, 221, 222–23, 275; as soldiers, 20, 50, 144; as spies, 37–38, 143
Woodward, Anthony (alleged thief), 166
Wright, Anthony (Lieutenant), 60

Wright, Thomas (cook), 140
Wykoff, Henry (inspector), 103
Wyoming, Pa., 96, 99, 135, 137–38

Yates, Donaldson (deputy quartermaster), 198

Yorktown, Va., 48–50, 55, 90, 99, 110, 137, 140, 164–65, 166, 173
Young, Joseph (physician), 222
Young, Mrs. Peter (washerwoman), 141
Young, Samuel (volunteer), 180

www.ingramcontent.com/pod-product-compliance
Lightning Source LLC
Chambersburg PA
CBHW021143160426
43194CB00007B/674